FLAUBERT: A LIFE

Geoffrey Wall teaches French at the University of York. He also works as a translator, travel writer and literary biographer. His acclaimed translation of *Madame Bovary* was published in 1992.

FLAUBERT
A Life

GEOFFREY WALL

faber and faber

First published in 2001
by Faber and Faber Limited
3 Queen Square London WC1N 3AU
This paperback edition published in 2002

Typeset by RefineCatch Limited, Bungay, Suffolk
Printed in England

A CIP record for this book
is available from the British Library

ISBN 0–571–21239–5

2 4 6 8 10 9 7 5 3 1

For Sara

Contents

CONTENTS

FLAUBERT
A Life

CHAPTER ONE

The Family Name

ACHILLE-CLÉOPHAS FLAUBERT, doctor of medicine and father of Gustave Flaubert, was a man whose whole life could be read as an illustration of the bourgeois virtues. Born in 1784, he survived the heroic high-mortality decades of Revolution and Empire by cultivating a modest public rectitude. He worked hard and won prizes, and soon accumulated a large fortune in the pursuit of his profession. Achille-Cléophas Flaubert became one of the princes of the new realm of scientific medicine. It would surely have dismayed the good doctor if anyone had ventured to tell him that he would be remembered principally as the father of a boy whose only obvious talents were for writing odd, disreputable novels, spending other people's money, and generally satirising the bourgeois virtues.

Being Gustave, the younger son of such an eminent and irreproachably successful man, was a complicated destiny. Gustave was given wealth and comfort and a certain social importance, but he was expected, in return, to live a life that would add lustre to the family name. Prolonged exposure to moralising tales of his father's exemplary youth, even when they were recited in a gentle, well-meaning tone, may have had an unexpectedly dismal effect on the young listener's mind.

On the evidence of the journal that he kept when he was eighteen, Flaubert loved his father passionately, even in adolescence. And yet all the awkward old Oedipal questions arise from the shadows. How can a boy challenge such a perplexingly powerful figure? How is it possible not to *turn into* that father? What do you have to do to become *Gustave* Flaubert? Disheartening questions. No wonder that Flaubert liked to boast of the Iroquois Indian blood that supposedly flowed in his veins, courtesy of an audacious seventeenth-century ancestor.

No wonder that fathers are swept aside so effortlessly in Flaubert's writings. They generally die before the story begins, or else they are despatched to an obscure grave.*

Flaubert's *Dictionnaire des idées reçues*, that wonderfully dubious compendium of nineteenth-century attitudes, has the following entry under the topic of 'Father': 'You say "My late father . . . " as you take off your hat.' If only the gesture had such power to seal up the chambers of memory. Achille-Cléophas Flaubert, the real father, was not quite so easy to lay to rest. This tender, troublesome, disobligingly dead character must be summoned back to life if we are to understand the time and the place and the family from which Gustave Flaubert sprang forth with the great raucous wounded howl of laughter, wonder and fear that echoes all through his earliest writings. Where did Flaubert begin? How did he find his way, under such a prodigious hereditary burden, to the marvellous places of his imagination? And how did he find his way back again from that remote and bewildering country, back to the indisputably prosaic world of a nineteenth-century provincial city in which he was referred to, if at all, as *cet original de Monsieur Flaubert*.

The story of Achille-Cléophas is a lumpy mixture of biographical fact and family legend. I shall tell it now, to draw you into the bizarre, heroic world of early nineteenth-century medicine in which the son first came to consciousness. Religion and Science, to be conceived in the person of a priest and a doctor, are the superbly opposed heroes of this tale. Unintimidated by these thunderingly quarrelsome characters, the son will eventually find his way, after great tribulation, towards Literature.

E VEN as a child Achille-Cléophas Flaubert was possessed by a fiercely competitive spirit. Whether he was playing with the other boys down by the river, or learning his letters from an indolent priest, Achille-Cléophas simply excelled. The modest country town of Nogent-sur-Seine, where his father doctored the cows and the horses, was far too small an arena for energy and talent such as his. Everyone agreed that Achille-Cléophas was a boy who might go far. Those of a more critical disposition, such as his two elder brothers, might well have added, under their breath, that such *damned superiority* would be sure to end miserably.

---

* Charles Bovary's father is a shadowy, cantankerous figure; Frederic Moreau's father dies 'from a sword wound' before the birth of his son; Monsieur Aubain disappears in the third paragraph of *Un coeur simple*.

Trouble came upon this modest, respectable family in January 1793, when Achille-Cléophas was nine years old. Nicolas Flaubert, his father, was arrested in a local inn. He had been observed weeping as he read in his newspaper that the foul tyrant Louis Capet, formerly known as Louis XVI, had recently been beheaded using the scientific 'instrument of separation' devised by Dr Joseph Guillotin. These were anxious days. England had just declared war on France in response to the execution of the King. The authorities of the besieged infant republic had imposed a ferocious revolutionary vigilance. The political opinions of vociferous royalists like Nicolas Flaubert could no longer be ignored. Here was an educated man with a significant local influence. He had to be silenced.

The Société populaire de Nogent-sur-Seine, the local republican committee, voted to send Citizen Flaubert to face the Revolutionary Tribunal in Paris. He would probably be sentenced to death or deportation. But Nicolas Flaubert was rescued by the intervention of his youngest son, Achille-Cléophas. Tutored by his mother, the nine-year-old boy delivered a speech which swayed the hearts of the Société populaire. We may pause to imagine this scene. It has all the ingredients of a genre painting in the elevated political-sentimental style of the 1790s. The pure-hearted and precocious eloquence of the child prevails upon the moral sympathies of his father's accusers. Rescuing his father from death was undoubtedly the formative experience of Achille-Cléophas's childhood, and it duly became a cherished family legend. As an image of the dark days of the Revolution, as a story passed down from father to son, it offered a sharply memorable lesson in the perils of political enthusiasm.

However, there was worse to come. Citizen Nicolas Flaubert, so evidently unreliable, so lacking in public virtue, was arrested once again in February 1794 and carted to Paris to receive sentence. This was not the moment to step forward as an enemy of the people. The country was at war. Political hatred was in full flood. *La patrie*, the fatherland itself, was in danger. Patriots were stripping the lead from the roofs of churches and melting it down to make bullets to fire at invading Prussians. Nicolas Flaubert was duly sentenced to death. His wife came to Paris to plead for his life, equipped with 'certificates' from influential persons in Troyes and Nogent. The sentence was commuted to deportation, a kind of civic death, with a good chance of actual death from hardship and tropical diseases.

Nicolas Flaubert now languished in prison. He was one of 8500 political prisoners being held during that fearful summer of 1794. The guilty were now so numerous that they had to be herded into dungeons improvised in convents, hospitals and barracks. The prison regime was harsh: no visitors, no letters, no newspapers, one clean shirt a week and daily roll-call of those listed for the guillotine. Young men awoke to find their hair turning grey.* In mortal terror, many committed suicide; but Nicolas Flaubert was one of the fortunate survivors. He walked from prison in the month of Thermidor, August 1794, saved by the fact that Robespierre and his faction had been ousted from power, thus bringing the most radical phase of the revolution to its close.

Nicolas Flaubert, like a man rising from the grave, made his way back to the village of Nogent and set about planning his family's future. He resolved to send his youngest son, Achille-Cléophas, to the best school that he could afford. It was a shrewd investment. All the exclusive old careers were opening up. Though there was little to spare, the family saved up what they could and in the autumn of the year 1794, a little before his tenth birthday, this promising child was accordingly transported the thirty-odd miles from the scene of his boyhood to the neighbouring town of Sens. A slow and fatiguing day's journey, it pitched the boy into the dangerous, quickening flow of national life. His brilliant career was about to begin.

Achille-Cléophas was educated, for the next eight years, as *pensionnaire*, a boarding pupil, at the Collège de Sens. Sens was an ancient cathedral town standing on the river Yonne. Seven centuries of archbishops and cardinals had built their palaces and town houses around the main square. The results were monumental, opulent, and exquisitely ecclesiastical.

For all its tranquil historic dignity, Sens was not cut off from the larger world. The old road from Paris to the south passed through the town. Travellers came to the coaching inns on the square, bringing the news from the great cities of Dijon, Lyon, and Geneva. In the summer of 1792 the boisterous ragged army of the Revolution, the *fédérés*, had marched through Sens on their way from Marseille to Paris, raising a giant cloud of dust and singing the fiery new anthem of the republic, the

---

* Twenty-five years later, in his medical thesis of 1810, Achille-Cléophas recalled precisely this effect of physical terror: 'The young man whose hair turns suddenly grey, a phenomenon which we have seen repeatedly during the bloody weeks of the French Revolution.'

'Marseillaise'. In 1793, at the height of the revolutionary campaign to de-Christianise everyday life, the town's ancient cathedral of Saint Stephen had been stripped of the great company of stone saints that had adorned its west front ever since the twelfth century. Only Saint Stephen himself, holding the book of the law in his hand, had escaped the hammer.

Image-breaking was an unmistakable sign of the times. Militant anti-clericalism was in the ascendant. When he arrived in Sens the youthful Achille-Cléophas could see the great fact of the Revolution written all over the cathedral. The young priests from the local seminary had prudently fled the wrath of the infant French Republic and a godless new college was now officially housed in their abandoned residence. Here, in a handsome old building set into the medieval city walls, embedded in the old, but instructed in the new, Achille-Cléophas Flaubert observed the slightly quieter closing years of the eighteenth century.

Already we may discern the larger historical pattern of his life. The ardent young men of science pursued their enlightened trade in premises recently vacated by the somnolent old men of faith. The principal scenes of Dr Flaubert's life would all be set in buildings that had once been church property. Priests could be expropriated and ridiculed. Catholic rituals could be abolished by decree. But the ancient poetry of religion could scarcely be erased from the national mind for ever, even by the most stern and conscientious efforts. It was exasperating for the rationalist. Something archaic and inexplicable, some little superstition from the past always survived. So it is no surprise that the baffling, seductive, ridiculous, stubborn experience of the sacred was to be one of Gustave Flaubert's major themes.

The events of the 1790s, viewed from the window of a school classroom, offered much to ponder, even for a boy not given to sustained introspection. If Achille-Cléophas had kept any private written record of his early days, he may have laid his journal out according to the newfangled republican decimal calendar. Certainly he was quick to acquire the official language of the new world.

With its curious location, the Collège de Sens offered a double view. You could look down, within the walls, along the narrow echoing streets of the city. You could look out, beyond the walls, to a grove of trees and the open countryside beyond. Somewhere far away to the north, at the end of a white dusty road, there lay the great city of Paris. A newly arrived schoolboy, gazing towards that horizon, would soon calculate how many hours the hundred-mile horse-and-cart journey to the capital might take. The only question was *when?*

Achille-Cléophas had yet to prove himself in this strange new world. He felt no hesitation. At the end of his first year at the school he won a prize for good behaviour, 'morale et bonne conduite'. He sought and soon found a father-figure, attaching himself to the principal of the college, a man called Salgues. Jacques-Barthelmy Salgues, currently Citizen Salgues, 'that chameleon priest', as his enemies scornfully referred to him, was a talented man in his mid-thirties who had already played many parts. In just ten years Salgues had been priest, man of letters, schoolteacher, delegate, magistrate, fugitive, prisoner, journalist and pamphleteer. Now he had turned headmaster.

Intellectually and politically agile, an eighteenth-century Voltairean salon intellectual, full of wit and malice and energy, unencumbered by deeply held principles, Salgues was a powerful mentor. Here was a man who might open doors for you. Salgues had contacts, in the church hierarchy, in provincial journalism and in Parisian literary circles. For Achille-Cléophas, the younger son of an impecunious village vet, a real nobody 'whose only patrimony was his intelligence', such patronage was indispensable. He soon fashioned himself into the most congenial kind of student: respectful, discreetly affectionate, and wonderfully zealous in his urge to acquire knowledge.

Salgues taught eloquence, experimental physics and natural history. Here was yet another sign of the times. The knowledge officially offered to the young citizens of the future had been thoroughly de-Christianised. The class of 1794 could enjoy the most progressive secular education available anywhere in Europe. The Republic of France was at war with all neighbouring monarchies; in the Republic's recently reformed schools there was great emphasis on high-minded patriotism and applied mathematics, a potent combination for anyone preparing to mount an artillery barrage. There was room for literature as well. Achille-Cléophas studied the classic authors in French and Latin and assembled a useful little stock of quotations, the kind of solid cultural capital that a busy practical man might draw upon for the rest of his life.

How many candlelit late eighteenth-century evenings did the boy spend in conversation with Salgues? We may picture the older man reading Voltaire aloud to his young disciple, for we know that Achille-Cléophas acquired an abiding passion for Voltaire. His library would one day include the complete works, seventy-two expensively bound volumes, displayed in pride of place alongside the works of Buffon and Rousseau. Achille-Cléophas was a loyal admirer of Salgues, and remained in contact with him for many years to come. He learnt to emulate his adoptive father's sharply combative, no-nonsense, Voltairean tone. The imitation was so successful that a certain imperious paternal irony became the native habit of his mind. It was a tone of voice that Gustave Flaubert fittingly compared to the action of a scalpel.

IN November 1803, in an atmosphere of world-historical excitement, victorious French armies were marching across Europe. The tricolour citizen-soldiers were strong in the virtues of liberty. It was their delight to wake the old kingdoms from their centuries of sleep and rewrite their constitutions. Perhaps the universal Republic of Reason was at hand. Whenever it came it would undoubtedly express itself in French.

It was in this same month that the ambitious nineteen-year-old Achille-Cléophas Flaubert finally rattled and splashed his way along the road to Paris. He travelled light, for the patrimony of his intelligence was still his only possession. He had resolved to study medicine, a choice of career that was nicely consistent with the pattern of his family's steady social ascent. His grandfather had been a blacksmith-cum-farrier, a village artisan practising inherited skills. His father was a vet, formally educated in veterinary medicine, a man with a certificate that allowed him to charge his customers accordingly.

Achille-Cléophas had aspirations beyond the imaginings of his forefathers. His intelligence and energy were augmented by superb good luck. He was in the right place at the right time. That year was a supremely favourable moment to enter the medical profession. In the progressive slang of the late eighteenth century, medicine was 'the religion of humanity'. Doctors rather than priests were loudly acclaimed as the true benefactors of the human race. Their status and their incomes were both rising. The bloody practicalities of revolutionary warfare had forced ingenious technical improvements in the art of surgery. The theoretical speculations of the Parisian philosopher-scientists had culminated in the word 'biology', coined by the French naturalist Lamarck in 1802.

The French medical profession had come of age, intellectually, in the years since 1789. Before the Revolution, medicine was chaotic. The qualified elite of physicians, surgeons and apothecaries had always been in fierce competition with a charismatic tribe of pseudo-medical charlatans; the marketplaces of country towns were crowded with them. They were scruffy, noisy miracle-men: the urine-sniffers, the wig-makers, the gelders, the bone-setters, the hernia-menders, the execu-tioners, the false-teeth-makers, the oculists and the mesmerists, who travelled the land in search of the afflicted and the merely credulous. Boasting and cajoling, perched up on old barrels, these colourful itiner-ants had no real qualifications apart from an ability to perform. They had been curbed (though not banished) by the recent reforms. From all these changes there had emerged a medical profession that was liberal in its ethos, independent of politics, and miraculously lucrative for the fortunate few at the top. By the early years of the nineteenth century Paris was universally regarded as the medical capital of Europe. Enter, unobtrusively, Achille-Cléophas Flaubert.

The life of a medical student was not easy. The years of newly codi-fied medical training were expensive. In 1800 it could cost about five thousand francs. Then you would have to find another thousand francs to pay a substitute to do your military service. Every year over a thou-sand students enrolled to study medicine in Paris and they were all in fierce competition with one another.

In this professional jungle what was to become of a young man who, as Achille-Cléophas liked to remind those around him in later life, had no patrimony? He prevailed, as he was accustomed to do, by the simple force of intelligence and hard work. For three years in a row he won first prize at the prestigious Ecole Pratique. It was a conspicuous suc-cess and it entitled him to have his fees paid by the state. For all that, he endured an exceptionally harsh apprenticeship. Parisian medical stu-dents lived in great poverty. They wore shabby clothes, ate a meagre diet and lived in cold, dismal rooms. Most of them wore cheap wooden clogs rather than shoes. Achille-Cléophas used to raise extra money by selling to his friends, in advance, the textbooks that he invariably won as prizes.

N APOLÉON was crowned Emperor of the French in 1804. The Empire was a period of frivolous elegance after the anxious and austere years of the Republic, a time for resplendently embroidered military uniforms, cavalry parades, and the cult of national glory, *la gloire*. Achille-Cléophas, now in his early twenties, was busy making his way up the ladder of his chosen profession. He formed the habits of work that would see him through the rest of his life. According to his biographer, 'His mind was focused on practical matters, and he took no serious interest in anything that was not imperative or had no specific utility.' He spent his days in the hospital, among the dying; all too many of his nights he spent in the gloomy stench of the dissecting room, among the candlelit dead.

Anatomy and physiology were his supreme intellectual passions. He was living at a great moment in the history of science when the foundations of modern biology were being laid. He read all the latest books. He read Françoise Bichat's *Recherches physiologiques sur la vie et la mort* (1800) and quoted copiously from it in his own published work. He read Pierre Cabanis's *Rapports du physique et du moral de l'homme* (1802). Bichat and Cabanis were his inspiration. Their writings, suffused with a distinctly sombre medical eloquence, expound the physiological perspective. Their analysis of biological processes reached down to the level of tissues and organs. Only in the next generation, once microscopes had improved, did analysis reach down to the level of the cell. Achille-Cléophas Flaubert, like most of his early nineteenth-century medical contemporaries, appears to have ignored the possibilities of the microscope.

'Open up a few corpses,' Bichat suggests casually, in the foreword to his *Anatomie descriptive* of 1803. He promises that it will be a revelation. 'For twenty years, from morning to night, you have taken notes at patients' bedsides . . . and all is confusion for you in the symptoms which refuse to yield up their meaning . . . Open up a few corpses: you will dissipate at once the darkness that observation alone could not dissipate.'

When Gustave Flaubert read Bichat, seventy years later, in November 1871, he found it 'most entertaining'. He relished the satirical possibilities of this one-eyed view of the world. At the end of *Madame Bovary*, when Charles has been found dead, sitting in the garden, the officious Dr Canivet is called in to investigate. 'He opened him up and found nothing.' It's a quietly devastating criticism of medical pretensions to knowledge of the inner world. The joke, such as it is, falls on the physiologists. They think there's nothing there. In the words of the *Dictionnaire des idées reçues*, 'they can't find our souls with their scalpels'.

Achille-Cléophas attracted patrons and won recognition. In his second year he was nominated *interne*, the equivalent of a modern houseman, at the Hôtel-Dieu de Paris, the foremost hospital of the day. There the celebrated Guillaume Dupuytren, soon to be elected professor of clinical surgery, took him up and began to exert himself for his pupil's advancement. Reading between the lines of his career, I surmise that Achille-Cléophas now made an important moral discovery. Dupuytren, so helpful to his disciples, so generous in his dedication to the poor and the sick, was in fact notoriously vindictive towards all potential rivals. The great prince of science, with his abnormally large burden of vanity and malice, was all too human.

Flaubert family legend has it that the great Dupuytren now talked Achille-Cléophas into taking up a medical post in Rouen. It was a splendid post. He would leave Paris and it would be excellent for his health. Dupuytren would procure him a medical certificate. That would give him exemption from military service. And he would lend him the six hundred francs to pay for the journey to Rouen.*

It worked beautifully. In the guise of doing his pupil a great favour, Dupuytren arranged for Dr Flaubert to vanish into the provinces for ever. Achille-Cléophas spent the next forty years in Rouen, getting richer every year but forever grumbling about Paris and everything Parisian. For all his talent and his driving energy, Achille-Cléophas was never truly at ease in the metropolitan medical world. He didn't speak the same language. He was the eternal provincial: too serious, fierce, awkward and outspoken to make his way among the polished salon-pleasers. Dedicated, competent, successful and exceptionally humane, Achille-Cléophas sulked in secret over the fact that he had been out-manoeuvred by lightweight professional rivals. It was his favourite grievance. It lent a characteristic edge of malice to his wit, stoked his devilish bad temper, and imparted an interesting unspoken moral lesson to his observant younger son.

A CHILLE-CLÉOPHAS arrived in Rouen, after a three-day journey in the *diligence*, the fast public stagecoach, on 27 November 1806. He was twenty-two years old, 'with few possessions but a rich future ahead of him'. Quite fortuitously we know what he looked like from

---

* The medical certificate, dated July 1806, specifies that Achille-Cléophas had the symptoms of tuberculosis. See Bosquet 1955. It has been argued that Achille-Cléophas could not have survived if he had really had the symptoms as described. The medical certificate must therefore have been a discreet favour from Dupuytren. Dr Germain Galérant, interview, March 1998.

the sketchy physical details recorded on his certificate of exemption from military service. He was five feet nine inches tall, with brown eyes, an oval-shaped face, a long nose and a small chin. The father clearly did not share the features of his tall, blond, green-eyed second son, Gustave.

From later testimony we also know something of the moral nature of the man. He was 'opinionâtre' – 'Opinionâtre en toutes choses', said one of his professional contemporaries. He was diligent, tenacious and persistent. But he was also stubborn, inflexible and unyielding. These were moral qualities that his second son displayed in abundance. It's perfectly familiar now, this melancholy-mad relentlessness, this sombre passion of men devoured by their work. In 1800 it was still rather a sinister psychological novelty.*

The demonic world-transforming energies of bourgeois individualism are already deeply inscribed upon the youthful face of Achille-Cléophas Flaubert as he looks out for the first time, like an ardent young nineteenth-century hero, on the provincial city that is to be the theatre of his ambitions. To a man with an unaccustomed weight of money in his pocket, a young man just released from long years of student poverty, the city wore the aspect of a feast spread out before him. Achille-Cléophas might now begin to acquire a taste for the civilised pleasures appropriate to his station. The latest books, a sober wardrobe of well-made clothes, several pairs of elegant shoes, an evening's tasteful entertainment – they all now lay within his reach.

At the bookshop of Vallée frères he could buy, for 25 francs, the new translation of Adam Smith's *Wealth of Nations*, in five octavo volumes. Or he might browse through the pages of the *Letter on the Perils of Onanism*, an edifying work 'useful for fathers and teachers'. Rouen's Théâtre des Arts was offering *Le Caravane de Caire*, grand opera on an oriental-imperial theme. At the other end of the cultural marketplace, the Equestrian Amphitheatre was playing *Don Quixote*, billed as a

---

* Balzac was probably the first to identify it. Achille-Cléophas displayed something of that fierce mysterious willpower that fascinated the novelist. Like Achille-Cléophas Flaubert, Balzac's Dr Roubaud, a character in *Le Curé du village* (1838), escapes from Paris to the provinces. 'Roubaud was one of those superbly educated young doctors, the kind they produce these days at the Medical School in Paris, a man who could certainly have made a name for himself on the vast stage of the metropolis; but daunted by the pace of ambition in Paris, having more of a taste for knowledge than for intrigue, more aptitude than avidity, his gentle personality had led him onto the smaller provincial stage where he hoped to be recognised sooner than he would have been in Paris.'

burlesque pantomime in two acts with battles and gymnastic interludes featuring Monsieur Forioso's elder sister dancing upon the tightrope.

But these were mere frivolities. The official mood of the hour is caught in the closing words of the local newspaper announcement for *The Dream*, a topical-patriotic Christmas miscellany that would be playing throughout December at Rouen's Théâtre des Arts. 'The high deeds which continue to distinguish the genius of the emperor and the courage of his great and valiant army offer to the imagination such wonders that we are inclined to think we are dreaming when we read the bulletins which set out each glorious circumstance, were it not for the fact that we are in the century of marvels, quite accustomed to seeing ever new and ever more extraordinary things brought about.'

A century of marvels: The week before Achille-Cléophas arrived in Rouen, Napoléon had entered Berlin and begun to issue proclamations. The Emperor's victory bulletin was printed on the front page of the *Journal de Rouen* for 5 November 1806. On the inside page there was a *Patriotic Ode on the Prussian War* in eight stanzas. According to instructions from Paris, the latest imperial victory was to be celebrated in the nation's churches, 'in gratitude to the Supreme Being who so visibly guides and protects the invincible armies of His Imperial Majesty'.

In that winter of 1806 the fashionable patriot, with one eye on the supreme being, and the other eye on the value of his investments, could be observed wearing a long-tailed and white-buttoned version of the Napoleonic greatcoat. In Rouen the linen merchants were selling great quantities of an elaborately festooned lace *jabot*. In *Les Halles*, Rouen's great seventeenth-century Cloth Hall, there was brisk trading in fabrics whose very names evoke a lost world of exact social nuance: *siamoise*, white thread and worsted, fustian, drill and check. These were the city's commercial speciality: plain everyday fabrics for the masses, the no-nonsense stuff of a peasant woman's skirt or a soldier's uniform.

Though he spent his formative years in Paris and Rouen during the tumultuous days of the First Empire, the *gloire* that illuminated Dr Flaubert's dreams was never Napoleonic. He was exempt, as already explained, from military service. But we may surmise that even as a young doctor he saw too much of the human damage, smelt and touched too many prosaic horrors, too much torn flesh and shattered bone, to be seduced by the magnificent illusions of his empire-building contemporaries. Unlike many men of his generation Dr Flaubert did not take part in that particular world-historical adventure. The paternal legend, as served out after dinner to his two sons, encompassed neither the grandeur nor the servitude of military life. The whole Napoleonic episode figures in Flaubert's fiction only as an inert memory, as something from a vague prehistory. His father had been exempt from service, and so it was that the high drama of Revolution and Empire had no great imaginative resonance for him.

Like many of his professional contemporaries, Achille-Cléophas was a liberal, though it was a genteel philosophical liberalism that certainly did not imply democratic convictions of any practical consequence. He was also a freemason, a mildly republican anticlerical, attached to the sceptical deism that was the dominant religious attitude among late eighteenth-century English, French, and German intellectuals. Attached to the principles of 1789 while deploring the excesses of 1793, like many doctors he was pragmatically indifferent to the political regime of the day. He did not greatly care about governments, as long as they respected his principles and didn't interfere with him.

From the month of his arrival in Rouen his career followed a smoothly ascending curve. As *prévot d'anatomie* he was now established in the School of Anatomy and Medicine that was annexed to the Hôtel-Dieu. At a salary of 1200 livres a year he was apprenticed to an illustrious new master, Jean-Baptiste Laumonier. Laumonier enjoyed a great reputation for the wonderfully repulsive life-size waxen effigies of the half-dissected human form that he put together in his Laboratory of Artificial Anatomy. He drew in the best medical students from all over France, though they generally stayed in Rouen for only a year or two before moving on to higher things.

Achille-Cléophas was required, among his other duties, to assist Laumonier in the Laboratory of Artificial Anatomy, making the famous wax figures. He thought the whole thing a ridiculous waste of time. It had nothing to do with real anatomy. One day he would be able to enjoy venting his scorn, but for the moment he had to play his cards carefully. Laumonier, though indolent and old-fashioned, was a man of some influence. He had friends in high places and his wife's relatives were prominent in Parisian politics. He also had an orphaned niece, a sad-eyed, dark-haired girl of thirteen called Caroline Fleuriot, who would eventually become Dr Flaubert's principal reason for staying in Rouen.

Working with Laumonier, Achille-Cléophas realised that there was no proper medical education available at the Hôtel-Dieu; he promptly 'set up a school on his own and taught anatomy without charging, on his own initiative, driven by the need to share the light of his generous and sympathetic mind with others'. Results were excellent and he soon established an independent reputation for himself as an inspiring teacher.

O
N 27 September 1810, towards the end of his fourth year in Rouen, Achille-Cléophas presented his thesis to the five examiners of the Paris Faculty of Medicine. Dedicated 'To My Father' and written in the unadorned aphoristic style of the day, the thesis deals with 'the care of the sick before and after surgical operations'. Browsing through the seventy printed pages of this modest but elegant volume, we may open a small door into the distant world of early nineteenth-century medicine. In his thesis, surprisingly his only publication, Achille-Cléophas 'formulated the principles from which he never departed', a phrase that may suggest either a magisterial consistency or a one-eyed fixity of opinion. Dr Flaubert was concerned with what might now be called the psychosomatic aspects of medicine, all the curious traffic that runs between the body and the mind. His professional ideal was a humane, healing wisdom grounded in the best scientific knowledge of his day; his thesis is accordingly different in its scope and its method from other medical theses of the same year, technical treatises on some specialised aspect of surgery, complete with illustrations and detailed case-histories.

Uniquely Achille-Cléophas combines a precise physiological notation of bodily symptoms with a vividly sympathetic perception of the patient as a fellow creature, subject to feelings of terror and desire, hope and despair – feelings that the enlightened doctor-surgeon must not ignore. Drawing upon his own aspirations and upon the example of his masters, Achille-Cléophas portrays an ideal doctor who brings many gifts to the task of healing. He must have a knowledge of anatomy, exceptional manual dexterity, a certain *finesse* or delicacy of the five senses, and a real strength of mind. He will observe the temperament and the physical condition of his patient. He will attend to the many factors that influence recovery.

Allow the patient, says Achille-Cléophas, to relax for several days beforehand in the place where the operation is to take place. Keep a special eye on 'debauched' patients. They must be prevented from masturbating. The oversensitive types, who can be recognised by their plumpness and the whiteness of their skin, will benefit from cold baths. Talk to the patient attentively before the operation. Reassure him. Tell him that it will be quick and not very painful. Imaginative patients, especially those who have read medical books, pose a special problem. Their excess of sensibility is the enemy of the doctor. Anxiety and terror render them more susceptible to infection. In a state of anxiety the heart beats more slowly, the breathing becomes laboured, the skin goes cold, the muscles relax, sweat covers the body, and there is copious diarrhoea. In a state of terror the pulse races, the patient blacks out or bursts into sardonic laughter. Some lose blood, some have convulsions.

All surgical instruments should be concealed from the patient's eyes and you must never discourage the patient from screaming during the operation. The scream always alleviates pain. In the first phase after the operation, the spasm, the patient's skin is dry and cold, the pulse is weak and rapid, all secretions cease, there is shivering and vomiting and the mind itself seems exhausted. In the second phase the skin is warm and damp, the face is pink, breathing is easy, the pulse is strong and regular, the mind revives, blood seeps back into the veins and floods the open wound.

After the operation we may give the patient half a glass of wine, remembering to change the patient's bloodstained sweat-soaked shirt as often as necessary. Narcotics such as opium, camphor or quinine can now be used to induce and control sleep. Sunlight will 'augment the vital forces'. Humid air, heavy with 'animal emanations', will increase post-operative mortality. The doctor is advised to assume a calm and confident manner whenever approaching the patient.

In the days before anaesthesia and antisepsis, when surgeons prided themselves on being able to amputate a leg in less than ten seconds, often to polite applause, all these little niceties listed by Achille-Cléophas might well make the difference between life and death.

Achille-Cléophas proclaimed the virtues of scientific medicine. Why should he not? Paris had given him the best medical education in Europe. The medical sensibility that speaks from the pages of his 1810 thesis is sternly materialist, lucidly impersonal and authoritative. But it is obvious from the testimony of those who had seen Achille-Cléophas at work that intuition and empathy played a large part in his therapeutic success. Beneath the brilliant, educated surface his mind was disturbed by invisible currents of pity and horror. The same tension, between explicit impersonality and unspoken compassion, animates the mature style of his son.

Achille-Cléophas returned to Rouen after the success of his thesis in 1810. What lay behind that decision? By returning he was effectively excluding himself from the Parisian medical elite. Had his superior, Laumonier, nearing retirement, tempted him with promises of advancement? Or was it the prospect of a liaison with Laumonier's young niece, Caroline Fleuriot? Perhaps it was both.

Of course it was still common practice, in medicine as in other fields, to marry the master's daughter. Such marriages were supremely convenient. But in Flaubert family tradition, the father's decision to stay in Rouen is carefully explained as a psychological oddity, the supremely impulsive moment in an existence otherwise governed by rational calculation.

Instead of staying a couple of months, the young doctor stayed there all his life. The frequent appeals of numerous friends, the hope of attaining a high position in Paris, a hope justified by his early achievements, nothing persuaded him to leave his hospital and the people to whom he had become deeply attached. But love was the initial reason for this extended stay, love for a girl he glimpsed one morning, a child of thirteen, Madame Laumonier's goddaughter, an orphan who lived in lodgings and came to visit her godmother every week. [. . .] She had just arrived [. . .] when they first met; a few months later they confessed their love and exchanged promises.

No doubt he impressed her greatly – impressed her with his energy, his ambition, his intelligence, his simple relentless belief in himself. They were married in February 1812.

CHAPTER TWO

A Very Queer Place

THE CITY stands on a wide bend of the River Seine, halfway between Paris and the ocean. The river is tidal here. You can smell the salt, like a bright, pleasant memory of the open sea, lost among the thick, damp folds of that ubiquitous, excremental, nineteenth-century urban stench. Wooden sailing ships – a thousand ships every year – are moored at the busy quayside. What currents of money must flow, swift and exhilarating, into the coffers of these citizens. The imposing remains of city walls, a multitude of elegant church spires, the rows of solidly handsome stone-built town houses, they all testify to five centuries of God-fearing prosperity and contentment. The merchants and the manufacturers of Rouen draw excellent profits from cheap textiles, mass-produced pottery and the regional cider market. Frugal types, the sword-carrying, silk-stockinged, land-owning aristocrat means nothing to them.

A large walled city, huddled around a busy port, it was always the perfect place to catch the plague. Smallpox, dysentery, scarlet fever, raw sewage and horse dung were the ingredients in this witches' brew of urban mortality. The charitable citizens of Rouen had therefore decreed, long ago, that a religious hospital, the Hôtel-Dieu, was to be built in the shadow of their great cathedral. There, in the Hôtel-Dieu, a medieval receptacle of all human misery, you might pray to Saint Roch for a miracle and prepare your soul for the quiet of the afterlife. As the city grew, so the dangers of contagion increased and it became evident that something more modern, more sensibly remote was required.

In July 1758 the sick were lifted, coaxed and bullied from their beds in the old Hôtel-Dieu. Singing psalms, carrying crosses and candles, they were carted across the city in a symbolically edifying procession and shown to their new quarters, a splendid neo-classical Hôtel-Dieu, situated on open ground just beyond the city walls.

The sick now found themselves, on that eighteenth-century July day, installed in cavernous rooms with the names of saints: Louis, Madeleine, Sebastian, Marguerite, and Ambroise. Bright, spacious rooms, they were heated by massive cast-iron stoves. Here in these church-sized spaces the sick were crowded together, five in every enormous bed. Their mattresses, irregularly stuffed with fresh straw, gave off a nostalgic smell of summer fields. There the godly and the ungodly alike were watched over by the nuns, Augustinians, dressed in white robes, black veils, and black capes decorated with the large scarlet cross of Malta. The nuns did all they could. They brewed rich herbal potions in the giant vats of the *tisanerie*; they recited Latin prayers over the dying; they stitched together the rough sacks in which the plague corpses were hurriedly laid to rest. It was consoling but it was not enough, not nearly enough for the generation of philosophical physicians who were dreaming up, encyclopaedically, their new religion of humanity.

In August 1790 the nuns were expelled from the Hôtel-Dieu, along with all the discredited, superstitious trumpery of the *ancien régime*. Under new management, the Hôtel-Dieu became the Hospice de l'humanité. But mere humanity was not enough, and the nuns soon returned, with fresh trumpery, in 1802. The sick complained at being disturbed by the bells incessantly calling them to mass. Polychrome effigies of the saints now gazed into the strange blind eyes of life-size medical heads made of wax, crazily complicated things of pink and blue intended to convey the hidden intricacies of the human skull. Science and superstition would have to coexist, thus transfixed in mutual disdain, for at least another generation or two.

Here, within the high walls of the Hôtel-Dieu, between the old gods and the new, exposed to all the dismaying evidence of mortality, Gustave Flaubert spent the early years of his life.

THE HÔTEL-DIEU was undoubtedly a very queer and a very splendid place in which to be a child. As big as a palace, it's a great geometrical complex of neoclassical public buildings that still breathes an austere French grandeur. Built in several stages between the years 1650 and 1770, the Hôtel-Dieu had been a prison, a warehouse and a barracks, before it became a hospital. The last doctor left the Hôtel-Dieu in 1962. Expensively renovated in the 1990s, the Hôtel-Dieu now serves as the regional *préfecture*, a labyrinthine urban chateau housing the elegant and genial administrative elite of the day.

Here we have to picture Gustave Flaubert, 'the doctor's little boy', a brave, sturdy, daredevil, dressed in the little white apron and the padded helmet of the nineteenth-century child. Taking his younger sister Caroline by the hand, he explores this puzzling world, piece by piece: a sunlit corridor, an endless staircase, a walled garden, a damp courtyard, a malodorous cellar, a shadowy attic, a hushed chapel. Everything around him, from the tasteful gold monogram on the family's Sunday-best porcelain to the daily mystery of the deference accorded to his father, it whispers the same pleasant message. This is your father's house and you are a Flaubert. You are still only a little Flaubert, but you are an immensely important person, to be treated with a prudent smile and a measure of teasingly humorous respect.

In defiance of the general oblivion that soon closes over the scenes of early life, certain moments of Flaubert's boyhood have survived. His selection from his own past is, of course, highly significant. 'I can remember', Flaubert wrote to George Sand in 1869, 'when I was five or six wanting to "send my heart" to a little girl I was in love with (I mean my actual heart). I could see it on a bed of straw, in a hamper, a hamper full of oysters.'

In a darker vein, Flaubert assailed Louise Colet, his new lover, with the following impressive anecdote:

The first time I ever saw the mad, it was here in the public asylum [. . .]. In the cells, sitting in chains, naked to the waist and all dishevelled, a dozen women were howling and clawing at their faces with their nails, I was about six or seven years old at the time. It's a good thing to have such experiences at an early age; they make a man of you. I do have such strange memories of that kind. The dissection room at the Hôtel-Dieu looked onto our garden. How many times did my sister and I climb up the trellis and, holding on to the vines, gaze curiously at the corpses all laid out. The sun was shining on them; the very same flies that were buzzing around us and the flowers in our garden were going to settle on them, again and again, buzzing away [. . .]. I can still see my father looking up from the dissection table, telling us to go away.

There is, Flaubert adds, 'a *moral density* to be found in certain forms of ugliness'.

Whatever else they may tell us, however steeped in the bitter and indignant sensibility of adolescence, these early memories are consistently tendentious. The experiences that Flaubert recalled were predominantly painful: *amour fou*, death and madness and the interesting ways that human bodies can be taken apart. One might even try to build an aesthetic on the fact of being a surgeon's son. 'External reality', he wrote, 'has to enter into us, almost enough to make us cry out, if we are to represent it properly.'

THE little boy's bedroom was hidden away high above the real world, tucked away somewhere under the roof. The walls were made so thick and so solid that the room was a place of perfect quiet. It had a window that looked out north-north-west upon a patch of sunless grey Normandy sky. You could see out across all the different grey roofs of the great city of Rouen: church spires and factory chimneys, the very old and the very new all mixed up together. Sixty feet below the window was the great courtyard. It was big enough, they said, to parade a regiment. Tall green trees shaded the benches where the poor sick people sat out in the summer to take the air.

His father was a very important man in the hospital. Dr Achille-Cléophas Flaubert had warm hands and a kind voice and he was a father to the poor, but when he was angry he was a demon and his eyes could look right inside you. Mother had a sad face and sometimes her head hurt. She stayed in bed all day and that was one of her migraines. His big brother was called Achille, and that was father's name too. Achille was a very clever boy. He went to the Collège Royal and won lots of prizes. They all said that Achille was a real Flaubert.

He had a little brother who died, and then he had a little sister and her name was Caroline. The summer she was born they all went to live in a castle by the river. It was his earliest memory. 'I remember a circle of lawn and a butler in a black coat crossing the lawn, some tall trees and a long corridor with a room at the end on the left where I slept.' Inside the castle there was a special feeling of pink-and-blue silk-embroidered chairs, very large and very soft. Outside the castle there was an old moat, planted with apple trees, and in the grass you found great pieces of stone that had fallen from the walls. He remembered the sad sound that the wind made in the chimney and then the owls calling as they flew up and down in the wide dark spaces under the roof. That was a very frightening sound.

All day at home he sat by the big, bright kitchen fire. He liked his nursemaid Julie. He was Julie's favourite. It was the way she laughed when she called him *Monsieur* Gustave and sometimes she carried him on her back just like a horse. Mother told Julie to stop kissing him all the time. On New Year's Day, Julie took the children visiting. Hand in hand they went, Gustave and Caroline, along the great cold boulevards, their legs freezing, their teeth sticking together with toffee. Then they had to be hugged six times by old women in strange bonnets. Julie's real name wasn't Julie. She had a different name. She said she'd lost it somewhere. But that was just for a tease. She came from Bourg-Baudoin, a little village half a day along the road, high on a hill at the edge of the forest. Once she lay in bed for a year and read books.

One day he was frightened of the thunder and Julie gave him a sprig of white thorn and said to hold it in his hand for a charm against lightning. Then she told him about the fairies and their mischief. They'd come and pinch the baby's bottom and make her cry when she was sleeping in her cradle. Julie knew such strange sad things and made them into stories. She took him to the night world where the giant Gargantua still walked, where druid stones came alive and big fat snakes lay coiled asleep in dark pools. She told him about talking animals, elves and changeling children, goblins, werewolves, witches and decapitated saints who wandered the lonely country roads carrying their own heads in little baskets.*

City children of the 1820s were not yet insulated from the older rural world and its mental habits. Julie, 'a simple daughter of the people', took her favourite child with her into another world. She introduced him, in his earliest years, to a superlative kingdom of miracles, visions and prodigies. Though he never wrote about childhood, Flaubert often wrote about these dark things that had so precociously excited his imagination. He accumulated a vast, leisurely erudition on the subject of saints, heretics and goddesses. He was fascinated by all the wilder varieties of religious experience. Perhaps it was a clever way of staying on, a way of lingering in that glorious first world that unfolded for him beside the kitchen fire in the years before he could read. 'Early impressions', Flaubert wrote, 'never fade [. . .]. We carry our past within us; all our lives we still smell of our nurse's milk.' If we are looking for the

---

* This is an unashamedly speculative paragraph based on the storytelling scenes in Flaubert's juvenilia and on Amélie Bosquet's contemporary compilation of rural Normandy folklore, *La Normandie romanesque et merveilleuse*, published in 1845. According to Bosquet, marvel tales are 'familiar to us from our earliest days . . . and though our rational intelligence has long grown out of such credulity, our imaginations gladly submit to them once again.'

traces of Flaubert's first world, we may find them, transformed and elaborated, in the landscapes of his more exotic fictions. The emotional generosity of the smiling storyteller who warmed the days of his boyhood was laid deeper in his memory. He celebrated Julie eventually in the figure of Félicité, the loyal family servant in the story *Un Coeur simple*. The tacit excellence of the simple-hearted is one of his profoundest themes.

T HE city child soon knew the gentler pleasures of the country. In February 1821, the year of Gustave's birth, the family acquired a country house. Dr Achille-Cléophas paid 52,000 francs for his new domain, only an hour's journey by carriage from the Hôtel-Dieu. It was a modest, handsome property standing on the hillside just above the village of Déville. Set fifty yards back from the road, shaded by tall trees, the house had a long terrace and gardens that looked out across the fields and down into the valley below. Discreetly delighted by the magnitude of his worldly success, Dr Flaubert bought a bust of Hippocrates and put it on display in a niche just above the front door. In the distance, just beyond the village houses and the church tower, a cluster of factory chimneys stood as a reminder of the crude, encroaching powers of the new industrial order. Standing under the trees in the garden at Déville you could hear the sound of a steam engine in the next valley. The Déville house remained in the family's possession all through Flaubert's childhood. It was a pleasant refuge, a world away from the family's cramped, melancholy quarters in the Hôtel-Dieu. During the long cheerless months of his student exile in Paris, the spacious garden at Déville was one of the places Flaubert remembered most fondly.

F LAUBERT soon grew tired of Julie's ghost stories and folk tales. He discovered stories in books. In pursuit of this sweet new pleasure he would now make his way through the big door in the garden wall, down six steps and across the road, to find Uncle Mignot, a benign elderly neighbour who was content to play grandfather to this bright, responsive child. Here was a man who had time for the boy in a way that his own father, so heroically and obliviously busy, did not. Mignot took him on his knee and told him stories, glorious exotic tales that surpassed anything of Julie's. Most memorably he read to him *Don Quixote in Pictures, being the Adventures of the Hero of La Mancha and his Squire Sancho Panza.* Cervantes abridged for children and adorned with thirty-four large illustrations, this was the favourite book of Flaubert's early childhood.

He coloured in the pictures, with the help of his sister, and he soon knew the story of Don Quixote off by heart, long before he could read. Cervantes always delighted him. 'Sancho Panza, you can see him up on his donkey, eating raw onions and digging his heels into his mount as he talks to his master. You can see those Spanish roads though they are never described.' Flaubert clearly cherished the Sancho Principle: the ironic realist (with his donkey and his onion) pursues a friendly conversation with the exalted visionary. The tragicomic theme of the romancer at odds with the real world is such a complete premonition of both *Madame Bovary* and *L'Education sentimentale* that we are left to marvel at this happy, fertile coincidence of boy and book.

After a slow start, asking why he should bother to acquire a skill that Uncle Mignot exercised so competently on his behalf, Flaubert was soon a great reader with a superb memory for what he had read. He made notes on Don Quixote – 'Uncle Mignot says they're very good' – and he was soon planning his own novels based on Cervantes.

Prodigiously single-minded, Flaubert began to compose as soon as he could write, 'asking my nurse to say the letters you needed for the words in the sentences that I made up'. He found his first admiring audience near to hand in the person of his sister Caroline. By the age of ten he was dreaming of glory, and he displayed an imaginative intensity that could be oddly disconcerting. 'So immersed in his reading, twisting a lock of hair in his fingers and nibbling at his tongue, that he used to fall flat on the floor. One day he cut his nose when he fell against the glass door of a bookshelf.'

They began to wonder about him. The child seemed to drift away into a world of his own. Was it a form of epilepsy? *Le petit mal?* The 'little sickness', characterised by brief absences? Or was he, as some have suggested, practising a form of spontaneous self-hypnosis?* Perhaps both conditions were present simultaneously. Whatever the psychiatric explanation, Flaubert treasured his self-induced hallucinations.

---

* Dr Germain Galérant has suggested the possibility of self-hypnosis. He points out that no para-epileptic symptoms (fugues, amnesias, somnambulism) made their appearance in Flaubert's childhood. According to Galérant, minor brain damage leading to epilepsy may have occurred in late adolescence as a result of a fall. A notorious daredevil, Flaubert may have fractured his skull. G. Galérant, interviewed by the author, Rouen, March 1998.

He describes such experiences very clearly in *Mémoires d'un fou*, written in 1838 on the eve of his seventeenth birthday. Walking alone, thinking of a girl, the hero drifts away: 'The regular movement lulled me to sleep so to speak, I thought I could hear Maria walking by my side ... I knew very well that it was a hallucination which I was producing for myself, but I could not help smiling over it and I felt happy.' Romantic reverie was a pleasant psychological reality. It could also become a dangerous addiction. The artist's lucid and joyful powers of vision would have to be disentangled, somehow, from the other mysterious aberrations of consciousness that brought lesser visions.

EVEN the most surly of romantic individualists has a selection of aunts and uncles and cousins to anchor them to the common life. Flaubert boasted fancifully of his exotic Red Indian ancestors. His true affinities, he was sure, were with gypsies, nomads, barbarians and one or two of the more flamboyant despots of classical antiquity. But the real family of his early childhood was irreproachably bourgeois and provincial.

From his father's side, Flaubert inherited a substantial collection of country cousins; not a complete set of relations, for there was only one survivor of the older generation: his paternal grandmother, Marie-Apollonie Flaubert. She figures pleasantly in his early history as the distant source of regular New Year parcels packed with good things to eat. Marie-Apollonie died in 1832 when Flaubert was ten, thus breaking his last intimate family link with the eighteenth century.

That whole generation, the protagonists of the immense national drama of revolution and empire, is absent from Flaubert's fiction; as if those great events had tangled and snapped all the delicate threads of family history, leaving behind only an enticingly poetical image of the late eighteenth century as a world that was both more elegant and more audacious than the queasy culture of constraint that had taken its place. Emma Bovary's brief glimpse into that earlier world, when she attends the ball at the country house of the Marquis d'Andervilliers, is her undoing.

If there was any continuity with the past perhaps it was to be found in small country towns. Flaubert's paternal cousins lived in Nogent-sur-Seine, and the Rouen Flauberts made the journey to Nogent almost every other year. It was a great distance, a great adventure, going to Nogent in the years before the railways. They took it slowly, in little stages, travelling by chaise de poste and sleeping in village inns. Travelling was to become one of Flaubert's special pleasures, the source of abiding memories and the very stuff of bittersweet romantic reverie. His boyhood journeys to Nogent left a pleasantly vivid image of 'the vines . . . and the white houses, the long dusty road and the pollarded elm trees all along the way'.

When the family reached their habitual destination they found a small prosperous market town of about 4000 inhabitants. Goods on their way to Paris passed through Nogent to the sound of heavy wagons rumbling along the main street. The long-distance coach service, the diligence, called at the inn on the square. Sailors disembarked from the riverboats and headed for the brothel near the quayside. A few miles north of Nogent Dr Flaubert owned four acres of meadow down by the Seine. The purchase is interesting. It suggests the strength of his attachment to the distant scene of his boyhood.

The Nogent Flauberts lived in a large and solidly inelegant bourgeois town house shaded by an immense chestnut tree.* Among the indistinct but convivial crowd of Flaubert's Nogent relations only one is of individual significance. François Parain, known affectionately as Père Parain, was Flaubert's uncle by marriage. But he was definitely not a Flaubert. Slightly older than Dr Achille-Cléophas, François Parain was a *bon viveur* with a mischievous, boyish taste for smut. He was well qualified to play the classic part of the favourite uncle. 'He loved me', wrote Flaubert, 'with a love that was dog-like and exclusive.' Parain was *un original*, a gentle, undemanding, good-humoured eccentric, 'a splendid man whose slightly crazy juvenile vivacity was the source of his charm'. Flaubert needed such friendships. They served to lighten the burden of family ambition laid upon him by his critical, loving, disappointed father.

Flaubert retained an affectionate attachment to Nogent. As the scene of virtuous domestic boredom it would eventually supply him with a strongly contrasting background for *L'Education sentimentale*, his great novel of metropolitan modernity. Frederic Moreau, the principal character, comes from Nogent. Madame Moreau's house is modelled on the Nogent family house. The feuding, gossiping neighbours, the tranquil evenings down by the river, the mysterious enticement of the local brothel – all these first-hand small-town details are worked into

---

* The house still stands. It was bought by the Banque Commerciale de Champagne in 1965 and it carries a modest commemorative plaque.

the richly intimate texture of the story. Flaubert knew this world at first-hand: '. . . all the tittle-tattle, the backbiting, the slander, the jealousy and all the pettiness which are the exclusive ingredients of bourgeois life in small towns.'

THE strange story of the Rouen textile millionaire Pierre Dutuit deserves a small place at the end of this chapter. A modern fairy tale, it shows how quickly the coarse, energetic capitalist spirit can sicken and then decline into sterile, miserly obsession. Pierre Dutuit came from a modest artisan family in a poor quarter of Rouen. He went into business with his uncle Étienne, married a nice bit of money and made his first fortune down in Marseilles. In 1821 Pierre was back in Rouen with money to invest and a visionary enthusiasm for mechanisation. Thirty years, three water-powered factories and a spinnng works later, Pierre Dutuit died and left 2.3 million francs to his three children. Parvenu vanity required a large commemorative window in the basilica Bonsecours. There he is in stained glass, Pierre Dutuit, framed by a tasteful Gothic canopy, his family kneeling around him, forever giving thanks to the good Lord for the riches showered upon them.

But something went wrong, after Pierre. Eugène, Héloise and Auguste Dutuit were crushed by the weight of their riches. Perpetually unmarried, trying to keep the inheritance intact, they all lived together in splendid isolation in their large comfortable *hôtel* on the quai du Havre, juggling their capital, selling the factories, investing in land and shares. Éloise died first in 1874 with 2 million. Eugène died in 1886 with 6 million.

Auguste, the sole survivor, became ever more eccentric. He lived down in the cellar of his riverside mansion, paid starvation wages to his two old servants and entertained rare visitors around the kitchen table. Auguste's passion was collecting Renaissance masterpieces. Dressed in a threadbare overcoat with sagging pockets, he would travel all over Europe – third class, of course – in pursuit of some rare and expensive item. He wrapped his purchases in old newspaper, headed back to the quai du Havre and put them straight into boxes to be stored away. Auguste filled the house up to the attic with his collection. But he never looked at his nice things. He much preferred leafing through the receipts.

Auguste Dutuit, 'the Rouen Croesus', died in 1902 leaving 17 million francs, thirteen separate wills and six codicils. He had no known heirs.

Thus began a gold rush. Who would inherit the Dutuit millions? There were 5000 claimants in Rouen alone. After nine years of legal argument and passionate genealogical research 1350 Dutuits, scattered from Normandy to North Africa, received a meagre 3500 francs each. The Dutuit millions, so avidly scraped together and so piously hoarded, had finally rained down upon the city once again.

CHAPTER THREE

Awakenings

FLAUBERT'S earliest writings date from the revolutionary year of
1830. This small coincidence is all the more compelling for being so
unexpected. We may picture the artist roused from the soft and timeless
sleep of boyhood by the sound of wild political excitement. Looking
back on his youth, from the 1860s Flaubert fondly awarded himself an
honorary place alongside the insurgent romantic writers of 1830. It
was a comfortable fiction. Eighteen thirty was so heroically simple.
Eighteen forty-eight was so horribly ambiguous.

Rouen's revolution of 1830 was symbolically consummated at one
o'clock on the afternoon of Sunday, 1 August. The white *fleur-de-lis*,
emblem of the Bourbon kings, was ceremoniously lowered from the
Hôtel de Ville. In its place appeared the national red, white and blue of
the tricolour. Royal insignia were hastily removed from the city's public
monuments and street signs. A large crowd gathered on Rouen's main
square, the Place Saint-Ouen. Old soldiers who remembered Waterloo
were wildly excited.

The long, cold political winter, so miserable for every disenfranchised
freethinking liberal citizen, was over. Humiliated by the defeat of
Napoléon, then bullied into obedience by an ultraconservative monarchy, the political nation now exploded into life. In just three glorious
summer days, long to be celebrated as *les trois glorieuses*, the old order
had been swept away. What would take its place? He was called Louis-
Philippe, a constitutional monarch who carried an umbrella (a sign of
democracy). We can be sure that Louis-Philippe's sudden elevation to
the throne was the subject of animated conversation around the large,
highly polished liberal dinner table of Dr Achille-Cléophas Flaubert.
The mood of the hour was generously optimistic. Professional men

welcomed the new order. But would anyone have the power to contain the crude effervescence of popular expectation? That might be difficult.

Popular expectation soon made itself heard. A few weeks later, less than a mile from Dr Flaubert's liberal dinner table, a small crowd of Rouen textile workers began to gather on the banks of the Seine. They marched along the waterfront, moving from mill to mill, throwing stones through the windows and breaking down the doors. Soon all the mills were closed and a crowd of 3000 had gathered. The *garde natio- nale* was hastily mustered on the other side of the river. A police agent addressed the excited crowd, promising to bring their grievances to the attention of the mill-owners. The workers regrouped. They marched peacefully to the Hôtel de Ville and then dispersed. The prefect organ- ised a commission of mill-owners to consider the workers' demands. He was being lenient, moving cautiously. He knew that the new king was anxious to avoid any unfortunate 'incidents'.

Unorganised textile workers were easily hushed. Schoolboys inspired by their reading of Robespierre were a different matter. In October, returning for the new school year, the older boys of the Collège Royale de Rouen were in audaciously high spirits. The new king was going to change everything. He had already abolished censorship of the press. Catholicism was no longer to be the state religion. France was on the move. How was it that the little world of school was standing so per- fectly still? There had been a few changes of the tantalisingly symbolic kind. The Cross had been taken down from the top of the school bell- tower. The *fleur-de-lys*, now an obnoxious relic of the past, had been removed from the school shield. But none of this amounted to much. There was such great excitement in the air. Lessons were disrupted by the music of barrel organs in the street. They were playing the old patriotic tunes that marked moments of national danger. The new gov- ernment had just repudiated the humiliating peace treaties of 1815 and it was feared that France might be invaded by a coalition of indignant neighbouring states. On every square in the town men were parading and doing arms drill.

Gustave's stolid elder brother, Achille, may well have been among their number. The students of the college were all urged to play their part in this collective costume drama. Equipped with flintlock rifles and gold-tasselled police helmets the boys paraded up and down the main yard at the end of the school day. The teachers feared that this surge of popular military enthusiasm might undermine school discipline. Political excitement ran dangerously high among the day boys. They demanded a holiday to coincide with the Saint-Romain fair. Their discontents simmered all through the winter, giving off a delicious political fragrance that soon found its way into Flaubert's earliest writings.

Flaubert's first distinctively personal letter, dated December 1830, opens with a great salvo of indignation. He denounces reactionary manoeuvrings in the Chamber of Deputies against the citizen-hero Lafayette, 'the brave the white-haired Lafayette, liberator of the old world and the new'. This is just the kind of satisfyingly progressive political emotion that Flaubert will eventually satirise in *Dictionnaire des idées reçues*. At the age of nine, Flaubert was already deploying the phrases he heard at home, declaimed with a fresh and lively emphasis from the pages of the *Journal de Rouen*. The boy had observed the game and he understood its importance. A serious man was entitled to his political opinions. Indeed it was his social duty to declare them.

Flaubert's earliest literary efforts were being taken seriously too. An indulgent friend of the family gathered up Flaubert's loose pages then had them copied out and 'published' under the title *Three Pages from a Schoolboy's Notebook: The Selected Works of Gustave F.* 'Entertainments vented by his nascent muse', they were offered to the author's parents and his friends 'so that they might judge of his progress and his talent in every genre'. This collection includes a promisingly ingenious piece of schoolboy scatology, entitled *Splendid Explanation of the Famous Constipation*.

'Constipation is a tightening of the turdicarious hole, and when the passage is sterile, that is to say when the outlet is constricted, this is called constipation. It then resembles a sea that makes no foam and a woman who has no children. The substance that comes from the hole is called turdicalia, large and small. That is what the famous hole produces.'

A wonderfully solemn imitation of his father's official tone, it suggests that Flaubert already had ambitions as a mimic, and was happy to entertain his small circle. *The Selected Works of Gustave F.* also included a 'brilliant romantic epitaph for a neighbour's dog' and a satiric comedy in seven scenes called *The Miser*, which portrays 'the hideousness of avarice, the power of love in a man and its dissimulation in a woman'. Constipation, avarice and love, they are an irresistibly comic conjunction. It requires little ingenuity to suggest that Flaubert's richest satirical-aggressive impulses were rooted in the fascinations of anality. His subsequent reading of Rabelais and de Sade would suffice to bring this infantile theme to its full maturity.

Meanwhile, the political hopes so easily ignited during the summer were being carefully dowsed. The new government was moving swiftly to the right. The superbly harmonious social vision celebrated in Delacroix's allegorical image of *Liberty Leading the People* would survive for only a few months. In December 1830 the press laws were tightened up. In February 1831 there came news of deplorable 'disturbances' on the streets of Paris. 'People in rags have been perpetrating chaos.' The *Journal de Rouen* urged its leisured, liberal readers to visit the *Hôtel des Augustins* where, for one franc, they could admire a large history painting entitled *Barricade Scene*. Based on a heroic incident from the July Days, the painting captured 'the excitement and the energy which presides over the mighty deeds of the people when roused to Anger'. Not all the mighty deeds of the people could be so cheerfully endorsed. In the first week of March 1831 a crowd of unemployed workers gathered in front of Rouen's Hôtel de Ville. Sensing that history was not yet on their side, they dispersed without incident when faced with a troop of the National Guard.

Meanwhile, a few streets away, behind the walls of the Collège de Rouen, where the sons of the city's professional and merchant families came to be fashioned into citizens, a lamentable drama of insubordination was unfolding. The trouble began when half a dozen students refused to go to confession and then refused to accept their punishment. A sign of the times! The boys took a heroic oath of defiance and barricaded themselves into the dormitory on the top floor of the school. The National Guard was called in and all lessons were suspended. Declaring a state of siege, the students broke their dormitory windows and bombarded the staff room from above. Soaked by the fire brigade, fainting from hunger, the rebels eventually surrendered. Their ringleaders were expelled from the school and an official inspector, Monsieur Naudet, 'a sincere friend to the young', was appointed to conduct an inquiry. An open letter, deploring the recent troubles, was read aloud in class. 'There have been grave disturbances, serious offences and great imprudence.'

Discipline in French schools was already harsh. Ever since the restoration of 1815 the nation's schoolboys had been metaphorically chained down, enduring a regime of relentless surveillance, minute regulation, and harsh reprisals. Schoolboys lived in an atmosphere of continuous mutual suspicion. Now, in the aftermath of this failed revolt, discipline in the Collège de Rouen became even stricter. The educational institution that would soon enfold the young Gustave Flaubert was now a mature miniature despotism. Something in between an army barracks, a prison and a madhouse, school was a place where a young boy might experience the scorching action of the darker psychic forces that lay compressed beneath the phrase 'new industrial age'.

If the defeated insurgents of the Collège de Rouen had been looking for a manifesto, they might have found it in a book published that very month: Victor Hugo's *Notre-Dame de Paris*. A timely fable of rebellion, the novel is full of wild, joyful crowd scenes. It describes a secret urban world peopled by dwarves and demons whose reckless energy threatens to turn everything upside down. Flaubert especially admired Hugo's description of the underworld. It mingled the real and the fantastic in a powerful new way. He remembered Hugo's Quasimodo, the gentle monster, when he created the priapic primitives of his own adolescent fiction.

The month before Flaubert's tenth birthday, in November 1831, Hugo published another book that soon wove itself into the memories and the dreams of the rising generation. *Les Feuilles d'automne* was a collection of intimate meditative lyrics exploring family life and memories of childhood. Alert to the mood of the hour, Hugo equipped his apparently innocuous poems with a deliciously subversive political preface, inviting his readers to thrill to 'the muffled sound that revolutions make, still buried beneath the earth, as they extend their subterranean galleries under every kingdom of Europe . . . ' Hugo was offering his readers the intoxicating Poetry of Premonition, a passionate schoolboy version of the thwarted political aspirations of the day. Swiftly acclaimed as the hero of a new Romantic counterculture, Hugo stood for perpetual insubordination. He was forbidden in schools. Schoolboys read him, of course, after dark in their dormitories. Poetry by candlelight was yet another sign of the times.

GUSTAVE Flaubert was ten years old when he entered the Collège de Rouen in March 1832. He was unlikely to be daunted by the neoclassical grandeur of the place. As a child of the Hôtel-Dieu Flaubert already felt quite at home in big buildings. The college was impressive. It stood in one of the healthiest quarters of the city (an important selling point); it had a handsome portico, a fine courtyard, an enormous chapel in the baroque style (ideal for prize-givings); its dormitory, designed for ease of surveillance, was a vast barn-like space on the third floor of the main building, just beneath the curve of the roof.* Still in use as a school, the building projects a powerful, slightly bullying impression of sober, high-bourgeois dignity.

As an *interne*, Flaubert lived here for the next six school years, until the great day in October 1838 when he became a day boy. His school record suggests that he was initially a compliant, industrious, eager schoolboy. Surprisingly, he only began to hate the place when he was fourteen. His recollections of school are therefore predictably tinged by that later vision in which he appears as a solitary, disaffected hero.

There were evenings of reverie:

What did I dream of during the long evenings of prep, when I sat there, my elbows on my desk, gazing at the wick of the Argand lamp [. . .] whilst my classmates' quills were squeaking across the paper [. . .]? I used to do my homework at top speed so that I could devote myself uninterruptedly to these cherished thoughts. [. . .]. I used to push as far as possible into my mind, exploring in every direction [. . .]. I devised adventures for myself, I set up stories, built myself palaces and lived in them as emperor [. . .].

There were sleepless nights:

And when the evening came and we were all laid in our white beds with our white curtains and the house master was walking alone up and down the dormitory, how I drew back into myself again, delightedly hiding in my bosom that warm bird with the fluttering wings! I always took a long time to fall asleep, I listened to the chiming of the hours, the later it was the happier I felt [. . .].

There were cold awakenings: at five in the morning, summoned from sleep by a roll on a drum, thirty boys sprang promptly from their beds, dressed and washed in silence, then formed up in a line and were closely inspected before walking downstairs in silence. School was a junior version of military life. Discipline, sir! Petty, relentless and mildly sadistic discipline. It was the only way to drive out the crafty devil hiding in every sweet, pink, twelve-year-old heart. The punishments ordained for the young were long remembered by those who had endured them.

* In 1998 the dormitory of 1832 was still a dormitory, though the school ethos was slightly softer. A cheerful individualism prevailed, with giant photo-posters of rock stars and football heroes decorating the wooden screens that separate the beds.

There was standing outside on a frosty day without stamping your feet. There was kneeling on a thin wooden rod. There was holding out two heavy books at arm's length. Flaubert worked his way, instructively, through the whole repertoire.

The classroom left its own assortment of uncongenial memories: an enormous bare room with oak benches around the walls, a cast-iron stove, only ever lit at the beginning of November, and scarcely casting any warmth beyond a radius of six feet. The ink froze in winter and if you came top of the class you had to sit, inexplicably, furthest from the stove. You wrote, shivering, with your knee for a desk, an excruciatingly awkward arrangement.

Only one happy school memory made its way into Flaubert's writing. It deserves to be included as a corrective to the romantically darkened picture that he preferred to paint in later years:

[. . .] it was winter, a really cold day, we had just come in from a walk, and because there were only a few of us we were allowed to sit around the stove; we warmed ourselves lazily, we toasted our slices of bread on our rulers, the chimney was humming; we talked about everything under the sun: the plays we'd seen, the women we'd loved, leaving college, what we planned to do when we were grown up.

The pleasures of masculine conversation, though largely absent from his fiction, were always dear to Flaubert's heart.

FORTUNATELY for Flaubert, the Collège Royale de Rouen was not the whole of his life. He was soon writing and performing plays at home in the holidays. At the age of ten, in March 1832, he was working on a farce to be called *The Miser* and urging his friend Ernest Chevalier to collaborate with him on further stories. Elaborate theatrical preparations were in hand. The family billiard table was commandeered for a stage. It was going to be just like a real theatre. There were posters and tickets, a man on the door, armchairs all set out, fancy decorations and a proper canvas backdrop. Four short pieces, one by Molière and one by Scribe, were performed to an audience of ten or a dozen people consisting of Ernest Chevalier and his mother, family servants and school friends.

Outdoors, walking the streets was an education. The boy had a big city to explore, a whole world of urban enterprise, novelty and entertainment, the happier face of the 'century of miracles'. Go south from the Hôtel-Dieu, towards the river. At your back was La Madeleine, an immense neoclassical church, with four great pillars, a dome, and a triangular gable decorated with the emblem of the sun. The warm yellow stonework was still scarcely blackened by the smoke. Ahead of you there was a wide, tree-lined avenue leading down a gentle slope to the Seine. You strolled past the iron gates of the great wine and cider market, the Champ de Foire aux Boissons, a picturesque industrial enclave of brewers, barrel-makers and spirit merchants, an odd place to find on the doorstep of the Hôtel-Dieu. Here was animation: ships loading and unloading their cargo of barrels on the quay, carts rattling across the cobbles, men in heavy boots leading their massive draft horses, Brabants and Percherons, straining to pull their loads up the slope. At the far end of the avenue, out in the river, there was a little island, l'Ile du Petit-Guay, with a swimming school. Flaubert spent many summer afternoons there, 'under the little avenue of poplars, naked, in a swimming costume, with the smell of the nets and the tar and the sight of the sails'. In later years there would be little glasses of rum, supplied by the congenial proprietor.

The city of Flaubert's boyhood, though dedicated to hard work, still made time for play. Every year, braving the autumnal damp, the Foire Saint-Romain drew crowds of people on to the streets. 'Faire la foire' meant 'to have a wild time'. It meant bells and drums and trumpets and steam organs and the smell of grilled herrings, roasted chestnuts and *pain d'épice*, a warm, promiscuous, festive mixture drifting here and there on the cold November air.

All along the boulevards and down the city streets it went, under the doors and up the stairs and into the salon where it tickled the ears and the noses of sober, prosperous Monsieur et Madame, pulling gently at their purses and whispering to them the names of the bright, foolish things they had loved as children: puppet shows, performing dogs, magic lanterns, Turkish wrestlers, Bengal lights and ladies in little pink dresses dancing implausibly on the tightrope.

Rouen's Foire Saint-Romain was an archaic taste of the carnivalesque and Flaubert loved it. Molière, when still a hungry strolling player, had played his first gig at the fair in 1643. Peasants came in from miles around, blocking the way with their enormous baskets of produce, playing billiards in the open air, drinking cider. Village priests warned their simple flock against the depredations of pickpockets and prostitutes. Mangin, the pencil-seller, was always there, enthroned on a cart with his antique helmet, his ruff and his breastplate, sharpening the pencils with a cavalry officer's sabre. On a square of painted canvas, an athletic-looking man, naked as a savage, is lifting an enormous weight on his back; the banner scrolling from his mouth says: I AM THE HERCULES OF THE NORTH.

At the fair there was something for every taste, for every pocket. A singer under a big red umbrella. A band of musketeers in doublet and hose. A quack doctor, haranguing a crowd from the top of a barrel, resplendent in '... a green coat laced with gold, a broad scrubby wig ... imitation diamonds on his fingers, breeches of worn black satin ... and shoes with enormous buckles'. With their colourful costume and the boldly fanciful eloquence of their patter (like Rabelais) the fair-ground doctors offered a gloriously disreputable parody of the paternal-medical mystique. There were freaks and oddities to delight and disgust. A seven-legged calf. A hydrocephalic foetus, grimacing inside his great jar of alcohol. The Schmidt Menagerie advertised a dozen lions, a Bengal tiger, leopards, hyenas, and bears both black and white, an elephant, snakes and crocodile. After dark there was loud music and the flare of gaslights. In later years, as the high point of the entertainment, people paid to see naked women.

Here was a world of fairgrounds and cider works, a provincial urban world that Flaubert knew in intimate detail. Why did he choose not to portray it in his mature fiction? Perhaps because the urban-picturesque already belonged to Victor Hugo. Baudelaire would raise it to a new aesthetic intensity, but Flaubert would turn it in an entirely different direction. The bits-and-pieces immediacy of the Paris of *L'Education sentimentale* points forwards to *Ulysses*. It's the next chapter of the inner history of the city.

Most miraculous of all the engines of modernity was the steamboat, *le pyroscaphe*, an American invention that reached France in the late 1820s, bringing the message that the coming century would be unlike all others. As a boy Flaubert would have seen the steamboats, the *Charles-Philippe* or the *Elise*, racing each other as they turned the bend in the river on their way to Paris. Steam was the new magic, the force that would one day undo the ancient powers of gods and kings. For the moment, though, its effect on the social fabric of Rouen was limited. Business was still on a small scale. Mechanised textile production required little capital in the 1820s; the sale of a farm could finance the start-up, a converted barn could house the enterprise, and families still commonly worked together in the new mills. A close friend of the Flaubert family, Paul Le Poittevin, Alfred's father, was just such an industrialist, a man who came up 'from nothing' in the space of twenty years. Arriving in the city around 1800, Le Poittevin started off as the foreman in a dye works, went into business on his own account, married the daughter of a rich ship-owner, expanded into weaving, prospered enormously and bought farmland on the coast. The business was dissolved soon after his death and the children all married into the rural nobility, begetting a third generation of rentiers, artists and writers, including Guy de Maupassant.

IN April 1832, the city of Rouen was struck by an epidemic of cholera. This was the very first of the catastrophic nineteenth-century European cholera epidemics. Many of its poorer victims died within the walls of the Hôtel-Dieu and Flaubert long remembered living in the midst of it all: 'A simple wooden partition with a door was all that separated our dining room from the sick ward where people were dropping like flies.'

The disease had appeared in Paris on 26 March, spreading within a week to all quarters of the crowded, unsanitary city. It then ran across northern France, carried by migrant workers. In a typical case, a traveller from Paris would fall sick and die at the village inn. The disease would then spread to the whole village.*

The cholera epidemic was a social and political crisis as well as a medical problem. Because cholera killed the urban poor in great numbers it inflamed class hatred to fantastic dimensions. There was fear and panic below, heavy-handed ignorance and prejudice above, a combination that spawned rumours almost as virulent in their effects as the disease itself. On the coast, in Dieppe and Le Havre, pious fishermen said it was all a punishment from God for having deposed the rightful king. Perhaps the end of the world was near. In cities and villages the destitute said it was a plot to exterminate the poor, a plot organised by the rich, by the government, by the doctors. They were putting poison in the bread they gave away to the hungry. In the hospitals the doctors were putting poison in the salt. Provincial crowds turned against

---

* Cholera begins abruptly and runs its whole course within a week. Copious but painless diarrhoea, four gallons or more in the first 24 hours, is followed by vomiting and dehydration. The skin becomes cold and withered. The face is drawn and the pulse weakens. The limbs are locked as the muscles go into spasm and then death comes with a stupefied burning thirst.

medical students sent from Paris to help the local doctors. Any educated stranger might be part of the plot. Suspicious characters were lynched on the streets. Whole populations fled into the surrounding countryside. The National Guard were posted, to protect drinking fountains and to drive away gangs of fugitives arriving from neighbouring villages. Overworked prefects were worried that the poison rumours might be the work of malevolent agitators. One minor official consoled himself with the observation that the disease only struck 'individuals of little use to society'. The editors of provincial newspapers were prosecuted for exaggerating the scale of the epidemic. Doctors disagreed bitterly with each other over the mode of the disease's transmission. The contagion theory, substantiated only half a century later, was angrily denounced.

The cholera epidemic of 1832 was a modern *danse macabre*, a procession of disgustingly animated corpses crowding into the Hôtel-Dieu. Together with folk memories of the plague and the artistic revival of the Dance of Death, 1832 left its morbid traces in Flaubert's later writings. The faint, sad, inescapable corruption of the flesh is his darkest theme.*

A T first he was a great success. In August 1833, at the age of eleven, Flaubert won a school prize for excellence. Top of the class five times, his name was there, in print for the first time, in the local newspaper, the *Journal de Rouen*. It was a most auspicious beginning. The boy might yet bring honour upon the family name. The prize ceremony, attended by the social elite of Rouen, took place among the seventeenth-century Jesuit splendours of the school chapel. This was the great moment of the school year, a little taste of *la gloire*. Prizewinners were accorded elaborate honours. They received crowns of oak leaves, proudly preserved through the year; they were given calfbound volumes of the edifying kind, with the city arms embossed in gold on their covers; drummers from the National Guard played outside their houses. It was all an excellent preparation for the rigours of meritocracy.

Whatever the implications of his public debut, Flaubert was also beginning to think for himself. We catch sight of him fleetingly, in the summer of his eleventh year, reading Walter Scott and Victor Hugo,

---

* The artist and writer Eustache Langlois, a close friend of the Flaubert family, was an expert on the iconography of the Dance of Death. See Yvonne Bargues-Rollins 1998, *Le pas de Flaubert: une danse macabre*. Paris: Champion.

rehearsing plays, enjoying an excursion to a Parisian theatre, or attending a family baptism in Nogent at which he didn't recite the *credo*. In September King Louis-Philippe made an official visit to Rouen. No expense was spared. Civic loyalty took the form of artillery salvoes, peals of bells, maidens in allegorical costume, and bread for the poor. The queen and the princesses visited the Hôtel-Dieu, met the staff, inspected the kitchens and tasted the soup. Flaubert stayed away, resolutely unimpressed. 'The people are so blind!' he wrote, resolved to ignore the parades, the orchestras and the fireworks. It was all such a waste of money.

Later that same week, something more interesting than a constitutional monarch came into view. At noon on Saturday, 14 September 1833, by courtesy of steam, a large piece of old Egypt arrived in Rouen. It was the *Louxor*, moored down at the quai d'Harcourt with its singular cargo: 250 tons of uprooted granite obelisk, the gift of Mehmet Ali, Pasha of Egypt, in transit from the Temple of Sesostris to the Place de la Concorde, now awaiting the autumn rains that would raise the level of the River Seine. Two transplanted female vultures, also on board, appeared to be surviving the drastic change of climate.

Did Flaubert visit the obelisk and its attendant vultures? How could he resist their allure? Orientalism, both the fashionably poetic and the merely political, was in the air. Flaubert had reached the very age at which we first learn to draw down whatever is 'in the air'. It was at this moment, in the early 1830s, that he took on the exuberant, insurgent identity of his generation. He always remembered it with undiminished enthusiasm. In 1860, he wrote,

I have a great respect for what I was then (even though I was perfectly ridiculous) – and if I am still worth anything it may well be because of all that? We were a little coterie, boiling and blazing, I swear to you, with a most ferocious hyperbolical excitement, both literary and sentimental. We slept with daggers under our pillows. We committed suicide, literally. We were angelically good-looking! Why the devil am I telling you all this?

By 1872, at a distance of forty years, the memory of those days had reached its autumnal ripeness. 'Our dreams,' Flaubert wrote,

were superbly extravagant – the last ripples of romanticism [. . .] compressed by the provincial milieu, made a wonderful ferment in our brains. Some eager souls yearned for dramatic love-affairs, with gondolas, black masks and great ladies fainting in post-chaises somewhere in Calabria. The more sombre

41

amongst us had set our hearts on the rowdy world of journalism or politics, on the fame of the conspirator. One of the older boys composed a *Vindication of Robespierre* which circulated outside the school and so scandalised a certain gentleman that there ensued an exchange of letters with a challenge to a duel in which the gentleman came off the worse. I remember one brave boy forever sporting the red liberty-bonnet; another lad swearing that later he would live as a Mohican; one of my close friends wanted to turn renegade and serve in the army of Abd-el-Kader. But we were not simply troubadour, insurgent and oriental, we were artists above all else; once our extra homework was finished, then literature began; and we all ruined our eyes reading novels in the dormitory, we carried daggers in our pockets like Antony; and we went even further: B***, disgusted with life, blew his brains out with a pistol, A*** hung himself with his necktie. We were not especially praiseworthy, certainly, but what hatred of mediocrity! What splendid aspirations! What reverence for our literary masters! How we admired Victor Hugo!

Flaubert's great mentor in the hatred of mediocrity was his friend Alfred Le Poittevin.

Several years older than Flaubert, Alfred was the antithesis of Ernest Chevalier. Ernest was robust, competent, cheerful and energetic, 'the Gendarme', destined for worldly success; Alfred was sensitive, refined, fragile and lethargic, a precociously decadent pessimist who met a premature death. Flaubert was enthralled by Alfred. He was eager to learn whatever this ideal elder brother deigned to teach him. It was a strenuous curriculum consisting mainly of Spinoza, Satanism and cunnilingus; their conversations, of which nothing has survived, were horribly exhilarating. Flaubert remembered these long adolescent afternoons most appreciatively:

We lived in an ideal hothouse with our *ennui* poetically fired up to a temperature of 70 degrees. There was a man, indeed. I have never ever managed such journeys in the real world. We ventured far without ever leaving the fireside. We mounted high, though the ceiling of my room was low. Certain afternoons remain in my mind, conversations that went on for six hours at a stretch, walks across the hills [. . .].

Fired by Alfred's example, Flaubert turned mildly Byronic. He admired the noble faces of the men condemned for their part in the recent Paris riots and he bought himself a copy of Dumas's latest play, *Antony*, the very symbol of advanced Romantic taste. *Antony* was a tale of violent adulterous passion in a modern setting, perfectly designed to catch the youthful imagination. The melancholy, sarcastic hero was a bastard and an outcast. Every schoolboy copied him, acting the part with a burning passion. It was easy to do Antony. The role was a medley of wild emotions: 'desperate attitudes, sombre glances, fatal brows, mocking laughter, convulsive sobs, fists raised to heaven, blasphemies and maledictions'. Dumas, the author, still in his late twenties, became rich and famous from his triumph in the theatre. This fact did not escape Flaubert. He immersed himself in the new Romantic theatre, woke up at three in the morning to read *Othello*, followed all the Parisian gossip, deplored the re-imposition of play censorship, founded a literary and theatrical journal of his own, and chose a pen-name with a nice Polish ring to it, Gustave Antursekothi Kocloth.

Moving faster and faster now, Flaubert had the great good luck to encounter an inspiring teacher. Pierre-Adolphe Cheruel, a pupil of Michelet, the greatest of the French Romantic historians, was Flaubert's history teacher for five crucial school years, from 1834 until 1839. Loved and admired by his students, Cheruel was only ten years older than they were. He combined real intellectual distinction with an imposing physical presence. He was tall, with a high forehead, large bright eyes and a rich clear voice. Under Cheruel's benignly creative influence Flaubert acquired a taste for history that never left him. This was Romantic history, 'resurrection de la vie intégrale', history that a novelist might one day use. Reading Michelet's glowingly evocative *Histoire de France*, writing his own increasingly ambitious history assignments for Cheruel, Flaubert twice won the school prize for history. He remembered Cheruel with deep gratitude and sent him copies of all his published works.

IN the 1830s the Flaubert family usually spent their summer holidays in Trouville, a fishing village on the Normandy coast, increasingly fashionable with Parisians for its spacious sandy beaches and its cliff walks. There, in July 1836, the fourteen-year-old Flaubert encountered the twenty-five-year-old Elisa Schlésinger. It was, he always insisted, the great event of his life. The image of this voluptuously maternal woman possessed his imagination ever after.

We do not know exactly what happened between the boy and the woman in the course of that summer passion, though a whole fanciful department of Flaubert biography has been devoted to reconstructing it. (An archetypal tale of hopeless adoration, with a denouement for every taste.) Flaubert himself was decorously vague whenever he told the story. This was how it went in 1859:

In my youth I loved immeasurably, a love that was unrequited, intense and silent. Nights spent gazing at the moon, dreaming of elopements and travels in Italy, dreams of glory for her sake, torments of the body and the soul, spasms at the smell of a shoulder, and turning suddenly pale when I caught her eye, I have known all that, and known it very well. Each one of us has in his heart a royal chamber. I have had mine bricked up, but it is still there.

This is carefully posed, a clever studio portrait of the artist as melancholy romantic genius; Flaubert was trying to convince his correspondent, Amélie Bosquet, that he was not the heartless lecher she took him for. Hence the tragic narcissism.

Somewhat closer to the event, in 1838, Flaubert wove the real Elisa Schlésinger and her husband Maurice into the dark fabric of his first real novel, *Mémoires d'un fou*. In this version there is a village by the sea, '[. . .] charming with its houses piled one on top of the other, black, grey, red and white, facing in every direction [. . .] like a pile of shells and pebbles that the waves have left on the shore'. At low tide the hero walks across the great expanse of wet silver-grey sand that shines in the sun. On the shore one morning he finds a red-and-black *pelisse* with silk fringes and rescues it from the advancing waves. Eating his lunch at the inn, he receives gracious thanks from the beautiful woman at the next table. Her voice, her eyes, her shoulders, her lips, are burnt into his memory; every morning thereafter he goes to watch her bathing in the sea. One day he sees her breast-feeding her infant daughter. Devouring her breast with his eyes he imagines bringing his own lips towards it, kissing and biting it in a frenzy of passion.

This delicious primal reverie is interrupted, comically, by the presence of the Husband, a vulgar, jovial man, 'something in between an artist and a commercial traveller'. The Wife gives the boy cigarettes and talks literature, 'inexhaustible topic of conversation with any woman'. The Husband organises a boating party for the evening. There is moonlight on the sea. Sitting beside her, touching her dress, feeling the warmth of her shoulder, the Boy is enchanted by the sound of her voice. Walking back with her to the inn, he is too timid to speak. He gazes up at her window. When her light goes out he is stricken with jealousy, imagining her in her husband's arms. His thoughts – bitter and vengeful, obscene – keep him awake until dawn.

Looking at a portrait of Elisa Schlésinger we may readily envisage the erotic power of her presence. She was an opulent beauty, with large eyes, full lips and big breasts. Plumply maternal and pleased with life, she radiates that warm, fertile, physical contentment for which the word *Junoesque* was aptly devised. If we place her alluring image alongside a portrait sketch of Madame Flaubert, executed in 1831 when she was in her late thirties, we shall observe a striking contrast. Swathed up to the chin, the real mother has a small, unsmiling mouth and a small head on a large, shapeless body. Looking for the Mother was already the great theme of Flaubert's erotic quest.

CHAPTER FOUR

Coming of Age

BACK at school again, Flaubert felt 'lonely isolated suspicious low jealous selfish cruel'. Only two more years, he grumbled, in this 'shit-awful god-awful madhouse of a college'. He was now leading a singularly complex existence: winning prizes, writing precociously sophisticated tales of adultery, exploring new worlds of feeling in Goethe and de Sade, and all the while observing the strange wilting of his own genius. On top of this, the once rose-pink schoolboy had magically acquired a truculent public character as the hard-drinking, foul-mouthed, pipe-smoking habitué of the Café National, the fearless explorer of every idea, every vice, declaiming advanced political opinions and exhaling a generalised disgust with the world.

Let us follow him through the closing scenes of his schooldays, the time when habitual diligence coexists with rebellious anger. In August 1837 Flaubert won first prize for his work in natural history – 'the just reward for his unremitting efforts' – with a twenty-five-page essay on the history of mushrooms, conscientiously copied up from an encyclopaedia . It suggests an affinity with the imaginary intellectual labours of *Bouvard et Pécuchet*.

In September 1837, a few months before his sixteenth birthday, Flaubert ventured briefly but unforgettably into a social world that he had never seen before. With his family he attended the autumn ball given by the Marquis de Pomereu, 'the greatest landowner in France', at the Chateau du Heron. Here was aristocratic magnificence on a scale to corrupt the thoughts of even the most austere egalitarian. Flaubert, never particularly austere or egalitarian, was thoroughly corrupted. 'I spent the whole night watching the dancing [. . .]. I didn't go to bed and in the morning I took a boat out on the lake, on my own, in my school uniform. The swans watched me as I went by and the leaves were falling into the water. It was just a few days before school started again. I was fifteen years old.' Flaubert uses this scene again and again in his fiction, a mark of its extraordinary importance in his own life. It goes through many transformations, but the basic elements are always the same. The young hero is captivated by his first taste of aristocratic luxury; he drifts into a solitary early-morning reverie and creates for himself a fantasy future, a glorious dream of elegance and pleasure that leaves him thereafter utterly forlorn and discontented. It's the delicious, ruinous, bittersweet essence of *Bovary*-ism.

Troubled by his chateau visions and by his impossible desire for Elisa Schlésinger, Flaubert now created his first great heroine, Mazza, a married woman at the centre of a drama of adultery and suicide. *Passion et vertu*, based on a recent court case, is a remarkable early sketch for *Madame Bovary*. The man is brutal and cynical in his seduction. The woman is exquisite and ferocious in her passion, so ferocious that she frightens the man away. He runs away to America and she kills herself with acid procured from the chemist, after the deaths of her husband and her children. *Passion et vertu* was Flaubert's first sustained effort to describe the psychology of his characters. Just as in *Madame Bovary*, Flaubert twists his tale to make it a vindication of the heroine, destroyed by the dark power of romantic love. On this occasion, though, Flaubert loses the thread after the moment of betrayal. He makes the denouement too black. He had found his theme but he was not yet sure what to do with it.

A different kind of inspiration came to Flaubert in the form of Goethe's *Faust*.

He read it the very day before Easter on his way back from school; instead of going home he found himself, he had no idea how, in a [. . .] beautiful promenade with an avenue of tall trees on the left bank of the Seine, a little way out of town. He sat on the bank; the bells of the churches on the other side of the river were ringing out through the air and mixing with Goethe's splendid lines: 'Christ is risen . . .' His head was spinning, and he went home bewildered, in another world.

That was how Flaubert told it to his niece. When he told the same story to the cynical de Goncourt brothers in 1866, he omitted the exaltation of the church bells and gave his tale a more terrestrial ending, claiming that he 'found himself a couple of miles outside Rouen, near a shooting gallery, in the pouring rain'. It is entirely plausible that Goethe's Easter-morning scene took the Rouen schoolboy into 'another world'. Celebrating the Resurrection it went right against Alfred Le Poittevin's bitter cult of scepticism and despair. Goethe's eventual influence on Flaubert was even more pervasive. His poetic polytheism and his Romantic science of morphology offered agreeable nourishment to a mind weary of the more desiccated varieties of rationalism.

When the new school year began in September 1838 Flaubert was no longer a boarding pupil. He was *externe libre*. This was freedom of a kind, but it was not enough to mitigate the servitude he now began to detest. His closest friends, Alfred and Ernest, had both left for Paris and he was eager to join them there. 'What a splendid trio we would make!' So he made a world of his own, in books and in daydreams, but this was not enough either: 'I spent hours sitting with my head in my hands, gazing at the floor of my study [. . .] and when I woke, with wide staring eyes, people laughed at me, the laziest boy in the class [. . .] the one who showed no aptitude for any profession [. . .] the good-for-nothing who would at most be a clown, a showman with performing animals, or a maker of books.' He was afflicted by 'a nervous irritation which made me abrasive and bad-tempered [. . .]. I used to stand apart, with a book of verse or a novel [. . .]. Often after one reading I retained whole passages and I used to say them to myself [. . .].'

Flaubert spent the autumn of that year writing *Mémoires d'un fou*, a tale aspiring to be a novel, distinguished by its autobiographical audacity and a certain delirious comic energy. It was to be a book 'neither instructive nor amusing, neither chemical, philosophical, agricultural or elegaic [. . .] a book with no mention of railways or the stock-exchange or the secret places of the human heart [. . .]'.

In February 1839, demoralised and isolated, with the question of his future career hanging over him, Flaubert began writing a journal.* 'My usual character', he observed, 'is what they call cheerful, but there are blanks, a dreadful emptiness, I fall in broken exhausted destroyed! I no longer write – I used to – I used to be enthralled by my ideas, I knew what it was to be a poet [. . .]. And now though I still have a sense of my own vocation, or is it the fullness of an immense pride, I waver more and more [. . .].' This journal entry coincided with Flaubert's first

---

* This is the only journal to have survived. There were undoubtedly others, but they were destroyed, probably by their author.

reluctant declaration, in a letter to Ernest Chevalier, that he would *eventually* take up the study of the law. Alongside this, he also declared his true vocation: 'If ever I play an active part in the world it will be as a thinker and a demoraliser. I shall simply tell the truth, but it will be horrible, cruel and naked'. Anxious doubts and inflated certainties jostle their way across the page. The outcome is a sour, constipated acquiescence. 'I am incapable of imaginative work, everything I produce is dry, difficult, forced, torn painfully out of me [. . .]. My life which I had fancied so beautiful, so poetic, so ample, so amorous, will be just like any other, monotonous, sensible, stupid. *I will do my law, I will be called to the bar* and then in a worthy finale I shall go to live in some little provincial village [. . .].'

Somewhere behind these words we may picture a series of unhappy Christmas conversations between a benignly concerned father and his indignant son. To a boy in this vengeful, morally defeated condition, the realm of the monstrous might now begin to beckon with a most seductive charm. *Epater le bourgeois?* Who could be better qualified for that joyful task than the Marquis de Sade? De Sade accordingly makes his first ghostly appearance in a letter written on 15 July 1839. The name comes up in connection with a recently executed murderer, one Lacenaire. 'I like to see men such as this, like Nero, like the Marquis de Sade.' Such men, Flaubert tells Ernest Chevalier, are 'like the little priapic statues which the Egyptians placed alongside the immortals [. . .]. To my mind such monsters explain history, they are the complement, the apogee, the morality, the dessert.' It emerges in this same letter that Flaubert had not yet read de Sade. Merely a recent pamphlet – by Jules Janin – denouncing him in the most enticing fashion. 'De Sade', thundered Janin, 'is everywhere; he is in every library, hidden away on a certain mysterious shelf [. . .].'* Flaubert asks Ernest, in Paris, to find him some. 'I'd pay you their weight in gold.' Flaubert was ready for what he hoped was in de Sade. Did Ernest, 'the Gendarme', oblige him? Though there is no further mention of the request, we may assume that Flaubert was soon in a position to judge for himself. He came to regard de Sade as a great comic writer. Comic in a dark and uncomfortable sense that will be fully explored hereafter.

* Janin 'made his mark around 1830 with novels that exemplified the younger generation's taste for horror, mixed with humour, cynicism, and some despair'.

Back at school once again, in October 1839, Flaubert was now in *philo*, the great year, the one everybody looked forward to. Now he could study philosophy, 'the supreme science, the flower, the cream, the summit, the excrement of all the rest'. Philosophy amounted to making copious notes from the official textbook, Mallet's *Manuel de philosophie à l'usage des élèves*. Flaubert hated it. 'It gives me such a cudgelling that all my bones are broken. But I refresh myself by reading Montaigne in great quantities, he's my man.' He persevered with Mallet and toiled through all sixty-two chapters. He even came top of the class before he was crushed, morally, for attempting to apply the philosophical method to a small question of school discipline.

It happened towards the end of his first term. One Monday evening in December when Bezont, a replacement teacher, was taking the philosophy class, all the boys came into the classroom talking loudly, delaying the start of the lesson. Bezont had some difficulty imposing silence. Flaubert and two of his friends kept interrupting. They were given impositions but 'disorder continued' with much whispering and shuffling of feet. Bezont gave out a general imposition, one thousand lines for everyone in the class.

But Flaubert was not to be silenced. On Wednesday there appeared a letter to the headmaster, Monsieur Dainez, signed by thirty pupils, with Flaubert's name at the head of the list, announcing their refusal to write their lines. On Thursday Flaubert celebrated his eighteenth birthday. Later the same week there was another letter, written in Flaubert's hand, with thirteen signatures. As their numbers diminished, so their tone became more ceremonious, more defiant and more dignified. The thirteen now complained that the authorities were treating them insultingly. 'You said [. . .] we were behaving like children.' They deplored the proctor's threats to expel the three students who had been the cause of the original disruption. Expulsion was serious. It meant 'spoiling their future prospects and excluding them for ever from the careers which they might have followed'. They appealed for justice. They were simply students of philosophy, attempting to put high theory into practice: 'Philosophy students who have reflected and considered carefully before taking a step which they feel is justified and which they are resolved to pursue to its conclusion.'

Anxious to avoid another scandal of the kind that had befallen the college all too recently, Monsieur Dainez responded with decisive measures. Those who refused to do their impositions were immediately expelled. They were to be allowed back only if they submitted to their punishment. By Monday the thirteen intransigents were reduced to eight. By Tuesday there were only five, including Flaubert. They were all expelled from the Collège de Rouen. At this point Flaubert family influence came into play. The heroic impasse in which the son now found himself was resolved from above by his father. Dr Flaubert and the head of the college worked out a discreetly amicable arrangement whereby the boy was to be allowed to complete his studies at home and then sit his exams independently in the summer. His future career as a lawyer need not be prejudiced and the illustrious family name could still shine forth untarnished.

Though he had played a glamorously intrepid role in the events at school, Flaubert now kept oddly quiet about the whole business. We do not know the details of the serious father-and-son conversation that may have taken place, but in his letters to Ernest Chevalier, Flaubert sounds distinctly chastened: 'If you want to hear some news, or at least a piece of news, I can tell you that I am no longer at the college and since I am so weary of the details of my story and I'm just fed up with it I refer you to Alfred for the narrative. I am therefore going to work hard for my *baccalaureat*, though for the moment I am supremely lazy and all I do is sleep.'

The price of salvation was Good Behaviour.

EIGHTEEN FORTY was to be one of the great years of Flaubert's life. But it began rather badly. Christmas was over and it was January and he was stuck at home, working on his physics and his maths, his Greek and his Latin. Studying Seneca, he said, but thinking about de Sade. 'Read him from cover to cover,' he instructs a friend, 'it will complete your moral education and give you a brilliant insight into the history of philosophy.' Apart from his official tasks Flaubert was pondering a facetiously egalitarian novel in the style of Goethe. It was to be the story of a king and a cesspool-cleaner. They meet and converse in a brothel. Here we touch upon one of Flaubert's cherished secrets. The comic truth comes ludicrously spattered with traces of blood, shit and semen. De Sade, Rabelais and a childhood spent in the confines of Rouen's hospital, the Hôtel-Dieu, all seemed to confirm this harsh but interesting fact.

Predictably, Flaubert was lonely in Rouen. His best friend, Ernest Chevalier, was in Paris. Flaubert's letters to Ernest overflow with winter memories of summer mornings when he and Ernest lay together in the shade of some great tree, their faces shining, their pipes going, talking about the future: 'Looking at each other and smiling with the laughter that comes from the heart, the silent laughter that lights up the face.'

Flaubert pleads with Ernest. The conversation must never stop. He must have longer letters, 'a mass of witticisms, of rudenesses, of passions, all jumbled up in a heap without style or order – in bulk – as when we talk and the conversation goes, runs, capers, when we take flight, when laughter explodes and hilarity seizes hold of you'. Such uninhibited letters – by turns convivial and sentimental, cerebral and physiological – hint at the emotional substance of Flaubert's most intense masculine friendships. This particular friendship, an intimate link with his early years, had by now almost run its course. There was no dramatic break-up, no quarrel, just a slow drifting away from each other, with many a happy reunion. Ernest Chevalier, true to his nickname, 'the Gendarme', had simply decided that it was time to be serious, time to make a name for himself. Increasingly he would ignore Gustave's frivolous, demanding loyalty to the things they had shared in their boyhood.

Quite characteristically, Flaubert wouldn't let go. When he realised what was happening, a few years later, he accused Ernest of keeping out of his way, accused him of hiding behind legal busyness. It was a sour lesson, and he later incorporated it into *Madame Bovary*. Emma's lover Leon, the young lawyer, turns his back on passion and settles down. 'He gave up the flute, exalted feelings, the imagination. For every bourgeois, in the heat of youth, if only for a day, has believed himself capable of immense passions, of heroic deeds; every solicitor carries inside him the ruins of a poet.' For the moment the solicitor in Ernest Chevalier had not entirely prevailed over the poet. At Easter, Flaubert went to Andelys to stay with him for a few days. It was the only pleasant interlude in these arduous, empty months. At Chateau-Gaillard, the old castle on the hill overlooking the Seine, the two old friends lay among the ruins and smoked their cigars in the sunshine. They went out on the Seine in a little boat. They stretched out, gazing at the sky and singing a song.

Once he was back in his attic in Rouen, Flaubert felt 'horribly sad'. He sat down to paint the scene of his departure from Andelys in richly glowing colours.

I was sitting outside up on the roof of the coach, in silence, with the wind in my face, rocked gently by the rhythm of the horses galloping, and I could feel the road speeding away beneath me along with all the years of my youth; I thought about all my other journeys to Andelys, I reached deep into all these memories vaguely comparing them to the smoke from my pipe streaming out behind me and leaving its scent upon the air.

Chateaubriand's sonorously sentimental prose had left its mark.

The next four months would be 'sterile, banal and laborious'. Many hours of relentless, solitary hard work lay ahead of him. He would be stuck at home, sitting at his books, in the little bedroom under the roof, 'the cave where my thoughts struggle and expire'. There we find him, on an unseasonably cold grey day, towards the end of May, in his cave. The comedy of being serious – as he began to call it – had left him in a state of anguished lassitude, incapable of sustained thinking. He opened his school notebook and he wrote: 'I am now in a bizarre position on the eve of leaving the schoolroom and entering what is called the world [. . .]. My eight years at college pass before my eyes [. . .]. A period of unspeakable boredom and idiotic sadness along with a few spasms of buffoonery – one day I shall write that story down, for I take an avid pleasure in telling myself the story of my life.'

There were one or two pleasant distractions from the business of passing exams. He read Gautier's *Voyage en Espagne* as it was published in *La Presse*, one of the new daily newspapers. Gautier was the creator of a new form of travel writing, an exuberantly clever blend of anecdote and fantasy, landscape and art history. The mixture was made all the more pungent by Gautier's nicely facetious assault upon the banality of bourgeois taste. Instalments of *Voyage en Espagne* ran all through the summer, a bright thread of Spanish-ness to alleviate the disheartening Rouen grey.

Fantasy also came to town in the person of Rachel Felix, a girl of nineteen. Rachel (her stage-name) was already acclaimed as the greatest classical actress of the day. At the Théâtre des Arts, only a few streets away from the Hôtel-Dieu, she played Andromaque, Camille and Emilie, the great roles of the tragic repertoire. Flaubert attended several of Rachel's performances and wrote an admiring review that marks the beginning of his enthusiastically miscellaneous passion for actresses. Conventionally ardent, Flaubert celebrates the magic of Rachel, the *grande tragedienne*. She resurrects classical antiquity. She is the prophetess at Delphi. She writhes when the god speaks through her mouth. She is the itinerant Homeric bard singing to the sound of the lyre. Rachel was only a few months older than Flaubert and this admiring encounter with the great actress excited his abandoned dreams of theatrical glory.

Much later, in the *Dictionnaire des idées reçues*, Flaubert paid his definitive comic tribute to the erotic myth of the actress. 'The ruin of respectable young men. Appallingly lubricious, frequently engage in orgies, squander millions, end up in the workhouse. Excuse me! Some are excellent mothers.' Rachel Felix is only the first in a series that includes Marie Dorval, Madame Sabatier, Alice Pasca and Sarah Bernhardt. Flaubert's fictional actors, Lagardy, the opera star in *Bovary*, and Delmar, the pin-up turned politico in *L'Education sentimentale*, are both glamorous, narcissistic charlatans. Significantly they are also Flaubert's only representatives of the romantic myth of the artist.

As the day of academic judgement drew closer, Flaubert laboured ever more zealously. In July he rose at three in the morning and worked all day, memorising chunks of Demosthenes and several books of the *Iliad*. As a reward for all this exemplary hard work, Flaubert's father promised him a great journey. His elder brother had been to Scotland. Gustave would go to Spain. A modest introduction to the pleasures of travel, it would mark the passage from boyhood into adulthood. His first real excursion, two months in the Pyrenees – he would be walking in the footsteps of Gautier. It was a most alluring prospect, even though he would be closely chaperoned by a friend of the family, Dr Jules Cloquet. Flaubert confided his doubts about this arrangement to Ernest Chevalier. 'Rationally I want to go, but my instinct which I usually follow [. . .] tells me that while the journey itself will certainly be a pleasure my companion will not, though I may be wrong, entirely wrong. As far as character and temperament are concerned he is an excellent man, but what about all the rest?'

Jules Cloquet turned out to be the ideal mentor. He had no sons of his own. He was worldly, handsome, and indulgent, a sophisticated Parisian with high social connections everywhere and a medical career that looked both illustrious and effortless. The human contrast between Dr Cloquet and Dr Flaubert is very striking. Here was a splendid addition to Flaubert's collection of favourite uncles. They enjoyed an easy, affectionate friendship and, over the next ten years, Cloquet played an important though intermittent part in Flaubert's life.

H IS RESULTS APPEARED. He had passed. Flaubert slept for several
days, then began his preparations for the journey. There had
been a change of plan. They were going to Corsica, with only a brief
look at Spain. Cloquet's unmarried sister and her companion, the abbé
Stepani, were also to join the party.

When Flaubert boarded the paddle steamer for Paris he was escaping
from his family for the first time. His loyal sister Caroline soon wrote to
say that she was travelling vicariously alongside him. Madame Flaubert
found it difficult to let go of her younger son. Her first letter voices the
full tragic chorus of maternal anxiety. Has he had an accident on the
way? Has the travelling made him ill? 'I shall only feel less anxious once
I have received your letter.' This was a very familiar sound. He and his
sister made jokes about it, though one day he would find himself bound
irrevocably to his mother. Knowing what was required of him, Flaubert
diligently wrote a string of letters home.

His father was more serious. This journey, he pointed out to his son,
was not a holiday but a kind of assignment. He was expected to treat it
conscientiously. 'Look, observe and take notes; don't behave like a
shopkeeper or a commercial traveller. Remember that you are the
youngest member of the party and that you ought to be the most
cheerful and always ready first.'

Flaubert paused in Versailles to visit his old teacher and confidant,
Gorgaud. Master and pupil strolled through the sunlit palace gardens
together. 'I announce my doubts about my literary vocation and he
reassures me.'

Bordeaux, their first stop, was a disappointment, an uncongenial
southern version of Rouen, memorable only for the Montaigne
manuscripts in the town library. Flaubert touched the pages 'with as
much veneration as if they had been a religious relic'. Dutifully they
visited a large porcelain factory, a thing still regarded as a great
novelty. Flaubert was stubbornly unimpressed. He dedicated several
pages of his journal to denouncing this dismal symbol of modernity.
Thanks to Cloquet's social connections the small party dined with a
field marshal, though the evening's conversation left no significant
traces.

One melancholy evening at Pau, a town on the edge of the Pyrenees,
Flaubert made the mistake of reading his travel notes aloud to Cloquet
and his sister. They showed very little interest and Flaubert felt humiliated. He wrote a letter to his mother and sat at the dinner table, holding

back his tears. Leaving home was going to be more difficult than he had expected.

He put the incident aside when they crossed the border into Spain. This was the first time that Flaubert had left French soil and he was eager to make the most of it. 'Yesterday I was in Spain, I saw Spain, I'm proud and I'm happy and I'd like to live there. I want to be a mule driver (because I saw one) [. . .]. I opened myself entirely to the impressions that came my way [. . .] and savoured them with a gluttonous relish.' His father would have approved.

Then they turned west, travelling to Nîmes and to Arles, site of the finest Roman remains in Europe. Primed by his classical reading, Flaubert's imagination was powerfully moved. 'For two days [. . .] I have lived in the midst of antiquity [. . .].' He walked along the dry bed of the three-tiered aqueduct at Pont du Gard. At sunset he explored the galleries of the Roman arena at Nîmes, still wonderfully intact. Writing it up in his journal, Flaubert crammed the scene with the smell, the sound and the colour of two thousand years ago: panthers roaring in their cages, fresh blood spattered on the sand, the setting sun, a corpse being dragged off, an elegant courtesan climbing into her litter. Pure Delacroix. It was a heady sadistic-erotic-historic brew. Flaubert was already sifting and gathering the future ingredients for *Salammbô*.

There were richer visions yet to come. Flaubert's eyes, accustomed to a pale northern light, were willing to be dazzled by the splendours of the south. Early one morning, from the hills above Marseilles, he saw the Mediterranean Sea for the first time, sparkling blue in the distance. 'I had just woken up. I stepped down from the carriage to take the air and stretch my legs. I walked a little way along the road. I felt a virile pleasure such as I have never known since. What a sweet love I felt for the sea, the antique sea that I had seen so often in my dreams.'

In 1840 the mail boat for Corsica left from Toulon, a naval station just along the coast from Marseilles. When they reached Toulon Dr Cloquet engineered a visit to a ship of the line. The experience confirmed Flaubert's conviction that the tightly buttoned, highly polished military life was largely futile and lacking in poetry. Seeking out convivial company of his own age, Flaubert spent his last day in Toulon with Lauvergne, a local man, a fellow spirit, 'half poet and half doctor'. Sitting in the shade, in the garden of an old farmhouse, they ate lunch, smoked cigarettes and played on a swing. Then Lauvergne told the tale of Napoléon's triumphant exploits as a young artillery officer at the siege of Toulon in 1793. Flaubert, like his father, had witnessed too many amputations to be beglamoured by the military life. Yet he was sufficiently impressed by Lauvergne's tale to record it in his travel journal. It's the only piece of the Napoleonic legend that ever made its way into his writings. In the evening they sailed around the islands in a little boat while Lauvergne recited some of his own poetry. As they walked back through the late-August twilight, their meandering conversation was 'a mixture of everything, solitary daydreaming in the depths of the woods as well as joking gossip by the fire'. Flaubert cherished the expansive pleasures of masculine conversation, and he remembered this as a day of great contentment.

'Next morning we embarked for Corsica.' The late-summer sea-crossing to Ajaccio was utterly wretched. The little paddle steamer took sixteen hours to reach the island. Flaubert lay below in his cabin, wracked with nausea, dripping sweat and vomiting into a tin bowl. The ground was still moving many hours after he had disembarked. Once they arrived in Ajaccio, the diminutive capital of the island, Cloquet's social connections came into play. The travellers were welcomed personally by the Prefect, Jourdan du Var. Extricated from their scruffy hotel, they soon found themselves 'installed in fine comfortable rooms, sleeping in good beds and feeding at a good table with horses, carriages and servants at our command'.

Their host, Jourdan du Var, was a powerful, energetic man, a cut above the average provincial bureaucrat. 'Stirred by political passions in his youth', he was a man with an interesting story to tell. Appreciatively, Flaubert listened and observed. A stubbornly loyal supporter of Napoléon, Jourdan had escaped from prison in 1815 and fled to Italy where he joined the *carbonari* and became the leader of a secret society. An illustrious liberal exile, he was appointed Prefect of Corsica a few months after the revolution of 1830. Ever since then Jourdan had been at war with Corsica's bandits. It was a futile game, even when played with conviction. Regiments of French light infantry, the *voltigeurs*, endlessly pursued elusive and defiant bands of armed Corsican patriots across the *maquis*. Jourdan du Var was a survivor from the heroic age, a man whose life illuminated the moral history of the previous generation. An instructive exception to the bourgeois rule? Flaubert often voiced his scorn for public men, disgusted by their banal self-importance. Yet he was always impressively skilful at collecting powerful allies.

Not that he behaved himself in Ajaccio. Flaubert's truculent table talk, berating the still-popular patriot-poet Béranger, made a most unfavourable impression on the company. Flaubert took such pride in the story of his indiscretion that he was still telling it thirty years later: 'In Ajaccio I dared to maintain in the presence of about fifteen people (it was at the prefect's) that Béranger was commonplace and a third-rate poet. I am quite sure that the whole company thought me a most ill-bred little schoolboy.'

Literary opinions aside, Corsica was splendid. It was, Flaubert told his sister, a magical, fertile land of cloudless skies, clear blue waters and the great fragrant expanse of the *maquis*. 'Make a little bouquet of oak, chestnut, broom and reeds, you'll be holding a miniature maquis in your hand.' Jourdan, their host, put all his influence and local knowledge at the disposal of his guests. He arranged their main itinerary from Ajaccio to Bastia. He also organised a military escort for them. They would be crossing bandit country.

For their first small-scale excursion the little party set off from Ajaccio early on the morning of 7 October. Ahead of them lay a ten-hour trek on horseback to Vico. Heads bent low, dazzled by the light, they moved slowly along the empty road that wound its way north across the peninsula, following the contours of the mountains. At noon they came down to the sea again and there they followed the track along the coast, walking across the sand. The light was sparkling on a calm, translucent blue sea, and there Flaubert experienced a moment of authentic rapture, long remembered:

The sea has a scent more delicious than roses and we sniff it up avidly; we breathe in the sunlight, the sea-breeze, the line of the horizon, the smell of the myrtles [. . .]. You fill yourself with sunlight, with pure air, with sweet unspeakable thoughts; your every fibre tingles with joy and flutters its wings in sympathy with the world, you take hold of it, you breathe in time to it, the quickening essence of nature seems to flow into your body in an exquisite pagan marriage; you smile at the sound of the wind in the tops of the trees, the sound of the waves on the sand; you run with the breeze across the surface of the sea, something vast, something delicate and soft is floating in the very light of the sun, dissolving into a radiant immensity like the morning mist that rises back into the sky.

Intensely conventional, Flaubert's prose seems to be striving after effect. He was not yet ready. In 1840 he had not yet discovered how to weave such experiences into the mundane texture of narrative fiction. Not for another ten years, not until *Madame Bovary*, would he do that successfully.

At Sagone the party turned inland, for the third stage of their journey. They reached Vico, their destination, by evening. This was bandit country. The peasants they met along the way were all romantically equipped with daggers or pistols. Flaubert's guide sang him the ballad of the famous Theodore, a Corsican Robin Hood who had spent twelve years hiding in the *maquis*. As a reader of romantic outlaw fiction, Flaubert was properly appreciative. As he explained later in his journal, 'It is impossible to travel in Corsica without coming across former bandits, whom you meet socially, as we might say in France. They tell you their story with a laugh and far from feeling ashamed they all take pride in the fact [. . .].' Increasingly receptive to the human detail of the scene, Flaubert relished and recorded the sombre antique dignity of a Corsican shepherd, leaning sadly on his long stick, a dog asleep at his feet. A conscientious footnote even records that Corsican sheep have 'much larger and more ardent eyes than ours'.

This was Flaubert's first real glimpse of a culture not quite French and not quite nineteenth-century. His Corsica is a nice mix of realistic detail and romantic heightening. Corsica, as he later described it, was 'a fine country, still untouched by the bourgeois, who has not yet sullied it with his admiration [. . .].' Richly ironic cultural contrasts lay all about. Flaubert was intrigued by the florid, plump, down-at-heel figure of Monsieur Lefrançois, the manager of the local sawmill, a reluctant expatriate from Rouen who traded lewd anecdotes and dwelt nostalgically on the fancy-dress balls and the restaurants of his home town. 'This little man. . . looked like a vaudeville alongside an antique tragedy.' Travel taught a tolerant appreciation of human oddity – especially the innocent comic oddity of the petit-bourgeois, with his little habits, his odd costume and his peculiar turns of phrase. Alongside the romance of the primitive, Flaubert was discovering the social-moral world that so beguiled Balzac and Dickens.

THE real journey across the interior of the island began next day. At three in the morning they set off from Ajaccio, heading north-east, in the direction of the far corner of the island. Captain Laurelli (an ex-bandit) was their guide. Laurelli told Flaubert his best bandit stories as they made their way up through the chestnut forest where they met up with their official escort, consisting of two French soldiers. Climbing up the valley they entered the Vizzavona, a glorious forest of beech and pine. The road became ever more steep and narrow until at four in the afternoon they paused on a high plateau.

Here Flaubert and Dr Cloquet separated briefly from the main party and began a wild game that illustrates the congenial side of Cloquet's character. Corsican shepherds often used to set fire to the living trunks of pine trees, leaving them burnt-out but still standing. Flaubert and Cloquet discovered that with one hand they could easily pick up thirty-foot-long pine trunks and hurl them at each other. They smashed harmlessly, to great laughter. After half an hour of this, the truant pair caught up with the main party. They said they had been 'making botanical observations'. For Flaubert it was a rare and happy moment of complicity with a man old enough to be his father.

It was already dark when they arrived at the inn in Ghisoni. They were not expected and dinner was served in silence. Rough and grey with dirt, the bed-sheets sheltered a bustling population of fleas. Flaubert undressed by the light of a single candle and rubbed olive oil into his saddle-sore thighs. It was one of those wretched moments, familiar to even the least adventurous of travellers. The fleas kept him awake for hours, but then the moon came up and a superb silvery mountain landscape unfolded before his eyes. He stared at it for half an hour, 'like an idiot' (a characteristic pose), fascinated by the transforming play of moonlight over the mountains.

The next day they headed south, through the forest, along the zigzag road that ran high above the River Orbo. By late afternoon they had reached the summit of el Prato, one of the highest mountains on the island. To the east he saw mountains in every shade of green, descending to a blue sunlit sea, the Tyrrhenian Sea. On the far horizon there was a white line: 'I stood for half an hour without moving, gazing like an idiot [. . .].' It was Italy. A distant prospect, and all the more alluring for that.

It was a steep three-hour descent from the peak to the village of Isolaccio on the floor of the valley. The party had to scramble down over chaotic slabs of granite, stumbling among the roots of giant beech trees, followed by their reluctant, trembling, sweating horses. They were well received in the village. In bestial, joyful silence they fed on pieces of goat roasted on an open fire. At the end of the evening their guide, Captain Laurelli, introduced his young nephew, a man who had fled into the *maquis* three years previously, having murdered one of his enemies. The bandit, like his fictional counterparts, was a model of handsome, well-dressed, nonchalant affability. To help the bandit escape from the island, Flaubert offered his own passport. It was not required, for he already had one in another name.

They set off again at four next morning, heading east, towards the coast, down through the *maquis*, across the wide desolate coastal plain. There was the ancient derelict port of Aleria, 'like one of those long-dead cities of the Orient which we imagine to have been so beautiful and so sad'. Beyond Aleria was the exotic blue immensity of the Mediterranean. Beyond the blue, on the far horizon, was the white line that was the coast of Italy. This conjunction prompted a wonderfully languid, richly orchestrated reverie:

Our guide was singing some *ballata* or other but I wasn't listening, letting my horse stumble his way across the stony ground, dazzled and dazed by so much sun, so many images, and all the thoughts that came to me, one upon the other, serene and limpid like waves falling upon waves. The wind was blowing, a warm wind that had come racing across the waters, from over there, from beyond that horizon, bringing with it the smell of the sea and a kind of memory of places I had never seen. I could have almost wept when I buried myself among the mountains once again.

That was the high point of Flaubert's Corsican journey. What followed was mostly unremarkable. Their destination, the port of Bastia, was a dreadful place, modern and commercial and all too reminiscent of Rouen. The return sea crossing from Bastia to Toulon was wild and sickening. Flaubert soon abandoned his cabin and spent the night up on deck under his Corsican greatcoat, watching the moon over the sea. Then he slept and dreamt of the Orient.

When he woke he could see the coast of Provence. Symbolically, this was the end of his journey. Flaubert's journal of his travels finishes here, with a ceremonious farewell to the Mediterranean, then a postscript in which he puts aside his unused notebooks, sealed with the inscription 'blank pages for future journeys'. Yet this neat finale is mysteriously speckled with erotic allusions. The writing is haunted by indistinct female presences, women seen, remembered and imagined. There was, undoubtedly, something more to tell.

CHAPTER FIVE

Something the Matter

Arriving back in Rouen on 1 November 1840, after ten weeks away, Flaubert spent the next week at his desk writing up his Corsican journal. Under grey northern skies, walking the damp, narrow streets of his home town, his memories of the south seemed ever more vividly alluring. He was harvesting, working through his notes, fashioning his material into something that a family audience might appreciate. He wanted to make a good impression. It was part of the agreement. This was an opportunity for a conscientious, cheerful, intelligent young man to impress a sceptical but essentially magnanimous father. He intended to show off his precocious skill in the lively and fashionable genre of travel writing. There are glimpses of more private themes: romantic evocations of antiquity, intimations of the Orient, all the deep, romantic harmonies of a Mediterranean landscape.

Once the task was finished, he paused ceremoniously. He remembered it, ten years later, as a turning point in his life, a moment of infinite possibility:

It was over. I had left college. What was I to do? I had dozens of plans, a hundred hopes, a thousand aversions already. I wanted to learn Greek. I was pining to be a pirate. I was tempted to turn renegade, mule-driver or monk. I wanted to be away, out of myself, somewhere, anywhere, like the smoke going up my chimney [. . .]. Eventually, with a deep sigh, I sat back down at my desk. I placed a fourfold seal on my little supply of writing paper and on it I wrote 'Reserved for my next journey' with a large question mark at the end. Then I put it in my drawer and locked it away.

In the journal thus locked away there is, of course, no mention of Eulalie, Flaubert's great *amour de voyage*. The secret fact of his sexual initiation was withheld. It was not for the profane eyes of his family. What had happened? And what did Flaubert make of it?

He always remembered the wonderful bed. It came from South America, a mahogany bed inlaid with brass and mother-of-pearl. On an October evening in 1840, in a small hotel near the old harbour in Marseilles, in that memorable bed, Madame Eulalie Foucaud had taken him, the handsome, youthful guest, into her warm, aromatic, maternal embrace. Twenty years later, when Flaubert told the story to Jules and Edmond de Goncourt in 1860, the ashes were still glowing with sexual nostalgia:

Sitting by his fire, Flaubert told us the story of his first love. He was on his way from Corsica. He had previously lost his virginity with his mother's chambermaid. He happened upon a small hotel in Marseilles where the women, who were just back from Lima, had brought with them some sixteenth-century furniture made of ebony inlaid with mother-of-pearl, a thing that bedazzled the guests. Three women in flowing full-length silk dressing gowns; and a little black boy, dressed in nankeen and oriental slippers. For a young lad from Normandy who had only ever been from Normandy to Champagne and from Champagne to Normandy this was alluringly exotic. Then there was a patio with lots of exotic flowers and a little fountain splashing in the middle.

One day returning from a swim in the Mediterranean, steeped in those magical waters, he was lured by the woman into her room, a magnificent woman of thirty-five. He gave her one of those kisses which draw out the very soul. The woman came up to his room that evening and began by sucking him off. There was some delectable fucking, then tears, then love letters, and then nothing.

There was also a suitable postscript to the story. It took the form of a failed romantic pilgrimage that was both tenderly sentimental and bleakly ridiculous:

Went back to Marseilles several times. Nobody could ever tell him what became of those women. The last time he was there, on his way to Tunis for his novel about Carthage – he went to see the house every time – he couldn't find the place. He looks about and he searches up and down and he realises that it's been turned into a toy shop. There's a barber's shop on the first floor. He goes upstairs and they shave him and he recognises the bedroom wallpaper [. . .].

THE next three years of Flaubert's life, his Paris student years, stand out as an episode of anguished obedience to his father's wish that he follow a respectable career in the law. It all ended, as Flaubert feared, in disaster. Academic failure added to sexual humiliation led to a serious 'nervous' illness. Flaubert was trying to lead a double life. Outwardly, he complied with the utterly reasonable demands of his loving father. Inwardly, he had dedicated himself to a higher purpose. He had ideas beyond his station, beyond the imaginings of his family. By day, he was a reluctant but dutiful student of the law. By night, he was an aspiring artist. It was a life of everlasting duplicity, an impossible life. A dismal mixture of grandiosity, ambition, fury, grief, and self-hatred, one dark night it all exploded inside his head.

RETURNING home late from a ball, on the night of 2 January 1841, 'a gentle rainy winter night, all damp and misty', in the seclusion of his tiny bedroom just under the roof of the Hôtel-Dieu, Flaubert began to write in his journal. He looked back to the month of August:

How I have lived since then and how many things have happened in the interval [. . .]. I shall try to sum up these five months of my life which bring to a close what is called childhood and begin this something which has no name, the life of a man of twenty years [. . .]. When I hark back to my beloved journey and when I find myself here then I do ask myself if I am the same man [. . .]. Today is Saturday, it happened on a Saturday, one day in a room rather like mine with a low ceiling and a red-tiled floor, at the same hour of the day, because I have just heard it striking half past two.

The memory of Eulalie Foucaud, 'la belle tetonnière', was pleasant to contemplate. Her love letters, discreetly relayed to him from Paris by a friend, were a small but intriguing diversion from the sour facts of his current position. Rouen was not Corsica. Its winters were grey and damp. Flaubert complained to Ernest Chevalier,

I'm pissed off at being back in a sodding country where you see the sun up in the sky about as often as a diamond in a porker's arse-hole [. . .]. I think I must have been transplanted by the wind to this land of mud, and I was actually born somewhere else, because I've always had some sort of memory or instinct for scented shores and seas of blue. I was born to be the emperor of Cochin China, to smoke pipes a hundred and fifty feet long, to have six thousand wives and 1400 concubines, a scimitar to chop off the head of anyone I take against, Numidian mares, and pools lined with marble [. . .].

However splendid Flaubert's fantasies, however imperial their dimensions, the prosaic demands of adult bourgeois life were pressing in upon him. He was not Ghengis Khan, Tamburlaine, or Nero. Ridiculously, lugubriously, he was nineteen years old, still at home, still waiting for the real life to begin:

> Better to choose a career and get on with it, grab your share of the collective cake and eat it up appreciatively, rather than go down this sad path which I have walked alone. I used to think I had genius, I walked along with a head full of magnificent thoughts and style flowed from my pen like the blood through my veins [. . .]. But when I found that others had had my very thoughts [. . .] then I lapsed from the intoxication of genius to a desolate feeling of mediocrity, with all the fury of a king deposed [. . .].

Stripping away the narcissistic eloquence of this fictional alter ego, we touch upon the everyday dilemma of an aspiring writer wondering what he might do next.

Somewhere in the future was the study of law. But that was not yet, not for many months. Luxuriously detached, Flaubert was nonetheless 'wearied by dreams, pestered by plans, soaked in thoughts of the future'. By now it was too late for him to register in Paris with the Faculty of Law for the current year. Flaubert had made an agreement with his father, an agreement allowing him to defer his legal studies. We do not know the terms of the agreement; it was never mentioned. But Flaubert's indolent year at home would otherwise be a bizarre departure from the energetically self-improving traditions of his family. Was he required, one evening, beneath the keen paternal gaze, to explain himself? Virtuous dedication to the task – that was what the world expected from the sons of Dr Achille-Cléophas Flaubert.

FLAUBERT'S principal secret occupation over the next two years was the intermittent writing of *Novembre*. A conscientiously lurid autobiographical romance, it was the most sustained and the most ambitious project he had yet undertaken. He finished it off with a ceremonious inscription on the title page: 25 October 1842. Though he never published it, for he had no intention of rushing into print, he thought very highly of *Novembre*. It was the first of his writings that he showed to anyone other than Alfred Le Poittevin. It was also the last thing he wrote before illness irrevocably altered the course of his life.*

Reduced to its essentials, *Novembre* tells the story of an unnamed

---

* Over the next ten years he showed *Novembre* to his sister Caroline, to Maxime Du Camp, and to Louise Colet.

but very Gustave-like young man who visits a beautiful Eulalie-like prostitute called Marie. Exploring boyhood memories of home and school, as well as reworking his recent experiences, *Novembre* is a vividly confused and inconclusive first-person-singular poem of sexual initiation, masculine-style. Chateaubriand and Byron were Flaubert's models. More promisingly, it also 'contains' Marie's story, as told in her own voice, prompted by her new lover. Eliciting the erotically autobiographical, coaxing women to talk about themselves, was already one of Flaubert's talents. He loved listening to women. He liked to 'do their voices'. Sometimes, for a joke, among friends, he *was* a woman. His habitual simulations of the feminine, whatever else they signify, underlie the wonderful psychological intimacies of *Madame Bovary*.

For the moment, though, Flaubert's innermost model of the feminine, as revealed in *Novembre*, was still split. That tediously bickering mythological couple, the virgin and the whore, parade across its pages. The sweet pleasures of purity are celebrated in a memory of boyhood summer days in Trouville. The boy walks across the fields at sunrise, towards the sea. He lies in the corn, listening to the sound of the waves. A vision of the morning light playing on the sea fills him with love and joy. Nature, he knows, will mother him. He makes his way to a candle-lit chapel and there he prays to a statue of the Madonna. She holds the little baby so tenderly in her arms.

Then the scene shifts and the boy tells another Trouville story, a story with a different kind of ending. He climbs a dark staircase that leads up to a room with long yellow curtains where a voluptuous woman in a thin white dress is waiting for him. In a golden light, on an inlaid mahogany bed, she takes him. Afterwards she plays with his hair, 'like a mother with a child'. Her name is Marie. Their farewell is brief and inconclusive. Walking the streets, the boy struggles with disappointment, indignation, nausea, and the desire for more. 'So that was it,' he exclaims. 'That was love! That was all there is to a woman! [. . .] I kept turning her over and over in my mind, trying to discover something more, something I'd missed, something I hadn't explored the first time.'

When he returns to Marie, for another go, the boy is tongue-tied with wonder. Unexpectedly, he realises that he is the object of *her* desire. She tells him, 'How beautiful you are, my angel. You are the kind of lover I want, so young and fresh!' Her delight in his physical beauty is disconcertingly authentic. It's Eulalie speaking, the older woman, the woman who had so deliciously, so rapaciously and so unforgettably *taken him*.

ONLY four of Eulalie Foucaud's passionate love letters to Flaubert have survived. None of his letters to her have ever been found. Their correspondence ended in August 1841, having lasted less than a year, when she returned to South America with her mother and her daughter. Her farewell letter to Flaubert speaks the language of high romantic passion.

I hope that heaven still has a few good days in store for me. At my age, Gustave, your love and your feelings are more ardent than at your age; the passions are much more urgent, much more vivid! Yes what I am telling you today may seem a little strange but, unless you squander your youth in late nights, orgies and promiscuity, in ten years' time you will find that I am right and if you feel a violent passion that is the age at which you will know the meaning of love, that is when you will realise that the woman you love is the image of all the joys and all the pleasures that man can hope for [. . .]. Friend, you will never love like the woman who is writing to you. You would need a soul of fire, a temperament which I would not wish upon you [. . .]. Farewell, do not forget me, write to me.

Her letter is written with an alluringly wholehearted naivety that has brought down upon its author the accusation that she probably copied her phrases from some printed source, perhaps a novel or a manual of epistolary style. An amusing thought, especially for readers of Flaubert, so attuned to the ironic inauthenticity that bedevils our most earnest efforts of self-expression.

FLAUBERT didn't mention *Novembre* to Ernest Chevalier. The boyish intimacy of their schooldays was dwindling slowly, giving way to something more meagre and conventional. Ernest's increasingly successful legal career was not compatible with serious literary ambitions. It was better to talk about something else. Flaubert still visited his old friend in Andelys at Easter, but it was already a nostalgic pleasure 'to link myself once again to my own past, to walk along the same paths where we laughed together'.

Eighteen forty-one turned into a time of officially cheerful procrastination. After Andelys, Flaubert spent most of the summer in Rouen. He portrayed himself to his friend as greedy, lethargic and prodigiously fat: 'I'm becoming colossal, monumental, I'm an ox, a sphinx, a booby, an elephant, a whale, everything that is enormous and fleshy and heavy, morally and physically.' It was the first instalment of the great Flaubert bestiary, an intimate comic device, and a good way of being simply enormous. Enormity might also offer intoxicating artistic possibilities, if only one could stay sober enough to bring it off.

Caroline Flaubert, pale and fragile, had always applauded her brother's enormities. Flaubert now lamented the fact that the character of his 'poor sister' was 'turning gloomy as a result of a long and irritating illness which recurs every so often'. With the aim of diverting her from her ailments, the family spent a month at the seaside, in Trouville, from the middle of August. Flaubert dedicated himself, if we are to believe his letters, to prodigious feats of eating, drinking and sleeping. He gave particular attention to the smoking of pipes. Was this a serious *lethargy*, an ominously real symptom of an impending organic crisis? Or was it just a pose, a game that he played with his lean and diligent friend, Ernest Chevalier? With Flaubert we never know, and such sparkling uncertainties are the primary substance of his fictional world.

In November 1841, as if to mark out his real future, Flaubert went to Paris to register as a law student. This was not his initiation into the wonderful immensity of the metropolis. It was an academic formality. Flaubert continued to live in Rouen until July 1842. A peculiar, unhappy, bewildered reluctance speaks out from every version of Flaubert's days in Paris. The letters and the novels tell much the same story. In the most notable example, the hero arrives in Paris, with his mother, then sits in an armchair in a hotel room, and sinks ever deeper into a reverie, 'gazing stupidly at the [. . .] old veneered commode'.

His mother said to him, 'Well what are you daydreaming about then?' And when he didn't move an inch she shook him by the arm and asked him the same question again. 'What's the matter? The matter with me?' he said sitting up with a start. 'There's nothing at all the matter with me!' Yet there was something. Even though he would have found it very hard to say what it was, because he didn't know himself.

CHAPTER SIX

Mainly Parisian

JANUARY 1842. Isolated in Rouen, stranded somewhere between boy and man, unable to open his law books, distracted by the desire to write, Flaubert was in trouble. The question of his own talent was the most perplexing. He turned to one of his former teachers, Gorgaud-Dugazon, a perceptive and indulgent man in his early forties who had previously encouraged his pupil's literary ambitions. Flaubert had successfully confided in him once before. He could be trusted. He wrote:

I have reached a decisive moment. Now more than ever I need your experience and your friendship. My moral position is critical. Either I must go back or I must go on, everything is at stake. It's a question of life and death. [. . .]. When people talk to me about the bar and they say: this strapping fellow will do well in court, because I have broad shoulders and a resonant voice, I confess to you that I am filled with silent scorn and I feel that I'm not made for that kind of trivial materialistic life. [. . .] consequently this is what I have decided upon. I have in mind three novels, three tales of quite different kinds, each requiring a particular way of writing. This will be enough to prove to myself if I have any talent, one way or the other.

I'll put everything I know about style into them, all my passion and my wit, and then we shall see. In April I expect to have something to show you.

Was Flaubert already looking beyond his still-unfinished novel, *Novembre*? In this same letter he scoffs at it defensively. 'It's that sentimental and amorous stew I mentioned to you. The action is non-existent [. . .]. It consists entirely of psychological analysis and dissection. It may be splendid [. . .] it may be just a sham, somewhat pretentious and stiff.'

A month later, still 'unable to do anything constructive', he teased

Ernest Chevalier with a farcical account of his legal studies. 'I've made a start on the *Code civile*, having read the title page which I didn't understand, and the Institutes, just the first three articles which I've forgotten.' Flaubert was distracted by more convivial objects. 'Went to a masked ball [. . .] had supper with two old courtesans [. . .] kept women from among the aristocracy of Rouen, one of whom I shall cultivate for her wit and as a study of the human heart. You have to get into the habit of seeing people around you simply as material for books.' At least he was developing his professional skills.

Ernest Chevalier was probably a lost cause. That was not surprising. But alarming symptoms of bourgeoisification had begun to appear in Alfred Le Poittevin. He was taking his legal career all too seriously. 'He spends his afternoons drawing up bills of indictment.' To cheer himself up, Flaubert jumped into the role of *le Garçon*, nature's anarchist. It was a wild performance: 'make a racket in the night, break a few street lamps [. . .] bugger the dog, crap in your boots, piss through the window, shout merde, fart loudly and smoke a big pipe. Drink without paying, dent a few hats [. . .]. And thank the Lord you were born in a happy century [. . .].' The idea was not to create real chaos, but to collaborate on an aggressive comic fantasy of outraging one's fellow citizens. The imaginative immorality of *Madame Bovary* disturbed the respectable and provoked a prosecution. That was an achievement worthy of *le Garçon*.

Self-doubt could be stifled in various ways. Clowning was a relief. Dissipation was also remarkably effective. It was around this time that Flaubert acquired a congenial new drinking partner, Anton Orlowski, a musician, director of the Rouen orchestra and a friend of Chopin. Orlowski lived only two doors away from the Hôtel-Dieu and was employed to give Caroline Flaubert her piano lessons. He and Flaubert often worked their way through a bottle of absinthe together. Orlowski even gave him a couple of bottles of the excellent Black Forest variety.

In April Flaubert went to Paris for his statutory third inscription as a law student. He was greatly looking forward, he said, to the sight of the prostitutes in their low-cut dresses strolling along the boulevards at twilight. It reminded him of antiquity. He was clearly not reconciled to the law. 'In the name of God,' he grumbled, 'in the name of shit in the name of twenty-five thousand thundering pricks of God, in the holy name of a fart, may the devil strangle jurisprudence and those who invented it!' However extravagant his lamentations, he never criticised his father. Alfred Le Poittevin, meanwhile, made a brilliant legal debut and was soon enrolled as barrister in Rouen.

In July 1842, after eighteen months at home, Flaubert finally moved to Paris, taking Ernest Chevalier's old rooms at 35 rue de l'Odéon. His first exam was in August; he wanted to be at the seaside with the rest of the family. His father wrote him a gently encouraging letter: 'I hope that you are feeling more cheerful and that your thoughts are turning to the School of Law rather than to Trouville [. . .]. Work like a good boy and come back fresh and frisky with some good marks'. Flaubert replied reassuringly. 'I'm working like a navvy and I go to bed in the evenings with the bestial satisfaction of the ox who has done a good day's ploughing [. . .].' Only another month, said Madame Flaubert, and he could join them. He was expected to stay and pass his exams. But his prospects were not good. He would spend the greater part of the day messing about, start work at seven in the evening. 'The Law,' he told Ernest Chevalier, ' leaves me in a state of moral castration which is almost inconceivable.'

That phrase was not lightly chosen. Flaubert was 'imperiously possessed' by the idea of castrating himself. 'In the midst of all my vexation in Paris [. . .] I wanted to do it.' He used to stare at mutilated male statues in museums, and he could long recall standing outside a shop in the rue Vivienne, one evening, struggling with the impulse. He resisted the 'mystic mania', as he called it, and chose instead to avoid 'seeing women', a resolution that lasted for several years.

What was it, the problem to which castration was the solution? We do not know, nor did Flaubert. We do know that sacred horror is at the heart of his darker works, all of them set far back in time, at a safe distance. Defying all parental expectation, Flaubert announced that he was not well enough prepared for the August exam and then promptly left Paris for Trouville. The joy of his arrival in Trouville, the scene of seduction and oceanic reverie, was a measure of how unhappy he had been in Paris. 'I arrived, on foot, in wonderful moonlight, at three in the morning. I can still remember the canvas jacket and the stick I was carrying and the exhilaration I felt when I caught the salt smell of the distant sea.' He soon adopted a gloriously indolent routine: eating, sleeping, swimming and smoking, with an occasional glance at Ronsard, Rabelais and Horace.

Back in Rouen, Flaubert finished writing *Novembre*, then returned to Paris on 10 November 1842. He had to prepare for the exam at the end of December. This time he had new lodgings at 19 rue de l'Est, 'superb lodgings', more congenial and probably more expensive than his previous quarters on the rue de l'Odéon.* Up on the second floor, he had 'a small sunny set of rooms which looked out onto the miniature orchard in the Luxembourg Gardens'. There was a fine view out across Paris. 'In the summer, at night, I used to look at the stars, and in winter at the luminous haze of the great city hovering above the buildings. You could see gardens, rooftops and the surrounding hills [. . .] those sad and beautiful twilights in the year 1843 when I used to take the air at my window, utterly bored and depressed.'

The official picture was more cheerful. At the end of the first week, Flaubert wrote reassuringly to his father: 'I'm working like a wretch and I have just bought a new set of bookshelves to display the *innumerable* volumes which fill up the space in this little jar which I inhabit. Me and my books in my room – like a gherkin in its vinegar.' To combat his loneliness, Flaubert wrote copious letters to his convalescent sister, letters in which she is cast in the role of the strong comforter. Or he would spend the afternoon with Gertrude Collier, reading *Atala* to her while she had her portrait painted. 'I used to promise myself a day with you as if it were a holiday. They were the best moments of my life in those days.'

To add to his incipient sense of deprivation, there was never enough money to eat on the scale he enjoyed. In the interests of economy he had negotiated a deal with a cheap restaurant on the rue de la Harpe: thirty meals at thirty sous each, paid for in advance. He ate very fast, affecting a look which was 'simultaneously sombre, preoccupied and casual' – then burst out laughing once he was alone in the street. After a week of exemplary restraint he had only 36 francs left in his pocket and he had to ask his father, self-consciously, for extra funds.

Flaubert's letters to Caroline for November and December 1842 tell a sad story. As his exam approached he developed an array of distressing symptoms that spoilt his concentration. He spent many a sleepless night, weeping from the pain of toothache. 'I'm getting nowhere, I'm losing ground, I still have the whole lot to learn [. . .]. Sometimes it sends me into a deadly cold sweat [. . .].' But the worst of the toothache

---

* The rue de l'Est had already disappeared when Flaubert came to write his great Parisian novel, *L'Education sentimentale*. It was demolished in 1855 to make way for the Boulevard Saint-Michel. See Hillairet, J. 1963. *Dictionnaire historique des rues de Paris. Editions de Minuit*

was as nothing to the 'atrocious spasms' caused by the study of the law. The unlovely legal prose of the *Code civile* made everything worse. 'I want to be finished as soon as possible because it just can't go on like this much longer, I shall end up in a state of imbecility or a state of fury. This evening, for instance, I am experiencing both of those pleasant states of mind.'

Despite visiting his mentor Gorgaud in Versailles, despite an invitation to the big annual dinner given by Maurice Schlésinger, Flaubert was longing to be back in Rouen. 'The walls of my room in the rue de l'Est still remember the terrible curses, the stamping of feet and the cries of distress that poured from me when I was alone. How I roared and how I yawned there.' In his letters he pictured his homecoming. He would run up the wide curving staircase of the Hôtel-Dieu, up to the family salon on the first floor. Shouting for joy he would hug them all with that reckless exuberance they always found slightly frightening. 'I cannot resist hurting you,' he tells Caroline, ' just a little bit, just like the times when my great big nanny kisses make so much noise that mother says "Just leave that poor girl alone!" And you feel faint and you push me away with both hands saying "Away boy!"'

Flaubert returned to Paris on 9 February 1843. He portrayed himself to Caroline sitting alone in his room, with his law books spread on the table, 'feeling like an imbecile', and not knowing what to do with himself. His thoughts kept wandering back to Rouen, to the sitting room where he imagined his family convivially gathered around the fire, joking and playing dominoes. Caroline, in her reply, corrected this cheerful picture. Family meals, since his departure, have been sad silent occasions, clouded by mother's migraine.

MONEY was the great problem. How could he, a man of such taste, a man with such a need for luxury, survive on an allowance? Only rich men are allowed to have a good time in Paris.

They make love to marquesses or to the strumpets of princes, and the buffoon of a student loves a shop girl with chilblains on her fingers or once in a while has a quick fuck in a brothel, for the poor devil is as sensual as the next man, but not too often, like me for instance, because it costs money and once he's paid his tailor, his boot-maker, his landlord, his bookseller, his fees, his porter, his coffee-shop, his restaurant, then he has to buy boots, a frock-coat, his books, pay registration fees, pay a quarter's rent, buy some tobacco and he hasn't a penny left, he's a worried man.

The poverty of student life could always be remedied by some judicious visiting. Flaubert soon became a regular visitor at the Schlésingers', dining with the family every Wednesday, delighted to find ten kinds of mustard on the table. Their 'exquisite hospitality' was a memory he cherished. Flaubert also began to frequent the studio of the sculptor James Pradier. If anyone could plausibly embody the great bourgeois fantasy of the Artist it was Pradier. He was a rich, flamboyant, cheerful, expansive man in his fifties, one of the most successful sculptors of his day. He welcomed interesting and admiring young men to his circle. Indeed he preferred to work in a busy studio full of people coming and going. Engaged on several commissions at once, he thrived on noise and laughter and clever talk. He dressed fancifully, to look like Poussin, wore a wide-brimmed hat with a steel buckle, long curly blond hair, a black velvet jacket, and a frilly shirt. Success had given him a very high opinion of his own talents. He furnished his studio with musical instruments, composed symphonies, painted mediocre pictures and wrote amateurish poetry. His work as a sculptor was elegant, sensuous and smoothly conventional. Beautiful naked women, portrayed as nymphs and goddesses, were his speciality. Pradier's studio breathed an atmosphere of infinite sexual opportunity. 'It's a place I like very much,' Flaubert told Caroline, 'very free and easy and definitely my kind of thing.'

To add to the fascination of his company, Pradier also had a beautiful young wife. At the age of twenty-eight, Madame Louise Pradier was notorious. She was 'a statue made flesh, beauty in its prime, voluptuous enchantment, the most desirable woman in Paris'. From their luxurious house on the quai Voltaire, Madame Pradier presided over a salon that brought together poets, painters and musicians, as well as the merely fashionable. 'Beauty is *de rigueur*,' she wrote on her party invitations. The evening's entertainment would always be scandalously lavish. There were musicians dressed in antique costumes. There were grand fancy-dress processions of gods and goddesses. The high point of the evening was the appearance of Venus, embodied in the divinely voluptuous person of Louise Pradier herself, making her entrance in a diaphanous classical tunic held together by a large diamond. With her tight amber-red curls, her dazzling blue eyes, her powerful shoulders and the curious golden down on her breasts, this was a woman who could plausibly play the goddess. When Flaubert first encountered the fascinating Louise Pradier, her scandalous infidelities had already estranged her from her husband. Her history would one day feed into the story of Emma Bovary.

But the event that dominated this chapter of Flaubert's life was his first meeting with Maxime Du Camp. It took place in March 1843, inaugurating a friendship that shaped the next ten years. Du Camp was the perfect replacement for Alfred Le Poittevin and Ernest Chevalier, the friends who had so recently 'abandoned' him. The orphan son of a famous surgeon, Du Camp was well endowed with money, talent and charm. The perfect Parisian, he dressed elegantly, told a good story, sang in tune, wrote for the newspapers and was on first-name terms, he said, with the great men of the day. A splendid companion over a bottle or a whore, he was that classic mid-nineteenth-century type, the gentleman-adventurer who could turn his hand to anything: photography, journalism, poetry, politics – the list was impressively various. There was an audacity, an energy, a generous intensity about Du Camp that drew men and women alike.

Flaubert was soon deeply attached to this new friend. He read *Novembre* to him, confidentially, an occasion that Du Camp recalled fondly in his memoirs:

One evening when we had eaten together, I walked home with him as far as his door; as he was about to say goodbye he stopped, hesitated, and then said brusquely, 'Come upstairs with me. I want to talk to you.' Once we were up in his rooms he unlocked a small box and took out a manuscript, dropped it on the table and said with a certain pride, 'I'm going to read this to you. Only I beg you to keep it a secret; the present state of things requires us to conceal our literary efforts as though they were some disgusting infirmity.'

The street lamps outside in the rue de l'Est were turning pale in the early light when Flaubert eventually finished reading and locked his manuscript away in its little box. The two friends spent the rest of that day together, sharing their dreams of literary success, encouraging each other with lavish praise. From that day, said Du Camp, they were inseparable. As a gesture of romantic friendship, they exchanged rings. Flaubert was given a Renaissance ring with a little cameo of a satyr. Flaubert gave Du Camp a signet ring with a monogram and the motto *Solus ad solum*. 'It was,' said Du Camp, ' a kind of intellectual engagement which was never broken by divorce.'

They had great plans. They were both in their early twenties. It would take them nine years to learn everything they needed to know. At thirty they would begin publishing. At forty, the age when the imagination dies, they would give up literature and retire to the country where they would pass their remaining years compiling a massively erudite history of European languages, to be called *The Transmigrations of Latin*. Flaubert was especially keen on this idea. Indeed he never abandoned the idea of a fraternal alliance. The scheme of life imagined in 1843 coincides, in its essentials, with the plot of Flaubert's last novel, *Bouvard et Pécuchet*. The action has simply been transposed, for comic effect, from *haut* to *petit* bourgeois.

WITH Du Camp for company, Flaubert began to enjoy being in Paris. He now had a sustaining circle of friends. As well as the glamorous bohemians who gathered around Maurice Schlésinger and James Pradier, he had contact, through Jules Cloquet, with the world of Parisian medicine. His friendship with Cloquet was flourishing. 'Our mutual affection is growing, I think, day by day, to the extent that he is now offering me lodgings. . . We chatter [. . .] like a couple of parrots who would be deputies.' Though he often declared a taste, in later years, for inviolable solitude, Flaubert never forgot the importance of the address book. For a misanthropic hermit he was remarkably well connected.

Paris prompted him to begin work on an ambitious new novel, a task that would occupy him for the next two years, with occasional gaps.* Both his novel and his new social life were pursued at the expense of his legal studies, which were ever more perfunctory and seemed ever more odious to him.

He had certainly adopted a strange approach to the task in hand. He would copy out, quite mechanically, long passages of the books he was supposed to study, without giving the material his attention, accumulating masses of useless papers. His exams were in August and as the day drew nearer, Flaubert's letters to his sister contained odd premonitions of disaster. Tormented by toothache, 'I launch into silent monologues in which I swear a great deal.' The growing power of his anger was a mystery to him. 'Sometimes I want to beat the table with my fist and break it all to pieces; then when the fury passes I see from the clock that I've lost half an hour weeping and wailing [. . .].' If only he were with his

---

* The precise chronology of *L'Education sentimentale* is contentious. According to the most plausible account, it was begun in February 1843, continued in September and October 1843, abandoned in January 1844, resumed in May 1844 and completed in January 1845.

family, out at Deville, sitting on a bench in the woods, enjoying the sunshine. 'I'm working like a mad thing and from now until the month of August I shall be in a state of permanent fury. Sometimes I start to twitch and I thrash about with my books and my notes as though I had Saint-Guy's dance [. . .] or the falling sickness.' He began to sleep for excessively long periods of time, '14 or 16 hours at a stretch'.

Early in June 1843 he decided to renounce all sexual activity, a decision that may have been connected with his recent premonitions. He mentioned it, in later years, as if it had been a conscious moral necessity, a step towards artistic maturity. 'I was so often humiliated,' he explained to Louise Colet, 'so often created a scandal and caused pain that eventually I realised [. . .] that to live peacefully you have to live alone [. . .]. That is why, for several years, I systematically fled the society of women. I did not want anything to impede the development of my native principle, nothing to burden or influence it. I lived without the palpitations of the flesh and the heart, without even being aware of my sex.'

He dreaded the approach of August and his law exams. His toothache returned, he couldn't sleep, he couldn't concentrate. He felt 'cruelly harassed by all kinds of things'. To add to his miseries, it emerged that he had recently been cheated out of a large sum of money. When the secret came out, it provoked a stern letter from his father. 'You are a fool twice over, first for letting yourself be swindled like some country boy [. . .] secondly for not trusting me [. . .]. I had thought I deserved to be told as a friend whatever was happening to you good and bad [. . .]. Farewell my Gustave, be a little kinder to my purse, look after yourself and do some work.'

'I think I'll be pleased just to have it over with, even if they fail me.' The exam took place on the afternoon of 21 August. Flaubert failed, just as he had expected, and a discreet family silence descended over the whole episode. They went to Nogent, as usual, and Flaubert wrote nonchalantly cheerful letters to his friends.

He was back in Paris by the end of November, glad to find that his room still smelt of old pipe smoke, but missing Du Camp, who was away. At Pradier's he met Victor Hugo, the hero of his youth, 'the man who has most often made my heart beat faster'. Unintimidated by genius, though gazing at its magical writing hand, he acquitted himself well. 'The conversation was all about punishment, revenge, thieves and so on. Myself and the great man were the ones who did most of the talking; I can't remember if the things I said were any good. But I did have plenty to say.'

Meanwhile, at home in Rouen, an oppressively melancholy atmosphere had gathered above the heads of the remaining members of the Flaubert family. Caroline reported the details to her brother.

Mealtimes pass in lugubrious silence. Mother has a headache. Miss Jane, the English governess, never changes her clothes and never speaks. Worst of all, Father has now decided that she, Caroline, spends too much of her time writing to Gustave. Caroline's attachment to her favourite brother was regarded as a problem. She liked to spend the day up in his room, reading, and remembering the sound of his voice. Perhaps it was at this point that the family decided to encourage the discreet attentions of Emile Hamard, one of Flaubert's school friends.*

These everyday family uncertainties, added to his deeper worries, were enough to push Flaubert towards a crisis. The signs were there. The last letter that he wrote before the events of January 1844 is mildly peculiar. He remarked on it himself: 'I think this letter of mine is rather silly [. . .] it's made of bits and pieces like a harlequin's costume – it's a mosaic.' Towards the end of the letter, Flaubert reports dining with the Portuguese ambassador to Paris and thinking, 'What a pleasure it would have been to spit in his face, to give him a thrashing, and to finish him off with a punishment fit for the lowest of the low.' The imagined punishment jumps straight out of the unconscious. Who was its real object? Who was the guilty one who had to be brought so low?

---

* In a letter dated 26 November 1844 Maxime Du Camp says that he had been predicting Hamard's marriage to Caroline for more than a year. In other words, since at least November 1843.

CHAPTER SEVEN

The Fall

> First an indeterminate anxiety, a vague unease, a distressing sense
> of expectation, as in the moment just preceding poetic inspiration,
> when you feel that 'something is about to happen', a state that can
> only be compared to the point when you are fucking and you feel
> the sperm coming just before the discharge takes place.

AT NINE O'CLOCK on a January evening (let the year be 1844) two
young men were driving along a French country road in a lightweight two-wheeled cabriolet. Gustave Flaubert, the younger and the
sturdier of the pair, was holding the reins. Sitting beside him was his
slender, red-bearded elder brother, Achille, a man whom Flaubert disliked with a peculiar fraternal intensity. The air was cold on their lips.
The moonless winter night was unusually dark and the puddles in the
ditches were growing a fragile skin of ice. It was the darkness that
Flaubert remembered when he told this story. 'It was so dark', he said,
'you couldn't even see the horse's ears.' A real cave-black supernatural
nineteenth-century pre-electric dark, with only the light of a distant inn
to dispel the perfect illusion of nothingness.

The little cabriolet turned a corner and the brothers heard a rumbling
and a jingling coming towards them. It was the iron-bound wheels of a
big wagon carrying a single night-lantern up in front. The bright flame
of the night lantern moved slowly across their field of vision,
away from the distant light of the inn. The conjunction of the two
lights, near and far, moving and stationary, sparked something inside
the skull of the big man holding the reins of the cabriolet. It was,
he said, like an explosion behind his eyes, 'like being swept away in
a torrent of flames [...] sudden as lightning [...] an instantaneous

irruption of *memory* [. . .] a letting go of its entire contents. You feel the images pouring out of you like a stream of blood. It seems as if everything in your head is going off at once like a thousand fireworks [. . .].' Gustave Flaubert fell to the floor of the cabriolet and lay there as if he were dead. He was twenty-two years old.

The family hoped that it was simply an accident, unlikely to happen again. But it was no accident. It came back. In the course of the next two weeks Flaubert had four further attacks. What had happened to him? What name could medical science give to the golden fire that had burnt such a dark hole in the fabric of his life? Was it epilepsy? apoplexy? hysteria? Or was it 'just his nerves'?

For Flaubert himself, there was no word for it. 'Never,' said Du Camp, 'did I hear him speak the name of his malady. He said, "my nervous attacks", and that was all.' Such poignant reluctance is not surprising. Epilepsy was not yet understood. The symptoms of the disease had been described in antiquity, by Paracelsus, but there was still no effective treatment for it. It was a hopeless, loathsome, incomprehensible thing and its victims were subjected to a drastic regime. In Flaubert's case, a device like a small tap, known as a 'seton collar', was attached to his neck to facilitate regular bleeding. Purgative mercury massages were applied. Alcohol, tobacco, caffeine, and meat were forbidden. The patient was secluded and carefully watched over. It may be a measure of his fears for his sanity that he renounced masturbation in June 1844. Was he sealing himself in? Or trying to keep the demons out?

His treatment wore a rational, modern disguise. Yet from beneath that disguise it spoke in the older language of religious symbolism. Flaubert's treatment, however unscientific to our eyes, makes good sense if we consider it as a ritual of purification. Victim and family moved to Croisset, a holy place beside a great river, thus escaping all the malignant impurities that hung in the air of the Hôtel-Dieu. At Croisset the victim was symbolically cleansed of his pollution, through repeated washing, bloodletting, and swimming.*

---

* The stigma of epilepsy was so powerful that Flaubert's condition was kept a secret, from all but family and close friends, for the next fifteen years. It was only in the early 1860s, when Flaubert emerged from his prolonged seclusion with the publication of *Salammbô*, that rumours of his epilepsy began to circulate beyond his immediate circle. One of the de Goncourt brothers heard it first in November 1860. By December 1862 Flaubert's secret was the stuff of Paris newspaper gossip. There was an attack on Flaubert published in *Le Figaro*, which ended with a disparaging reference to epilepsy. Soon after his death,

Flaubert subsequently observed and described his nameless condition with great acuity. We might say, from the evidence of his letters, that he learnt to live with it, to inhabit it imaginatively as a unique province of his mind, dark and dangerous though it was. Perhaps a name would have kept him out, discouraged him from undertaking that terrifying quest. Once he knew that he could survive the recurrent intimate disaster of the attack, he could begin to learn from it, even to experiment with it. His epilepsy, or rather what-he-did-with-what-they-called-epilepsy, confirmed in him a curious early affinity for the most extreme varieties of religious experience, the ecstatic visions and the diabolical torments of the saints. How could he make use of it, this suddenly acquired sixth sense?

THESE vague possibilities still lay somewhere in the future. For the moment, tediously confined, Flaubert had to face up to the difficulties of a long convalescence. This is how he described it to Ernest Chevalier, about a month after the first attack:

I've had a cerebral congestion, in other words a miniature attack of apoplexy, accompanied by nervous disorders [. . .]. I nearly plopped it in the bosom of my family (where I had come to spend two or three days recovering from the horrible scenes I had witnessed at Hamard's). They bled me in three places at once and I eventually opened my eyes again. My father wants to keep me here for some time and look after me very carefully [. . .]. I'm in a wretched state, the least sensation and all my nerves quiver like the strings on a violin [. . .].'

Somewhat to his own surprise, Flaubert turned out to be a remarkably compliant patient, under the strictly loving care of his father. But then, only a few days after his first attack, there occurred a most bizarre incident which greatly added to his sufferings. As part of the treatment Dr Flaubert was applying warm water, from various kettles, to his patient's hands. In a moment of carelessness, he picked up the wrong kettle and poured boiling water over the back of Gustave's right hand, inflicting a serious burn. It was, of course, the writing hand, now left permanently scarred, 'the skin all wrinkled like a mummy [. . .] less

---

Flaubert's secret became common knowledge. In May 1880, Dr Pouchet informed de Goncourt that Flaubert had died of an epileptic attack. Maxime Du Camp finally 'betrayed' the secret in his memoirs, published in 1882. Since then, the posthumous speculative diagnosis of Flaubert's condition has become a thriving speciality.

sensitive than the other hand to heat and cold'.* Was Dr Flaubert trying to put a stop to the writing? The unconscious meaning of his painful 'mistake' is all too evident.†

For almost a year, apart from a brief visit to the seaside, Flaubert hardly ever left the safety of his father's house. His symptoms were subsiding, but all too slowly. He often felt dizzy and he was never to be left alone. In February Du Camp came to stay for several weeks. He wondered to see the young giant laid low, stricken with migraine, sitting with his feet in a bowl of water and a damp towel wrapped round his head, 'every evening [. . .] in that position, while your mother and your sister warmed your long woollen socks by the fire'.

Du Camp was with him during his attacks. 'He would lie on his bed shouting out – "I'm holding the reins. Here comes the wagon, I can hear the bells jingling. Ah! I can see the lantern at the inn." Then he gave a terrible cry [. . .] and went into convulsions.' Flaubert was also subject to endless minor disturbances of his vision. 'Not a day goes by without my seeing things in front of my eyes like big pieces of hair or Bengal lights. It lasts quite a long time, more or less. However, my last real attack was less serious than the others.' By the end of April Flaubert was well enough to travel with his parents to the seaside. He began to use his right hand again, for shaving, though he still could not bend his fingers.

Flaubert had to say a sad and affectionate farewell to Maxime Du Camp. 'Ah what long letters I shall write to you!' Maxime was going to Constantinople, and he would be away for nearly a year. There would be long letters, but Flaubert was losing his best confidant at a vulnerable moment. To make matters worse, somewhere in the background, perhaps unnoticed by Flaubert, Emile Hamard was wooing his sister.

Alfred Le Poittevin, estranged for some time, stepped into this empty space. With Du Camp far away, the old friendship with Flaubert could be revived. 'My dear child,' wrote Alfred, 'if I seem to have been keeping my distance from you recently that is because I had the impression that you were being rather less frank with me than I expected [. . .] something seems to be trying to put obstacles in our way [. . .]. Why

---

* The accident must have happened some time before 14 January 1844, according to the internal evidence of a letter from Caroline to Flaubert. Du Camp placed it in the week after the first attack.

† It is also worth adding that Flaubert's letters never mention his father's carelessness in connection with the injury to his hand.

have we never met up in Paris?' The obstacle had been Du Camp, the new Parisian friend.

Temporarily reunited with Alfred, Flaubert resumed work on *L'Education sentimentale*. What does it mean – *Sentimental Education* – a title so evocative and so generically modern that Flaubert used it again twenty-five years later? Potentially a great novel, certainly a great artistic advance, it's spoilt by its own chaotic abundance. Keen to show off what he could do, Flaubert tried to do too much. The novel also betrays the broken history of its composition. Begun before the first of Flaubert's nervous attacks, it was completed during the gloomy early months of his convalescence. This makes for crude thematic contrasts that pull the novel apart at the seams. It was another false start. Another book written but never to be published.

IN June 1844 Dr Flaubert bought a *property* (his son's mischievous emphasis) situated at Croisset, a cluster of houses a few miles downstream from Rouen, just around the first bend in the river. Expensive, though scarcely an extravagance, it was a large, handsome old property of the kind that any big man of medicine might acquire in the closing years of a triumphantly lucrative career. Croisset, his just reward, stood on the right bank of the River Seine. It had spacious terraced gardens with an avenue of lime trees (where Pascal had once walked) and an open aspect to the south-east. The low, white, eighteenth-century house looked out on to the great silver-grey curve of the river, little wooded islands out in the stream, and the green meadows of Normandy beyond. Only half an hour away, by paddle steamer, from the malodorous streets, the raw smoking chimneys, the huddled church-door beggars and the snorting, lunging industrial engines of nineteenth-century Rouen, Croisset was the pleasant patrician face of the bourgeois century. It would soon play a most important part in Flaubert's life.

'I can see you from here,' Du Camp wrote affectionately to Flaubert, 'in your white burnous, walking along under the tall lime trees.' This was Croisset: a place of picturesque seclusion where the stricter proprieties were suspended, a place where a respectable man might stroll about, unencumbered and unembarrassed, in his white burnous. This is our first glimpse of Flaubert in a burnous. (There are several more still to come.) It was a long, loose-fitting, hooded garment, which Flaubert adopted for its practicality when sitting at a desk, but also as a richly symbolic alternative to the standard male gear of the day, which was a costly, all-constricting, all-chafing artefact of black serge held together by innumerable fastenings. A burnous was both comfortable and play-fully exotic. It spoke of Oriental languor. It hinted at superior pleasures. It announced *un original*. Was it also in some sense a ritual garment? A sartorial sign of convalescence and purification? The burnous fits comfortably around the prominent fantasy-self of Flaubert's later years: the monk, the hermit, the saint, the man who carries all the sufferings of a stupid and sinful world.

THE workmen were busy renovating the fabric of the old house, and Flaubert was re-reading his favourite authors, with a fine, ravenous intensity. He relished the generously impersonal epic realism of Homer and Shakespeare. He prized Rabelais, Montaigne and Voltaire for the muscular, masculine qualities of their style. Voltaire's *Candide*, that staccato satiric parable of education, held a very special place for Flau-bert. He'd read it, he said, twenty times *and* translated it into English. Old books and the easy pleasures of summer – these were all he had. 'One day soon I'm getting a little boat from Le Havre. I shall go floating along the Seine with sail and oar. The hot weather is on its way and I shall soon strip off to go swimming.' He was not yet allowed to go sailing alone.

By the middle of July, Flaubert's outward condition was improving. The seton collar had been removed from his neck and the mercury massage treatment had finished. 'Now my ring can go back on your finger,' remarked Du Camp. But then Flaubert's mood darkened and he wrote a letter so unhappy that it earned him a tender rebuke. You have everything, Du Camp argued. Why are you so unhappy? 'You are a surprising mixture; despite your rather false and unreal demoralisation you have a heart, believe me, of adorable simplicity. You have been in love once, and the second time, when it happens, you will be greatly raised in your own estimation and I swear I'd love to be the woman you'll love.'

Du Camp also offered his friend some generously inept artistic advice. 'You have to see things as far as possible with the eyes of your own century. You may regret the poetry of antiquity but it is now impossible, and to look for it in the things of today is almost an absurd-ity.' Mere talent, presumptuously lecturing genius? Journalism dictat-ing to art? It's a spectacle that raises a knowing smile. In this instance, though, it measures the invigorating difference between the two men. Without Maxime Du Camp's annoyingly energetic passion for the modern, Flaubert might have stayed forever loyal to Alfred Le Poittevin's languid antiquarianism.

Ever active, Du Camp encouraged Flaubert to throw off his state of lassitude. A long journey might help. 'If ever you travel to the Orient [. . .] I'll do it with you, and then the two of us, friends as we are, seeing with the same eyes, perfectly alone together in the midst of everything, we will have some splendid excursions [. . .].' The Orient, that peculiarly nineteenth-century object of desire, still lay some years away. Flaubert was currently struggling with things nearer to home: the fact of his sister's imminent engagement to Hamard, the problem of Dr Flaubert's attitude to his son's artistic aspirations, and his own slow progress with *L'Education sentimentale*. 'Have you finished your novel?' Du Camp asked him. 'How far have you got with it? [. . .] And you [. . .] what are you doing? Are you in your boat softly rocking on the little waves, are you walking under the avenue of green trees that goes up the hill, or are you in a state of *kief* in the room where we agreed you would think of me [. . .]?'

In September Flaubert made 'a great decision'. He was going to talk to his father and tell him of his plan to be a writer. He would read him some of his new book. His father would *surely* understand. Du Camp agreed. 'Don't worry about reading your book to him. He is kind and above all he's intelligent [. . .].' Flaubert went ahead, but his father's reaction was unexpectedly discouraging, possibly even scornful.* Flaubert was full of 'sorrow and discouragement'. He confided his feelings, once again, in a letter to Du Camp, a letter that expressed 'in every line [. . .] a sort of bitterness which I have never seen in you before [. . .].' He would withdraw, he said, into the higher, purer world of art.

Du Camp, detecting Alfred Le Poittevin's influence, tried to argue him out of this idea. He wrote back: '[. . .] the life you dream of, a life which is dry and sterile in spite of its grandeur, it's a selfish life, impossible to a man with a heart such as yours [. . .] you want a large

---

* In his memoirs Du Camp offers a vividly circumstantial account of the fateful interview between father and son. Claiming, against the facts, that he was there in Croisset with Flaubert at the time, Du Camp invents a whole scene in which Dr Flaubert plays the part of the comic philistine, falling asleep during the reading, and then laughing cynically at his son's pretensions. This humiliating Oedipal 'scene of the interview' has enjoyed a prominent place in Flaubert's biography. It remains impossible to determine which parts of it were true, because Flaubert never referred to it in any of his letters.

independent existence free of all hindrance [. . .] your life will become solitary, so you say [. . .] art is a great thing [. . .] but art has never contented the heart [. . .].'

Du Camp went further. He urged Flaubert to detach himself from Alfred, 'a corrupt creature' whom he detested.

You have imagined beauty where there was no such thing, you have let yourself be carried away by wretched things whose artistic aspect should not be allowed to obscure the horror and the ridicule; you have lied to your heart, you have joked pitilessly at the expense of things that are sacred; with your superb intelligence you have played the ape to a corrupt creature, a Greek of the late empire, as he says himself. And now I give you my sacred word Gustave he is making a mockery of you and he does not believe a word of anything he has said to you. Show him this letter and you will see if he dares to contradict me. Forgive me, my dearest child, I say these things reluctantly – but friendship is relentless and I had to say these things.

Alfred as Mephistopheles, drawing Flaubert towards his damnation? There is no knowing precisely what it all meant. Yet it does suggest, at the very least, an earnest struggle between Du Camp and Le Poittevin for Flaubert's affections. Du Camp, who was now in Rome, went to the Forum and wrote their two names, 'Gustave' and 'Maxime', on a pillar in the Temple of Fortune. 'It was,' he told Flaubert, 'like a silent prayer to the goddess that she never separate us.'

WE know that Flaubert finished *L'Education sentimentale* at one o'clock on the morning of 7 January 1845. This was to be his last sustained piece of writing until he began work on *La Tentation de Saint Antoine*, a gap of nearly two years. 'The cure', he complained, 'is so slow, with these infernal nervous illnesses, that it is almost imperceptible [. . .]. I never leave my room. Apart from Alfred Le Poittevin I don't see anyone. I live alone like a bear [. . .]. I have been reading and working [. . .]. My illness will always have the great advantage of allowing me to get on with things as I choose.' But 'getting on' was more difficult than it used to be. Writing was painful, both physically and mentally. He still had that large red scar on his writing hand.

In February his sister Caroline went to Paris, shopping for her wedding. Once the dress, the corset, the linen, the silverware and the guests were all assembled, the wedding took place and the couple moved to a flat in Paris. Their child was conceived later that month. Caroline Flaubert, the beloved companion of his boyhood, had now departed from his life. His first letter to her as Madame Caroline Hamard was a denial of their separation. He dwelt fondly on little memories, 'those nice places where we used to go to do drawing', and he persevered with the pet names of their childhood. She was still 'old rat'. He was still 'your old Boun'.

The whole family was soon busy with preparations for the honeymoon journey to Italy. Everyone was going. It had been decreed that the happy couple would have company, the bride's father, mother and brother. Preposterous perhaps. But Dr Flaubert insisted. He was concerned for his daughter's fragile health. Their agreed itinerary was Rouen, Paris, Nogent, Arles, Marseille, Genoa. In Genoa, if all went well, the party would divide. Caroline and her husband would go south. The others would turn north for 'a leisurely trip through the Midi'. Flaubert, obedient to his father's advice, packed his whole wardrobe. He was to travel with a trunk of his own.

It was the first time he had left Rouen for over a year. Flaubert was delighted to be back in Paris again. He pulled on his best boots, caught a bus and went visiting some of his old friends. The list included the Darcet family, Maurice Schlésinger, and even Du Camp, back in Paris after his travels. 'I have seen him. He is coming to Croisset this summer.' Flaubert also paid an interesting visit to 'the fallen woman', Louise Pradier, now living alone in greatly reduced circumstances. Their conversation was gratifyingly intimate. 'I approved of her conduct [. . .] she was extremely flattered by my visit and she invited me to supper next time I'm in Paris [. . .]. They have taken away her children, taken everything she had. She lives [. . .] in furnished rooms with no chambermaid, in misery.' How she had come down in the world, since separating from her husband. Flaubert remembered her, in the days of her social glory, presiding over a double salon with gilded ceilings and purple-silk-upholstered furniture. This impulsive, voluptuous woman, haunted by memories of opulence, would make a splendid subject for any novelist who knew what to do with her. Flaubert was fascinated, but as yet he had no idea what to do with Louise Pradier.

Flaubert also made his way along the Champs-Elysées to call on the Collier sisters, Henriette and Gertrude, the daughters of an English naval captain. In the old days he had been a frequent visitor, lingering all through the afternoon, reading aloud to them from the great romantic books of the day, Hugo's *Hernani*, Chateaubriand's *René*. Henriette Collier, the perennial invalid reclining in her armchair, still gave him her warmest smile. This was the woman he might one day be expected to marry. He appreciated her, rather warily: a superb beauty in the Christian-Gothic style, a charming, conventional girl with an uncomplicated, emotional nature, pure in heart and easily moved by his words. 'I still see her with her head on her pink cushion looking at me with her big blue eyes as I read to her.'

The party headed south and Flaubert soon discovered that travelling *en famille* was not ideal. 'Hardly had we left Rouen', he wrote, 'than my father began to have recurrent problems with his eyes that forced him to stay in his room whenever we stopped in a town and he had to use leeches [. . .].' This may have been a serious unacknowledged symptom of Dr Flaubert's failing health. There is some evidence that he was developing diabetes.* Caroline endured the rigours of travel only as far as the city of Toulon. At that point her mysterious sufferings returned and her mother, predictably, began to worry herself sick. Dr Flaubert, for his part, was bored. He missed his work. He thought the food was awful and he didn't like any of the hotels. Achille, left in charge at home, wrote to complain of being overwhelmed by the work at the Hôtel-Dieu.

'It wasn't real travelling, it was scurrying about; no sooner arrived, they were off again.' Flaubert, the most junior member of the party, scarcely had time to look properly at anything. To Alfred he wrote, 'If you knew all the thoughts that are being unwittingly aborted, torn out of me, lost for ever, then you would almost feel indignant [. . .].' It was only the veneration he felt for his father that kept his irritation in check. Flaubert worried that his true feelings might be evident to his family. 'Perhaps they have leaked out in spite of my efforts.' At least he would see the sunlit Mediterranean once again. Flaubert's travel journal records one splendid solitary moment, sailing down the Rhône. 'Full of hope going down the swift-flowing river which leads you on towards the sea of your dreams. In sunlight, I sat for a moment by the funnel, and I read Horace. The sky was blue.'

Flaubert was looking forward to reaching Marseille. He would pay a call on Madame Eulalie Foucaud, his *amour de voyage*. Their reunion, he informed Alfred with gloomy relish, would be bitter and farcical. That was as it should be. Readers of Byron, youthfully sophisticated, knew that such romantic pilgrimages were destined to fail.

---

* Evidence of diabetes may be found in the slightly swollen features to be seen in the portrait of Dr Flaubert in the Musée Flaubert. I am indebted to Dr Germain Galerant for this observation.

Flaubert was not disappointed. He made his way late one evening down to the old harbour. It was raining when he arrived at the rue Darse. 'The Hôtel Richelieu: all dark, no more lights, no mother-of-pearl shining in the gaslights; had trouble finding the square. Rain, cold grey weather, like the Sunday evening I left her [. . .].' Madame Foucaud wasn't there. 'They don't keep the Hôtel Richelieu any more. I walked past, I saw the steps and the door. The shutters were closed; the hotel is empty. I scarcely recognised it. Symbolic, don't you think? [. . .] with a little more determination I could perhaps have found out where she lives. But the information that they gave me was so incomplete that I let it be.'

Lingering by the door, Eulalie's absence was his inspiration. He began to remember all kinds of little details: the women down by the harbour, their brown stockings, the way they wore their skirts gathered at the hips, their easy rolling walk, the little yellow flowers they held in their teeth. There on the rue Darse, past and present seemed to merge together. They were both equally real.

After Marseilles, somewhere between Toulon and Genoa, pestered by memories of happier days and distressed by the worsening tensions in the group, Flaubert had a nervous attack, 'several hours of the most horrible anguish, when I suffered as I have not suffered for a long time [. . .]'. It was decided to cut the journey short. They would travel only as far as Genoa, then all come back together via Milan. It was a great relief. 'My father was thinking of going as far as Naples. I thought that I'd be going too. Thank God it won't be happening. We are coming back through Switzerland. In three weeks, a month at most, we'll be back in Rouen [. . .]. The journey so far, though excellent in the material sense, has been too deficient in the poetic sense for me to want to extend it further.'

Deprived of the pleasures proper to travelling, Flaubert had a keen sense of what he was missing. Writing to Alfred, he described how it ought to be.

When I go I want to be able to feel that old antique world in the very marrow of my bones, I want to be free, on my own, alone or with you, not in a group. I want to be able to sleep under the stars, to set off without knowing when I might be back. Only then [. . .] will I let my thoughts flow white hot because they will have time to rise and come to the boil, I shall coat myself in the colours of the objective world, engross myself in it with an undivided love. Travelling ought to be a serious business. Otherwise, unless you get drunk every day, it is one of the most bitter and inane things in the world.

Flaubert resolved to make the best of Genoa. It was a truly beautiful city, a great temple of luxury. 'You walk on marble, everything is made of marble: staircases, balconies, palaces [. . .] as you walk along the street you can see those high patrician ceilings all painted and gilded.' Such opulence, as ever, kindled his imagination. 'I kept on thinking about the ceilings in those palaces [. . .] and the sumptuous fucking one might do there.' Such sentiments, more decorously expressed, would find their way into *Madame Bovary*.

Flaubert spent many hours in Genoa's churches, just looking, gazing at the costumes, the altars, the statues. He kept his eyes wide open, 'naively and simply', taking it all in, without needing to reflect. This was new, this immersion, this 'coating himself' in the colours and the shapes of the material world. A radically innocent, vividly dissociated mode of vision, it may have had its organic source in the altered brain functions characteristic of epilepsy. Whatever the explanation, Flaubert's odd habit of 'just looking' would eventually become a powerfully original way of deciphering the real world.

In church Flaubert's thoughts turned to Don Juan. 'This is the place to dream about him, how I like to imagine him when I'm walking around these Italian churches, in the shadow of the marble tombs, in the pink sunlight that filters through the red curtains, looking at the tanned necks of the kneeling women.' These thoughts, after a long incubation, produced a scenario for a story about Don Juan.*

Genoa had its official treasures too. In the picture gallery of the Palazzo Balbi, ignoring Titian and Rubens, Flaubert was enthralled – the word is exact – by a painting that would occupy his mind for many years to come. It was Brueghel's *The Temptation of Saint Antony*, a large allegorical canvas that portrays in repulsive and exuberant detail the fiend-sent visions endured by the fourth-century Christian saint. For the moment, Flaubert made only a brief note of the painting. 'Naked woman lying down, Love in one corner.' A few days later he wrote a much fuller description, from memory.

Saint Antony with three women, turning away to avoid their caresses; they are naked, white, smiling, about to put their arms around him [. . .]. The whole composition is swarming, crawling, sniggering, in a quite grotesque and

* The Don Juan story was eventually mapped out in 1850.

frenzied fashion, beneath the geniality of the individual details. This painting seems confused at first, then it becomes altogether strange [. . .] for me it obliterated the rest of the paintings in the gallery, I can no longer remember any of them.

Flaubert told Alfred Le Poittevin he was toying with the idea of arranging *The Temptation of Saint Antony* for the theatre, but concluded that it would 'require a different sort of fellow from me.'

Brueghel's *Saint Antony* was a powerful symbolic image of Flaubert's inner world. He returned to it again and again, over the next thirty years, in between other things. Why such an inexhaustible fascination? Brueghel's *Saint Antony* spoke immediately to his sexual imagination, blighted and inflamed by the previous two years of anxious abstinence. 'These days,' he confided to Alfred Le Poittevin, 'fucking has nothing further to teach me. My desire is too universal, too permanent, too intense for me to have any such desires. I have no need for women [. . .]. I just use them to look at.' *Saint Antony* was equally a challenge to his historical sense. It offered a splendid opportunity to visit a dark corner of the ancient world, a faraway place crawling with exotic heresies, perverse mortifications, and feverishly ambiguous visions of the divine.

A few days later, dismayed by Caroline's worsening health, the party turned north, towards Milan. Flaubert himself was in exceptionally low spirits. For three days he 'felt like dying'. With everyone's anxious eyes upon him, he hardly spoke a word. They must have been asking themselves if he was about to have another attack. For him it was a moment of intense self-scrutiny and self-definition. He was considering his thwarted vocation, the very shape of his future life. He announced his provisional conclusions, not to those around him, but to Alfred, in a manifesto-like letter:

The only way of not being unhappy is to lock yourself in the tower of Art and dismiss the rest as worthless [. . .]. I'm really doing rather well ever since I consented to being perpetually ill [. . .]. And everyone is astonished to see me so well-behaved. I have said an irrevocable farewell to practical life [. . .]. All I ask from this day on is five or six hours of peace and quiet in my room [. . .]. I shall resume my peaceful uniform existence, between my pipe and my fire, at my table, and in my armchair.

Intimate collaboration with Alfred Le Poittevin was still vital to Flaubert. His original vision of artistic self-sufficiency always included a friend.* Perfect fraternal seclusion was one of his most cherished fantasies, to be explored in his final novel, *Bouvard et Pécuchet*. 'On our own, you and I, unmolested, far from the throng, away from the bourgeois, like bears in a cave, growling under our three layers of fur. I'm still pondering my Oriental tale which I shall write next winter.'† Alfred approved. 'We are two Trappists who speak only when we are together.'

'I have no need for women [. . .] I just use them to look at.' This was surely only a disdainful pose, an Alfred-like attitude, a factitious piece of misogyny. 'Just looking' was put to the test when, in a villa outside Como, Flaubert encountered Canova's delicately voluptuous statue of Cupid and Psyche. The pair of white marble figures moved him deeply.

I didn't look at anything else in the gallery; I came back to it several times and on my final visit I embraced her, the swooning woman who is reaching out to Cupid with her two slender marble arms [. . .]. May I be forgiven, but it was my first sensual kiss in a long time; and it was something rather more than that, I was embracing beauty itself, and my ardent enthusiasm was dedicated to genius. I threw myself upon the form, almost without thinking what it was saying.

Nobody was looking, I hope, when Flaubert placed that kiss on the cold, delicate lips of Psyche. His father might have thought it odd. It was a great moment, a moment of high antithesis. If we place Canova's *Cupid and Psyche* alongside Brueghel's *Saint Antony* we shall see two utterly different visions of the flesh. The one is a turning away from lascivious saint-pestering naked women. The other is a magical awakening followed by a tender mutual embrace.

Later that day, as if to complement the sublime erotic delicacy of

---

* Ernest Chevalier, Alfred Le Poittevin, Louis Bouilhet – they all played the same part. They were Horatio to his Hamlet. Though Alfred – the senior partner – undoubtedly saw himself as Hamlet.
† This is Flaubert's first mention of an Oriental tale, though it is already known to Alfred. The tale always posed great difficulty and the writing of it was frequently deferred. By April 1846 Flaubert was telling Du Camp that he was giving it up for good. But he's still thinking about it in 1849. Thereafter it comes up now and again. In August 1853, whilst writing *Madame Bovary*, Flaubert mentions his Oriental tale to Louise Colet. There it figures alongside the preface to the *Dictionnaire des idées reçues* as the repository for everything he loves. Maurice Bardèche suggests that Flaubert modelled his tale on those of Voltaire – in which lots of characters have complicated adventures – and on *Don Quixote*.

Canova's Cupid, Flaubert encountered three mute idiot women along the way. They were paupers, begging for alms, 'frightful creatures, disgustingly ugly and cretinous'. Though these women could hardly walk they put on a curious show of love and affection directed at Flaubert. 'They smiled at me, blew kisses to me.' Intrigued and gratified, he observed, 'I attract fools and animals. Is that because they know that I understand them. Because they feel that I enter their world.' Observing his son at such moments, childishly consorting with such riff-raff, the feelings of Dr Flaubert might have been rather less charitable.

The family group reached Paris on 8 June where they remained for three days. Each day, Flaubert visited Henriette Collier, not realising (or perhaps not acknowledging) the fond hopes he had inspired in her heart. It was a great shock when he finally discovered his mistake.

One day we were alone together, sitting on a sofa. She took my hand, twined her fingers in mine. I let it all happen without really thinking about it because I am very innocent most of the time, and she looked at me with a look [. . .] which still turns me cold. Her mother came in at this point, took it all in and smiled as she pictured the imminent consummation of a marriage. I shall not forget that smile [. . .]. You cannot imagine my feelings of terror. I left in great distress, reproaching myself for being alive [. . .]. I would gladly have given my life to atone for that sad look of love which I could not reciprocate.

'What a fine story they make, these visits! They showed me the flaw in the cuirasse I wear upon my soul [. . .].'

It was not a perfect fit, the cuirasse. The factitious serenity of sexual abstinence (ever since May 1843) could not last for ever. 'A singular thing it is,' he told Alfred, 'how I have kept away from women. I'm satiated with them [. . .]. I've become impotent on account of those splendid secretions which have bubbled away inside me too long ever to be uncorked. It will soon be two years since I gave myself to the act of coitus, and in a few days time it will be a year since I engaged in lascivious deeds of any kind.'

Temptation might take many forms. Flaubert had a visit from Louise Pradier, in her straw hat and her black dress. Here was a different kind of woman, a different kind of love. Flaubert found himself, like another Saint Antony, assailed by erotic imaginings. Henriette and Louise, the pure and impure. The meeting with Louise prompted paradoxical reflections. 'The poetry of the adulterous wife is only true because she herself is at liberty though caught in a larger fatality.' Louise also prompted cruder thoughts.*

Before he left Paris, Flaubert saw James Pradier, Louise's husband. Pradier, a cynical connoisseur of women, offered Flaubert a piece of 'medical advice'. He advised him, in the idiom of the day, to take a mistress. He may also have suggested a few names. Perplexed and provoked, Flaubert confided his worries to Alfred Le Poittevin. He was not yet ready to abandon his vow of chastity.

If I were to take it seriously and devote myself to fucking, I'd be humiliated in the process. However, that is what it would require and that's just what I shall not do. Normal, regular, steady, solid copulation would draw me too much out of myself and disturb me. I'd find myself involved in active life, physical truth, common sense, and that is what has been harmful to me every time I've tried it out.

What was this humiliation? What was so frightful that it could keep him away from women for nearly two years? Was it the fear of suffering an epileptic attack whilst in a woman's arms? If sexual excitement could bring on an attack, if he *believed* that it could do so, then sexuality would have to be suppressed. Such a decision would explain the forlorn physiological theme, so common in Flaubert's letters, of premature senility. It might explain the attraction of Saint Antony. It might also explain why Flaubert stayed with his mother. She was the only woman in the world with whom he was safe.

'BACK IN MY CAVE!' 'I'd rather like to buy a nice painting of a bear, get it framed and hang it in my room labelled *Portrait of Gustave Flaubert*, to indicate my moral and social disposition.' Settling down in Croisset, Flaubert felt a wary optimism, tinged with self-disgust. 'I'm recovering, I'm on my way up, and sometimes it surprises me that a man so solid should have nervous ailments.'

This cave of his, figuratively so dark and close, was in reality light and spacious. Croisset was the perfect place to spend the summer. It offered security, solitude, and a leisurely domestic routine. We may glimpse Flaubert, at this point, through Alfred Le Poittevin's eyes. 'I often see you – in your long dressing gown – on the terrace or in the

---

* Flaubert's journal for that day places the odd phrase 'Welcome to the cellar' next to Louise's name. I take this to be a piece of cryptic but obvious sexual slang. Was it something she said? Something he thought? Or something they did?

orchard – looking out through the gaps in the trees at the passing riverboats and their passengers.' It's a characteristic pose, observing his fellow citizens from a safe distance.

Croisset had its active pleasures too. Flaubert went out on the River Seine every day in a little sailing boat. It was especially enjoyable when there was a strong tide. 'I cut through the swell that splashes over me as it comes bouncing off the side of the boat, I let the wind fill my sail and I feel how joyfully it shivers and slaps, I'm alone, without a word, without a thought, subject to the elements [. . .].'

Flaubert was keen to read his recent novel to Alfred. He needed to know what it looked like after six months. Caroline had already read it and praised it. Maxime Du Camp said he was most eager to read it, though he was so taken up with a new love affair that he kept postponing his promised summer visit to Croisset. He kept Flaubert waiting for weeks and finally arrived in August.

Long summer days could turn sour. 'Everyone apart from me', Flaubert complained jokingly, 'is getting married.' Ernest Chevalier was established, serious, and responsible. Caroline was in Paris. He wrote to her, long letters richly loaded with remembered details of their sibling games. 'I have nobody here to strangle, both my hands at your throat, saying old rat! old rat, or "I have bestrangled many a man worthier than thou" [. . .]. We could start on a play. You can come and roll around on my bed like the dog, and I can play the Negro: "Yes me love missy, me love her." [. . .] sometimes my mouth is itching to kiss your smooth and shell-like cheeks.'

Alongside items of local news and gossip, brother and sister could still share their intimate thoughts. Flaubert confided one of his recent resolutions: 'I have cast off the foolish pretension of wanting to grope my way about in those dark places of the heart which are indeed sometimes revealed in a sudden flash but at the cost of many hours of blindness.' This sounds like a cryptic version of his attack, the darkness, the flash of light and the blindness that follows.

It was a surprisingly compliant gesture of renunciation, from one so constantly drawn towards 'the dark places of the heart'. Flaubert was still suffering. His body was soon covered in boils. He had poultices placed on his buttocks, his legs, his head. He was being dosed with quinine, as a tonic. In the midst of all this, Flaubert announced quite casually to Alfred that his principal occupation was analysing Voltaire's plays. 'It's boring but it could be useful to me later on.' It was a very strange thing to do. Voltaire's plays were completely out of fashion in 1845. Flaubert's friends must have thought it an inexplicable waste of time. Unknown to them, doing Voltaire was probably another gesture of compliance, a display of meritorious drudgery by which he hoped to win his father's elusive approval. Play-writing was the most lucrative literary trade of the day. Perhaps the rudiments could be acquired, apprentice-fashion, from a close study of the master.

It was an impressive sight, the expensively bound seventy-two-volume edition of Voltaire, the pride of his father's library. Bizarrely conscientious, Flaubert spent several months burrowing his way, scene by scene, through all thirty-three plays. He made nearly 500 pages of notes: detailed summaries of each play, plus an array of quotations. Flaubert ventured only one or two critical observations, most of them very hostile. He particularly disliked Voltaire's habit of constantly parading his opinions. He soon decided that such authorial preaching was simply 'pitiful'. Impersonality might mean *not* sounding like Voltaire.

In the intervals of annotating Voltaire, Flaubert read Shakespeare. He was delighted by a scene in *Timon of Athens*. Timon lures his false friends to a feast, serves them up a surprise consisting of stones and hot water, then chases them all away with blows and curses. The appeal is obvious. The play is a darkly satirical fable of misanthropy, and this particular scene sings the glory of revenge, allowing the hero a bitter comic farewell to his fellow citizens.

Flaubert told Ernest Chevalier towards the end of the summer, 'My life is still surprisingly chaste [. . .]. I'm like a piece of wood, which I do not mind in the least. Passion, excitement being what I dread, I think that if happiness is to be found anywhere it's in stagnation. No storms over a pond. I'm almost set in my ways. I live a life of calm, regular, routine. Exclusively busy with literature and history.'

Since his sister's marriage, the big house often felt sad and empty. His parents were showing their age. His mother was worrying about her son's health, making herself worse. Flaubert, for his part, was looking forward to a winter with Alfred. 'We can see each other every day and we'll write scenarios.'

CHAPTER EIGHT

Under the Knife

B Y the autumn of 1845 it was clear to Flaubert that his father, now in his early sixties, was beginning to show his age. Even the most loyal of Dr Flaubert's colleagues had begun to think that it was time for him to step down. The last two or three years, painful years of worrying about his younger son, had undermined his health. In recent months he had quarrelled bitterly and irrevocably with his old enemy and colleague Leudet. By November, after suffering in silence for months, Dr Flaubert was obviously too ill and too tired to work effectively. But it was equally obvious, to those who knew him, that he was far too obstinate ever to leave the great arena of his profession. He would work to the bitter end. He would never relinquish his position, to his elder son or to anyone else. There was nothing the matter with him, he declared.

But Dr Flaubert walked like a man bent beneath a great burden. His limbs were so heavy and he staggered as if he were drunk. On Saturday, 10 November 1845 he did his usual ward round at the Hôtel-Dieu. He taught his students and performed all his regular duties. That evening when he returned to Croisset he was exhausted. He had no appetite and he seemed broken in body and mind. Next day, acknowledging his condition, he had himself carried into Rouen, to the Hôtel-Dieu, and put himself into the care of his elder son.

A deep abscess was discovered in his thigh. In a rare moment of clumsiness, Achille-Cléophas must have dropped his scalpel whilst dissecting a corpse. It was the accident that every surgeon dreaded. The contaminated blade had pierced his skin, inflicting a tiny wound that had now grown into this secret horror.

Drastic measures were required to save the man's life. Dr Flaubert called upon his two closest friends, Dr Cloquet and Dr Marjolin. They were fellow surgeons, men who had studied with him. They agreed what had to be done. The only hope was to cut open the great abscess, drain the pus from the cavity in the thigh muscle, and then simply trust in the body's natural powers of recovery.

But who was going to perform the operation? Cloquet or Marjolin? It was impossible to decide. Who was going to concede the superiority of the other? Professional etiquette; personal loyalty; self-importance. There was too much at stake. Dr Flaubert resolved the issue. He decreed that his son, Achille, would hold the scalpel.

The surgeon's hand trembled for a second but then moved decisively. The blade of the knife cut deep into the leg. For some days there was hope. Then it became clear that it was too late to save him. 'For ten weeks', wrote an eyewitness,

neither the tender care of a wife who never left his bedside for one second, nor the attentions of his children, nor the knowledge of his son and the other doctors who attended him during the final hours, nothing could arrest the decline [. . .] persistent vomiting drained the patient's strength. He succumbed on the fifteenth of January, at half past ten in the morning, in the midst of those he had loved so much.

A PUBLIC funeral was held two days later in the Eglise de la Madeleine, the grand eighteenth-century church attached to the Hôtel-Dieu. The men who worked in the harbour wrote to Madame Flaubert, requesting the honour of carrying their great benefactor's coffin to its place in the cemetery. Dr Flaubert was known locally as 'Father to the Poor', a secular saint, a man of inexhaustible compassion and wisdom, 'a man who practised virtue without believing in it'. His death was widely regarded as a catastrophe for the town. It generated a collective grief that looks strange to modern eyes. 'The town', Flaubert wrote, 'will pay for his tomb and the public will put up a statue to him.' The statue never progressed beyond being a good idea.

His father's premature death had a profound effect upon Flaubert. His mourning took a curious form. Henceforth he regarded himself as an old man. His youth was now over. There was, so he declared, a great division in his life, a division marked by his first epileptic attack in 1844, but subsequently consummated by the death of his father. The two events were surely connected. They took place at almost the same time of the year, in January, and perhaps, at some deeper level, the prodigal son had been the death of his father. To make amends, however belatedly, Flaubert idealised the dead man. Loving admiration could dilute but could not take away the fear he felt for the man who walked into his dreams with a sharp knife in his hand.

In Rouen six days after her father's death, Caroline Hamard gave birth to a daughter. Within a week of the birth, Caroline had 'a dangerous attack of fever', undoubtedly puerperal fever. She survived and her doctors declared that there was no cause for alarm. Believing that his sister had virtually recovered, Flaubert threw himself into 'a great struggle' to defend the professional interests of his brother Achille. Flaubert family honour, no small matter even for Gustave, required that the succession be secured. Surely the son was to replace the father. A great position, a large cultural capital, the conscientious accumulation of a lifetime, was suddenly at risk. 'They simply wanted to push him out of the hospital in return for all the services rendered by his father.'

Flaubert now began to show a surprising talent for intrigue. 'I have taken command of the situation, been twice to Paris (and again tomorrow), and I have been so successful that at present we have no doubt at all that Achille will succeed his father in every respect.' Flaubert went to Paris for a further week of negotiation. He was in a strange, wild, shifting mood. Du Camp was alarmed by his friend's behaviour. 'He went rapidly from a state of exaltation to a state of collapse without any apparent cause.' Flaubert walked so fast that nobody could keep up with him, then slept so deeply that nobody could rouse him. He didn't realise that his sister was sinking. They kept it from him, until it was clear that she was going to die. Leaving in a wretched hurry, he embraced Maxime and gave a sob as he climbed into the railway carriage. Two days later Maxime received an urgent message. He was to find Raspail, the famous Parisian doctor, and bring him to Caroline's bedside in Rouen.

Caroline was slowly dying. Her husband, her brother, her mother and her doctors were all gathered at the deathbed, the delirious, wide-awake, pre-pharmaceutical, nineteenth-century deathbed. In her delirium, the week before the end, Caroline thought her father was still alive. She wanted to see him. Why was he not there? She was remembering scenes from her childhood. Flaubert wrote about it to Maxime Du Camp.

Caroline is talking, smiling, fondling us, with gentle and affectionate words for everyone. She is losing her memory, everything is confused in her head [. . .].

What grace they have, the sick, and what peculiar gestures they make. The little baby suckles and cries [. . .] my eyes are as dry as marble. It is strange, how I feel expansive, abundant, overflowing, in the face of fictive suffering, while the real thing sits in my heart, acrid and hard, crystallising there as it comes.

Caroline Flaubert died on 21 March 1846. In Paris, Dr Raspail confided to Du Camp that the local doctors had perforated the patient's stomach by giving her enormous doses of quinine. In Rouen, Flaubert kept the traditional vigil.

I was at her bedside; I was looking at her laid on her back in her wedding-dress with her white bouquet [. . .]. She looked much taller and much more beautiful than she did in life with the long white veil that came right down to her feet [. . .]. I was reading Montaigne and my eyes kept moving from the book to the corpse; her husband was asleep, moaning softly; the priest was snoring; and I said to myself, as I gazed upon this scene, that all things pass away, that the idea alone remains and I shuddered with excitement at certain turns of phrase in my book.

That night, as he watched over the candlelit dead body of the woman he had so loved, memories of Eulalie Foucaud came back to him. He unsealed the small bundle of her love letters, the four letters that he had kept. It was a curious tender ritual of reminiscence. He read them through and then, on the envelope, he wrote, 'With a special feeling of regret. Poor woman! Would she have really loved me?'

The day after Caroline's death, Flaubert returned to Croisset. 'What a journey, alone with my mother and with the weeping infant.' It was a desolate day. The empty house was cold and damp. The wind was blowing through the bare branches of the trees in the garden. The Seine was brimming with yellow muddy water. Then they returned to the Hôtel-Dieu and Flaubert spent another night beside the body. 'In the morning when everything had been done I gave her a long final farewell kiss in her coffin [. . .]. It was I who had the death-mask done [. . .]. I shall have her hand and her face. I shall ask Pradier to make a bust of her for me and I shall put it in my room.'

To add to the perplexingly tangled patterns of death and birth, the infant Caroline was now baptised in the village church, just over the hill behind the house at Croisset. It was a peculiar, sombre occasion. The officiating priest, pink in the face from the wine he had taken with his lunch, mumbled through his Latin at top speed. 'Not one of us really understood what we were doing. Contemplating all those symbols, devoid of significance for us, I felt as if I were present at the ceremony of some obscure religion that had been exhumed from the dust.'

Flaubert now found himself alone, in the big white house by the river, alone with his widowed mother and his infant niece. Dejected and angry, he turned to his books. There was some solace to be found in Greek grammar, Michelet's *Histoire romaine* and the *Bhagavad-Gita*. 'I read or write regularly for eight or ten hours a day [. . .] and if anyone disturbs me for a few moments it makes me feel quite ill. Many a day passes without my going even as far as the end of the terrace [. . .].' The shape of his future was still uncertain. He told Maxime Du Camp, 'I very much doubt if I shall compose anything this summer [. . .]. I dream of great journeys on horseback [. . .]. If my mother dies, my plan is laid, I shall sell up and go to live in Rome, Syracuse or Naples.' As the weather grew warmer, his health was slowly improving. In May he noticed that he had had no attacks in the seven months since his father's collapse in November.*

To add to his losses, Flaubert found out that Alfred Le Poittevin, under pressure from his family, had finally made an effort to secure an official post for himself as a lawyer in Rouen. Alfred would be far too busy for literature. It was a betrayal of all the ideals they had shared since boyhood.

ENTER Louis Bouilhet, in the summer of 1846, auspiciously on cue. He was a great discovery, 'an old school friend who writes poetry; he gives Latin lessons in Rouen [. . .] comes here on Saturday evening and leaves on Monday morning'. Here was the friend who would swiftly replace Alfred Le Poittevin and become Flaubert's principal literary confidant over the next twenty years. Bouilhet looked so uncannily like Flaubert that people used to say they were brothers. Du Camp, who knew both men and probably felt excluded by their intimacy, was disdainfully amused by the fusion of their personalities. 'They lived the same life for so long [. . .] pursuing the same ideal, that they eventually copied each other's gestures, attitudes, phrases and tones of voice. Both of them were tall, broad-shouldered, prematurely balding, with long moustaches of the same colour, and the same regional accents [. . .].'

---

* His epilepsy was only in temporary remission. The next documented attack occurred in February 1847.

This rapprochement could only have taken place after the death of Flaubert's father. A medical student under Dr Flaubert, Louis Bouilhet had been expelled for a trivial act of insubordination and would scarcely have been welcomed at Croisset. Flaubert and Bouilhet had been in the same class at school; they had survived the same harsh regime and shared all the nicknames, the jokes, the rituals, and the catchphrases that constitute the secret language of the tribe. There were also profound social differences between the two men. Louis Bouilhet was from a poor family, a charity boy with no father; he knew he had to behave if he was to rise in the world. In the classroom he was ambitious and compliant. Bouilhet won first prize for rhetoric; his medals were displayed on a shelf at home, in the shabby sitting room. He so needed to please his mother and impress his aristocratic benefactors by a relentless show of diligence. Flaubert, on the other hand, being the second son of a rich, influential doctor, was allowed to mess about, show off and generally make lots of noise.

These original differences, these inequalities of talent and fortune, persisted all through the later years of a friendship that was miraculously untainted by envy. When Flaubert looked at Bouilhet, he began to count his blessings. 'In the midst of my weariness and my discouragement when the bile kept rising in my mouth, you were the Selzer water that made life digestible for me. You reinvigorated me [. . .]. When I was groaning with self-pity [. . .] I used to say to myself: "Look at him" and I would get back to work with renewed energy. You were my supreme moral emblem and my perpetual edification.'

F LAUBERT was still fragile, recovering slowly from his symptoms. 'My boils are going down a bit, my leg is looking better, my nerves are quiet. Soon it will be seven months since I had my last attack.' He was still dutifully confined to Croisset, and there his mother's anguish weighed heavily upon him. 'My courage wavers sometimes from carrying this great burden of her inconsolable despair all alone.' He needed some refuge from sorrow and adversity. He found it near to hand, in his mind, in reading and writing. He had adopted the large first-floor room overlooking the Seine, and there he spent long summer days, studying Greek, reading Latin and devouring Michelet's *Histoire romaine*. 'I'm doing my best to live in the ancient world.' It seemed to work. 'My tide is running full. I have a craving for long study and eager work. The inner life I have always dreamt of is finally beginning to flow.' Though there might be a price to pay. ' I worry about becoming desiccated from too much erudition [. . .].'

Indeed his misfortunes were not quite over. Flaubert was wounded by the sudden discovery that his dearest friend, Alfred Le Poittevin, was about to get married. It was deplorable. 'Another one lost!' he exclaimed to Ernest Chevalier. There would be no more of those gloriously meandering arcane conversations. No more precious secrets of exalted mutual feeling. Bewildered but acquiescent, Flaubert wrote to Alfred: 'Are you quite sure, great man, that you will not ultimately turn into a bourgeois? In my mind I associated you with all my artistic hopes. That's what I find so painful.'

In defiance of his absent friend's sour predictions, Alfred married his *bourgeoise*, Louise de Maupassant, at Neuville on 6 July 1846.* Three weeks after Alfred's wedding Flaubert began his tempestuous liaison with Louise Colet, a coincidence that is interesting but ultimately indecipherable.

---

* There is no positive evidence that Flaubert absented himself from Alfred Le Poittevin's wedding. I deduce his absence only from the fact that he never alluded to the occasion.

CHAPTER NINE

Louise

CROISSET, midnight, 4 August 1846. It was a warm summer night, with a moon shining on the river, when Flaubert wrote the first of his many impassioned letters to the beautiful older woman he had just inexplicably abandoned in Paris. In the opening lines of Flaubert's letter to Louise Colet we hear a new voice. He writes to her in the sentimental, sensuous, passionate tones of a man who has been suddenly roused from the long, cold reverie of his grief and is now awakening to the dangerous pleasures of love. 'Twelve hours ago we were still together. This time yesterday I had you in my arms [. . .] do you remember? [. . .] How far away it is already!!' Quickened by long separation, conducted principally by letter, the love between Flaubert and Louise Colet was destined to be an ideally imaginative, superstitious, ceremonious, frustrated love. In the deepest and most comprehensive sense, it was the source of *Madame Bovary*.

Let us observe for a moment Flaubert's fastidious first-night performance as the letter-writing lover. When everyone else in the house is asleep he unlocks the drawer of the little cabinet where he hides his treasures. There, on his writing table, he arranges the precious mementoes of love. The collection includes a miniature portrait, a lock of blonde hair and a handkerchief, evocatively stained with a woman's blood. Folded away in a little embroidered bag, here are two letters from Louise, the pages faintly scented with musk. And here is the most precious relic of all, a pair of her slippers. He gazes at them so fondly as he writes. His hand trembles as he reaches out to touch them. He inhales their subtle bouquet of verbena. He imagines the warm feel of her foot inside them. Endearingly ridiculous, he eventually confesses to her, 'I think I love them as much as I love you.'

In the early weeks of the affair, Flaubert showed a promising fluency in the little language of the artfully erotic gift. He sends Louise a rose picked from his mother's garden and asks her to sleep with it between her thighs. He promises to sprinkle her breasts with a bottle of water drawn from the Mississippi. How eagerly Flaubert remembers the scene of their first encounter in the studio of the sculptor James Pradier. Among blocks of marble and plaster casts from the antique, Louise Colet had stood posing alongside her own half-finished statue, 'your curls touching your white shoulders, your blue dress [. . .] the light falling on you from one side, I was gazing at you and you were gazing back at me'. The rich, erotic ambiguities of this scene, cold white marble being shaped and polished to the contours of warm white flesh, would scarcely have been wasted on such a viewer. He may have wondered, in his more sober moments, if it had all been set up for him.

Who was she, this superlative statuesque object of desire who gazed back so alluringly at the viewer? Notorious in her day, the perennial subject of metropolitan gossip and misogynist fantasy, Louise Colet has left copious but enigmatic traces of her presence. There is a painting by Courbet. There is a statue by Pradier.* From her own hand there are journals, stories and poems. However, because all but a few of Louise Colet's letters to Flaubert have disappeared, we have only one side of their actual conversation. We can only reconstruct Louise Colet's voice from the echoes that it generates in Flaubert's letters. Her effect (rather than her life) is thus the proper subject of our inquiry.†

The Colet Effect – for we may call it that – was generated by the volatile, hazardous substance that she herself compounded with lavish care from echoes, images and reflections, blue dresses, blonde curls, voluptuous shoulders and incurably minor poetry. Though he had not

---

* Pradier's Louise still stands on the Place de la Concorde – representing the city of Strasbourg.
† Louise Colet's letters to Flaubert were supposedly destroyed after Flaubert's death by his prudishly pious niece, Caroline. The niece herself repeatedly denied the deed, and her denial raises several teasing possibilities. Flaubert may have destroyed the letters himself. From a sour and vengeful impulse of disgust? Most unlikely, considering his infinitely retentive habits with all pieces of paper. I greatly prefer the theory that Flaubert prudently hid the Colet letters. The obvious moment arrived in December 1871 when Flaubert 'buried a large box full of letters' in order to keep them safe from the group of victorious Prussian soldiers who had just arrived to take possession of his house at Croisset. If this ingenious speculation were true, then a fabulous nineteenth-century biographical treasure may still lie buried a few feet below the twentieth-century steel and concrete of Rouen's commercial dock land, the land that was formerly Flaubert's garden.

yet experienced the full elemental force of the Colet Effect, Flaubert was already feeling 'shattered, dazed, bored to death, like after some great orgy [. . .] I who was once so calm, so proud of my serenity, working away avidly [. . .]'. For a man 'charitably rumoured to be incapable of it, I used to manage it so rarely', this renaissance of sexual passion was overwhelming. 'Now I feel within me the appetite of a wild beast, an erotic instinct which is carnivorous and lacerating.' Their first consummation had been somewhat complicated. 'Do you realise', Flaubert wrote, 'that what happened to me with you has never happened to me before? (I had been so weary the three days before, wound up as tight as the strings of a cello.) [. . .] I was grateful for your spontaneous intelligence which was not at all perturbed by something that astonished me as being an utter monstrosity.'

His quiet convalescent existence in Croisset, alone with his mother and his Latin and his high intellectual ambitions, had been thrown into disarray. 'I have no heart for work. I do nothing. I lie on my green leather couch and I think about you.' Problems began the moment he got back from Paris. 'My mother was waiting for me at the railway station. She wept when she saw me arrive. You wept when you saw me leave.' Like Charles Bovary hopelessly striving to please his wife and his mother, Flaubert found himself caught between two bewilderingly powerful women. 'The two women I love the most have fitted a bridle to my heart , and they hold it on a double rein. They take it in turns to pluck at me with love and pain.' Not surprisingly, Flaubert was keen to keep his two women forever apart, an unconscious stratagem that would subsequently bring many troubles down upon his head. The Croisset compartment of his double life was to be perpetually filial, infantile, and asexual.

At first he even tried to keep Louise Colet a secret from his mother. The unusual number of letters arriving from Paris posed a slight problem. He reassured his mother that they all came from Du Camp. But Madame Flaubert was rather more astute than her son allowed for. She soon guessed that something was happening. Within two days of Flaubert's return from Paris, her condition became much worse. Flaubert reported the fact to Louise Colet. 'Mother was in a terrible state. She was having hallucinations about funerals. I stayed with her.' He insisted to Louise that he could not return to Paris, even briefly, until he had an excuse in the form of a letter from Pradier. 'This winter there will be no other way of getting to see you.'

Louise Colet was urging Flaubert to leave Croisset and live in Paris. She wanted to draw him into her metropolitan circle. He protested. 'Can I drop everything and go to live in Paris? It's impossible.' His first loyalty has to be to his widowed mother. His place is at her side. He risks a few discreetly discouraging noises, rebuking Louise Colet's generously exaggerated enthusiasm for his writings. 'I don't know what it was that pushed me into reading you something. Forgive me that weakness. I couldn't resist the temptation to win your esteem. [. . .] It was a sweet idea of yours to suggest that we write a book together, I was touched. But I don't want to publish anything.'

Within ten days of the beginning of the affair, a thrillingly turbulent pattern of feeling was established. It could deservedly wear the motto *coitus semper interruptus*. Brief and extravagant scenes of passion, squeezed into a single afternoon, were cut short by Flaubert's stubbornly insulting departure for Croisset. There followed a separation, lasting weeks or even months and prompting much luxuriously reflective letter-writing.

Reduced to its essentials, the exchange of letters between Paris and Croisset unfolds along the following lines: he insists that he cannot possibly leave his mother. He tells her, for her own good, not to come too close. He's damaged, wounded, frightened, impotent, unworthy. He uses alarmingly literal images of physical contamination to frighten her off. 'I began by displaying my sores.' 'I did warn you. My misery is contagious. I have the scab and the itch. Woe to anyone who touches me!' He criticises her sentimental credulity, her *womanly* exaggeration, her democratic enthusiasms. Stung by these asperities, she attacks furiously. Everything about him is vile. He's a Voltairean, a materialist, an admirer of de Sade, a heartless, treacherous, swaggering poseur. Slightly chastened and perhaps secretly amused, he apologises in proud, indignant tones. It was fraternal criticism. Why can she not take it like a man? Unexpectedly, she relents. Her letter is tearful, affectionate, wearily magnanimous. She offers to forget him. He capitulates with a capricious display of abjection and a promise that he will come and see her soon. Something gets in the way. He cancels. Then suddenly it *can* go ahead. Passionate reunion. Departure. Separation. Recriminations. Apologies. Endearments. This was an ideally economical arrangement for both parties because it encouraged the most ingenious imaginative elaboration of all the material available.

FOR all his new-found impatience with the things of the mind, Flaubert's thoughts were not exclusively focused on Louise Colet. He was settling into his new quarters. He had taken early possession of the best room in the house, a spacious, many-windowed first-floor room with a splendid view out across the garden to the River Seine. Characteristically, he was already imagining himself irrevocably attached. 'Destined to pickle myself here, I have had my jar embellished to my specification and here I live like a dreamy oyster.'

The embellishments were modest but carefully chosen. There was a sofa of green morocco leather, an essential aid to serious literary composition, designed for *sprawling* upon, between sentences. On the wall there soon hung a portrait of Louise Colet, conveyed from Paris by Du Camp, in his new role as go-between. Flaubert reported that his mother seemed to approve. 'My mother has seen it, she liked your face, thought you were pretty, animated, open and kind, those were her words. I told her that the engraving had just been printed, as I happened to be visiting, and that you gave copies as presents to everyone who was there at the time.' One of Louise's great rivals was also emblematically present in the form of a grotesque seventeenth-century engraving, Jacques Callot's *Temptation of Saint Antony*, which hung on the wall in his study. As Louise Colet would have realised, Saint Antony is the man who turns away from the female flesh so alluringly offered up to him. Flaubert explained to her the power that the image held for him. 'It is a picture I love greatly. I have wanted it for a long time. The melancholy grotesque holds a special charm for me. It answers to the intimate needs of my buffoonishly bitter nature. It does not make me laugh, it sends me into a dream. I notice it wherever it occurs [. . .].'

On 14 August 1846 Maxime Du Camp, the other rival, disembarked at Croisset. The fact that he stayed there for a month was not lost on a certain jealous observer. Tactlessly, Flaubert instructed Louise to address her letters to Du Camp, so as to avoid stirring up Madame Flaubert's suspicions. It had been two weeks since they were last together and his promised visit to Paris was imminent. But it could only happen, Flaubert insisted, if Pradier sent a letter summoning him 'on business'. No letter arrives and Flaubert stays in Croisset, renewing his promise to visit her later in the week. He has developed a boil on his cheek, so big that it closes up his eye. He's looking hideously and ridiculously ugly. Soon his whole body is covered in boils and he has to lie down with his head wrapped in bandages. Unable to send word in time, he disappoints her again. Miraculously cured of his boils, and slightly scarred, he eventually finds his way back to her bed. They spend a tumultuous twenty-four hours together, then he is back home in Croisset again, at his desk, writing to her – his preferred position.

On the desk, he has a precious new memento, one of her poetry-prize medals. But love's pure tenderness has been sadly and irrevocably alloyed. Beneath the endearments, we hear the infernal grinding note of complaint. 'You criticise me,' he writes, 'for always analysing [. . .] you do not like the way my mind works, its fireworks annoy you, you'd prefer a smoother tone, a more monotonously tender idiom [. . .] you're just like the rest of them, just like everyone else, finding fault with the only good thing about me, my flights of fancy and my artless exuberance.'

In her next letter Louise Colet swept aside all such subtleties. She's pregnant and she's delighted. Flaubert is horrified. A child? It would tie him to her for ever, which is, as he knows, probably what she has in mind. 'I'm turning cold at the very idea.' He imagines, impressively, throwing himself into the river, 'with a 36-pound cannonball tied to my feet'. The pregnancy scare lasts a full three weeks. Flaubert is angry. He believes that Louise Colet has a plan to ensnare him and that visiting his mother in Croisset is a vital part of her plan. If ever the two women get together they'll concoct something clever and they'll have him cornered. Flaubert leaves Louise Colet in no doubt about his true situation. 'I'm always trying to think of something that will prove my love to you and the kind of proof you want from me is exactly the kind I cannot give you. My life is shackled to the life of another, and will be so for as long as she lives.'

A spirit of growing antagonism is evident from his letters to Louise Colet. Having delighted her with a gift of flowers on her birthday he spoilt the fine gesture when he told her that it had all been Du Camp's idea. When she wrote to him about things in the news he retorted sourly that he never read newspapers. To annoy her, he expounded the lofty universal perspective, far above the human here and now. Louise Colet did not greatly appreciate what she called Flaubert's 'fastidious dissertations on art'. A recurrent feature of his letters, so appreciatively quoted by posterity for their intimate eloquence, these 'impromptu aesthetic dissertations' evidently exasperated their original recipient. She soon regarded them, however myopically, as a series of muted insults.

Louise was perplexed, 'astounded' she said, by his 'jeremiads' about the pregnancy. She hit back in a letter that startled Flaubert with its 'bitterness, vitriol, obscenity!'. 'You reproach me endlessly,' he complained in reply, 'for posing, for being theatrical, for being arrogant, for parading my sorrows like a ruffian showing off his scars. You say that I vex you wantonly, pretending to cry so that I can watch your tears flowing.'

Ominously, the name of Elisa Schlésinger, Flaubert's adolescent *amour fou*, had come up between them at some point in the course of their recent reunion. Anxiously possessive, even of her lover's past, Louise Colet now took hold of that name again. 'You believe', Flaubert responded, ' that another woman is still in my heart, that she has remained there so radiant that you have vanished into her shadow. It's all in the past now [. . .] it even feels as though it happened in the soul of another man.' He had 'two quite distinct existences', he explained, divided by 'external happenings' (meaning his first attack of epilepsy). Madame Schlésinger belonged to the first life, the 'active, passionate, emotional life' that came to an end when he was twenty-two.

Of course he wanted desperately to persuade Louise Colet that this other woman belonged to the distant past. For this purpose he expounded yet another version of the double life. Between the lines, for all that, we sense a fascinating half-truth, a symptomatic autobiographical myth that describes the indescribable thing that had so divided and damaged his life. In the writing of *Madame Bovary* and especially in the person of Emma, we may safely surmise that Flaubert was intimately yet ironically reconciled with his own 'active, passionate, emotional life'.

Disconcertingly Louise Colet's next letter was kind and gentle. On pages stained with tears she still pursued the fatal theme. 'You want to visit this house, my heroine [. . .]. What is the use of imagining such folly! It's impossible. The whole town would know by next day. There would be endless odious rumours [. . .].' The best he can offer is an afternoon together in Mantes, a village on the River Seine, halfway between Rouen and Paris. He'll arrive on the 11.19 and leave on the 6 o'clock. Less than six hours together. But that will have to do. They must resolve, sensibly, to put up with this 'infirmity'. Try throwing yourself into art, he suggests.

Incensed by his little plan, she wrote a stinging letter. 'So!' she exclaimed. 'They keep an eye on you like a little girl do they?' Unperturbed, he tried to explain his persistent refusal to allow her to visit Croisset. He is not, he says, deterred by his mother's jealousy. It's all for Louise's sake. 'For your name, for your reputation, to avoid seeing you besmirched by the banal pleasantries of the casual visitor, to spare your blushes in front of the customs men who walk along the river bank, to avoid you having servants sniggering at you.' They will meet in Mantes and she must promise not to cry, beautiful though she is with tears running down her cheeks. He also announces a prudent future policy of *coitus interruptus*. She felt angry, obscurely insulted by his chilly, bourgeois spirit of calculation. It was as if he didn't believe she was pregnant.

They spent the afternoon together at the inn in Mantes, a white inn with a deer painted on the weathervane. What glorious memories. He recalls her crying out, 'Bite me, bite me!' But for all their sexual eagerness, things were not well between them. Flaubert often seemed oddly absent. Several times Louise Colet exclaimed, 'What a peculiar person! What are you dreaming about?' 'I have no idea,' he replied. 'In fact,' he added, 'this is my habitual state. I am not with anyone, wherever I am. I think I am not of this land, perhaps not even of this world.' There was also, of course, a more mundane explanation. 'My mother', he explained, 'is in a truly dreadful state. I think it's the bust of Caroline which has upset her so much. I've never seen her so distressed.'

In spite of his stern resolutions, Flaubert stayed the night at the inn with Louise; then he took the morning train back to Croisset. When he saw his mother, he realised his mistake. She was waiting for him, on the landing stage outside the house, in a state of great anxiety. She said nothing, but her exhausted, sleepless look was a sufficient reproach. At lunch he made up a little story to explain away his absence, ate prodigious quantities of sirloin, laughed at himself and then fell asleep stretched out on his green morocco couch. None of this, he had decided, could be allowed to happen again for a long time. Love is like music. It has its *andante*, its *scherzo* and its *finale*. Louise would have to resign herself to their separations.

The next forty-eight hours were miserable, almost like the worst days of his boyhood, 'when you want to throw yourself out of the window so as to put a stop to it', or run away and be a pirate. Eventually, on the third evening, he forced himself back to work. His letter to Louise was brisk and cheerful. 'In the six weeks since I have known you (decorous phrase) I haven't done a thing. Must do something about that! Let's get down to work and give it our best.' He scolds her affectionately. She has such a low regard for art, 'the only good thing and the only true thing in life'. He suggests, finally, that she contact Du Camp and he gives her his Paris address.

Louise now announced that she was organising an abortion. Relieved, Flaubert gave her cool, sensible advice seasoned with a grim joke about 'bringing the redcoats ashore'.* He was moved by the passion in her letters, but he was determined to keep his distance from her. He lays down his conditions. 'We cannot live together [. . .]. We cannot sustain these convulsions of the soul which bring such sick dejection in their wake.' She must stop telling him to come to Paris. 'One might think it was your deliberate intention to torment me with that refrain.' And she must stop trying to gain entry to Croisset. 'You must never come here, it would be impossible topographically speaking for us to meet privately [. . .].' Yet having slammed that door, he relents and leaves it slightly open. 'It would be better if you stayed in Rouen [. . .]. I would make a pretext of going into town on some errand or other, and I would be back here at about six o'clock.' There was also the more immediate matter of Louise's condition. Her next letter brought good news. 'The redcoats have landed.' Flaubert's response was a study in inverted grandiosity. 'All the better if I have no offspring. My humble name will perish with me [. . .]. It is an idea I find pleasing, the idea of an absolute nothingness.'

ONCE he discovered that Du Camp had made contact with Louise Colet in Paris, Flaubert immediately began to imagine them in bed together. He pictured strange, farcical scenes of abjection and betrayal, then he described them in gleeful detail to Louise. 'I should love to make myself ill over you,' he wrote. 'Kill myself for you, make a beast of myself for you, become a kind of Sensitive Plant that only your kiss could keep alive.' The idea of a Third Party was powerfully exciting. It was a new phase. It offered all the sour, sophisticated pleasures of conscious duplicity. It also marked the beginning of the end, the first of all the many endgames that were played out between Croisset and Paris.

Over the next few months, with Flaubert's encouragement, Du Camp became ever more deeply involved in his friend's affairs. A complicated triangular postal service was set up. When Flaubert wrote to Louise Colet he addressed his letters to Du Camp in Paris, allaying his

---

* Redcoats, as worn by the English soldiers of the day: in this context, it was a euphemism for the appearance of menstrual blood.

mother's suspicions. Du Camp then delivered the letters to her in person when she was sure to be alone, thus avoiding awkward questions from both her husband and her official lover. Flaubert explained to her the benefits of this arrangement. 'I would like to have someone to talk to about you, someone who knows you, who has been through your door, who can tell me about you [. . .].' Their meeting was in his thoughts. 'I would like to have been there. I'm sure you were both feeling equally awkward [. . .]. Did you like him? Did you talk about me? Have you worked out your arrangements?'

Released from the odious prospect of paternity, feeling that he was once again in control of his fate, Flaubert began to look towards his literary future. His oriental tale had come to nothing. For the moment he floated in a luxurious state of creative indecision. 'Winter is upon us, the rain is falling, my fire is burning, this is the season of long hours of seclusion. Here come the silent evenings in the lamplight, watching the logs burning away, listening to the sound of the wind.' In November Flaubert decides that next spring he can start on something new. 'I'm still afraid of writing [. . .] a sort of religious terror that comes upon me just before I begin [. . .].' In preparation he ordered a special armchair. 'A big writing-chair, with a tall back, Louis XIII style, covered in green morocco, with fancy woodwork.' 'I'm awaiting a book I have in mind before I decide on my own worth, but it is quite possible that this book will never come to pass.' Flaubert imagines himself, in a parable of art, playing the most obscure part. 'I am the obscure, tenacious pearl-diver who explores the lower depths and surfaces empty-handed, his face turning blue. A fatal attraction pulls me towards the dark places of the mind, down into the inner deep, so perpetually enticing to the stout-hearted.'

He spent many hours sitting motionless. Reading Hottinger's *Historia Orientalis*, published in Zurich in 1660.* Reading Virgil. 'I'm rereading the *Aeneid*,' he told Louise Colet, 'repeating certain lines to myself endlessly [. . .] there are certain sentences which stick in my head and haunt me [. . .].' He came across verses he had copied out as a punishment 'a hundred times' as a schoolboy. Sustained repetition could release the uncanny powers hidden beneath the old Latin words on the page. Revision and declamation might one day work the same magic with sentences of his own. Floating in language, he could reach

* Bruneau suggests that the chapters on heresies led Gustave to abandon his Oriental tale and embark on the research for *Saint Antony*.

back into his own boyhood. 'One day', he promised, 'I shall unfold to you the long story of my youth; it would make a fine book if there were anyone with the ability to write it.' Or – with a shift of emphasis – '[. . .] the story of the man of today between the age of seven and twenty [. . .] this unknown drama'. How did Louise Colet respond to Flaubert's autobiographical impulses? 'Gustave,' she complained, 'never speaks to me of anything except art – or himself.'

She sent him a poem, a lush fanciful evocation of their recent day in Mantes. In twelve parts, it began, 'O bed! If you could speak [. . .].' Flaubert corrected her geography, pointing out earnestly that the cray-fish that they ate could not have been caught in that part of the River Seine. Uncomplainingly, Louise revised her poem. Did she now accept that everything was going to be on his terms? He rebuked her for sending him funny stories. 'You must think me a very cheerful man [. . .] you are taking me for something I am not. Sometimes you treat me like a satanic creature from a melodrama, and next time we meet you turn me into a commercial traveller. Between ourselves I am not as high or as low as that; either you vulgarise me or you poeticise me.' It was, he concluded disparagingly, 'the old feminine rage to deny the halftones [. . .].'

FORBIDDEN to visit Croisset, Louise Colet inquired as to how Flaubert and Du Camp spent the days there. She may not have been very amused by the answer. 'We have spent three days with our maps working out a great voyage across Asia which would last six years and cost us [. . .] just over three million six hundred thousand francs. We had everything organised, purchase of horses, equipment, tents, wages for escorts, clothing, weapons. We had so heated our brains with the notion that we both felt rather ill: he in particular was in a fever.' This fantasy voyage was a symptom, he confessed, of his love of luxury. Madame Flaubert, who controlled all the family money, was scandal-ised by her younger son's recklessly expensive habits. She preserved the once-deprived child's disdain for luxury. 'She thinks of our father who procured for us by his labours a respectable ease.' Flaubert further confessed to a longing for a pair of special divans. One divan would be stuffed with swans' down. The second divan would be stuffed with the feathers of hummingbirds. Such divans were enough, he said, to fill his thoughts for a whole day and leave him feeling sad in the evening.

All this talk of great voyages and swans'-down divans was in fact a diversion. Flaubert and Du Camp were quietly planning a three-month summer walking tour in Brittany. Madame Flaubert, who was fond of Du Camp, gave her approval on condition that she would travel with them, at a distance, in her carriage, joining up with them every week or two in the towns. 'Thus,' declared Flaubert optimistically, 'we shall be totally free and alone.' He didn't mention any of this to Louise Colet. He kept it from her for another month, aware that such a plan scarcely accorded with his insistence that he must never leave his mother's side.

Family problems were worsening. Mortal disaster seemed to hang over the splendid house at Croisset. Caroline was a sickly infant. She might not survive. Emile Hamard, the bereaved husband, had begun to go mad. Ever since April, Flaubert had been contemplating the possibility of his mother's death. On top of all this, there came Louise's complaints and reproaches. When can she visit? When will he come to Paris?

Flaubert spelt it all out to her once again. 'I simply have to stay here. My mother needs me. Her sufferings impose an endless unimaginable tyranny on me [. . .]. I'm as weak as a little child and I give in because I don't like reproaches and plaintive sighs.' 'Since I am all she has to live for my mother spends the entire day brooding over the accidents and misfortunes that might happen to me.' 'Last year [. . .] I used to go out every day in a little sailing boat [. . .].' 'I have put all my gear away in the attic, and not a day goes by without my wanting to get it out again [. . .]. In just the same way for ten years I used to do my writing in secret to spare myself the teasing I expected to get.'

Louise's grievances, large and small, had begun to dominate the conversation. Some were ridiculous. 'Can it be possible that you criticise even my innocent affection for my armchair!!' Some were more substantial, as when Flaubert informed Louise Colet that he was writing 'a sentimental letter' to his old flame, Madame Foucaud. 'She's an old acquaintance, don't be jealous, you can read the letter if you want, on condition that you don't tear it up.' Having promised Louise not to mention Madame Foucaud and the letter ever again – 'because it's a subject that upsets you' – he immediately sent the letter to Louise anyway. It arrived along with an elaborately self-incriminating, half-hearted explanation. Eulalie Foucaud, he calmly reassured Louise, was just a good fuck. Big tits, but not very intelligent. 'We really had nothing much to say to each other.'

Louise was not reassured. She was scandalised. She forbade all further affectionate written reference to her breasts. She was sarcastic. She predicted that Madame Foucaud would ask for money. Flaubert, disingenuously, pleaded artistic license. 'You thought my letter was too fond? I cannot imagine why. On the contrary, I thought there were several little touches of insolence and the general tone was lightly aristocratic. [. . .] when I was writing to her, given my capacity to induce feelings in myself solely by the use of the pen, I was taking my subject seriously but only while I was actually writing. [. . .] It's one of the effects of my charlatanesque character.'

Against the background of this dispute, the question of Flaubert's next visit to Paris became highly charged. It had now been a month since their last meeting in Mantes. Louise was ever more insistent. Like her fictional counterpart, Emma Bovary, Louise wanted them to run away together. They could live somewhere in the east, in Rhodes or Smyrna. Deftly, as he thought, he fended her off. 'Ah, dreams such as these make for unhappiness. I have had all too many of them.' Flaubert became evasive. He was planning a couple of weeks in Paris, on business to do with his father's memorial. 'But when it will be I really don't know.' It depended, he said, on the date of the meeting of the committee.

She found it exasperating, first the anguish over the letter and now this uncertainty. Resenting her indignation, he did his best to hurry things up. 'It was as though I could hear your voice [. . .] shouting in my ear with your childish petulance [. . .].' Inexplicably, the committee meeting was deferred. He hated to let her down, though it was not his fault. 'My mother is not at all well. I hardly ever leave her side. When I'm not in her room she's in my study.'

At this point the scene changed. Du Camp left Croisset and returned to Paris. There he met Louise Colet for the first time. Du Camp's letters to Louise, which began several days later, were full of deviously confidential advice about how to manage Flaubert. The effect of Du Camp's presence was soon apparent in a certain darkening of the sky.

A big storm was brewing. Louise's dreadful sickly encumbrance of a husband, Hippolyte Colet, Professor of Composition at the Conservatoire, was back in Paris. Flaubert was wasting her time with his excuses, insulting her with his evasions, taunting her with his crude commercial traveller's jokes. ('I'm like a cigar,' he wrote. 'It takes a good pull to get me going.') Louise Colet had had enough. She stopped writing to

Flaubert. After four days of her silence he fell into a panic. When her letter arrived it was a stinker, à la Colet. He was instructed never to say that he loved her. He was required, furthermore, to decide on a day to 'collect his things'.

For a whole week, pages of exhausting dramatic eloquence flew in both directions. 'You are quite right,' Flaubert conceded wearily. 'You would have been better off not loving me.' Louise had a new complaint, the most preposterous yet. 'If I had never met you,' she wrote to him, ' I would possibly have accepted, once I were free, a position that everyone would have thought dazzling.' She meant that she could have married her protector, Victor Cousin, once her husband, Hippolyte Colet, was dead. (He died in 1850.)

To add to this museum collection of grievances, Louise now discovered, perhaps from Du Camp, that Flaubert had been planning that fraternal summer excursion to Brittany. Flaubert's self-defence was unconvincing. 'Do I even know if it will happen? There are so many reasons why it will fall through just like all my other plans large and small. In ten months any number of things could get in the way of our going, illness [. . .] lack of money [. . .]. I didn't mention it to you only because it was by no means certain and still is not.'

Flaubert ended this, his first openly reproachful letter, on a note of chastened formality: 'Farewell, dear comrade.' This elicited only a proud and injured silence from Louise Colet. Flaubert found her silences more terrible than her recriminations. After four days he cracked and wrote to her in tones of superb imperial indignation. 'Since my love is hateful to you (you said in your letter that I horrify you) [. . .]. Do you want me to help you loathe me? Shall I do something so ignoble, so petty, so coarse and so repulsive that it could never be mentioned?'

All of this was grotesquely inauspicious. Flaubert finally arrived in Paris on 9 November and left three days later on the 12th. The whole visit, coinciding with the first anniversary of the onset of his father's fatal illness, was predictably disastrous. He forgot to bring her the promised manuscript of *Novembre*, though he did manage to give her the paperweight that had once belonged to his sister. When he missed a rendezvous – 'out of modesty [. . .] in a party of four, it would have been a public event' – she turned on him, calling him traitor. He was fascinated, aroused and disgusted by the frozen emotional violence of the ensuing scene. 'Do you realise that there are no reproaches that can equal your tears, no words of insult or abuse more bloody and bitter to me than the lash of that harrowing despair you used on me. My heart still wears the marks.' The shade of the Marquis De Sade might have been there with them, in attendance. 'I still see you in the corner, against the wall, weeping and writhing. You were accusing me! I wanted to kneel before you and transform every sob into a cry of joy. Do you realise that we composed a *scene* and that I looked like a torturer?'

Refusing his farewell kiss, she threw him into a state of anguish. After his return to Croisset, after an unexpectedly forgiving letter from Louise Colet, Flaubert found himself speaking the language of guilt and abjection. He would do whatever she wanted. He would even go to the theatre with her, he said. He would also keep one of his earlier promises. 'I'll bring *Novembre* for you; I'll read it to you one evening, alone, at the hotel.'

Flaubert was soon back in Paris for a few days, with his mother. At some point, in an abrupt, dream-like, accidental street-corner encounter, Louise Colet probably met Madame Flaubert. Flaubert could only escape for brief moments with Louise. He read *Novembre* to her. 'If you were listening carefully to my *Novembre* you must have worked out thousands of unutterable things which may explain the way I am. But that part of my life is over. That book was the closing ceremony of my youth. What is left to me now isn't much, but it is solid.'

This reading of *Novembre* was an intimate gesture of reconciliation. We might suspect that it was also a deviously narcissistic performance of his secret history. *Novembre* described and dignified his problems, his afflictions, and his ambitions. 'None of it', Flaubert told Louise, 'is my fault.' If he seemed 'stupid, spiteful, foolish, selfish or unfeeling', it was not his fault. 'I was born', he explained once again, 'in a state of *ennui*. It's like damp eating away at me [. . .] by force of will I have finally acquired the habit of work. But when I succumb to distraction, all my vexation floats up to the surface, like a bloated corpse, exposing its green belly and poisoning the air all around. I have tried to avoid the passions. They came to find me.' Gloriously excessive, the image of the poison-corpse adds an authentic physiological touch. As the son of a surgeon, Flaubert knew what he was talking about. Like his great contemporary Baudelaire, he was instinctively at home in the dark and malodorous corners of Romanticism.

The reconciliation with Louise Colet soon turned out to be illusory. Flaubert returned to Rouen with Maxime Du Camp and there he became engrossed in precisely those intellectual passions that most excluded her. Flaubert began reading Saint Augustine, in preparation for the writing of *La Tentation de Saint Antoine*. 'I throw myself headlong into religious reading matter, not with any intention of acquiring a faith but in order to gaze upon those who have one.' He went to visit Alfred Le Poittevin, recently returned from his honeymoon in Italy. He spent long hours in fantastical conversation with Du Camp. 'We spend our time in talk of which I am almost ashamed, all kinds of folly and imperial reverie. We build mansions, we furnish Venetian palaces. We travel across the Orient with our escorts and then we stumble back into real life, utterly dejected, and, finally, we're as gloomy as a pair of corpses.'

Within a week or so of his return, urged on perhaps by Du Camp, Flaubert began to reprimand Louise Colet. Her crass, tearful enthusiasm for *Novembre* was her principal offence. He was 'shocked', he said, by the fact that she had compared his *Novembre* with Chateaubriand's *René*. 'It felt like a profanation.' When Flaubert took issue on literary matters he was always relentlessly outspoken. From such beginnings, ever more bitter reproaches began to flow in both directions. 'Why', he asked her, 'have you tried to encroach upon a life which does not belong to me, tried to alter this whole existence of mine to suit the requirements of your love?' She sent him a love-gift, an agate seal engraved with the motto *Amor nel cor*. 'What does this thing mean?' he demanded, obtusely. 'Is it a challenge? A retort? A joke? I'm lost [. . .].'

By the end of December the familiar endgame was being played out. Louise Colet took issue with Flaubert's 'aristocratic ideas' about women. His mockery had killed her love. He had treated her 'as a woman of the lowest order'. He responded to her accusations with facetious disdain. 'I find it impossible to continue with a correspondence that is turning epileptic.' 'Personally I've had enough of grand passions, exalted feelings, furious loving and howling despair.' 'If you could have been content with gallantry spiced up with a little sentiment and a little poetry, perhaps you would not have met with this fall which has caused you so much suffering.' 'Why do you, poor darling, stubbornly compare yourself, in the effect that you have on me, to a whore.'

Mollified by Maxime Du Camp, their Parisian go-between, Louise

Colet soon offered her forgiveness. 'Du Camp', Flaubert wrote, 'tells me that he is doing all he can to lift your morale.' Lifting Louise Colet's morale meant rather more than Flaubert realised. It meant treachery. Acting on a mischievous impulse of exasperation, Du Camp had promised to show Louise Colet one of Flaubert's letters, '[. . .] and I shall send it to you my poor dear sister whatever it costs me. There you will read [. . .] what he is and what he wants, and you will descend finally too late into this temperament which astonishes both of us.'

The letter in question has not survived. Its likely tone of exuberantly cynical mockery was enough to spark an explosion that brought the whole edifice clattering to the ground.* Louise's subsequent letter to Flaubert was charged with her most lethal scorn. 'There was enough in it to kill a man,' Flaubert remarked, showing a casual familiarity with her habit of invective. In his reply, Flaubert endeavoured to 'put things clearly once and for all'. 'Love', he said, 'is not the first thing in life for me, it comes second. It is a bed on which you lay your heart to bring it some ease. But you don't spend the whole day lying there.' 'You want me to roll around at your feet as if I were fifteen years old, want me to come dashing up to you, quivering and weeping.' After this withering caricature of amorousness, Flaubert tried to explain his incomprehensible reluctance. He had chosen to manage his nerves, he said, by cultivating 'an invincible apathy towards life'. It was better to feel nothing than to resonate and quiver like a violin. Her grief at the railway station, when they last parted, had rekindled his own 'nervous agitation'. Her extravagant emotionalism was a threat to his fragile defences.

The truth-telling, once-and-for-all mood of this letter coincided significantly with the first anniversary of Flaubert's father's death. Grief finds twisted expression in Flaubert's grandiose guilty curse directed against the Father. 'May his son be a torment to him and may [. . .] the colossal greedy *ennui* that eats away at the child, be to the father such a grief that he too shall repent having lived.' Whatever the deeper sources of the curse, we may be sure of its disconcerting effect upon Louise Colet. It was Flaubert's lurid way of saying *never*!

---

* 'I forgive Du Camp his treachery in showing you one of my letters [. . .]. I had not thought him so childish.' Du Camp was chastened by his friend's reaction. 'Gustave treated me so severely over the letter that I am not at all inclined to expose myself to any further satirical remarks from his direction.'

LOVE'S catastrophe soon arrived. It took the form of a scene in the bedroom of a Paris hotel, a scene that we can reconstruct in detail from Maxime Du Camp's letters. On the evening of Wednesday, 17 February 1847 Flaubert arrived in Paris. He had decided to conceal his presence from Louise Colet, persuaded that she had no real desire to see him. (Perhaps his secret intention was to see Louise Pradier; Louise Colet believed that this indeed was the case.) Unable to write, Flaubert had been feeling exceptionally sour and stupid. Nothing flowed inside him. He was just like a blocked ditch, he said. And he took no comfort from the fact that his splendid boils were closing up. 'The pus disappears back inside. All I ask is that nobody notices the smell.'

The next day, Thursday, Flaubert was busy with urgent money matters. He was negotiating the sale of a property inherited from his father. The farm, purchased in 1828, realised almost 23,000 francs, a substantial sum that largely paid for Flaubert's subsequent travels in the Orient. Early on Friday morning he received some sad news. An old friend of the family, Felix D'Arcet, Louise Pradier's brother, had died in Brazil, 'killed in his bed when a gas lamp exploded'. Stricken with grief, Flaubert spent the day with Maxime Du Camp, then returned to his hotel.

At six o'clock that evening Louise Colet found her way, uninvited, to Flaubert's room. In great distress she arraigned him for the fact that he had already been a whole day in Paris without seeing her. Flaubert was overcome by a murderous rage. 'I was beginning to lose my head, I was holding on so as not to explode, when I said *until tomorrow*, it was to get it over with, to put an end to it. I was choking, I was on the edge.' Maxime Du Camp subsequently explained it to her. 'What irritated him beyond endurance [. . .] was your saying to him that he'd been lying. He felt this was an unpardonable accusation [. . .] you seemed to be jealous of the fact that he was going to visit the D'Arcet family. He resented this bitterly.'

Flaubert dismissed Louise Colet and went to visit Madame Darcet. He called on Maxime Du Camp at around eleven in the evening and ten minutes later he had an epileptic attack. 'Which I am sad to say was entirely due to what took place between the two of you [. . .].' Humiliated, confused and exhausted, Flaubert spent the next day with Maxime Du Camp. In the evening a letter arrived from Louise Colet. Written in the third person, it expounded her suspicions about Louise Pradier. 'That's the limit!' he declared to Maxime Du Camp.

Flaubert left Paris early on Sunday, dreading another attack. Maxime Du Camp described the ominous scene to Louise Colet: 'When he is deeply moved his dreadful illness worries him greatly [. . .] he left feeling upset, desperate, ill and full of a silent intense anger which I found frightening: I had never seen him like that. At the moment his heart is full of torment and it's best to let him be.' Du Camp advised her to leave it for a whole year. He was angry with her for ignoring all his good advice. 'If you had allowed yourself to be guided by me I would have set up a never-ending liaison for you, sentimental on your side, intellectual on his, which would have made you both happy, I swear.' A few weeks later, Du Camp quietly delivered the coup de grâce to Louise Colet's hopes of a reconciliation. 'He doesn't mention you in his letters; he said in passing: *it's all over*, and that was all [. . .].' 'His letters are almost entirely about Saint Augustine, his current reading.' Weary of her angry accusations, Du Camp gave up trying to help her.

T HERE was inevitably a prodigious postscript to the 'scene' in the hotel. Several weeks later, on 7 March, Flaubert wrote to Louise Colet. Intending this to be his last word, he described to her in self-exonerating detail the history of his relations with Louise Pradier.* Flaubert blamed Louise Colet's suspicions on James Pradier, the much-cuckolded husband, who must mischievously have put the idea into her head. Flaubert insisted that he had only ever been a friend to Louise Pradier, keeping his distance, all the better to analyse and observe such a splendid specimen, 'the very type of womanhood with all its instincts, an orchestra of female sentiments.'

Like Emma Bovary's fictional seducer, Rodolphe, Flaubert ended his letter with the suggestion that Louise pretend he has gone away on a long journey. Instead of coming to an end, their correspondence now slowed to a more sedate pace. Now that the fury had subsided, a gener-ous and ironic tenderness came to fill its place. What had he been through, she asked, to have become the man he was? 'It's unutterable,' he replied. 'My soul [. . .] has been through fire [. . .]. Little wonder that it cannot be warmed by the sun. Regard it as my infirmity, a shameful inner malady which I contracted from having frequented unhealthy things, but do not distress yourself, there is nothing to be done about

---

* Louise Colet wrote 'last letter' in the margin, though it was by no means the last. There are twenty-two further letters to Louise Colet from the year 1847 and then two letters from the year 1848. Then nothing until May 1851, when Flaubert returned from Egypt.

it.' He concluded with a sombre thought. 'I ought not to have let myself be loved.' Then he described for her, with a kind of voluptuous sadness, how the years to come would efface the memory of their love. This quiet fading, this relentless decay of all human passion, will be one of his greatest and most original themes.

The week before Flaubert's departure for Brittany was further marked by two awkward and unhappy farewells. Flaubert visited Alfred Le Poittevin. Alfred's wife was pregnant, and their child was due in a few weeks' time. Alfred, though newly married, was 'vegetating as ever'. Flaubert found him in a 'deplorable' state, sinking ever deeper into apathy. Emile Hamard, the grieving widower, father of Caroline, posed a different problem. With his mind increasingly out of balance, Hamard went to England, probably for a whole year. 'Poor lad, he has taken more wind in his sails than he can manage [. . .].' Hamard was likely to return, ever more disturbed, ever more impossible, like one of the mad, disreputable relatives who inhabit the shadowy places of so many nineteenth-century novels. Both of these encounters – with Alfred Le Poittevin and with Emile Hamard – hovered in Flaubert's thoughts as he walked across Brittany.

CHAPTER TEN

On the Road

FLAUBERT always remembered the summer of 1847. For thirteen splendid weeks, dressed like insolent vagabonds, he and Du Camp tramped together across the rich green landscapes of the Loire and along the windswept cliffs of Brittany. Remarkably, it was the first time that Flaubert, now in his mid-twenties, had travelled any real distance with the companion of his choice. In a life so clouded by distress and frustration, this was a delectable experience of joyful creative energy. 'How many times did Gustave say to me, "That was the best moment of our lives."' Those summer days of 1847 remained in Flaubert's mind as a superlative experience of friendship. All of his major novels, apart from *Madame Bovary*, address this difficult but vital question of masculine friendship. Flaubert's fraternal couples – Jules and Henry, Matho and Spendius, Frédéric and Deslauriers, Bouvard and Pécuchet – play out their variations on this insistent, cherished theme.

Early on the morning of 1 May 1847, after many months of conscientious preparation, Flaubert and Du Camp set off at last. They had spent much of the winter devising their itinerary, reading the guide books, making lists of churches, buying new clothes, and doing their best to reassure an apprehensive Madame Flaubert.

The long-awaited day had arrived. It was a fine spring morning and both men were in excellent spirits as they set off from Du Camp's house. Rather than hire a carriage, they walked across Paris together, for the fun of it, heading south, from the Place de la Madeleine to the Place de la Concorde, over the river and along the quai d'Orsay, then down towards the splendid new Gare d'Orléans.

Now that they were on their way, at last, 'alone, free and together', their triumphant sense of mutual affinity expressed itself in a swinging, light-hearted stride, a clatter of hobnailed boots and an emphatic wielding of walking sticks. When we picture them together, at that moment of exuberant anticipation, they offer an arresting physical contrast. If they were animals in a comic fable they would be most aptly represented by a fox and a bear. Du Camp: the sophisticate, a smooth, slender, dandified, young man with a pleasing manner and a smile that might be remembered as insinuating. Flaubert: the ingénu, a boisterous, powerful, rough-edged giant with a resonant, boyish laugh that shakes his whole body.

They both felt pleasingly conspicuous in their new travelling clothes. 'Never', said Flaubert, 'was any party outfit chosen with greater loving care.' Self-conscious but undaunted, amused by the curiosity of their fellow citizens, they were determined to carry it off with a stylish bugger-the-bourgeois insouciance. With the pedantic relish of a connoisseur, Flaubert listed their equipment as follows:

> One grey felt hat.
> One horse-dealer's stick, sent specially from Lisieux.
> One stout pair of shoes (untreated leather, with hobnails).
> Ditto polished (for official visits in town, if there are any, or for excursions to Paphos if the geese who attend upon that goddess happen to snatch us up into her celestial chariot).
> One pair of leather gaiters, suitable for wearing with stout shoes.
> Ditto cloth to protect our socks from the dust, on polished-shoe days.
> One heavy linen jacket (stable-boy chic).
> One pair heavy linen trousers, enormously baggy, to be tucked into gaiters.
> One heavy linen waistcoat, elegantly cut to offset the vulgarity of the fabric.
> In addition, a special knife, two drinking bottles, a pipe, wooden variety, three silk shirts, and everything required by a European for his daily ablutions.

Everyone they met along their way, especially in the wilds of Brittany, was perplexed by these two odd young men. What were they supposed to be? Were they engineers or surveyors, sent by the government? Were they tax-inspectors? Undercover agents from Paris? Foreign spies? Landscape painters? It was impossible to say for certain. On their passports they were described as *rentiers*. But their interesting clothes and the fact that they were travelling on foot gave quite a different message. 'Nobody', Du Camp recalled, with some satisfaction, 'knew what we were.' Were they respectable young men with plenty of money to spend? Or merely itinerant riff-raff cadging their way across

France? These confusions were the fertile minor comic theme of their journey. Dressing up in something colourful and peculiar was a youthful, bohemian game. It was amusing and instructive to descend in jest from one's encoded sartorial niche in the mid-nineteenth-century class system, knowing that a set of nice clean clothes was always available should the game ever take an unpleasant turn.

To the sound of distant cannon-fire celebrating the official birthday of King Louis-Philippe, Flaubert and Du Camp arrived at the Gare d'Orléans. Like the rest of their generation they regarded the King as a great joke. The plump, pear-shaped, bourgeois monarch swinging his umbrella! How ludicrous! How unkingly! Louis-Philippe symbolised all the blighted hopes of the liberal revolution of July 1830, now no more than a distant memory of Flaubert's schooldays. The old King was the emblem of everything that the two young travellers were eager to escape, the embodiment of everything mediocre, prosaic and modern. However, the first stage of their journey required them to step aboard that most bourgeois contraption, the railway. It was just over a hundred miles to their first destination, the town of Blois, in the Loire valley.

WE may leave Flaubert and Du Camp, for the moment, defiantly unimpressed by 'this arid mode of locomotion', trapped in the uncongenial company of two rich and raucous Parisian grain merchants, along with a visibly syphilitic Englishman and his ugly daughter. As the whole company goes rolling towards Blois, in their deep-upholstered first-class railway carriage, cutting through ancestral parkland at a miraculous forty miles an hour, belching live coals, sparks, smoke and steam, we may pause to consider Flaubert's state of mind on the morning of 1 May 1847.

This summer journey was an escape. With a great surge of joyful energy, like some waking giant, he was breaking all the little chains that had held him down, so tightly and so long, at home. Since his fall in January 1844 he had come through a dark and painful time. His grief at the recent deaths of his father and his sister, his continuing artistic frustrations, all the perplexity of an unhappy love and the deeper fear of madness – all these he could cast aside for the next thirteen weeks.

Brittany and the Loire? Scarcely an exotic destination. Nothing like those grandiose journeys across the Orient that Byron and Chateaubriand had described so enticingly. Nonetheless it was an escape. From Croisset in particular, and from the bourgeois world in general. In his travel journal Flaubert waved farewell, with a reasonably good grace, to all the more alluring fantasies of his youth. 'Until another day, another time, those long journeys across the world, on a camel's back [. . .].' For Flaubert, always a great connoisseur of imagined journeys, this was enough for the moment.

Du Camp was a man of abundant energy and superlative charm, undoubtedly excellent company. Having inherited money from his father, he had long enjoyed an enviable independence and he was well versed in all the practicalities of travel. He could be trusted to look after Flaubert, if the need should arise. He could also smooth the way for them, socially, with his cheerful good humour. The two men shared their literary ambitions and their sexual attitudes. They were planning to write a book about Brittany together. They also enjoyed visiting brothels together, laughingly comparing notes afterwards. After nearly twelve months of Louise Colet's tearful, voluptuous intensity it would be a relief for Flaubert to espouse Du Camp's crassly mocking vision of womankind. Sustained by this warm, appreciative, teasing, mutual affection, Flaubert and Du Camp set out in high hopes.

For thirteen weeks Flaubert could escape – almost completely – from the lugubrious company of his widowed mother. He had the further satisfaction of turning his back on Louise Colet. Flaubert's absence, though relatively brief, announced to these entangling women, his grieving mother and his exasperated lover, that he was about to begin a new chapter in his life. He could not yet be sure of his destination, but his departure was at least an indisputable fact. He had reached his twenty-fifth birthday, some months previously, in December 1846, and now, according to the legal code of the day, he was no longer a minor. It was time to pocket some of the money he had inherited from his father and embark upon the agreeable adventure of spending it.

In the weeks before his departure for Brittany, Flaubert observed that his friends were changing, growing up, moving away and getting on. The bohemians were all returning to the bourgeois path from which they had strayed in the years of their youth. Condemned to the quiet life of the convalescent, living at home with his mother, Flaubert contemplated his friends' achievements with mixed feelings. There was Ernest Chevalier, Flaubert's earliest companion and schoolboy literary accomplice. Chevalier had just been appointed to the post of deputy public prosecutor in Corsica. The news prompted an affectionately mocking letter from Croisset. Though it was easy for Flaubert to satirise such impeccably conventional success, Ernest was taking the first step in the brilliant legal career that Flaubert himself had abandoned.

Flaubert, meanwhile, was stuck. He had written nothing since finishing the first draft of *L'Education sentimentale* back in January 1846. He felt so feeble and delicate, he confided to Ernest Chevalier, 'like a machine that grinds to a halt whenever a straw gets into its wheels'. It was now over a year since the death of his sister Caroline, and he needed to break the spell of grief, to take the air and see the world. Three gloriously irresponsible months of congenial masculine conversation, tramping the cliffs of Brittany in a pair of heavy boots, with the wind in his face and the sun on his back, smoking his pipe and gazing upon far horizons – this was exactly what he needed. It would clear his mind and help him to decide what he ought to do next.

IT was a hundred miles down the line to the royal city of Blois, time enough for Flaubert to ponder both the poetry and the prose of travelling. This grey, modern 'arid mode of locomotion' offered a sad contrast with the chaotic delights of the journeys of Flaubert's boyhood. Since that time, when the journey from Rouen to Paris had taken an epic three days, both travelling and travel-writing had changed. There were no more midnight sexual escapades in the shadowy bedrooms and corridors of country inns. No more erudite grand-tour aristocrats, like Byron and Chateaubriand, pursuing the sublime. The new travel-writers were career journalists, professional men of letters, writing for the new mass circulation newspapers. Impressions and opinions, little incidents and local details – this was the stuff of the democratic new style. Gérard de Nerval, writing from the Orient in the early 1840s, had adopted a tone of cheerful and lightly facetious ordinariness. Flaubert intended to master this, the prose of travel, before he attempted the poetry.

The city of Blois was their first stopping place. Rich in associations historical and literary, this was the perfect opportunity to try out one's prose style. Flaubert had passed this way once before, without stopping, in the summer of 1840 on his way to Marseilles. This time he was his own master. He responded deeply and idiosyncratically to the charms of the place. Shaking off the noise and the vexation of the previous day's journey, Flaubert climbed the silent, narrow streets that wound up the hill like a staircase, from the tree-lined quayside by the bright waters of the Loire, upwards, past the mansions that had once belonged to the rich and powerful, in the direction of the great castle on the hill.

The Sunday quiet of Blois elicited a mood of sweet provincial melancholy that had little to do with the kings and queens of the French Renaissance. For Flaubert the place was alive with pleasing associations, ghosts historic and literary, as well as private half-realised presences. These were the very streets where Victor Hugo had spent his boyhood. This was the city from which Balzac had taken his heroines. Flaubert described the streets of Blois as 'silent intimate streets in which one might place some tender and benign passion'. Contemplating the grass growing between the stones, the long grey walls enclosing large gardens, the discreet little door that opens at night to let in some mysterious visitor, Flaubert began to imagine a life somewhat like his own, a calm, monotonous, melancholy, disappointed life, lived out to the slow chimes of the church clock, the life of a woman buried alive with her sorrow, trapped in the desperation of her unhappy love, a woman like his mother, like Louise Colet, a woman like himself. 'Among these peaceful houses', he wrote, 'I entertain myself with dreams of some great deep intimate history, an unhealthy passion that lasts until death, the unwavering love of some old maid or virtuous wife; there in her appointed place, in spite of yourself, you invent some pale beautiful woman with long nails and slender hands, some coldly aristocratic lady, married to a peevish, miserly, jealous husband, dying of consumption.'

At least four women contributed something to this sketchy composite figure whom I shall call the Lady of Blois. We can picture their faces, crowding in, importuning Flaubert, pleading their forlorn and abandoned state. There is Flaubert's mother, so coldly aristocratic; Flaubert's sister, shackled by consumption; Louise Colet, the woman with the peevish husband; Elisa Schlésinger, the virtuous wife. Compounded from the spirit of the place and from Flaubert's recent emotional history, the Lady of Blois fascinated her creator. She kept coming back into Flaubert's mind over the next few weeks. She wouldn't leave him alone and he did not yet know what to do with her. He wondered, in his journal, if she might be one of Balzac's heroines, one of those superlative, voluptuous, mature, enigmatic 'women of thirty' portrayed so vividly in *La Femme de trente ans*. In 1847 such women were still the alluring new continent of the literary-erotic. Flaubert confided to his journal an ambition to outdo Balzac: 'We shall sound the depths of what has been merely touched upon [. . .].' It was a boast of impressive foresight.

When Flaubert reached the chateau, at the top of the hill, he emerged from this reverie to find the courtyard full of soldiers drinking up the wine given out to celebrate the King's birthday. It was his first glimpse of a social world dominated by a harsh, nervous, censorious ethos. The facts would all begin to add up, as he travelled on, as he approached the more remote regions of Brittany, where, for historical reasons, the presence of the French state was more obvious than it was in Normandy. Flaubert began to notice. Prisons everywhere, and barracks full of soldiers. Policemen and tax-collectors and customs officials in every village. Political mottoes inscribed on restored ecclesiastical monuments, letters of gold praising monarchy and good order. Renaissance statues emasculated by curators. Eighteenth-century books expurgated by bishops. Human bodies cramped into unlovely garments. All in the name of a narrow, insipid decency.

Flaubert's indignation bubbled up in a good-humoured witty tirade:

I feel an intense and perpetual hatred for all the restorers, the white-washers, the correctors, the expurgators, the chaste veilers of profane nudity, the devisers of abridgements and résumés; for all who would shave everything and make it wear a wig, ferocious in their pedantry, pitiless in their ineptitude, they set about amputating nature and spitting upon art [. . .] that nature which man carries within himself [. . .].'

Against the tide of this anxious bourgeois *discipline*, against the smooth, insidious flow of official religiosity, Flaubert resolved to cultivate the polemical vision of a human energy that was simultaneously artistic, sexual and religious. This resolution is first put forward here in Blois. Making trouble, like Byron, like Rabelais, had long been a vital part of Flaubert's artistic ambition. In Blois, it suddenly came into focus, sharp and clear.

In the main hall of the chateau, the scene of a notoriously bloody political murder in the late sixteenth century, Flaubert evoked an image of Montaigne, sceptically detached; 'unmoved in the midst of all those shrieking passions, unconvinced in the midst of so much violent conviction, he was there as the symbol of all that remains alongside all that passes away'. Lucid detachment was also part of the emerging vision.

TEN miles to the east of Blois was the village of Chambord, with its famous 440-room chateau. But Chambord was a disappointment. Flaubert and Du Camp lost their way while crossing muddy fields, searching for the place. When they found the chateau the rain had begun to fall and they were not at all impressed. The chateau had lost its woods and its park. There was not even a garden. Architectural masterpiece though it was, the building had been neglected for nearly a century. Stripped of its furniture in 1790, it had been passed from hand to hand until purchased by public subscription in 1821 as the residence of Henri d'Artois, comte de Chambord, the official Bourbon pretender to the French throne. The young count was currently living in exile and his symbolically decrepit chateau was the focus of intense royalist nostalgia. The visitors' book in the lodge offered the sceptical eye a rich feast of political absurdity. Its pages were full of forlorn and pretentious comments, bewailing the decay of France's legitimate monarchy. Flaubert, the true son of a self-made man from a great merchant city, had always known what to make of such archaic nonsense. It stirred him to appreciative satirical laughter: '[. . .] the whole rabble of sham nobility who live off the sempiternal poetry of turrets and miladies and palfreys, and the fleurs de lys on the banner of Saint Louis, and the white plume and divine right and a tall pile of equally innocent foolishness.'

Emma Bovary at the age of fifteen, starved of glamour, feasts on exactly these pseudo-historical memories. 'Emma dabbled in the remains of old lending-libraries [. . .] conceived a passion for things historical, dreamed about coffers, guardrooms and minstrels. She would have liked to live in some old manor house, like those chatelaines in their long corsages [. . .].' By 1847 this was a taste that Flaubert had long grown out of. He would soon be able to make use of it, artistically, as the deserted room in the house of his imagination.

ON the fourth day of their journey together, in the city of Tours, after a long and strenuous day on the road, Flaubert suffered a nervous attack, his first for several months. Du Camp acted decisively. He summoned an eminent and very expensive doctor who prescribed an enormous dose of quinine, enough to 'hit the body like cannon-fire'. The medical 'remedies' of the day could be as fearsome as the afflictions they were supposed to cure. Yet Flaubert seems to have endured them all without complaint. This attack, coming so soon after leaving the quiet safety of Croisset, was a humiliating reminder of his fragility. Their travel journal passes over it in silence. Perhaps Flaubert's reveries in Blois were a premonition. Such psychic receptiveness, increasingly associated with femininity, could be perilous. However, the attack was evidently not very severe, for it did not delay them. After a day resting in Tour, they embarked on the next stage of their journey.

They were beginning to enjoy the rhythm of the journey, walking along together through the rich landscape of the Loire. Du Camp paints a vivid picture of the best moments of their companionship:

The weather is warm; big white clouds gallop across the sky, spurred by the wind; the buds on the trees begin to open in the sun; our sticks ring out on the metalled road [. . .]. On we go then, walking along, merry and carefree, talkative and silent, singing and smoking; for us it was one of those days that make you love life, one of those days when the fog clears a little and reveals a bright patch of sky. We had left behind us the melancholy of the big cities; the countryside was intoxicating; in our hearts we felt infinite tenderness and profound pity. The Loire was shining, wide and calm, bordered by meadows; a few large boats were sailing upriver with their single sail swelling in the wind and from far away they looked like those classical galleys.

Once they reached the town of Nantes, the last outpost of modern urban France, they took rooms in a decent inn and settled in for the week. There they drafted the first two chapters of the book they had planned to write together, chapters that Flaubert regarded as the weakest of the collection. They soon realised that writing like this, en route, 'would have required six months and three times as much money as we had'. They therefore decided to write once they returned home.

THE real Breton journey began only when they left Nantes and began to make their way, mostly on foot, sometimes sleeping rough, along the jagged Atlantic coastline. Their itinerary can be traced out in two different ways: either as an evocative series of names – Guérande, Belle-Ile, Carnac, Lorient, Quimper, Brest, Morlaix, St-Brieuc, St-Malo – or as a sequence of scenes – the fair, the sea-caves, the slaughterhouse, the statue, the brothel, the castle. Either way, this was to be a journey into the other France.

Walking around the ramparts of Guerande, an ancient walled town at the edge of the salt marshes, they came across a mass of people and animals filling one of the public squares. It was the day of the fair. Drawn to one of the booths by the sound of a big drum, they saw a foxy-looking peasant in a blue smock calling in the crowds to see something called 'the young phenomenon. It was a sheep with five legs. Convinced that it would be a fraud Flaubert and Du Camp paid their two pence and went inside. There they found, disconcertingly, a sheep with five equally solid legs and a tail shaped like a trumpet. This was just the kind of homegrown freak that Flaubert loved. He was enchanted with the creature and its keeper. To Du Camp's growing dismay, Flaubert embarked upon one of his elaborate jokes. 'Incomprehensible,' he exclaimed, 'these tricks of nature!' In tones of mock solemnity Flaubert enthused over 'the young phenomenon' and began to ask its keeper a string of credulous questions. He had never seen anything so strange. The man should write to King Louis-Philippe. He would surely make his fortune. Flaubert invited the peasant in the blue smock to dine with them at the inn, where he plied him with great quantities of wine and called him by his first name.

Du Camp disapproved, but the joke was destined to live on. Flaubert loved monsters and he was infatuated with the five-legged sheep. It had entered his comic mythology and it would not lie down. Next day, as they marched across the bare landscape, Flaubert kept on mentioning 'the young phenomenon'. He addressed Du Camp himself as 'the young phenomenon', pausing along the way, in the empty countryside, to extol the virtues of the young phenomenon to an imaginary audience. Du Camp endured the obsessive joke as best he could. Flaubert's friends were often obliged to stretch their sense of the comic beyond its comfortable limits.

The five-legged sheep appealed to the whimsical, charlatanesque side of Flaubert. Yet Brittany also had a deeper and a darker side that spoke to him with a peculiar power. Death and the sea had a special place in Breton culture. From the dark rafters of village churches there used to hang intricately fashioned model ships, placed there as votive offerings to local saints. The dead bodies of sailors and fishermen were often washed up on to that wild coast. The cemetery was always to be found at the heart of the village. 'We live with our dead,' they said. 'If we bury them away from the village, they will hear neither the singing nor the services.' The dead remained on intimate terms with the living, like a black thread woven into the fabric of everyday life.

Flaubert, so recently bereaved, was duly fascinated by the archaic authenticity of the Breton symbolism of death. He kept noticing things: crypts and ossuaries and tombs, the candle light on the faces of the crowd gathered at a nocturnal funeral, the stillness of a beautiful young widow sitting staring through her window at the sea, the deathbed repentance depicted in a farcically naive painting. Here was a primitive folk decorum, deeply satisfying to contemplate. Brittany offered Flaubert a rich, brief, practical education in death. It showed just how the living might grasp their enduring connection with the dead. It was, in this sense, a preparation for his journey to Egypt.

Brittany also offered distressing scenes of violent grotesquerie. Flaubert was drawn, as ever, to the ugly, indecorous things that perplexed the human imagination by their 'moral density'. In a spirit of lucid and appalled compassion he observed the practicalities of the abattoir in Quimper. He remembered how the disembowelling of a great ox exposed the superb colours of the inner organs. He noted how the eyes of a calf filled with terror at the sight of the other animals being dragged towards the slaughterer's knife. Flaubert was possessed by the raw sound of death, 'the voices of those who were being slaughtered, those who were dying, those who were about to die; there were strange cries, intonations of such profound distress that seemed to be forming words you could almost understand'. Having lived in the Hôtel-Dieu, with its thin wooden partitions, the cry of agony was familiar to him. Inscribed on the intimate soundtrack of his childhood, it's a sound that rings out, with a terrible authenticity, in *Madame Bovary* at the moment of the amputation of Hippolyte's leg: 'a slow heavy wail, broken by a jagged screeching, like the far-off bellow of some creature being slaughtered'.

In the abattoir at Quimper, the whole experience was given a freakish imaginative twist:

At that instant I had the idea of a terrible city, an appalling enormous city, like Babylon or Babel, run by cannibals, where there would be human abattoirs; and on the scene of that slaughter I tried to recognise a human agony in the belling and the sobbing. I pictured troops of slaves being brought there, with ropes around their necks, tied to iron rings, to feed their masters who eat them sitting at tables made of ivory, wiping their lips on purple napkins [. . .].

The leap from the slaughterhouse to the human abattoir is worthy of the satiric fables of Voltaire, already a favourite. But Flaubert surpasses even his other mentor, de Sade – 'a dark comic genius' – by bringing together so many different worlds: the cannibal, the emperor, the vampire, the factory, the slaughterhouse, and the prison camp. In Quimper

Flaubert coined a new version of Gothic, a vision of the darkest of all possible worlds. He already had an extravagant and compelling satiric gift for reaching a few inches beyond the worst that the nineteenth century could provide.

From Guérande, on a very clear day, you can see Belle-Isle. The two travellers heard talk of the wonderful cliffs and the sea-caves, out there on the island, so they bought two places in a boat and had themselves rowed out across the bay, conversing with a poor soldier who was being transported, under escort, to the great star-shaped labyrinthine prison-fortress that dominated the island harbour of Belle-Isle. Here was yet another manifestation of the ugly modern passion for discipline.

Turning their back on le maréchal Vauban's military masterpiece, Flaubert and Maxime Du Camp set off together at dawn with a piece of bread and a slice of meat. They had no guide and no map and they were intending to walk as far as they could, returning as late as possible. At first they took the path along the cliff top, then they scrambled down on to the beach and waited for the tide to fall far enough to uncover the rocks. They slithered and clambered their way along the shoreline, eventually finding themselves trapped between the cliffs and the sea. Exhausted and alarmed, they found a valley that zigzagged its way deep into the cliff and then led them back to high ground, like a ladder.

They were soon lost again, inland, trying to cross the island, but they felt quite unconcerned, for this was a day of exceptional imaginative freedom. We see them, through the pages of their journal, making their way across the landscape: 'always a pleasure [. . .] to be out with a friend, tramping across the grass, through the hedges, jumping over ditches, beating down the thistles with your stick, pulling off leaves and seeds, going along in any direction as the fancy takes you, singing, whistling, talking, dreaming, nobody listening, nobody following you, as free as if you were in the desert'. In the depths of a cave they found a bed of white pebbles, polished smooth by the sea. It was, they fancied, the bed to which the Naiad once came to rest her beautiful, tired, naked body, sleeping in the moonlight. But now her bed was empty. She had gone for ever.

Towards sunset, as the shadows lengthened, the tide began to rise, making a blue mist. Tired as they were, they set off towards a distant chain of rocks that stretched out into the sea, ignoring the real danger of drowning. 'We needed', said Flaubert, 'to push our pleasure past the limit and to savour it without wasting a drop. Lighter than in the morning, we jumped and we ran tirelessly, unhindered, physical delight carried us along in spite of ourselves and in our muscles we felt strange and powerful shudderings of pleasure.' They felt a tenderness, an intensity of being, a receptiveness of the senses that was akin to 'the transports of love'. But it was too much, 'too dangerous for our fragile spirits'. It was madness, intoxication, ecstasy, idiocy. Such things were only to be found out at the edge, at the edge of the land, at the edge of night. Perhaps they came from the sea.

Flaubert tried to honour this experience when he wrote it up, later, in the high style, at home. But it came out too literary, too explicit, over-emphatic. His travel notes put it more soberly, and perhaps more authentically. But in his account of their return to the village the writing is distinctive. 'That evening our heads were not sitting square on our shoulders; we came back animated, moved, almost furious, our hearts beating, our nerves vibrating [. . .]. When we reached the town, just as they were going to close the gates, we had been walking for fourteen hours, our feet were showing through our shoes, and they wrung out our shirts which, even two days later, were still damp.'

The day's adventure ends on that distinctive, faltering cadence. We are left with a damp shirt and a pair of worn shoes rather than the rapture of a summer evening. The truth, for Flaubert, was in the tension, the contrast, the distance between the poetry of the edge and the prose of the everyday world of shoes and shirts to which even the pantheist must eventually attend. Thirty years later, when the walk around the island reappears in *Bouvard et Pécuchet*, the rapture has been erased.

A few miles from the little village of Baud, hiding in the middle of a beech-wood, stands the Venus of Quinipily. It's a granite statue, six feet high, representing a naked woman, with her hands over her breasts. [. . .] Seen in profile, with her fat thighs, her plump buttocks, her bent knees and her big head set deep into her shoulders, she has a sensuality which is both barbaric and refined. Her face is flat, she has a snub nose and bulging eyes, her mouth, her toes and her fingers are indicated only by a simple line. On her front they tried to represent her breasts.

At the foot of the pedestal there is a large basin, made of the same granite [. . .] they say it can hold sixteen barrels of water. [. . .] The Breton peasants used to worship her as an idol, and brought her their offerings. She cured the sick; women who had just given birth came to bathe in the basin at her feet, and young people keen to be married used to come and dive into the water, and then, under the eyes of the goddess they would engage in the solitary entertainment available to the melancholy lover.

This peasant Venus had a distinguished history. Scandalised missionaries had prevailed upon the local lord to overturn the idol. He had it tipped over so that it rolled down the hillside and into the river. The anger of the goddess engendered disastrous floods; the peasants hauled her out, reverentially, and put her back in her place on the hilltop. The bishop pleaded with the count to smash the statue. The count refused. He would abduct her instead. Venus would henceforth adorn the courtyard of his chateau. The soldiers who were sent to carry her off had to fight the peasants, who wanted to keep her for themselves.

Flaubert was delighted by the peasant Venus of Quinipily. She was the gloriously benign, massively indestructible emblem of the ancient powers that lingered on in Brittany. She was 'the invigorating, exciting, healing idol, the incarnation of health, of the flesh, and the very symbol of desire [. . .] the manifestation of that eternal religion rooted in the very bowels of man [. . .].' The Venus of Quinipily occupies a prominent place in Flaubert's imaginary museum, alongside Brueghel's Saint Antony, Canova's Cupid and Psyche, and the carnivorous iron deity of the Carthaginians, Moloch, who appears in *Salammbô*. For a myopic realist, Flaubert had quite a strange, insistent fancy for gods and goddesses. His vision could focus, with equal acuity, at six inches, at six feet, and at infinity.

'AND don't forget all about me for I often think of you, every day.' His farewell letter to Louise Colet, his April *ultima*, had been deliberately self-possessed, light-hearted, gently teasing. But Flaubert's composure was fragile. It soon began to feel, unbearably, as though one of them had died. Some reparation was required of him.

Less than two weeks after his departure from Paris, he wrote to her from Nantes, where he and Du Camp had paused in their travels. 'It will be a farewell then, a long farewell, as if one of us had gone to India and the other to America [. . .]. We'll think of one another and in our souls we'll send one another silent wishes and secret impulses of tenderness.' This fanciful scenario elicited a brisk, scornful reply from Louise. Has he nothing better to do with his time? Flaubert persevered. 'Yes I often think of you. I picture you, living your sad life, a life I have made more sad, alone in your little boudoir, alone in your house, with an empty heart, peopled only by troubles and sorrows that I have added to, my God!' Woven into this cluster of feelings we detect Flaubert's newly created female figure, the Lady of Blois. The fiction is folding back into the original.

When Flaubert reached Brest there was no letter from Louise Colet. Perplexed, he wrote to her again, from St-Brieuc, summoning her to him as his ghostly companion:

When I'm walking silently for hours at a time, whether it be along a path across a cornfield, or whether I'm striding along the sand [. . .] you come into my thoughts, you follow me, you walk with me, I see your face, I wonder what you are doing, what you are thinking [. . .]. If I were to see you now I would explain to you all kinds of things that would occur to me, and you would understand, and then you would stop accusing me, and your tears would cease.'

B REST was the end of the road, the first city of any size that they had seen for some weeks. The two travellers stumbled along, through the suburbs, weary and rainsoaked, trailing great clouds of pipe smoke, with jeering street boys following them at a safe distance. 'Bare-chested, our shirts billowing out, neckties around our waists, packs on our backs, white with dust, tanned by the sun, with our torn clothes, our shoes worn and patched, we looked like splendidly insolent and proud vagabonds.' Everyone gaped at them, stupidly, and they had to show their passports.

After the freedom of the cliffs and the beaches, Brest was lugubri-ously oppressive. A vast dockyard and a naval base – then as now – it's windswept, raw and bleak, and it has the heaviest rainfall in all of France. Flaubert hated it. Combining the arsenal, the prison and the barracks, it reminded him of 'administration, discipline, sheets of paper ruled with straight lines'. The streets were full of noise: convicts in their chains, soldiers marching, trumpets blowing. 'Not very entertaining, unless you are an engineer or a builder or a blacksmith.'

However, Brest did offer travellers the comforts of civilisation: hot water, clean beds, comfortable chairs, decent food and all the feverish pleasures of the local brothel. In Brest, as Flaubert soon discovered in the course of his meticulous researches, even *the streets of ill-fame* were all carefully classified. Brothels for the Navy. Brothels for the Artillery. Brothels for the Infantry. Brothels for the Jail (warders *and* convicts). Affecting the high moral tone of the intrepid nineteenth-century social investigator, Flaubert 'entered one of those establishments that Providence has placed in our cities to serve as *a fetid but useful conduit* [. . .]'. The atmosphere in the salon was polite and modest: four ladies in Parisian gowns sitting round a table, nice mahogany furniture with red velvet upholstery, tasteful military prints displayed on the walls. The effect was dispiriting and detumescent. Du Camp bought a round of drinks. Flaubert sat down in the corner, smoking a cigar, and launched on a silent but highly imaginative elegy for the lost glories of prostitution.

What do you most regret? Is it the monarchy? Or religious belief? The nobility? The priesthood? Personally, I miss the *fille de joie*. Out on the boulevard, one evening, I saw her walking along in the gaslight, alert and silent, staring boldly and letting her feet drag along the pavement. I saw her pale face at the street-corner, saw the rain falling on the flowers in her hair, heard her voice softly calling men to her as she shivers half-naked in her black velvet dress.

The streets, he sighed sententiously, are being cleaned up. Their glorious, melancholy, sordid poetry is being swept away. The prostitutes have vanished, along with the dancing bears, the jugglers, the tambourine men, the lovely tightrope walkers and the monkeys in the fancy costumes perched on the backs of camels. Such queasy righteousness, the ruling spirit of the age, was calling out for a new Aristophanes, a new Rabelais, a new Voltaire. Enter, ten years later, Emma Bovary, the new Candide.

SAINT-MALO: in 1847 it was place of romantic pilgrimage. One evening at low tide the two travellers walked out across the wide, wet sands to the little island, a hundred yards from the ramparts of the city, where the tomb of Chateaubriand had lain ready, since 1823, to receive his body.

A simple slab of grey granite, the stone was inscribed with the motto: 'Solitary in death, as he affected to be in life.' In spite of himself, Flaubert found this romantic narcissism deeply moving. His thoughts kept turning to Chateaubriand, all the time he was in Saint-Malo. As he explained to Louise Colet, 'That idea of being engrossed in your own death and of securing yourself a place in advance for the other world, which I had thought rather puerile, when I was there it seemed very grand and very beautiful.' 'We walked around the tomb; we touched it with our hands; we looked upon it as if it had contained its guest; we sat upon the ground alongside it.' Chateaubriand, of course, was *not* actually dead. It was merely as if. And this clever ambiguity allowed Flaubert a special freedom to re-imagine death.

The visit to the empty tomb prompted a splendidly oceanic paragraph:

There he will sleep [. . .] his face turned towards the sea; in this sepulchre, built on a rock, his immortality will be like his life, solitary and all set about with storms. The waves and the centuries will murmur long around this great memory. On days of tempest they will surge about his feet, or on summer mornings, when white sails are unfurled, and the swallow arrives from across the sea, long and gentle, they will bring to him the melancholy voluptuousness of far horizons, and the caress of the ample breeze; and as the days pass by, while the tides of his native shoreline flow perpetually between his cradle and his grave, so the heart that belonged to René, cooling slowly, will be scattered across the void, to the never-ending rhythm of this eternal music.

At sunset, before he left the magic island, Flaubert picked a flower. He sent the flower next day, as a gift, in a letter to Louise Colet. So aptly and so ingeniously sentimental, the gesture was very much to Louise's taste. It answered to the exalted etiquette of romantic love by which she aspired to live. (Like Emma Bovary, she greatly valued these little things.) And it meant all the more because it was so out of character. Within a year of Flaubert's visit, Chateaubriand died. He was buried on his island in July 1848. Louise Colet, though now ever more deeply estranged from him, sent Flaubert a lock of Chateaubriand's hair. His grudging thanks for this precious gift, so brief and so cold, added to her sorrows.

COMBOURG is a grey town, dominated by the ancient bulk of its chateau. Four massive circular towers linked by curtain walls ten feet thick enclose a gloomy labyrinth of staircases and galleries, corridors, dungeons and cellars. 'Everywhere was silence and shadow and an expanse of stone.' This was the boyhood home of Francois René, Vicomte de Chateaubriand, the French Byron, and the literary hero of Flaubert's youth. It was to be treated reverentially, as a place of pilgrimage. 'Nothing', wrote Flaubert, 'will convey [. . .] the shudderings and the contractions that future great works inflict upon those who bear them; yet we love to see the places where we know they were conceived and came to be, as if those places held something of the unknown ideal which once pulsated there.'

Yet the reality was perplexing. The illustrious house of Chateaubriand had been laid low by revolutionary pillage and the guillotine. The current owner of the chateau, a nephew of the writer, detested everything associated with his famous uncle. The travellers had come prepared. They produced a letter of introduction and a reluctant servant was found to guide them. The hinges of the great door were so stiff with rust that the visitors had to kick it open. The corridors were blocked with old ladders and chairs. The flagstones were broken. There was moss growing on the spiral staircase and the chestnut trees in the garden had grown so tall that they blocked out the light to the vast unfurnished rooms.

When they finally arrived at Chateaubriand's little bedroom they instinctively took their hats off, as if they were in a holy place. 'Flaubert had tears in his eyes and pressed his hand on the table as though to take hold of some remnant of that great spirit.' The dust and the cobwebs, the woodworm and the damp could not entirely dispel the romantic sense of place.

That evening, having borrowed an old edition of Chateaubriand's *Génie du christianisme*, the 1808 edition with the silly illustrations, Flaubert and Du Camp made their way across the park and then sat together on the grass beneath an oak tree, looking across the lake towards the great darkening mass of the chateau. This was the true vision they had been seeking. In the stillness of the early July evening, with the sunset reflecting upon the surface of the water, they read aloud to each other from *René*. It was the perfect moment.

Chateaubriand and his beloved sister had played together here, in the bright years before the Revolution, sailing on the lake, climbing the hills and running through the woods. This was the passage that Flaubert recited by the lake:

Sometimes we walked together in silence, listening to the faint moaning of the autumn, or to the noise of the dry leaves which dragged sadly beneath our feet; sometimes, in our innocent games, we chased the swallow across the meadow, pursued the rainbow across the glistening hills; sometimes we murmured verses inspired by the splendours of nature. In my youth, I cultivated the Muses; there is nothing more poetical, in the freshness of its passions, than the heart of a boy of sixteen. The morning of life is like the morning of the day, full of purity, full of images and harmonies.

Flaubert and Maxime Du Camp extracted an exquisitely gloomy

pleasure from Chateaubriand's sonorous prose-poem to time lost. 'As the shadows fell upon the pages of the book, the bitterness of those sentences reached our hearts, and we dissolved delectably into something large, melancholy and sweet.' Flaubert, like his hero Chateaubriand, had once had such a sister. He could remember their games. Yet when Flaubert wrote about the scene by the lake, some months later, in Croisset, *his* Chateaubriand walks alone. The sister disappears from the text. Flaubert had to take her out.

That night, at the inn where they were sharing a room, Du Camp was roused from sleep by the sound of a loud voice. It was Flaubert standing in front of the open window, reciting Chateaubriand to the night air. 'Man,' the rich voice intoned, 'the time of your migration is not yet come; await the rising of the wind of death, and then you shall unfurl your wings and take your flight towards the unknown world your heart has long been seeking.'

'Go to sleep!' said Du Camp. 'I want to talk!' said Flaubert. And so they talked of Chateaubriand until dawn. Except that in Flaubert's more romantic, more Chateaubriandesque version of this scene he is alone in the room, with the summer lightning flickering outside, and he holds the entire conversation with himself.

THE twenty-eighth of July 1847 was the first anniversary of Flaubert's meeting with Louise Colet. She assumed that he would be there, with her, to celebrate. Unforgivably, he wasn't. Louise Colet was predictably outraged by this casual indifference and she sent him, as he put it, 'more tears, more recriminations and, stranger still, insults'. He had made no promises, he said. Anyway, there were 'insurmountable obstacles' to his being there. He explained that they had come back from Brittany two weeks earlier than planned, at the urgent request of his mother, because the eighteen-month-old Caroline was dangerously ill. 'You think', he teased, ' that I didn't celebrate our Wednesday anniversary and that I didn't give it a second thought! Adieu.'

Flaubert offered Louise no further explanation of his absence. He left it, mischievously, to her imagination. But he did record elsewhere, for his own private satisfaction, in the notebooks he kept during the journey, his anniversary thoughts and feelings. He had spent the last evening alone, only ten miles from Croisset, in the village of Caumont, set on the wooded hillside just above the River Seine. There at the village inn, where he was still pleasantly anonymous, he passed the long July evening writing the last few pages of his journal.

Those pages describe his day's journey up the Seine, with Maxime, by steamboat, all the way from Honfleur, on the coast. It was their final day of travelling together. Wrapt in a sorrowful silence, Flaubert filled the empty hours with reverie. Watching the Normandy landscape pass slowly before his eyes, 'like a long ribbon being unwound', his memories began to flow and he thought of all the many other journeys he had made along this river. Six years ago, with his mother, his sister and her governess. And further back, on the steamer with Alfred, in the great days of their adolescent friendship, homeward bound, then as now, feeling equally dirty, weary and sad.

The last words on the last page turn towards the more recent past. 'A year ago I was in Paris fireworks celebrating the July revolution seen from the hilltop for G* I played the man of feeling now the feelings are real there is harmony in this anniversary.' The unpunctuated stream of reminiscence ends in a harmony, the powerful, commonplace romantic phrase for the music of the past and of remembrance – more complex than Louise could have allowed, guided by her conventional expectations about anniversaries.

Flaubert's harmony was more complex, drawing upon a tangled private poetics of river journeys and erotic memories. His thoughts did turn to Louise, on that evening in July 1847, though not in the decorously sentimental fashion that she would have applauded. What does it mean, the mysterious phrase 'for G* I played the man of feeling'? Deliberately cryptic, it must be a sexual reference, something that can only be written down in code. 'G*', in this context, stands for 'gamahuche', mid-nineteenth-century slang for *fellatio*. From the lucid distance of a year, Flaubert is savouring the comic confusion of the erotic and the sentimental. He had pretended, on the first night, for the sake of 'G*', to feel more than he was feeling. Twenty years later, writing the opening scene of *L'Education sentimentale*, in which the two lovers first encounter each other on a boat on the Seine, Flaubert would draw upon the powerful harmony of feelings that had come to him on the evening of his return from Brittany. He drew upon that scene and those feelings, feeding them into the great imagined encounter between Frederic Moreau and Marie Arnoux.

CHAPTER ELEVEN

French Revolutions

AUGUST 1847: Flaubert was back home, two weeks earlier than planned. Misfortunes old and new immediately came crowding in upon him. He'd spent far too much money, as his mother may have pointed out. There was a letter from Louise, ripely vindictive, exhaling recrimination in every line. The infant Caroline was seriously ill and, worst of all, Alfred Le Poittevin lay slowly dying. Flaubert felt as if he had been chained up, the victim of a gentle maternal tyranny. For the sake of the sick child, in search of healthier air, mother and son moved out of Croisset and took lodgings for a month in a 'hovel' in La Bouille, a cluster of houses ten miles upstream from Rouen. The whole situation was bad for his nerves.

Flaubert settled down, in the hovel, sorting through his notes from Brittany, but also reading Saint Theresa and Strauss's *Life of Jesus*. He was gathering material for his next project, *La Tentation de Saint Antoine*, a great escape from all the railways, the umbrellas, the frock coats and the newspapers to which the more prosperous citizens of the nineteenth century were so inexplicably attached. Declining the offer of a loan from Louise Colet, Flaubert refused to contemplate the idea of *earning* (disdainfully underlined) money from his writing. Writing, he declared, was an intimate, animal function.

Things were not much better once they moved back to Croisset. Family life was a source of constant vexation. His mother, now subject to nervous attacks and hallucinations, sat at the dinner table in the evening sighing over the empty places. The mad brother-in-law, Emile Hamard, had returned from England unexpectedly. He had come to live nearby, briefly, in Croisset, and he was so rough in his play with his infant daughter that Madame Flaubert was perpetually worried.

Amid this domestic gloom it is little wonder that Flaubert drew such dark comic satisfaction from a recent aristocratic scandal. The Duc de Praslin, caught up in an affair with the resident governess, had murdered his wife and killed himself by swallowing arsenic. Flaubert drew a distinctly Sadeian moral from these doings. 'The animal,' he wrote, 'in spite of the clothes that cover him, the cage that holds him, the ideas that are stuffed into him, the animal still retains his natural, old instincts which are base and bloody.' The animal, however caged, clothed and stuffed, was Flaubert's familiar. He was teaching himself to look it in the eye, without flinching. The imputation of sadism, though a significant embarrassment to Flaubert's biographers, misses this point.

The animal (let it be the emblem of his epilepsy) would not stay asleep. Even writing up the Brittany walking tour, though not especially demanding, could set it going. 'I had an attack a week ago [. . .]. The work I am doing at the moment – I'm writing at last, a rare thing for me – has not been conducive to a state of normality.' Flaubert was so out of practice, so viciously self-critical that *La Bretagne* (its informal title) gave him a great deal of trouble. After spending eight hours correcting five pages, he felt 'like a man with a perfect pitch who can't play the violin any more'. 'Next summer', he said, ' I shall see about attempting *Saint Antoine*.' *La Bretagne* required some precise descriptive writing. Otherwise it was a work of 'pure fantasy and digression', impossible to publish because 'the public prosecutor would take exception to certain passages'. When he looked back on it some years later, he said, 'It gave me a great deal of trouble. It was the first thing that I ever wrote laboriously.' He felt it sharply at the time: 'I hesitate, I worry, I vex myself, I lose my nerve, my taste becomes more exacting as my verve decreases [. . .].' Writing to the torrentially fluent Louise Colet, Flaubert could mock his precious difficulties: 'the humiliations that adjectives inflict on me, the cruel ravages of the relative pronoun'. Art (always capitalised) could now become his heroic epistolary theme. This was undoubtedly a good way to keep it out of the real writing. 'Art, what a great chasm! And we who are so small go venturing down into it.'

B Y the end of November Flaubert had been writing *La Bretagne* for three and a half months. November nights, nearly the longest of the year, were his favourite time. 'I dream of travelling, of endless journeys across the world [. . .].' Now he could savour the full poetry of a

Normandy winter, the fog, the cold wind, the long evenings spent gazing into the fire. 'At night I feel supremely calm. By the studious light of
a candle, how the intelligence flares up and burns brighter. That's the
only time I experience any real tranquillity at the moment. All day I feel
slightly ill and perpetually irritated.'

This nocturnal life did not entirely displace the daylight world. On
Christmas Day 1847, in the company of Louis Bouilhet and Maxime
Du Camp, Flaubert attended a Reform Banquet. It was, he declared, 'a
grotesque and lamentable spectacle'.* We have to picture Flaubert, a
bulky man in his late twenties, slightly constrained by his formal dress,
sitting improbably among his fellow citizens 'in front of cold turkey
and sucking pig', listening to eight hours of political speeches from the
liberal-opposition celebrities of the day. The worst thing, he said, was
the locksmith sitting next to him who tapped him on the shoulder at all
the best bits.

A lavish occasion, Rouen's Reform Banquet was held in a hastily
converted suburban dance hall, *Le Tivoli Normand*. Brightly lit and
draped in tricolour flags, the hall held nearly two thousand men, the
social elite of city. By three thirty they were all seated, and the presiding
lawyer, Maître Sénard, mounted the platform and gave the opening
address. This was a great day, he declared: 'A great day for France and
for liberty'. After a hasty collection for the poor, the orchestra played
the 'Marseillaise', and the eating began. Would Lamartine turn up?
Nobody really knew.

Maître Sénard was the first to speak. He denounced *la Corruption*, to
a 'thunder of applause'. He invoked the principles of 1830, the sentiments of 1789. 'Let them remember '93! The great giant is sleeping, but
it will wake sooner or later and its anger will be terrible.' Explosions of
cheering. Vive la reforme! Vive Sénard! Toasts were drunk. To national
sovereignty! To financial reform! To commerce! To industry! The
speaker begged to include another, 'equally dear to our hearts, equally
present in our thoughts, agriculture! Which a great minister has called
one of the breasts of the state'. (Very good!) Crémieux, the star speaker,
began with a resonant quote from Béranger, 'our immortal songster',
and then worked his audience up to a great pitch, regaling them with a
vivid, patriotic, pageant-history of France.

---

* Reform Banquets were political meetings in disguise, an important platform for official
dissent in the months before the revolution of February 1848.

The banquet finished at eleven thirty. Flaubert and his two companions, all of them connoisseurs of cliché, laughed and joked in disbelief as they made their way back along the riverside. 'What! Is that how you address a crowd? Is that really the kind of stupidity they like?' Surely, they said, such pretentious nonsense will never survive the scrutiny of common sense. It will expire. It will fall apart. Public ridicule will finish it off. Next day the *Journal de Rouen*, loyal advocate of the liberal-commercial interest, printed a special supplement reporting all the speeches *verbatim*. 'The joke', Du Camp realised later, 'was on us. That crude sweet wine is just the thing to intoxicate the weak-headed, which is to say the great mass of the population.'

When he came to write *L'Education sentimentale*, nearly twenty years later, Flaubert would lovingly resurrect all the dead languages, both political and sentimental, of his youth. The issues, from that later perspective, began to look rather different. Individual indignation, however noble, eloquent and humane, was now quite obsolete. A more ironic inquisition was required if the artist was to break the spell of received ideas. How does cliché come to wield such uncanny power? Why are we taken in? Why do we always sing along with the crowd? What else might we do? This would be the great tragi-comic theme of the modern novel that came after *Madame Bovary*.

W HAT were they doing meanwhile, the others? The ones who were not at the banquet?

January 1848: the thermometer is showing seven degrees below zero. The River Seine is frozen over at Rouen. Inside one of the city's many churches a sixty-two-year-old woman has been found dying of cold and hunger. She is taken to the Hôtel-Dieu. At eight thirty in the morning a small crowd has gathered on the place Bonne Nouvelle to witness the public execution of a young murderer. The boy is given hot wine to drink before he is led to the guillotine. Wolves, driven by hunger, have been coming out of the forests. A woman and a child have been attacked. The philanthropic freemasons of the local lodge, *Perseverance-Crowned*, have distributed 600 kilos of bread to the poor. From Le Havre, seventy-five Icarians of all professions, resplendent in the uniform of their utopian sect, have set sail for New Orleans. Working by gaslight, Eléanore-Victoire Lefebvre, aged seventeen, has had her right arm crushed to the elbow whilst trying to repair a machine in the textile factory where she works. Parts of the arm and the wrist remain in the machine. She is taken to the Hôtel-Dieu and her arm is amputated immediately.

THERE were *two* French revolutions in 1848. The February revolution was the beautiful revolution. Bourgeois and worker, readily identified for street-fighting purposes as frockcoat and smock, toppled the old monarchy and declared the Republic. The June revolution was the ugly one. Frockcoat and smock were quarrelling over the Republic. Was it to be the red republic, the true socialist republic? Or was it to be some vague, bogus republic that changed its colours every hour? Barricades went up, in the name of the Republic. Artillery smashed the barricades, in the name of the Republic. Large numbers of smocks were torn and stained. The face of the Republic henceforth took on a sickly pallor that could only be remedied by placing an impressively large, old-fashioned imperial crown upon its head.

The Second Empire (1851–70) was the ridiculous, Ruritanian outcome of three exhausting, audacious years of political experiment. The Second Empire, presiding over an era of hectic industrialisation, ever anxious to secure its own dubious legitimacy, always treated its writers suspiciously. Pedantic censorship to crush the disobedient, lavish patronage to reward the compliant – these were the blunt instruments of the state's cultural policy. Flaubert endured the full force of both. He was to be persecuted and patronised in almost equal measure.

The Ruritanian outcome was still a very distant prospect on the afternoon of 23 February 1848 when Flaubert and Bouilhet arrived in Paris, on a train from Rouen. Their purpose was 'to watch the riot, "from the artistic point of view"'. They met up with Maxime Du Camp at his house. Then, at five thirty, as darkness began to fall, the three men set off again. The streets were quiet. The crowds had dispersed. There were a few small groups of people, talking quietly, standing on the pavement. It all seemed to be over. At six o'clock companies of the National Guard marched past, shouting 'Vive le roi!' People appeared at their windows, applauding. The King, bowing to public opinion, had dismissed an unpopular minister, Guizot. Flaubert and his friends made for the Palais-Royal to have dinner at their favourite restaurant, Les Trois Frères provençaux. The waiter, with his neat whiskers and his glossy hair, was shaking with fear. When they reassured him that it was all over, he said, 'Not while the *people* are out on the street.' He spoke the word so scornfully that they all began to laugh.

By nine thirty they were out on the streets again. The boulevard des Capucines had been closed off, so they made their way along the rue Neuve-Saint-Augustin to the Foreign Ministry, Guizot's ministry. The building was curiously dark. Over the heads of the assembled soldiers they could see dragoons in the background, their helmets and their sabres glinting in the gaslight. Nothing was happening, so the three men made their way back to Du Camp's apartment. As they were opening the street door they heard a violent explosion only a hundred yards away. Flaubert said, 'They must have opened fire. Let's go and see!' 'Opened fire!' said Du Camp. 'You must be mad. That's just some children letting off fireworks to celebrate. Let's go upstairs.' They spent the rest of the evening sitting around the fire, pleasantly fatigued, listening to Louis Bouilhet read aloud the first section of his new long poem, *Melaenis*.

They had just missed one of the great mythological moments of nineteenth-century history. The explosion they had ignored was indeed the sound of gunfire. Disobeying orders, driven by anger, confusion and fear, the soldiers had suddenly fired upon the crowd gathered in the boulevard des Capucines. Once the smoke cleared there were eighty bodies lying on the ground. It was a massacre. Five corpses, still warm, were quickly piled onto a cart. Illuminated by torches, this improvised death-cart was paraded around the streets of central Paris. It was a dream-image from the national-political unconscious, it spoke so eloquently to collective fears and memories. The word went round: 'Vengeance! They're murdering our brothers.' The citizens of Paris, bourgeois and proletarian, remembered what they had to do. They rang the church bells and they dug up the cobblestones. By dawn the city was bristling with barricades.

Next morning Flaubert, Bouilhet and Du Camp began to walk the streets again, in search of picturesque historic detail. But now their mood was sombre and confused. Everyone was talking about the massacre. Nobody could say what it meant. Perhaps the King was finished. Bouilhet thought so, though Flaubert and Du Camp disagreed with him. Louis-Philippe was procrastinating. His soldiers were losing heart. Outside a wine shop the three of them looked on in amazement as a couple of soldiers glumly handed over their ammunition to a boy of sixteen. 'Yes, my bourgeois friends,' said one of the soldiers. 'This is how it is. They've left us in it, so we're letting go.' *Fraternising with the people*. That was the pamphleteer's phrase for it.

They went to the boulevard des Capucines, where the massacre had taken place. They stared at the wide and slowly darkening pool of blood. A man with a piece of chalk was drawing a line all around it. On the pavement he wrote, 'Blood of the victims of despotism.' They went for lunch at Tortoni's and listened in to the anxious alarmist conversations all around. After lunch they strolled along the boulevard des Italiens where the popular mood was coming to the boil. Two men appeared on horseback and made a smiling, godlike progress through the crowd. They spoke in the name of moderation, prudence and reform. It was Odilon Barrot, the new minister, accompanied by Horace Vernet, the famous painter, now ludicrously resplendent in the uniform of a colonel of the National Guard, bristling with medals, badges and gold braid. At the end of the boulevard Barrot and Vernet were met with a great volley of small stones and loud insults, as if to remind the big-name actors that the theatre of revolution encouraged every kind of passionate improvisation.

They saw the barricade being built on the corner of the rue Helder. They watched cavalry sabres being handed out from the door of a gunsmith's shop. They followed a column of well-armed insurgents along the rue de la Paix and across the place Vendôme. Passing the rue Saint-Honoré, they were drawn by the sound of a fusillade and ran towards it. As the crowd surged around them, the three men were separated. Bouilhet had disappeared. Du Camp soon found Flaubert again, he was conspicuously taller than anyone around him.

Settling themselves in a position with a good view, Flaubert and Du Camp observed the battle that had spilled out from the tangled labyrinth of little streets on to the place du Palais-Royal. A man dropped at their feet, hit by a bullet. The royalists of the 14th regiment, held responsible for the recent massacre, had taken refuge inside their barracks, the Chateau d'Eau, and now they were desperately refusing to surrender. Flaubert and Du Camp could clearly see the soldiers at the windows, calmly loading, aiming and firing at the insurgents who were sheltering behind the columns of the palace. It was fascinating: the futile bravery of the soldiers, abandoned by their superiors, defending to the death the lost cause of monarchy.

Suddenly it was a different drama. A picturesque band rushed into the square, led by a romantically dishevelled young woman. A flashback to Delacroix's icon of 1830, *Liberty leading the People*, she presented a formidable image of sexualised power. Her long brown hair hung loose down her back, 'her arms, her shoulders and almost all her chest were exposed; she was shouting and waving a great big butcher's knife'. She was closely followed by a barefoot urchin perched on a horse kitted out with an expensive saddlecloth. Shouting 'giddy-up', the urchin was waving a rifle with a bayonet and his head was disappearing into an enormous military hat – *chapeau du piqueur de la maison du roi.*

The shooting from the barracks was less frequent. Their ammunition was running low. Excited by the scent of victory, the crowd broke into the royal stables nearby and commandeered wagons loaded with hay, which they tried to set on fire, in the hope of burning the soldiers alive. Seized with horror and disgust, Du Camp turned to Flaubert and said, 'Let's go!' Just then a captain of the National Guard came over to them with a delighted smile and told them, 'Victory is complete, gentlemen. It belongs to the National Guard who will not let it slip through their fingers and will, henceforth, govern the country.' They nodded politely, puzzled by this announcement. The officer resumed. 'Yes, gentlemen. Excuse me, *citizens*. Our victory is complete and the tyrant is overthrown. The King has fled from the city, having abdicated. The Tuileries are free. The palace is open and anyone can go in.'

It was early in the afternoon when they entered the palace. At this stage the crowd was still in a good mood. A delighted, mocking curiosity prevailed. Two men sat eating the King's abandoned breakfast. 'This is our reform banquet!' they said. When Flaubert and Du Camp went up to the royal apartments on the first floor, bayonets had been put away to avoid damage to the furnishings. A well-dressed man was sitting on the throne, playing king and receiving mock homage. But the mood shifted when a vast crowd swept up the great staircase with excited cries of 'Death and victory!'. Shots were fired at the tall mirrors. Feeling uncomfortably and identifiably bourgeois, Flaubert and Du Camp pushed their way downstairs and made their way outside, into the private garden, where they managed to save a small group of soldiers who were about to be shot by the insurgents.

Ever more out of place, they left the palace and made their way back to the Palais-Royal, where they witnessed wild scenes of looting and burning. Gilded mirrors and delicate porcelain were being smashed. Du Camp tried to save an antique silver cup from the flames. The people broke into the cellars and drank the wine. When the fire brigade arrived to douse the flames, a staggering drunkard attacked the fire hose with his sabre. When it bounced off and slashed him on the forehead he began to shout murder. Laughing, his friends settled him in a corner to sleep. The victory of the people, the two observers noted, was a chaotic, farcical thing.

The servants up on the roof of the palace were tearing off their livery and throwing it down into the gardens below. At the barracks on the quai d'Orsay the dragoons were handing out sabres, rifles, pistols and ammunition to the people. Chanting 'Vive la reforme!', the dragoons walked away with the men in smocks, arm in arm. Exhausted, the two men returned to Maxime Du Camp's apartment, where they found an unhappy Louis Bouilhet. Unlucky as ever, he had been conscripted into barricade-building and had dropped a great stone on his foot.

Flaubert and Du Camp set off again, talking their way through the barricades, in the direction of the Hôtel de Ville. They wanted to hear the proclamation of the republic. It was a disappointment to find that only two hundred or so were gathered in the square. At twenty past ten a weary man with greasy hair read out the official decree, 'in the name of the sovereign people'. It was all over.

M AXIME DU CAMP drew a sour, simple moral from the events of February 1848. Revolution, he declared, is always the same: 'initiated by simpletons, helped along by fools, pushed through by rogues then taken over by the opportunists who do very nicely out of it'. Maxime Du Camp wrote his memoirs of 1848 in the early 1870s. By then he had read Flaubert's *L'Education sentimentale* and he had witnessed the bloody events of the commune of 1870. Inevitably, in the writing, the sour political disenchantment of a later decade was projected back on to the original events.

1 Rouen, *c.*1830: the view from the hill
2 Rouen: the view from the street

3 Rouen: the main gate of the Hôtel-Dieu
4 Rouen: the residential wing of the Hôtel-Dieu

5 The Father: Dr Achille-Cléophas Flaubert

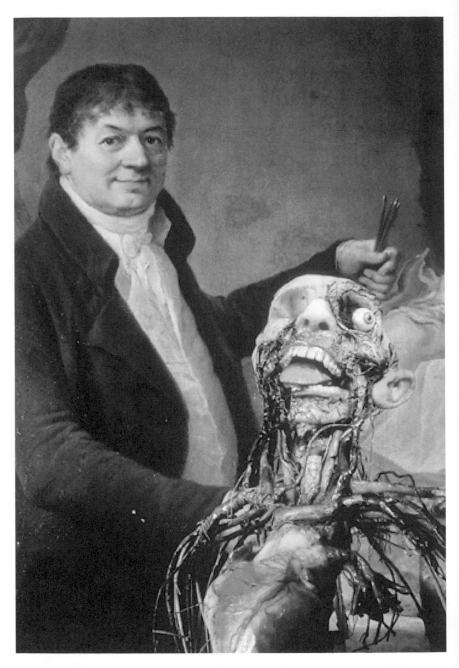

6 'Open up a few corpses': Dr Laumonier with wax anatomy model

7 The Mother: Madame Flaubert in 1831
8 The Boy: Gustave Flaubert, *c*.1830
9 The Boy: Gustave Flaubert , *c*.1830, as seen by his elder brother

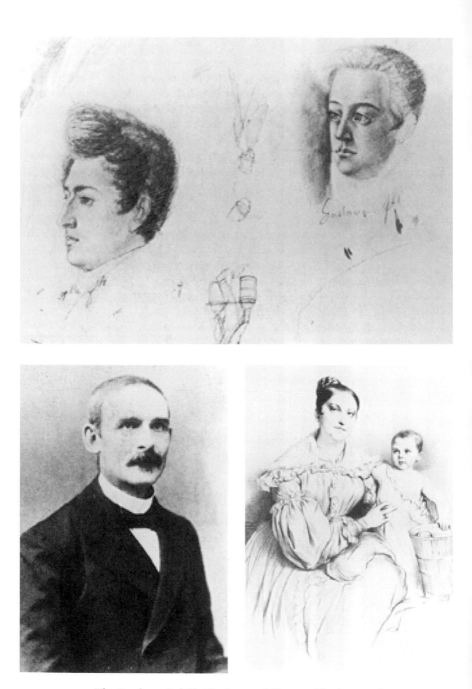

10 The Brothers: Achille Flaubert and Gustave Flaubert, c.1835
11 The Mentor: Alfred Le Poittevin, c.1845
12 The Older Woman: Elisa Schlésinger, c.1838

13 The Travelling Companion: Dr Jules Cloquet, c.1866
14 The Young Man: Gustave Flaubert, c.1845
15 The Dead Sister: Caroline Flaubert

16 The Lover: Louise Colet, *c.*1840

CHAPTER TWELVE

In Mourning

WITHIN a few weeks of his return from revolutionary Paris, Flaubert's thoughts turned away from public events. Louise Colet wrote to inform him that she was seven months pregnant. The father was a young Polish emigré. Flaubert's reply was cool, compassionate and carefully discouraging. 'Whatever happens, you can always count on me [. . .]. My *monstrous personality*, as you so amiably put it, is not enough to blot out every decent feeling in me [. . .]. Perhaps one day you will realise this and then regret having expended so much vexation and bitterness on my account.'

Louise Colet, her heart ever on the left, wanted Flaubert's opinion of recent political events. 'It's all very amusing,' he replied warily. 'I find people's long faces quite delectable. I am profoundly delighted by the spectacle of so much ambition so flattened. I do not know whether or not the new form of government and the social conditions it will create will be favourable to Art.'

Flaubert was not in the least engaged by the fate of the infant Second Republic. He had more immediate worries. Alfred Le Poittevin, still his dearest friend, in spite of their recent estrangement, died at midnight on 3 April. Flaubert arrived at the bedside soon after Alfred's death and there he kept a long, loyal, nocturnal vigil over the body.

I watched over him for two nights (all night long the second time), wrapped him in his shroud, gave him the farewell kiss and saw his coffin being sealed up [. . .]. On the last night I read *Feuilles d'automne*. I kept coming across his favourite poems [. . .] now and again I got up and went over to lift up the veil that had been put over his face, to have a look at him. [. . .] At dawn, around four o'clock, the attendant and I set to work. I lifted him, turned him and covered him. The cold stiff feel of his limbs stayed in my fingertips all that day [. . .] we put two shrouds around him. Once he was wrapped up he looked like an Egyptian mummy swathed in its bandages and I felt an immense, indescribable sense of joy and freedom on his account.

In a shower of spring rain, Flaubert followed Alfred's coffin to the cemetry. '[. . .] the ground was slippery. I went to the edge of the grave and I watched every spadeful of earth as it fell. It seemed as if there were a hundred thousand. [. . .] To get back to Rouen I sat outside on top of the carriage with Louis Bouilhet. The rain was beating down, the horses were going at full gallop, I was yelling to urge them on [. . .] the air did me much good. I slept all night [. . .] and I had a strange dream [. . .].'

The Republic, Flaubert observed to Ernest Chevalier, had no remedy for his sorrows. But for all that, it had designs upon him as one of its citizens. The week after Alfred's funeral, Flaubert reported for duty in the National Guard and went to watch the planting of Rouen's Liberty Tree.

Flaubert finally embarked on the writing of *La Tentation de Saint Antoine* in the weeks after the death of Alfred Le Poittevin. The mourning and the writing were so confusedly simultaneous that *Saint Antoine* is best regarded as an ingenious literary memorial to Alfred. In terms of Flaubert's artistic development, *Saint Antoine* was an indulgence, a dead end, an extravagant impasse. Full of glorious details, but lacking in unity, it was also the thing he had to keep coming back to, the thing he could never finish. The hallucinations of the fourth-century desert saint, however remote, were too close to home psychologically. It may well have been too soon to explore this strange new continent. In terms of literary history, *Saint Antoine* sits in a dusty corner labelled 'closet drama (nineteenth century)' alongside Goethe's *Faust*, Ibsen's *Peer Gynt*, and Hardy's *The Dynasts*. These works all share a desire to break with 'petty' realism, to break away from the merely contemporary, to break through to larger, deeper, visionary themes that require an epic treatment. Alluringly difficult, fatally miscellaneous, the genre makes supreme demands on those who take up its challenge. All too often, all too easily, in the name of a mighty torrent, the reader is sprinkled with something best described as a grandiose, erudite tedium. Our modern epic, we may protest, will not look at all like this. Only Wagner was able to make it work.

MAY 1848. Stuck at home, remembering Brittany, mourning Alfred, writing *Saint Antoine*, Flaubert engaged in melancholic orgies of masturbation, a nice comic detail omitted from all the more buttoned-up accounts of the scene of writing. An amusing, affectionate letter arrived from Louise Pradier, now in London. Her new English lover was a great disappointment. He detested cunnilingus, she said. Louise was ready to come and live nearby, 'on a farm'. A lovely but ridiculous idea.

The writing of *Saint Antoine* was now disrupted by the untimely reappearance in Croisset of Emile Hamard, the crazy, vagrant father of the infant Caroline. Hamard wanted to take his daughter away with him. He had plans, he said, to launch himself as an actor. He would be making his Paris debut in a few weeks' time. In the past few months Hamard had spent over 30,000 francs, a small fortune, as well as donating all his silver and his dead wife's jewellery to the Republic. Increasingly deranged, he brought 'shame and sorrow' into the family at Croisset, disrupting their immaculately ordered world with his wild notions.

Flaubert fled from Croisset to Rouen to escape from Hamard. It was an impetuous action that subsequently required an apology to his mother. He blamed it on his nerves and on the emotional demands of his writing. Somewhere beneath it all, Flaubert felt an anxious, compulsive fascination for Hamard. *Mon semblable, mon frère*: it was dangerous for him to be near the man, as he had discovered once before, in January 1844. Hamard made him feel fragile. The dreadful, chaotic extremity of his grief was too contagious.

Getting rid of Hamard was not very easy. At some point during the summer the whole family secretly fled from Croisset to avoid him. Then they sent Hamard off to Nogent. They even took out an injunction against him, but the injunction was impossible to enforce in the social chaos of the June Days. Sobered by the threat of the injunction, Hamard resorted to negotiation, a process that extended over several years.

Hamard embodied the 'madness' of 1848. All those wild dreams of human perfection – they could bring a man down in the world. Perhaps Flaubert was more deeply disturbed by Hamard than he cared to acknowledge. 'All around me,' he wrote, 'wherever I look I see only vexation, trouble, anguish, ruin, sadness and death.' He even relished the thought of going to war. At least it would be an escape from home. 'I don't give a damn if I get killed and in view of the political uncertainties of the hour I have been polishing up a formidable hunting rifle with a range of a thousand metres.'

Such apocalyptic, stay-at-home political fantasy is a familiar psychological condition, often brought on by the excessive reading of newspapers. Du Camp, ever the man of action, was now to be seen dressed in the uniform of the National Guard, rifle at the ready, playing a decently heroic bourgeois role in the great national-political drama that was unfolding on the streets. Besieging a barricade in the Faubourg Poissonière, Du Camp had taken a proletarian bullet in his leg. It cost him a few weeks in bed, and earned him the ribbon of the Légion d'Honneur, classe chevalier, a decoration that greatly impressed hoteliers and chambermaids.

R ETURNING from his recent travels in North Africa, Du Camp felt sorry for Flaubert. There he was in Croisset, 'cooped up alone [. . .] condemned [. . .] to live the life of some elderly small-town pedant'. When Du Camp described the next journey he was planning, to Egypt and Persia, Flaubert gave a cry of despair and said, 'It's hateful, not being able to go with you!' Du Camp gave the matter some thought and then approached Dr Achille with a plan. Even though Madame Flaubert was implacably opposed to the idea of parting with Gustave, it might be possible to persuade her that a hot climate would be the best thing for her son's health. Achille agreed to try. One morning at breakfast, with a face 'even frostier than usual', Madame Flaubert gave her permission. Flaubert turned red and thanked her.

Maxime Du Camp was annoyed to find that Flaubert was not bursting with delight at the prospect. He looked most dejected. Du Camp pointed out to the great armchair traveller that they would be going up the Nile together. 'Yes,' he conceded, 'but we won't bathe in the Ganges and we won't be going to Ceylon [. . .].' Flaubert insisted that he had to finish *La Tentation de Saint Antoine* before they set off. Maxime Du Camp agreed without protest. Unknown to her son, Madame Flaubert tried to persuade Maxime Du Camp to renounce the journey to Egypt. It would be so dangerous. Could they not go to Madeira for a few years instead? The tone of Du Camp's '*No!*' was brutally emphatic.

A LL through the year 1849 Flaubert worked obliviously at *Saint Antoine*. Beneath his window, the political life of the nation was an effervescent chaos. A multitude of fragmentary parties – Bonapartists, legitimists, socialists, Orléanists, fusionists, Republicans doctrinaire and democratic – were all eagerly competing for votes under a greatly extended franchise. Newspapers were being prosecuted and journalists were being imprisoned. The astounding discursive rumpus of 1849 may have prompted Flaubert's subsequent comic idea, the *Dictionnaire des idées reçues*.

Maxime Du Camp was napoleonically busy, attending to all the practicalities of travel. He assembled a great array of tents and saddles, tools and rifles. He talked to Nerval, dozing on Gautier's couch, about his strange experiences in Cairo. Master of the modern, he apprenticed himself to a photographer.* On the eve of their departure, in the midst of all this febrile activity, Maxime Du Camp's adored grandmother fell seriously ill. Flaubert came to Paris and they watched over her together. Her death left Du Camp desolate. 'When his grandmother died,' Flaubert recalled, ' I carried him like a child, tearing him away from her corpse where he was weeping, shouting, *calling on the angels, the great beyond* and so on, I put him under my arm and I spirited him away to the terrace.' His grandmother's death also left him a rich man. He told Flaubert that he was about to inherit at least 200,000 francs.

IT was the moment of truth. Three years' work in the balance. Flaubert's most trusted friends, Du Camp and Bouilhet, were about to pronounce judgement on *La Tentation de Saint Antoine*. They had listened in patient silence to four days of it, read aloud by the author in his powerfully resonant voice. It was Louis Bouilhet who spoke. 'We think you ought to throw it in the fire and never mention it again.'

Flaubert leapt to his feet and gave a cry of horror. 'Take a down-to-earth subject,' said Bouilhet. 'Some little incident from bourgeois life. Something like Balzac's *Cousine Bette*. Why don't you do the story of Delphine Delamare?'

Was it really like that? Perhaps not. Du Camp's *Souvenirs littéraires* are a colourful, devious mixture of truth, plausible fiction and outright lies. We only know that Flaubert set off for Egypt with a crushing artistic failure behind him. It left him feeling ill, he said, for the first four months of his travels. 'I saw everything through the veil of sorrow that this disappointment had cast over me, and I kept saying to myself [. . .] "What's the use?" '

---

* Photography was not for amateurs. It required considerable dexterity with various chemicals and a complicated array of glass tubes, bottles and porcelain bowls. Fragile and cumbersome, the whole apparatus had to be wrapped up 'like the crown jewels' in specially tailored sheepskins.

CHAPTER THIRTEEN

Oriental

I T was a Monday morning, 22 October 1849, when Flaubert set out for Egypt from the house in Croisset accompanied by his mother and his infant niece Caroline. They had agreed to spend a day in Paris together, and then travel on to the village of Nogent. There, surrounded by their relations, the passionate farewell drama of mother and son could be played through to its abrupt and sorrowful *finale*.

All the servants came out to see the family off, though Flaubert observed that only the gardener seemed truly moved. It was no surprise to him that his elder brother, Achille, being too busy to say goodbye in person, had sent his wife and daughter instead. Flaubert had already performed his own private ceremony of farewell, two days earlier, gathering up his pens and closing his cupboards, but otherwise leaving everything as it was. His books lay open on the table. His slippers were arranged beside his bed. It was almost as if he were not going away at all.

His mother was more difficult to arrange. He feared, quite plausibly, that she would make herself ill with worry. It had been agreed that Madame Flaubert was to stay in Nogent after her son's departure. There, among her relations, she could fret about her son more convivially, for the first few weeks at least. Thereafter Flaubert wrote to her with anxious, filial regularity, sixty letters in eighteen months, an average of one letter every nine days. 'Poor woman; she doesn't know what to do with herself [. . .] she needs just a little bit of the daily affection she was so used to having, affection which our poor dear father used to lavish upon her.'

Once they reached Paris, there were further goodbyes. Flaubert dined with Dr Jules Cloquet, the companion of his earlier travels to Corsica.

He then joined Maurice Schlésinger at the opera. Flaubert's poetic youthful desire for the wife, once so imperative, had ripened into a warm, proasaic friendship with the husband. After the opera he finished his evening with a visit to Mère Guerin's establishment in rue des Moulins, near the Palais-Royal. There, in the company of Antonia and Victorine, his favourite girls, he excited his senses and soothed his anxious mind with unspecified but fully satisfactory 'obscenities'.

Mother, son and infant arrived in Nogent-sur-Seine on Wednesday. The next day, the day of parting, was dreadful, 'the very worst day of my whole life'.

Supposed to be leaving on the Saturday. Decided to leave that day. Could not bear it. Endless walks around the little garden with my mother [. . .]. In the end I left – my mother was sitting in an armchair – near the fire – and as I was caressing her and talking to her I just kissed her on the forehead, hurled myself through the door – grabbed my hat from the dining room and left the house. What a scream she gave when I closed the door of the salon behind me! – it reminded me of the scream I heard her give when my father died, the moment she took his hand.

In the train from Nogent to Paris the sorrows of parting overflowed. Flaubert wept into his handkerchief. But his voice sounded strange. It reminded him of Marie Dorval, the actress he used to imitate. His head began to spin. He was afraid. He might be about to have an attack. He calmed himself by opening the window of the carriage, breathing the cold air and observing the moonlight shining on pools of water by the track. He pictured his mother with tears in her eyes and the corners of her mouth turned down. At a station buffet he drank three or four glasses of rum, just for something to do. At every stop he was tempted to turn back. Only the fear of looking ridiculous kept him on the train.

When Flaubert arrived in Paris, Du Camp was out. Flaubert lay down by the fire on the bearskin rug in the study. Exhausted by his own indecision, he wept. This was unlike anything he had known before. Maxime returned at midnight and was dismayed to find his colossal friend laid low, sighing and groaning. 'I shall never see my mother again [. . .] never see my country. It's too far to go, too far away [. . .] it's tempting fate, it's madness. Why are we going?'

Du Camp had it out with him. 'You are not under any obligation to come with me. You are free to decide. If this journey is more than you can manage then you must give it up. I can always go on my own.'

'No! I'd be so ridiculous that I wouldn't even dare to look at myself in the mirror.' The decision was made. There was to be no turning back. At one o'clock in the morning Flaubert sat down to write the first of many letters to his mother. Flaubert and Du Camp spent the next afternoon assembling their things, then Flaubert wrote to his mother again. He made her a promise. Max had now agreed that if things got too bad they would return from Egypt after a few weeks.

Du Camp produced a folder labelled *Ministerial Instructions*. It contained an official letter to Flaubert from the Republican minister of Agriculture and Commerce along with two notebooks setting out the details of his official mission. Flaubert was to collect any information that might be commercially useful. This mission, however implausibly un-Flaubertian, served several purposes. It reassured his mother. It dignified the whole adventure in the eyes of the world, and it gave him a pretext for making contact with influential French emigrés in Egypt.

To cheer himself up Flaubert spent the evening on his own at the opera. He saw Meyebeer's *Le Prophète* and came away 'refreshed, bedazzled and full of life'. Meyerbeer was the contemporary creator of Parisian grand opera. With its large choruses, elaborate scenery and expensive costumes, grand opera was the mid-nineteenth-century equivalent of the Hollywood film epics of the 1930s. Flaubert was an eager connoisseur of the whole genre, excited by its sensuous romantic vision of antiquity. His own distinctive contribution, *Salammbô*, was eventually turned into an opera in the 1890s.

On Sunday, his last day in Paris, Flaubert met up with Bouilhet and they visited the Louvre. There they inspected a newly arrived consignment of Assyrian artefacts, including a superb winged bull with a human head, the former guardian of the palace gates of the city of Nineveh. Here was a new fragment of the ancient past, something to complement the grandiose visions of opera. In the evening Flaubert and friends gathered for a meal in a private room at the Trois Frères provençaux, where they spent the evening talking about art, and literature, and antiquity. This was Flaubert's first meeting with Théophile Gautier, one of the literary masters of the previous generation. Gautier made Flaubert promise that he would convert to Islam. Flaubert talked excitedly about discovering the source of the Nile. Chewing morosely at his cigar, Bouilhet asked the travellers to think of him whenever they came across any relics of Cleopatra. After the meal Flaubert and Bouilhet made their way to Mère Guerin's, the second time in less than a week. That night he had Antonia, his favourite. His prodigious, pre-Egyptian consumption of food and wine and whores was a distraction. 'The senses bring a kind of tenderness and I needed to ease my poor tormented nerves.' Feeling sentimental and superstitious, he arranged to meet Antonia again, two years to the day, outside the Comédie Française.

Next morning, after saying farewell to Bouilhet at the railway station, he turned away with relief. 'Thank God that's over,' he recorded in his journal. 'No more separations. It was a great weight lifted from my heart.' Saying farewell to his mother had exhausted his capacity for feeling.

THEY were to leave Paris by the mailcoach. The sun was shining and his heart was full of hope. Striding across the coachyard, there was Pradier, with his artist's hat and his long hair, sympathetic and expansive as ever, like a good omen. He had come to see them off as he had promised. He was a man of feeling, a man who understood the anxious excitement of departures.

'Do you know what it said on my barometer this morning. *Set Fair*. Now that's a good sign. I'm superstitious you see, so I was delighted.'

Then the mailcoach rattled away over the cobbles and out along the banks of the Seine. The sky was clear, the day was bright and dry and the wind was blowing. From this very place at about the same time of day he had set off for Corsica in the summer of 1840. It was a reassuring coincidence.

Forty miles down the road, at Fontainebleau, their mailcoach was lowered on to a railway wagon. Their fellow passenger, a woman in her fifties, woke them all by screaming with terror in the belief that they were all going to be burnt alive. When she began to vomit out of the window Flaubert went to sit outside on top of the coach. It was swaying about like a ship at sea, with sparks and burning coals swirling down on to the track.

At Chalon, on the River Saône, they boarded a riverboat. Flaubert, consciously novelising his experience, paced the deck trying to place the passengers, reading the labels on people's luggage, eyeing an elusive, slender, fashionable young woman who spent her time leaning over the ship's rail, gazing down at the river. Then Du Camp arrived, 'grinning from ear to ear', to report a below-deck scene of lascivious grotesquerie. 'He had just wandered into the ladies' salon and seen our two mail-coach drivers secluded with two ladies from the first class kneeling down by the girls who were sitting on little stools, red in the face, excited, hatless, their hands wandering towards the *temple of Venus*, as they all soaked up little glasses of anis.'

At Lyon they boarded another boat along the Rhône. Delayed by the November fog, they took a passing mailcoach from Valence to Avignon and there they felt the road to the south opening before them. The light was perceptibly stronger as they passed through orchards of olive trees. At Avignon they boarded an empty train for Marseille.

It was raining when they arrived, but they were well received by Clot-Bey, a medical acquaintance of Du Camp's. The former organiser of the Egyptian army medical service, a member of the Société orientale, Clot-Bey had recently returned to France with an important collection of antiquities. He gave his guests useful letters of introduction to influential French expatriates in Egypt as well as a parcel of letters to be delivered.

Flaubert went to the rue de la Darse, of course, to look at the Hôtel Richelieu. But it was closed and he couldn't remember for sure which door it was. He consoled himself with a visit to a little canvas booth on the quayside where *Il Signor Valentino* paraded two prodigiously hairy girls. The public was invited to pull their hair and Signor Valentino then sang an aria by Donizetti. Wandering around the taverns at the end of the rue de la Darse, he came upon a transvestite cabaret act. The singer gave a splendid performance of 'Non so come si fa'.

Next day they went to visit their boat. It was superb, he told his mother, the biggest in the harbour. *Le Nil* was a 250-horsepower mail-boat belonging to the Messageries nationales. An ungainly, hybrid machine, it looked like a medium-sized sailing ship that had inexplicably acquired a tall funnel and a pair of paddle wheels. They were travelling first class, in the company of diplomats and their families. The second class was full of artisans, a bunch of wig-makers, gilders and mirror-cutters, making their way to Egypt to work for Abbas-Pacha. They often came to sit in the first class and there, as Flaubert put it, 'they bored us stiff with their speeches'.

They put to sea and hit bad weather. *Le Nil* was 'staggering along like a drunkard' in the strong wind and they made very slow progress. Flaubert standing at the rail, silently watching the coastline disappear, began to feel dizzy. Fearing an attack, he drank a glass of rum, which made him vomit almost immediately. He then went below and lay down in his cabin, motionless, for the rest of the day. Recovering slowly, he befriended lieutenant Roux, the second in command. Roux had a rich fund of sea-stories, including men being pecked to death by the albatross. 'It's funny', he observed to his mother, 'how I appeal to the rough sort.'

On the evening of the fourth day *Le Nil* docked in Malta to take on more coal. Flaubert wrote to his mother and portrayed himself to her reassuringly, walking the deck, unaffected by the rough weather, dining with the crew, standing watch with the captain, or gazing poetically out to sea, wrapped in his greatcoat like Byron's Childe Harolde. He was enjoying himself enormously. 'Everyone is on intimate terms. We chatter and we talk and we tell jokes. The gentlemen flirt with the ladies. We all throw up together and in the morning, looking deathly pale, we all laugh at one another again.'

One week and several storms later, nearing the coast, *Le Nil* sailed into superb weather, 'good enough for sketching up on the bridge'. When they were two hours away from land, Flaubert climbed high into the shrouds of the ship; on a distant promontory, sparkling in the sun, he could see the dome of a palace, black against the melting silver light on the surface of the sea.

Landing in Alexandria was an overwhelming experience: '[. . .] there was the most astounding racket, negroes, negresses, camels, turbans, sticks thrashing out to left and right, every blow augmented by earsplitting guttural exclamations. I gobbled up a bellyful of colour, like a donkey filling himself with oats.' The ship's dinghy took them ashore and they disembarked at a spot where camels were drinking at a fountain. Flaubert's 'solemn and anxious impression' was soon replaced by something more congenial. 'Scarcely had we set foot on land when the infamous Du Camp experienced an erection at the sight of a negress drawing water from a fountain. He is equally excited by negro boys. By whom is he not excited? Or rather, by what?'

THE two travellers were soon installed in the Hôtel d'Orient on Alexandria's main square. 'We go gently without tiring ourselves, living soberly and covered in flannel from head to foot [. . .].' They discovered a great Mediterranean city, a place as cosmopolitan as Marseille or Naples. For Alexandria had grown, over the previous fifty years, from a mere fishing village into a major port complete with opera house, colonial mansions, harbour, docks, warehouses and arsenal. Much of this new Alexandria had been built by the French, at the instigation of Mohammed Ali, the first great moderniser of Egypt. But Mohammed Ali had died in August 1849, only three months previously; crowds of French expatriates, soldiers and doctors, engineers and economists, many of whom had gone native, were now leaving the country in disgust at the new regime of Abbas-Pacha, the grandson of the great man. Abbas-Pacha, they said, was a comic-opera tyrant, an obese, bow-legged debauchee who had diamond collars made for his dogs, cared nothing for his grandfather's legacy and was generally allowing the country to fall into ruin.

November 1849 was an interesting moment to arrive in Egypt. The French expatriate elite, thrown into disarray by the death of their patron, were especially welcoming to their congenial young visitors. They felt the exiles' sudden eagerness to talk about home, the Paris theatres and the great political events of the day. The travellers were admirably received. Within a few days of their arrival they had been given a small military escort, 'to hold back the crowds when we are busy taking photographs'. They visited, conversed, observed, explored; they rested in shuttered hotel rooms, writing letters home.

'Set your mind at rest,' Flaubert told his mother. 'I'll come back to you in good condition. I've put on weight since I left, to the extent that my two pairs of trousers are with [. . .] a French tailor, busy being let out in the waist so that my paunch will fit comfortably inside.' He noted that one of the city's great monuments, Pompey's column, a splendid Corinthian capital, had acquired an elegant modern addition, 'the name *Thomson of Sunderland* written in black paint around the base in letters three feet high'. The oblivious effrontery of the bourgeois would become one of his great comic themes. If there were a hero worthy of the modern age, perhaps his name would be *Thomson of Sunderland*.

They spent ten days in Alexandria, staring into the urban face of the Orient. They also made a brief excursion to Rosetta, some forty miles along the coast, which gave them their first glimpse of the desert. Flaubert was delighted to discover that the regimental doctor at the barracks in Rosetta had heard of Dr Achille-Cléophas. It was as though his father were reaching out to protect him, a comforting thought. Prompted by a unique impulse of seriousness, Flaubert even visited his first factory and talked steam pumps with the manager. One afternoon they dressed up in frock coats and white shirts for an official visit to the French consul. He presented them to Artin-Bey, the minister of foreign affairs. They were given letters of introduction and 'treated like princes'.

THE journey from Alexandria to Cairo takes about four hours in a hot and chaotically crowded railway carriage. Sweat runs down the walls and fogs the windows and you understand, at last, the dire impracticality of trousers.

In 1849 Egypt still moved slowly. No railways had yet been built. Accordingly, Flaubert and Maxime Du Camp travelled by *cange* along the new canal that joined the city to the Nile and then changed to a small steamboat. It was so crowded that they took their beds up on to the top deck. 'First night on the Nile – state of satisfaction and lyricism, I wave my arms about, I recite some lines from Bouilhet. I cannot bring myself to go to bed – I think of Cleopatra – the water is yellow – the surface is very smooth – a few stars – tightly wrapped in my pelisse I fall asleep on my campbed, set up on deck. – with what delight! I woke before Maxime – as he woke up he reached out with his left hand to find me [. . .].' At about seven in the morning, as they turned a bend in the river, the pyramids came into view. 'Blue in the distance, bathed in a bright light which brought their outlines into sharp focus, they seemed to be made of transparent sapphire.'

They disembarked at Boulak, on the outskirts of Cairo, where the green fields reminded Flaubert of Normandy and its apple orchards. They made their way to Ezbekiyya, the European quarter at the edge of the old city. This was where Napoléon had lived, during his Egyptian campaign; this was where the best hotels were still to be found. It had a pleasant promenade, shaded with trees, little alleyways with chairs to sit and smoke and drink coffee; in the evenings tumblers came there to do tricks and parade African monkeys.

Here Flaubert and Maxime Du Camp settled in for the next two months, December and January. The contrast between the two travellers now emerged sharply. Du Camp was indefatigably busy, taking photographs, paying visits, talking politics and making notes. Flaubert, like an equal and opposite force, was supremely idle. After their first few days in Cairo, Du Camp realised that Flaubert's mood had changed. Now that the novelty of being in Egypt had worn off, Flaubert seemed to be bored and weary. 'If it had been possible,' Du Camp wrote in his memoirs, 'Flaubert would have travelled on a divan, lying down, without moving, watching the landscapes, the ruins and the cities passing in front of his eyes like the canvas unrolling in a panorama-machine.'

The expedition was already in jeopardy. It was unbearable. Du Camp decided to tackle Flaubert. 'If you want to go back to France you can have my servant to accompany you.' Flaubert replied, 'No; having come this far, I want to see it through; you take care of the itinerary and I'll follow you, I don't care if we go to the left or the right.' Flaubert was mildly depressed and deeply preoccupied. The recent failure of *Saint Antoine* had made it all the more difficult for him to find an answer to the urgent question of what he might do next.

Cairo expatriate society was an amusing distraction, and they soon collected several particularly choice specimens. There was Lubbert-Bey, the ex-director of the Paris opera. Now in his sixties, he was a gently ridiculous figure, a social parasite with a fund of scabrous anecdotes about the social world of the Restoration. There was Soliman-Pasha, a rough old soldier. Originally French, one of Napoléon's lieutenants, he had wandered away after the defeat of 1815, arriving forlorn and penniless in Egypt. There he became an instructor in the Egyptian army, converted to Islam, and installed himself with a harem in an old palace near the Nile. Noisy, cheerful, and formidably shrewd, Soliman-Pasha was warmly disposed towards his French visitors. Out of favour with the new ruler, he was currently lying low, playing endless games of billiards and reminiscing about his hero Napoléon. After only a few weeks in Cairo, Flaubert began to worry that Soliman-Pasha might decide to come with them.

But it was the gruesome Dr Chamas who most appealed to Flaubert, 'always and everywhere in search of the comic'. Amazingly ignorant and incompetent as a doctor, Chamas spent his idle hours writing neoclassical verse tragedies. Flaubert thought him a magnificent specimen: 'He has a nose like a parrot's beak and wears blue glasses [. . .] a creature swollen with vanity, a rogue, a thief, he bores everyone with his writings and is ostracised by his compatriots [. . .]. His family is frightened of him and when he reads out his tragedy everyone trembles in respectful silence.' Du Camp was less enamoured of their new acquaintance. 'Flaubert could not contain his joy; he went to see Chamas, he brought Chamas to see me, he invited Chamas to dinner: he and Chamas were always together. His tragedies were a jumble of weird situations, senseless dialogue, idiotic poetry; the worse the poetry, the more stupid the plot the more Flaubert applauded and the more Chamas swelled up with pride.' At Flaubert's insistence Du Camp sat through a reading of Chamas's play *Abdel-Kader*, a modern tragedy in five acts.

Chamas soon became a stubborn nuisance. He dropped in at all hours expounding his latest ideas, urging Du Camp to recommend him to the reading committee at the Comédie Française. Du Camp finally exploded. 'We're making fun of you,' he told Chamas. 'And we think you're boring.' Flaubert was furious. Du Camp simply did not understand, he said, the greatness of comedy.

Chamas was just another foolish distraction, an obsession, like the five-legged sheep from Guérande, the so-called 'young phenomenon'. Du Camp was too serious for such things. He sought and cultivated men of energy and influence. He was thoroughly at home in the expatriate salon, talking politics and swapping Paris gossip. Flaubert, though he dressed the part and accompanied Du Camp on these social calls, was much more interested in the low life of the city: the clowns performing out in the square, the male dancers in the hotel lounge, the madame of the nearby brothel, the old man in the *Turgish* baths, the antics of the snakecharmers.

By January they were well established in Cairo. They had their favourite places, their familiar things, their improvised habits. Feeling the need to look beneath the vivid surface of the life around them, they began to educate themselves. Up in their hotel room, overlooking the garden, they spent many afternoons in conversation with a French-educated Christianised Arab, Khalil-Effendi, who expounded to them the customs and the religions of the Orient. Du Camp was intending to write a book about Islam – *Les Moeurs musulmanes* – and Flaubert was gathering material for the oriental tale he had in mind.* Khalil-Effendi was so useful and so congenial that they decided to take him with them as an interpreter-companion on their journey up the Nile.†

THEY left Cairo at noon on horseback. After nearly four hours of riding the afternoon light was beginning to fade when they caught sight of the Sphinx. Wildly excited, shouting for joy, they tried to gallop towards it, their horses wallowing through the mud. 'Bigger and bigger it rose from the earth like a dog getting to its feet [. . .].' Buried up to its chest in the sand, 'pugnosed and tattered', Du Camp thought that it

---

* Flaubert made 63 pages of notes entitled *Islamic Life. Lectures by Khalil-Effendi. Cairo, January 1850* – but he never used them.
† Khalil-Effendi is mentioned twice in Flaubert's Egyptian journal.

looked 'like an enormous mushroom when viewed from behind'. It was pink and grey in the sunset. 'He was looking at us with a terrible power – Maxime is quite pale. I am afraid that my head will begin to spin, and I try to master my emotion.' They galloped away again, at full tilt, then walked their horses around the foot of the pyramids. Night fell and they sat down to wait for the servants with the tent and the luggage.*

This was their inaugural night out in the desert, a great occasion. Every little sensation was deliciously heightened: the light from the little lantern hooked to the roof of the tent, the sound of the canvas flapping in the night breeze, 'like the sail of a ship', the breathing of the horses tethered nearby, the Arabs sitting in a circle around the fire, chanting their prayers, listening to tales, sleeping in the holes that they dig in the sand, wrapped in their robes 'like corpses in their shrouds'. At two in the morning, Flaubert went out into the cold night air to smoke a pipe and gaze at the desert sky. Sirius was rising in the east, almost bright enough to be Venus.

They rose at five next morning for the great nineteenth-century ritual pre-dawn ascent of the Great Pyramid. Du Camp, slender and energetic, raced on ahead. Flaubert's progress was somewhat slower. Pushing him from below and pulling him from above, it took four Arabs fifteen minutes to propel his considerable bulk the five hundred feet up to the platform on the summit. Thoroughly winded, he reached the top half an hour before sunrise. This was the supreme spectacle, the great romantic set piece of all nineteenth-century travels in Egypt. Delicately appreciative though he was, Flaubert could not help noticing the comic underside of the experience. The ancient stones were scarred by modern graffiti, political slogans, obscene drawings, visitors' names. Everyone had left their little mark. 'The stones of the platform are disappearing under these ridiculous monuments of vanity and stupidity.'

Du Camp had also prepared a sublime suprise for him. 'Once I got my breath back and began to walk around the platform I saw a little white card pinned to the ground, and what was printed on it? HUMBERT FROTTEUR.' Here was an oddly familiar name. Humbert was a commercial floor-polisher in Rouen and this was undoubtedly his trade card. What was it doing here, up at the top of one of the Great

---

* There is a small but poignant irony in the fact that Flaubert and Maxime Du Camp were probably among the last Europeans ever to *see* the Sphinx without having already seen its photograph. Du Camp liked to believe that he was the first to photograph it.

Pyramids? This was Du Camp's doing. It was soon established that he had indeed filched Humbert's card from inside Flaubert's collapsible top hat, an ingenious spring-loaded contraption called a *gibus*, where it had been carefully stowed away, an odd little souvenir from home.

The future parting of the ways between Flaubert and Maxime Du Camp began quite inconspicuously: '29 December 1849. At three in the afternoon, to the Polytechnic School at Bulak, on the outskirts of Cairo, to pay our first call on Lambert-Bey.' In this odd expatriate world, full of mutually hostile, corrupt and mediocre men, Du Camp was delighted to discover the perfect mentor. Charles Lambert was a man he could love, trust and admire. Witty, benevolent and infinitely gentle, Lambert had an inspiring passion for philosophical discussion and he was, according to Du Camp, the most intelligent man he had ever met. Lambert, now in his mid-forties, had been in Egypt since 1832. He was a polytechnic-educated mining engineer who, along with many of the ablest men of his time, had espoused the Christian socialist doctrines of Saint-Simon. Du Camp's friendship with Charles Lambert eventually changed the whole direction of his life, turning him away from literature towards an enthusiasm for social questions. It was a change of heart, a new earnestness, a humanitarianism that Flaubert could only impotently deplore. He acknowledged that Lambert was 'a formidable specimen', 'a charming man of great intelligence'. It was just that he didn't understand about Art.

THE faint odour of latrines was hardly noticeable out in the court-yard where Bishop Boutros VII, the white-bearded Coptic patriarch, sat cross-legged and barefoot on a divan. With his books spread around him and three young black-robed priests in attendance, the patriarch was waiting for his European visitor to be introduced by their interpreter. 'This man is a French lord,' he began, 'travelling the earth in search of knowledge. He has come to visit you and to speak of your religion.' It was Flaubert, in search of a wisdom quite different from that professed by Lambert-Bey. The Egyptian Coptic church, an ancient Christian minority, cherished all manner of archaic theological notions. 'I began to ask him questions about the Trinity, the Virgin, the Gospels, the Eucharist. All my old erudition from *Saint Antony* came flooding back to me. It was superb [. . .] the old fellow ruminating in his beard before answering me, me sitting beside him, cross-legged, gesticulating with my pencil and taking notes [. . .].'

That same week Flaubert received a letter from his mother. Written in the days following his birthday, arriving on New Year's Day, it prompted some reluctant and inconclusive self-questioning: 'What shall I do when I return? What shall I write? What will I be worth? Where shall I live?' When his mother, in her next letter, asked him about his official mission he told her abruptly that he had done very little and intended to do very little. He had no worldy ambitions at all. 'What can satisfy me other than the endless pleasures of the writing table. Is that not the most enviable thing in the world? Independence, liberty of the imagination, my two hundred quill-pens and the knowledge of their use?'

But Madame Flaubert chose not to drop the subject of her son's future. At her prompting, he had to give further thought to this unpleasant subject. Indignantly, he wrote back:

What does this mean, that I must get myself a position, 'a little position', you say. First of all, what position? I challenge you to find me one, to specify which and what it might be. Frankly, without deceiving ourselves is there even one that I would be capable of taking on? You add: 'a little position that would not take up too much of your time and would not prevent you from doing other things'. What an illusion! It's exactly [. . .] what I said to myself when I began doing law and I nearly exploded with stifled rage.

But his most decisive argument was an appeal to his mother's emotional interests. Surely, he pointed out to her, a little position would inevitably take him away from her side? Henceforth, though his mother now dropped the subject, Flaubert continued to ask himself that same original awkward question: 'What shall I do when I return? What shall I write?'

CHAPTER FOURTEEN

Sailing the Nile

THEY were going south again. On 6 February 1850, with a fresh breeze and a clear sky, Flaubert and Maxime Du Camp set sail to the sound of a tambourine and a flute. It was a most auspicious beginning to their seventeen-week journey along the River Nile. They were travelling in a *cange*, a forty-foot boat with an immense triangular sail. The boat was painted blue and it had a small tricolour flag, courtesy of Du Camp, flying from the stern. There were two cabins, one with divans, for viewing the river, and one with beds. The *cange* had a crew of nine, all curiously minus their right forefingers. They had had them cut off, to avoid being taken for military service.

The wind dropped when it went dark and they moored for the first night in sight of the pyramids. Next morning they went hunting for duck on one of the small islands in the stream. But now the sky turned a dull grey and the boat was immobilised for several days by a sandstorm, the *khamsin*. They shut themselves in, the sand crunching between their teeth, their faces unrecognisable. Flaubert read the *Odyssey* (in Greek) and wrote a marvellously evocative account of Croisset.

To be on the Nile, after two months of urban noise, was to experience exquisite silence: only the sound of the river flowing, the oars dipping, the waterbirds swooping and settling to feed in the mud at the river's edge. Gazing at the gently changing landscape, living on a diet of pigeon, augmented by dates, oranges and figs, Flaubert was becoming 'ignobly plump'and sleeping for fifteen hours a night. Lulled by the peacefulness of the river, his thoughts turned 'endlessly' to Alfred. 'Instead of forgetting I remember more and more intensely'.

At the end of the first week they made a short excursion to El Fayoum, the provincial capital. It took eleven hours on a donkey to traverse the lush, green landscape of palm trees and orchards, watered by the ancient canal system. They arrived at sunset and were given lodgings by a local Christian, a prosperous, educated man, delighted to have such interesting guests. He served a very large meal and 'lots of little drinks were consumed in the name of religious solidarity'. Having sat through his host's wild enthusiasm for Napoléon, Flaubert turned the conversation to Saint Antony (born in this area), Arius and Saint Athanasius. They were joined by a bearded Catholic priest who lived with the family. Flaubert observed with mischievous relish that the priest was 'quite obviously getting it up the lady of the house'. He was further delighted to recognise two lithograph engravings of the Normandy countryside hanging on the wall. Egypt, he realised, was an excellent place to dream of home. Du Camp held back his dismay at this, the latest symptom of his companion's imaginative perversity.

Once they were back on the boat they enjoyed a day of rest. The sailors brought a prostitute on board and then Brichetti arrived with great news. He had found something special, a girl 'with a pair the size of pumpkins'. 'So off we went.' They found the place, a mud hut with a thatched roof. It was so low they had to crawl inside and stay squatting. The girl was dreadfully ugly but her sudden nakedness, on her back on a piece of matting, was irresistibly splendid. So they haggled her down, in spite of voluble protests, to ten piastres for two. It made a good story for Flaubert's next letter to Louis Bouilhet.

THE Orient also offered ecstasies more elevated and more hygienic than the ten-piastre shag-on-the-floor. Arriving at sunset, by water, at the ruins of Thebes, the veil of Flaubert's sorrow lifted for the first time. He was watching one of the sailors dancing on the deck of the *cange* to the sound of a drum and a flute. 'Then it was [. . .] that I felt rising from deep within me a feeling of solemn happiness which swept out towards the scene itself, and I thanked God in my heart for having made me capable of joy such as this – I felt it as a rich intellectual blessing even though my mind seemed to be empty – it was an intimate ecstasy of my entire being.' How could he work these intensities of rapture, horror and abjection that rose from deep within him into the fabric of his writing? How could fiction contain such experiences? *Saint Antoine* had failed because it was too direct. A nicely modulated obliquity – that might be the answer.

The *cange* didn't pause at Thebes. With the wind in its sails it was heading south, up the river, beyond Luxor, beyond Aswan and the first cataract, beyond the tropic of Cancer, into the Sudan, as far as Wadi-Halfa and the second cataract, a journey of exactly forty-six days. There would be ample time for antiquities during the subsequent ten-week descent of the river.

By the first week in March they had reached Esneh, a small town on a bend of the Nile, halfway between Luxor and Aswan. Most European travellers of the day had heard of Esneh. It was notorious. All of Cairo's legendary professional prostitutes had been exiled there by edict, ever since 1834. The *cange* came to its moorings at nine in the morning. Within half an hour, an invitation arrived. It came in the person of a blue-veiled woman with painted eyelids. She was leading a pet sheep, a voluminously fleecy creature with yellow henna patterns on its back and a black velvet muzzle. Flaubert was fascinated. Did they want to see women dancing? Well, yes. They did.

Later that same day, the messenger reappeared and led the two men through the streets, busy with soldiers in Turkish uniform. They reached a small house and passed through into the inner courtyard. There, at the top of a steep, narrow staircase, with the sun behind her, splendidly posed against the blue sky, they saw a woman in pink trousers with a transparent purple veil. 'It was,' wrote Du Camp appreciatively, 'like an apparition.' Kuchuk-Hanem (her Turkish name means *Little Princess*, or *Lady of the Dance*), had just come from her bath and the two men could smell the sweet turpentine oil on her skin. She was tall, youthful, and energetic. She had strong shoulders, ample breasts, and a verse from the Koran tattooed in blue all along her right arm. Du Camp followed her downstairs for some solitary entertainment and Flaubert soon took his place.

Afterwards, with much drinking of *raki*, served up in champagne glasses, the gift of an English tourist, the dancing began. Two musicians, a child and an old man, played a disagreeably strident duet on their little violins. Kuchuk-Hanem's dancing was an exception to the rule that 'beautiful women dance badly'. It was brutal and archaic, but curiously familiar; Du Camp thought of the Bacchantes and Flaubert thought of the figures on 'ancient Greek vases'. Kuchuk-Hanem then led her visitors back through the streets to their boat, jumping on their backs and pulling faces, 'like a proper Catholic tart'.

They came back for more, later that evening. The party lasted from six until ten thirty, and Flaubert made notes. 'Second shot with

Kuchuk-Hanem – as I kissed her shoulder I could feel her necklace against my teeth – her cunt milking me was just like rolls of velvet – I felt ferocious.' She agreed, reluctantly, to dance *the bee*, essentially a frenzied comic routine in which the dancer, attacked by the bee, has to take all her clothes off. Covered in sweat from the dance, Kuchuk-Hanem fell panting on the divan and pulled on a pair of enormous white trousers that covered her up to the neck. She did not want the two men to spend the night in her house. Their presence would attract thieves. She relented and then, after a memorable *gamahuchade*, she fell asleep holding Flaubert's hand. He 'sank into an endless mournful reverie' and entertained himself by squashing the cockroaches walking across the wall. 'How sweet it would be to a man's pride to be sure when you leave [. . .] that you will remain in her heart.'

Seven weeks later, on his way back down the Nile, piqued by the fantasy of being remembered, Flaubert visited Kuchuk-Hanem once again. Her messenger arrived, as before, at their boat. But the henna'd sheep had died and Kuchuk-Hanem appeared without her headdress or her jewellery. She looked tired and ill. The usual courtesies were exchanged. She had been thinking about them, she said. She criticised Flaubert's moustache, as she had done before. Why did he hide such a nice little mouth? 'We leave with the promise that we will return to say our goodbyes.' Infinitely sad in the knowledge that her face would fade from his memory, Flaubert spent the afternoon sitting in a café, soberly watching the crowds.

A T eight o'clock in the evening, forty-six days after leaving Cairo, the *cange* landed on the wide, sandy beach at Wadi-Haifa, six miles below the second cataract of the Nile. The moonlight shining on the sand looked like snow. Next day the two travellers made a short excursion across the desert to climb the great mountain above the cataract at Djebel Abousir. It was a hot three-hour climb to the summit. Their reward was a superb view out across the desert landscape, with the Nile far below their feet. From that height the river was a series of little pools edged with jagged rocks of coal-black granite that sparkled in the sunlight. This was a solemn moment. The two travellers had reached their furthest point south.

Here, on that summit high above the Nile, in a suspiciously neat piece of symbolism, Du Camp placed the great moment when Flaubert found the name for his heroine: 'He gave a shout: "I've got it! Eureka!

Eureka! I'm going to call her Emma Bovary!" and he repeated the name several times, savouring the sound of the word Bovary, pronouncing it with a very short o.*

Flaubert's version of what happened next is both more prosaic and more plausible. Together they went striding down the steep slope towards the Nile, sinking up to their knees in the soft flowing sand, drawn to the sound of the swirling waters below. They returned to the cataract by canoe a few days later, exploring the mountains, taking photographs and savouring the rich, mysterious conjunctions of heat and light, silence and swirling water. To a man with a passion for rivers, the second cataract of the Nile was a place of strong enchantment: twenty uninhabited miles of dangerous rapids, jagged rocks and thornbushes.

Three days later they set off back down the Nile. Imperceptibly but irrevocably they had turned for home. Every visitor to Egypt recalls the precise moment. Flaubert's thoughts had turned too. His associations began to point homewards. At Abu Simbel, the repeated cry of a bat at the temple 'sounded like the distant striking of a farmhouse clock – I thought of those farmyards in Normandy, in the summer, when every-one is out in the fields, towards three o'clock in the afternoon [. . .].' That precious, singular little detail – 'in the summer, when everyone is out in the fields, towards three o'clock in the afternoon' – surfaces several years later, perfectly intact, in *Madame Bovary*. Flaubert had found something, standing above the cataract, but it was something less obvious than the name of his next heroine.

THEIR journey into Nubia, the far southern edge of Egypt, was over. Their faces were dark from the tropical sun and now they were rowing slowly back down the river they had sailed up, visiting temples that were still, in that year, 'up to their shoulders' in sand. Everywhere previous travellers have carved their names deep into the stone. Du

---

* Too good to be true? This anecdote is usually disdained as a piece of fanciful invention. Heroines are not supposed to be born in such crude and dramatic fashion. And Flaubert's journal for that day makes no mention of Emma Bovary. Confusingly, there are two details of Du Camp's story which are plausible. Flaubert did shout out when he had made some comic discovery. The sound of the name chimes insistently. Bovary probably began life as Bouvaret, the name of a hotel-keeper in Cairo. In addition to Emma Bovary, Flaubert created a string of like-sounding characters. There is a Bouvard, a Bouvigny and a Bouvignard. The sound of the name also has aptly colloquial associations: *bavarder* – to chat; *buveur* – drunkard; *bouvier* – cowherd.

Camp has devised a little running joke. He greets all the temple statues in Arabic and asks after their health.

Thoughts of Europe and things European came crowding back to them. 'We spent the afternoon lying down in the prow of the boat [. . .] discussing, with a certain sadness and a certain bitterness, the old subject of literature, sweet and perpetual source of worry!' Often, late at night on the boat, gazing up at the stars of the Southern Cross, they discussed Flaubert's *Saint Antony*. Flaubert was possessed by the desire to find the subject of his next book. When they reached Aswan, he was bitterly disappointed to find letters for all the others but none for him. He had not heard from his mother since leaving Cairo, nearly three months before.

Early in the month of May they arrived in Karnak. 'I shall never forget my first impression of the palace at Karnak. It looked like a house where giants live, a place where they used to serve up men roasted whole, à la brochette, on gold plates, like larks.' They stayed in Karnak for three days, sleeping on a great stone slab, under the stars, listening to the nocturnal activities of tarantulas and jackals. Memories of Alfred kept coming back to him: 'Perhaps he was travelling with me,' he told his mother. 'In which case it was not that I was thinking of him but that he was thinking of me.'

They camped by the tomb of Ozymandias in the Valley of the Kings, bedazzled by the fantastical blue-and-gold images painted on the walls of the great chamber: 'serpents with several heads walking about on human feet, severed heads sailing along, monkeys pulling ships, kings with green faces and other strange attributes sitting on their thrones.' At the entrance to the valley they found an old Greek, dealing in antiquities. He was an odd specimen in his own right, with his white cotton umbrella and his *chibouk*, living all alone in a house packed full of mummies. Reluctantly Flaubert abandoned the idea of adding a mummy to his growing collection of oriental souvenirs. Exporting mummies had recently been made illegal; smuggling one out of the country would simply be too expensive and too complicated.

T HEY wanted to visit the Red Sea. So it was that they began making preparations for an excursion across the desert to El Koseir, a small town on the coast. To his friend's great amusement, Du Camp wore himself out enthusiastically greasing and stretching his riding boots, which had shrunk tight in the tropical heat.

They set off into the desert, a four-day journey, following the caravan tracks that ran parallel across the sand, delighted by the guttural
whistling song of the camel-drivers. Flaubert made conscientious
efforts to imitate the bizarre cry of the camel. 'I hope to perfect it before
we leave, but it is quite difficult because of the particular gurgling
sound that quivers somewhere beneath the screech they give.' Over-
taken by a desert sandstorm they spent hours held inside its pale red
cloud. A caravan passed them by in ghostly silence. The strangeness of
the desert was working upon his mind. 'I feel a wild mix of terror and
wonder flowing along my bones, I laugh nervously, I must have turned
very pale and I felt an extraordinary pleasure.' When they came down
to the Red Sea he ran across the dunes towards the water's edge,
amused by his own pointless impatience. Lover of waters, salt and
fresh, Flaubert went bathing in the Red Sea. 'It was one of the most
voluptuous experiences of my life. I lay basking on the waves and it was
like having a thousand soft juicy tits stroking me all over my body.'

Their host in Koseir was Père Elias, a delightful white-bearded Christian from Bethlehem. He lodged them in a little summerhouse. One
window looked on to the green sea with its exquisite melting colours
and its busy traffic of Arab ships; one window looked on to the road
where starving nomads came wandering in from the desert; one window looked on to the courtyard where sailors sat in the shade, playing
cards with little circles of embossed leather.

On the first day of the return journey across the desert there occurred
'a painful incident', the only serious quarrel of the entire trip. 'We did
not speak to each other for forty-eight hours [. . .].' It began with an
accident. At eight o'clock in the evening, the camel carrying their entire
supply of water in three goatskins fell over and broke its leg, crushing
the goatskins and spilling all the water across the desert sand. They
realised that they were at least seventy hours from the next oasis. On
the first day they sucked stones to cheat their thirst, but the wind came
from the south, bringing a fierce heat. Their mouths were dry, their lips
turned white and they travelled in complete silence.

As they were passing through a narrow place among the furnace-hot
pink granite rocks, Flaubert was seized by 'one of those irresistible
impulses that sometimes overcame him'. He turned to Du Camp and
said: 'Do you remember the lemon ices they serve at Tortoni's?' Du
Camp nodded. Flaubert continued. 'Ah those lemon ices. A lemon ice is
a splendid thing. Admit it, you wouldn't refuse a lemon ice. The white

frost that forms on the outside of the glass [. . .].You fill the spoon [. . .] you crush it gently between your tongue and the roof of your mouth [. . .]. It melts, slow and cool and delicious [. . .].' Nothing could stop him. He began shouting: 'Lemon ice! Lemon ice!' Suppressing the urge to put a bullet through his friend's head, Du Camp sent Flaubert away to ride ahead at a safe distance. Here was yet another instance of his companion's oddly compulsive sense of the comic. Would he never grow up?*

At some point during the excursion to the Red Sea Flaubert contracted a fever. His infuriating obsession with lemon ices may have been a symptom. For several weeks he lay on the boat, exhausted, sleeping for most of the day, largely indifferent to the ancient temples that lined the banks of the River Nile. Sitting on the prow, he gazed into the river:

I muse upon my life with a deep intensity. Many forgotten things are coming back to me, like the old tunes the nurse-maid used to sing, odd bits float up into your mind. Am I entering a new phase? [. . .] I have no plans, no projects, no ideas, and what is worse I have no ambitions [. . .]. Young Du Camp finds such ideas revolting [. . .] for after his return [. . .] he intends to throw himself into demonic activity.

B Y the end of June their boat reached Cairo and Flaubert's journal recorded a characteristic mood: 'that night immense nostalgia for the boat-journey and for the rhythmic sound of the oars dipping in the water [. . .] marking time all through the long dreamy days of the last three months'. They soon made contact with Charles Lambert, the most congenial of the Cairo expatriates, and in a long series of ardent conversations with him they argued out their positions on art (humanitarian or aesthetic?) and 'the future of society'. Suddenly, after three regressively tranquil months floating along the river, the mood had shifted. 'Bizarre psychological phenomenon, sir! I began to crackle with intellectual energy. The pot suddenly came to the boil, I felt a burning need to write.' Like it or not, Flaubert and Du Camp were the rising generation. The *Dictionnaire des idées reçues*, first mentioned a few months later, in September 1850, was Flaubert's first considered response to this compelling fact.

* Though it is often thought to be improbable, the *glâce au citron* episode looks persuasively circumstantial. And the teasing is perfectly in character. It may well be another of Du Camp's slightly disparaging tall stories. The evidence is thoroughly appraised in Steegmuller, *Flaubert in Egypt*, 195–6.

They left Cairo by steamboat on the morning of 2 July 1850. Their immediate destination was Alexandria. Their next objective was Beirut, then possibly Persia. At around three in the afternoon, on board the ship, Flaubert had an epileptic attack.* The strong emotions of the previous day, the sadness of parting from Lambert, the intellectual excitement of their conversations – it had all made the pot boil over.

They spent ten days in Beirut. In preparation for the next stage of their journey, mainly overland on horseback, Du Camp swapped the photographic equipment for ten feet of gold-embroidered fabric made of wool and silk. Sufficient, said Flaubert, for two divans (one each) of truly royal splendour. They stayed much longer than they had planned. The main reason was Camille Rogier. A fellow spirit and a recklessly convivial character, Rogier was a friend of Nerval's from the old days, 'one of the same artist gang'. A great connoisseur of the Lebanese varieties of organised lechery, Rogier now enjoyed a little sinecure as postmaster in Beirut. Characteristically he would challenge his European visitors to see who had the biggest cock, convinced that his own, a real monster, could humiliate all possible rivals.

* The words 'sale rage de nerfs' have been almost obliterated from Flaubert's journal, probably by his niece.

CHAPTER FIFTEEN

Countries of the Mind

IN Beirut there was a 'confidential' letter from Madame Flaubert waiting for Du Camp. Gustave was not supposed to know anything about it. The letter pleaded pitifully with Du Camp to abandon the whole Persian section of their journey. When Du Camp questioned him, Flaubert admitted that he had asked his mother to write the letter. Du Camp was displeased. Their original plan was to follow the route taken by Alexander the Great. It had all been agreed. Now Du Camp was placed in an impossible position. Either he must leave Flaubert to make his own way back to France, or he must to give up the Persian expedition. Flaubert was hugely relieved when Du Camp decided against Persia. 'It was never mentioned between us again, for I think he found it an unpleasant memory.'

That was Du Camp's version of events, as published in his memoirs. Plausible and interesting, but quite untrue. The whole story was in fact a demeaning fabrication, prompted perhaps by Du Camp's envy of Flaubert's subsequent literary reputation. The truth was much simpler. There were straightforward financial reasons on both sides for the decision to turn for home. The trip was beginning to go well over budget. Du Camp's inheritance from his grandmother had become legally entangled in Paris and he had reason to think he was being swindled in his absence; Flaubert, for his part, was reluctant to dig any further into his capital.

So they went south, along the coast, to Jerusalem. After the sleepy alluvial expanses of Egypt, this was an invigoratingly different landscape: humpback bridges across dry ravines, oleanders growing down to the shoreline. Nine days they travelled, on horseback, with spurs on their boots, galloping downhill for the hell of it. With four mules and their drivers, they set out at four in the morning, slept through the heat of the day, then rode on until sunset. Then, with a lantern hanging from the branches of some great sycamore tree, with the baggage and the horses arrayed in a protective circle, they slept under the stars, devoured by fleas. They reached Jerusalem early in the month of August. It was a solemn moment. 'We went in through the Jaffa Gate and I dropped a fart there as I crossed the threshold, quite involuntarily; I was even rather angered by the Voltaireanism of my anus.'

This mood of cold, sour irony, familiar to all travellers, persisted. 'Jerusalem strikes me as a fortified charnel-house; old religions are silently rotting away in there, you tread on turds and all you can see is ruins: it's immensely sad.' 'The Armenians curse the Greeks who detest the Catholics who excommunicate the Copts. It's sad rather than merely grotesque. Though it may be be more grotesque than sad. It all depends on your point of view.' Flaubert was intrigued to discover that he felt none of the expected emotions: 'neither religious enthusiasm, nor imaginative excitement, nor a hatred of priests [. . .]'; but he was amused to discover that a portrait of King Louis-Philippe had somehow found its way into the Holy Sepulchre.

On their first evening in Jerusalem Flaubert and Maxime Du Camp paid a visit to the French consul, Paul-Emile Botta, an ex-pupil of Dr Achille-Cléophas Flaubert and one of the great archaeologists of the day. In 1843 Botta had made a momentous discovery, an Assyrian palace thought to be part of the lost city of Nineveh. Some of Botta's Assyrian artefacts were already in the Louvre, and his book, *Monuments de Ninive*, had just been published. But the nomadic life had destroyed his health and he had become an opium-eater. He was a thin, anxious, embittered man in his late forties, a ferocious obscurantist immersed in cuneiform scholarship. Flaubert observed Botta closely: 'a ruin of a man [. . .] hates everyone except for the dead [. . .] weary of his various activities (his life is a patchwork: doctor, naturalist, archaeologist, consul) he's tried it all, he can't be bothered, he's had enough.' There was a lesson to be drawn from Botta. One of the foremost intellectuals of the day, still at the height of his reputation, he exemplified failure of vocation on a truly magnificent scale. Could he also have confirmed Flaubert's growing impulse of renunciation?

After the squalor of Jerusalem, Bethlehem was unexpectedly arresting. 'I lingered there, I could not tear myself away, it's beautiful, it's true, it sings of mystic joy.' Though there was, of course, another side to the holy places. Sitting in a café, somewhere between the Tomb of the Virgin and the Mount of Olives, Flaubert and Du Camp observed two capuchin monks drinking brandy among a company of splendid bare-breasted women.

At the end of August they made for Damascus, travelling north along the valley of the River Jordan. The nights were cold, the roads hard and rocky, the country difficult and dangerous. Eventually, afraid of being attacked from the mountains to the east, they had to travel by night across a great plain. They reached Damascus on the first day of September, covered in dust and looking like bandits. They now wanted to be in Constantinople by the beginning of November, before the weather turned. On the 13th they set off again, north-west, towards the coast, following the line of a wide, fertile valley between two high ranges of mountains. They camped by a stream, under a tree, opposite the ruins of the huge temple complex at Baalbek. Site of the Roman town of Heliopolis, Baalbek was a place of deep silence, with a cold wind rolling the clouds across the sky and snow-covered mountains on the far horizon. 'The stones of Baalbek seem to be deep in thought. Olympian effect. I stayed there two days walking around on my own [. . .] a historic landscape such as no painter to my knowledge has ever depicted.'

Here the two travellers separated, temporarily, for the first time. Du Camp had to take one of the party back to Beirut, leaving Flaubert and the rest to make their way towards the coast of Lebanon. They crossed the plain and began the long climb up into the Lebanese mountains, a limestone ridge that rises to 10,000 feet. Cold and disoriented, struggling through an icy wind among deep gorges and snow-covered rocks, the group lost its way during the descent, reaching their destination belatedly on 18 September. The lack of letters for this period is probably an index of the hardships encountered along the way.

From Tripoli they took a steamship, the *Stambul*, to the island of Rhodes where they lay quarantined for four days in the *lazaretto*. Flaubert wrote a long letter to his mother and began to think about a new subject, a tale about Don Juan. *Une nuit de Don Juan*, sketched out in 1851, was still too close in theme to *Saint Antoine*. The theme – let us call it carnal mysticism – required a more radical metamorphosis; it would have to be written from a woman's position if it was ever to come into focus. This fertile, bewildering, rapturous confusion of body and soul – let us call it the *physiology of the imagination* – would eventually become Flaubert's great subject. But it required him to turn into a woman before it could be divulged.

Once they had served their time in the *lazaretto*, they boarded a single-masted *caique* and made the crossing in seven hours from the island to the mainland. The leaves were falling as they rode across the great windswept plain of Anatolia; the October rainclouds came rolling down towards them from the mountains and they had thirteen days of hard riding to the city of Smyrna. It was an exhausting journey. Both men were nursing their more recent venereal wounds and Max Du Camp contracted a fever after being kicked by one of the horses. Tenderly and competently, Flaubert took good care of his friend.

As they approached the great imperial city of Ephesus, he felt *le frisson historique*, the full shiver of history. 'I'm thinking of Homer, the sound of the stream, it's murmuring lost verses in Greek.' But the modern reality of Ephesus was unremarkable and instead it was the opium-traders who delighted Flaubert's imagination. Tattered Europeans down on their luck, the opium men told grandiose tales of fortunes lost and found. Connoisseur of all shades of rascality, Flaubert bought them encouraging drinks and soaked up their experiences; he even conceived and often expounded (though he never wrote) a great picaresque comic novel set in the modern Orient, full of vagrant Europeans, all liars and swindlers. It was to be called *Harel-Bey* and its theme was the contrast between 'the Oriental who was becoming civilised and the European who was returning to a state of savagery'.

They arrived in the port of Smyrna (modern Izmir) towards the end of October. It was cold and wet and prosperous and boring; Flaubert was 'in a bad mood, morally and nervously'. At this point they decided against the thirty-day overland journey to Constantinople. It was perilously late in the season and they might well be unable to cross the swollen rivers. Besides, Du Camp's fever had left him weakened. So they took the steamboat to Constantinople. Flaubert passed the time eating great quantities of ham and reading the *Iliad* again.

THEY spent just over a month in Constantinople, though they had originally planned to be there for three months. The city is cold and damp in winter, 'like Siberia', said Flaubert, with a north wind coming off the Black Sea from across the Russian steppes. Confined by the weather and daunted by the immensity of the city, Flaubert wrote a series of long self-questioning letters to his mother and to Louis

Bouilhet. What should he do next? The letters sketch out possibilities, none of them very clear. There is, he tells his mother, *something* in the making: 'a second style perhaps? Some day before too long I must out with it. [. . .] Will I manage to retrieve what disappeared into Saint Antoine for some other work??' We catch this same note of creative uncertainty, variously expressed, in all the Constantinople letters. *Limbo-esque*, he calls it. Old and new projects jostle together. The *Dictionnaire des idées reçues*, though still distinct, merges into an ambitious political satire focused on socialist ideas.

In Constantinople Flaubert heard the news of the death of Balzac and he was surprised to discover that it affected him deeply. It may also have helped him to write a novel that would pursue Balzac's speciality, the 'study of women'. The 'woman question' was certainly in his thoughts. His niece Caroline would soon be five years old and decisions would have to be made about her education. 'Women', he wrote to his mother, 'are taught to lie shamelessly. An apprenticeship that lasts all their lives. From their first chambermaid down to the last lover who survives them, everyone does their bit to make them treacherous and then they raise a great outcry over it. Puritanism, prudery, bigotry, the whole system of strict confinement distorts and destroys in its prime the Good Lord's most charming creation.'

Flaubert marked his twenty-eighth birthday, 12 December 1850, with an adventure of pleasingly epic dimensions. In the company of Count Kosielski, the leader of the local community of Polish political exiles, Flaubert rode fifteen leagues out across the great snow-covered plains on the Asian side of the Bosphorus. Packs of dogs howled and gave chase as the two riders came crashing through the silent, frozen villages. In the cold, clear winter light the distant white mountains of Bithynia looked slightly unreal. 'The sound of our horses' hooves was muffled by the snow. [. . .] racing across that white solitude I was thinking about [. . .] Tibet, Tartary, the Great Wall of China.' A precious memory of boyhood also came back to him: being out in the country with his father, on a winter's day, visiting his patients and warming himself by the fire in a farmhouse kitchen. Flaubert and Kosielski returned to the city, spattered with mud, riding at top speed, just as the December sun was setting. There was moonlight on the Bosphorus and their little boat was nearly capsized by the waves. With its rich, clear, joyful harmony of the real, the imagined and the remembered, this was one of the great days of Flaubert's life.

Around this time there came a birthday letter from his mother asking him when he intended to marry. The question disturbed him and he wrote back with an emphatic *never!* He would live alone, a lucid solitude, but with his mother always there, somewhere by his side. 'I shall never love another woman as I love you [. . .]. You will never have a rival [. . .].' Thinking of his mother, thinking also of Alfred's marriage, Flaubert declared his intimate, artistic principle of detachment: 'You can portray wine, love, women, glory, on condition [. . .] of being neither a drinker, a lover, a husband or a soldier. Immersed in life, you cannot see it clearly, too taken up with its joys and sorrows. To my mind an artist is a monstrosity, a thing outside nature.'

FLAUBERT felt 'happy as a child' when he saw Athens for the first time from the deck of the *Mentor*. The sun was shining and there was the Acropolis, shining white, with the mountains behind it. He stood alone at the prow of the ship, alongside a cage full of clucking chickens. With his *lorgnon* on his nose, he allowed himself to 'indulge in great thoughts'. He felt a deep affinity for Classical Greece. It was one of the countries of his mind, 'dearer to me, closer to me' than the holy places of Christianity. The climate, compared to Constantinople, was mild and spring-like, with myrtles and olive trees. 'I am in a positively Olympian state, I inhale antiquity in great brainfuls.' This keen imaginative intensity came about, he supposed, precisely because the journey was nearly over. And, more prosaically, because he would never be able to afford anything like it again. 'My journey', he confided to Louis Bouilhet, 'has bitten deep into my slender capital.'

In Athens he realised, with some dismay, that the journey had also aged him. 'I'm not getting any prettier, far from it.' And he warned his mother: 'you must expect to find me three-quarters bald, with a wizened face, a big beard, and a pot-belly'. Teased by Du Camp, he made a joke of it: 'I'm about to join the ranks of the men that whores wince at when it comes to the shagging [. . .]. O where are you now, opulent curls of my eighteenth year, ye that hung down to my shoulders, the emblems of hope and pride.'

The travellers spent their first four days locked up in the *lazaretto* at Piraeus, being fumigated and dusted with sulphur. They had been in their hotel scarcely an hour when the first of their compatriots came to pay a social call. Colonel Touret, a pedantically immaculate old soldier, his sky-blue uniform bristling with medals, looked like a character out of a light opera. But he soon delighted them with great tales of the battles he had seen in the recent Greek wars of independence. Touret also introduced them to another partisan, General Morandi, a man who had fought alongside Byron in the 1820s. Du Camp, a great collector of celebrity gossip, regularly invited the two old soldiers to dine at their hotel with them. The conversations lasted well into the night. Touret and Morandi were characters who could have walked from the pages of the romantic poetry that Flaubert and Du Camp had read as schoolboys. To meet the heroes of your youth, in the year 1850, was a sobering, tragi-comical experience.

THEY reached Thermopylae, where Minerva had created a hot spring to refresh Hector in his struggle with the giant Antaeus. In 1850 the sacred waters were gainfully employed turning a watermill. Flaubert and Du Camp sat there, reading Plutarch's account of one of history's greatest battles, gazing at a suspiciously modern mound said to be the tomb of Leonidas. Putting all ironic reservations to one side, Flaubert was delighted. 'What a splendid story it would make!' Whilst Flaubert dwelt on the poetry of the past, his companion gathered up a handful of the yellow crystals from around the sacred spring. It would be very interesting, he decided, to send them for chemical analysis.

They set off across the Peleponnese, and it rained all the way to Sparta. The horses had to swim across swollen rivers with their riders on their backs. At night they all slept in the stables, bedding down amongst the animals, gathered around a fire of wet branches that blackened the beams overhead and filled the air with smoke. At this point in their travels, Flaubert and Du Camp both looked the part of the romantic nomad. Opulently bearded, their shirts in tatters, their boots falling to bits, wearing coats made out of goatskin held together with bits of foxtail, their outlandish appearance was enough to frighten the local children.

Money was running low but Flaubert was in excellent spirits. All along the way he improvised solemnly comic invocations to the great ghosts of antiquity; in Sparta he perplexed the local chief of police with a stream of preposterous questions about the ancient city. From their guide he was learning how to howl like a dervish, and he practised enthusiastically as they rode along in the rain. 'Maxime is sick of it. I carry on all the same. One evening my chest was literally caving in from it.' The travellers also invented a new game for two. Flaubert was the sweet, delicate, coquettish little shop girl who had to fend off the advances of a big, rough, crude, nicotine-stained soldier (Du Camp). Imaginative homo-erotic comedy was one of the pleasures that Flaubert and his friends never renounced.

They rode for fifteen hours through dense oak woods, hurrying towards their destination, the port of Patras, anxious not to miss the boat. Their boat was nine days late and so they had to sit it out, reduced to their last five hundred francs, killing time and gazing out across the bay to Missolonghi, the place of Byron's death in 1824. Missolonghi, gleaming white in the winter sun, was one of those subtly alluring impossibilities – the places you almost visited – that are woven into the bright fabric of every great journey.

They boarded the boat in the knowledge that this was the end of their real journey. From now on they were back among the tourists. After two days at sea they landed in Brindisi where officious customs men took against Flaubert's enormous bandit beard. Suspicious-looking foreigners, they were obviously up to no good. Their luggage was searched, their pistols were confiscated, their notebooks were anxiously scanned for subversive ideas.

It was their first unpleasant taste of Europe's post-1848 reactionary politics. The local despot, Ferdinand II, King of the Two Sicilies, mockingly known as *la Bomba*, lived in fear of being assassinated by liberal conspirators. The King's mercenaries had crushed a recent uprising and now his spies were busy everywhere. It was common knowledge that the jails of Naples held 35,000 political prisoners. For the next few weeks, all the way to Rome, Flaubert and Du Camp were carefully watched. On the back streets of Herculaneum there was a spy listening in to their conversation. In the museum in Naples there was a guard peering over their shoulder to check what they were writing in their notebooks. On Cape Misenus there was a policeman watching them as they ate their lunch. It was ridiculous, intrusive and exasperating.

Being back in civilisation was a shock. It felt like confinement. Du Camp described this feeling eloquently. 'No more tent, no more desert, no more palm trees, no more wandering river, no more horse-racing with the Bedouin [. . .] that free expansive life in the sun was coming to a close; time to come home, to the five-storey house, the busy street, the tight clothes, the routine, the decorum.' On the other hand one rediscovered cigars, clean clothes, fresh butter, and cutlets for lunch.

The pleasure of the latter, said Flaubert, was enough to reconcile him to civilisation.

IT was two hundred miles to Naples, three days and a night in a big, old, red-upholstered carriage, pushing north along the dusty roads of Calabria, with glimpses of blue sea, white houses, olive groves, little village squares with a fountain, a church and a statue. Then they turned inland, westward, crossing the Appenines. It was raining when they passed through the gates of Naples

There they spent two weeks, exploring the museums. This was a conscientious full-time occupation: looking all day, then writing all evening. 'Last night I couldn't sleep, my head was so full of the busts of empresses and votive bas-reliefs.' Flaubert wrote meticulous and oddly impassive descriptions of everything, the paintings, the sculpture, the bronzes, the temples and the ampitheatres. Was he compiling an encyclopaedia of objects that might one day be useful to him? Though he had no talent for drawing (unlike his brother and his late sister), he had a superbly retentive visual memory that ministered to his curiously obsessive passion for objects. This would become an insistent, distinctive feature of his vision of the human world: the rich stagnation of mere *things*, and all the magic powers that we bestow upon them.

It was a solemn moment when, on 27 February 1851, Flaubert shaved off his Oriental beard. 'My poor beard! Washed in the Nile! Blown by the desert wind! Scented by smoke from the campfire! Underneath it I discovered an enormously plump face [. . .] with two chins.' Along with the beard, he cast off his *tarbouch* and took to wearing a hat again: 'it had to be so [. . .] it would have been too great an affectation [. . .] everyone was turning to look at me.' He was in a peculiar state. The playful excitement of travelling was about to come to an end; all the sorrows and the uncertainties of his real situation were about to descend upon him. The last few weeks of freedom were marked by a quest for external danger. He fell in love with a French vaudeville actress; he climbed Vesuvius and looked down into the crater; he deliberately came close to drowning in the sea off the island of Capri. Soon he would have to be with his mother again. Du Camp, who joked about handing him over to her 'in person', was going to travel back directly to Paris, to sort out his financial affairs.

Towards the end of March the two travellers arrived in Rome on the diligence from Naples. Initially the city was a disappointment. Looking for the Emperor Nero, Flaubert found only Pope Sixtus the Fifth. Christianity had crushed all the life out of Antiquity. Even the stones from the Forum were being sold off as paperweights. His mind was elsewhere. He was expecting his mother some time around the middle of April and he soon began counting the days, even though he was not sure when she would appear. Every day he checked for letters at the post office. He had not seen her for nearly eighteen months and he was in a volatile, superstitious, susceptible state of mind.

It was at this moment, on the eve of the reunion with his mother, that Flaubert met with two erotic experiences that were both extravagantly compelling and yet chastely imaginary. The first encounter took place in the Palazzo Corsini when he saw Murillo's painting of a *Virgin and Child*. The image of the woman's dark eyes soon pursued him 'like a perpetual hallucination [. . .]'. He wrote about it, facetiously, to his mother. It was, he declared, 'enough to drive anyone crazy [. . .]'. But the image didn't fade from his memory. He mentioned the picture again, a month later. 'I'm in love with Murillo's Virgin [. . .]. Her face pursues me and her eyes keep appearing in front of me, like two dancing lanterns.'*

The second encounter took place about ten days after Flaubert saw Murillo's Virgin. Easter Monday (15 April) was a hot day, and the city was crowded for Holy Week. Flaubert was in the church of Saint Peter's when he saw the woman in red. She came walking slowly towards him, leaning on the arm of an old woman, like a convalescent who has ventured out for the first time. 'I took my lorgnon and moved forwards, something was drawing me towards her.' The pallor of her face, the whiteness of her forehead, the long red ribbon in her hair, the light in her eyes, every detail of her appearance was charged with mysteriously powerful feelings, as in a dream. 'I wanted to fall at her feet and kiss the hem of her dress [. . .] ask her father for her hand in marriage.'

She sat down on a bench and Flaubert gazed at her. 'You would have said that she had just woken up, that she came from another world.' Afterwards in his carriage, so often a place of languid reverie, Flaubert devised splendid scenes in which he magically imposed his presence: '[. . .] having her portrait painted, bringing Ingres or Lehmann from Paris to do it [. . .] if I were rich! [. . .] going to introduce myself to them

---

* The phrase 'like two dancing lanterns' evokes the moving lights on the approaching wagon that triggered Flaubert's first epileptic attack in January 1844.

as a doctor who would cure her? [. . .] and magnetise her! I was certain I could have magnetised her [. . .].' He wrote about her in his journal that same day, in the hotel, before supper: 'Already her features are fading from my memory. Farewell!'

These fleeting visions of ideal women, Flaubert's only Roman 'experiences', may have been a way of drawing a line across the page of his travels. A few days later his mother arrived to meet him. After they reached Florence there are no further entries in his journal, a fact that suggests sudden unhappiness. Madame Flaubert wanted to get back to Croisset as quickly as possible and Flaubert complied with her wish. They spent only four days in Venice, and Flaubert worked himself into a state of high exasperation. 'My mother [. . .] claims that I've changed and that I have become brutal. Which I am not aware of, though I often feel that I'm holding myself back.' In Venice Flaubert struck a sudden blow at a customs officer and was required to sign an apologetic declaration in order to escape arrest. Fearfully, his mother did her best to hurry him home. They reached Paris, via Milan, Cologne and Brussels, on 10 June 1851, a stage of his journey that left no significant traces. This was not the ending he would have chosen.

He had acquired along the way an interesting little collection of souvenirs, the wondrous residue of his travels. It was a disappointment, initially, to discover that the trunks dispatched from Egypt had not travelled well. All the gazelle skins and and the lizard skins had been devoured by worms; the pots of ibis – all but one – had been broken in transit; and the Nubian garments (female) were horribly rancid. But many other items, acquired later, had happily survived. The inventory might read as follows: Hashish, 'something special' from Cairo. One small crocodile, Nubian, embalmed. Ten feet of gold-embroidered fabric (wool and silk) from Beirut. Rosaries, eight dozen, from Jerusalem. One rose, ditto, blessed on the Holy Sepulchre. One Turkish scroll, inscribed *Louis Bouilhet* in letters of gold on thick blue paper, from Constantinople. Marble from the Acropolis, two pieces. Marble from the Temple of Apollo, one piece. Embroidered handkerchief, one, purchased from peasant woman on the banks of the River Alpheus. Flowers, for Louis Bouilhet, picked from just by the door of a brothel in Pompeii.

The item that was missing – the thing he regretted most of all – was the long gold-tasselled shawl that Kuchuk-Hanem had worn around her waist the night she danced for her visitors. Flaubert had been desperate to buy it from her, even though, as Du Camp had pointed out mockingly, the shawl was 'nothing special'. In the event he had failed to acquire it. His will had been mysteriously paralysed. 'We would have cut it in two,' he told Louis Bouilhet, 'and you could have had half.'

CHAPTER SIXTEEN

Intimacies

LOUISE Colet was short of money again. Belatedly informed of Flaubert's return from the Orient, she spent the evening of 24 June 1851 reading through her old love letters. 'Painful emotions, tears, regret, he loved me. [. . .]. I was irritable, extravagant, not very intelligent in stratagems for charming him. [. . .] I shall go to Rouen tomorrow.' Putting aside her recent humiliation at the hands of a loudly scoffing Maxime Du Camp, she wrote to Flaubert pleading for one last brief meeting. This was the moment, so she insisted, for the ceremonious return of all letters and love-tokens. Flaubert's reply is lost – perhaps she destroyed it in her passion – but it clearly told her not to come to Rouen.

She decided to go anyway. The train from Paris took only a few hours. Once she was installed in the Hôtel des Anglais she spent the afternoon writing another letter to him. '[. . .] I want to see you before I make a decision which will change the whole course of my life.' She quoted, in self-justification, the grandiose lover's promise he had made five years ago in his very first letter to her. She ate a meal and rearranged her toilette, and then at around six in the evening she went down to the quayside and hired a boatman to take her down the river to Croisset. It was the first time she had ever seen the beautiful white house. The tall windows, the spacious garden, the tree-lined terraces, they spoke of substantial wealth and elegance. She realised, looking through the railings, that she had no idea how she would be received.

In the event she was scarcely received at all. Monsieur, they told her, was not available. After some delay a chambermaid brought word that Flaubert was at dinner with his guests. He could meet her later, in

Rouen. She was to leave her address and depart. In desperation she now began to walk up and down the quayside, on the far side of the tall railings, in full view of the group sitting at dinner, hoping that Flaubert would see her. When he emerged through a door in the garden wall he addressed her as 'Madame' and he was humiliatingly polite. Abjection burning in her cheeks, she made her exit.

When they met again, later that evening, in her room at the Hôtel des Anglais, she wept and she pleaded with him. She wanted to live nearby. She would be available, whenever he wanted to see her, if only he loved her. 'I would be a wretch', he said, 'if I were to deceive you. But there is nothing I can do to make you happy.' He advised her, repeatedly, with a cynical smile, to solve her little problem by marrying her official protector, Victor Cousin. Refusing to accept defeat she walked back with him, along the gaslit boulevards, halfway to Croisset, under the warm, starry splendour of the summer night. Despite all her stratagems, her smiling, seductive, cheerful talk, her tears, her embraces, her sudden tragic intensity, there was no avoiding his final word, an infinitely ambiguous *au revoir*.

She wrote to him but she had no reply and he was still in her thoughts three weeks later when she travelled to London. The Great Exhibition had just opened in the Crystal Palace and she was hoping to turn a good profit by selling her album of celebrity autographs. In Windsor Park she picked a convolvulus, 'for Gustave'. He finally wrote to her, towards the end of July, one month after her peremptory reappearance at his garden gate. 'You must have thought me very cold. I was doing my best to be kind. Tender, no. That would have been an outrageous piece of hypocrisy [. . .]. I like your company when it is not *tempestuous*.' He would soon be leaving for London, he said, just for a few weeks, with his mother, at her insistence, to visit the exhibition.

Flaubert appeared to be in no hurry to see Louise Colet. His going to London rankled with her. Obviously, she declared, he was already tied back to his mother's apron strings. They met again in Paris, early in September, and Louise's journal recorded two pleasant and calmly convivial evenings. 'Gustave arrives, handsome and charming. We go for a walk in the Bois, we have dinner together chez moi, etc. The sadness remains. I feel that I am not loved as I love him [. . .] he was gentle and kind, but no deep feeling [. . .] always so in control of himself [. . .]. He said goodbye to me without any mention of my situation.' Her situation was increasingly uncomfortable. She had only ten francs left to last her the next two weeks.*

FLAUBERT and his mother arrived in London late on the evening of 27 September. The journey from Rouen had taken three days, two days longer than usual, because of the absurd itinerary imposed by an increasingly querulous Madame Flaubert. They took a Sunday walk around Highgate Cemetery and Flaubert mocked its dismal tidiness. It looked as if everyone had died in full evening dress. Flaubert spent Monday in the British Museum, where he took notes but inexplicably failed to introduce himself to Herr Marx, the impoverished but industrious European correspondent of the *New York Tribune*, usually to be found at the same favourite desk, working his way through another large pile of books. Next day mother and son set off in a thick fog towards Hyde Park, to visit the Great Exhibition housed in Paxton's Crystal Palace, 'a truly splendid thing, even though everyone admires it'.

Flaubert made copious notes on the Chinese and Indian exhibits, a most pleasant form of creative procrastination. The artefacts were exquisite, a little mirage of the Orient, all the more evocative for being thus suspended upon the yellow and grey of a London fog. Flaubert was enchanted by the decorative extravagance of carved and gilded ivories, embroidered shawls, stuffed elephants, filigree silver necklaces, chariots, saddles, parasols, fans, musical instruments, and mannequins; fascinated by the women's clothes and the great array of ingenious feminine accessories, the layers of gold-braided white muslin, the sequins, the tassels, the fringes. He took notes. They were minutely objective, designed to seize and hold the forms and the colours of these fantasy objects, to store them away for later use. Flaubertian reverie is always this: documented, verified, *legitimate* reverie. Once you had seen an elephant's harness, then you could embark, properly equipped, on your dream of being a maharajah.

FLAUBERT was taking his time, dallying with Louise, making notes, coaxing his next subject into existence. Du Camp, on the other hand, was a man in a hurry. On his return to Paris he had set to work with fiendish energy. It was time to stop dreaming, time to make a big

---

* Flaubert did lend money to Louise Colet on two occasions over the next few years: 500 francs in August 1852 and then another 800 francs some time late in 1853.

splash, to make a name for himself, to catch up on the political ideas of the day. Installed in his new apartment, with his recent inheritance in his pocket and his ribbon displayed on the lapel of his fashionable coat, Du Camp set about copying up his notes, unpacking his trunk, printing his calotypes, visiting government offices, advising Louise Colet how to handle Flaubert, launching a new liaison, spinning out several old ones, and energetically pursuing the many influential acquaintances he had made in the course of his travels. By the middle of August Du Camp was negotiating the purchase of a literary journal, the *Revue de Paris*. The first monthly number appeared six weeks later, on 1 October, with an editorial by Gautier declaring that politics would never usurp their pages. This was to be a literary journal.*

Flaubert could only look on in wonder. Du Camp regarded himself, only half-jokingly, as the new Rastignac, the aspiring youth at the end of Balzac's *Père Goriot*, the one who was going to *take* Paris single-handed. Somewhere in the midst of all this activity Du Camp lost Flaubert's friendship ring, the ring he had worn ever since 1843. If one believed in omens, this might be significant.

For Flaubert, the week after his return from London was a time of anguish. He was 'used up from over-indulging in solitude, swooningly nervous, troubled by stifled passions, full of uncertainties inside and out'. Getting going was always horribly difficult. He wrote a plaintive, vulnerable letter to his purposeful friend in Paris. Should he go ahead, as Du Camp suggested, and publish *La Tentation de Saint Antoine* in the *Revue de Paris*? Bouilhet was advising him against it. *Saint Antoine* was the wrong debut. It would strike the wrong note. To really launch himself he would have to go and live in Paris, pushing and scheming, just like Max. But the very idea sickened him. It was against his nature. He lacked the worldly qualities: the audacity, the finesse, the savoir-vivre. Flaubert's letter to Du Camp ends on a strangely abject note: I've told you everything. I trust you. Tell me what to do.

Du Camp's reply arrived a week later. It was a twenty-page tirade of a letter in which all the long-suppressed antagonisms of their friendship were released simultaneously into the air. Du Camp, sensitive to the implied criticism of his own conduct, was triumphantly aggressive. He

---

* In the seven years from its launch in 1851 until its suppression in 1858 the *Revue de Paris* published work by many of the major writers of the day: Baudelaire's essays on Edgar Allan Poe, a posthumous tale by Balzac, writings by Nerval and George Sand, as well as *Madame Bovary*.

refused on principle to tell Flaubert what to do. The public, he declared, would find *Saint Antoine* boring. 'If you want success [. . .] come out of that lair of yours because nobody is going to come looking for you in there [. . .].' With every conceivable advantage in life, Flaubert had reached thirty and so far he had done absolutely nothing. Du Camp ended with a confession designed to mortify its recipient. He had discovered, he said, that Flaubert was not the man he had supposed him to be, the man he had loved so dearly. He felt betrayed and that was why he was being so severe.

Had it failed, this great romantic friendship? We may suspect that Du Camp was attacking with questionable vigour the very thing that he himself had once been: the dreamer, the artist, the tragic failure. For several years there would be no more letters, no more meetings, no more pleasant expeditions together. For the moment there was nothing more to be said. Wounded by this acrimonious exchange, both men retreated into a proud silence that neither of them could sustain for ever. Mildly perfidious, Du Camp showed Flaubert's letter, along with his own reply, to Louise Colet. 'Nothing at all about me,' she grumbled. 'What monstrous preoccupation with their own troubles! [. . .] Maxime is right. Gustave dries up those who come near to him [. . .].' Then she wrote him a reproachful letter, to drive the point home.

There was no further communication between Flaubert and Du Camp until June 1852, when Maxime broke the silence. Too soon, as it happened. The exchange of letters that ensued was brief and decisive. Maxime wrote 'bitterly deploring' the fact that Flaubert would not come and live in Paris. 'Only there', he decreed, 'is the breath of life.' Flaubert came back at him with a dignified, good-humoured riposte. Max was 'singing the same old song' and it would have no effect on this listener. 'May I die like a dog rather than try to rush through even one sentence before it is perfectly ripe.' Du Camp's reply, 'good-natured and aggrieved', provoked Flaubert into delivering the epistolary coup de grâce. 'I find your distress on my account comical,' he wrote. 'Reconcile yourself to my premature decay, to my irremediable crustification [. . .]. We are no longer travelling along the same road.'

It was a satisfying gesture. 'I do not think he will forget the shock of a punch like that for some time,' he told Louise Colet. Indeed this exchange marked the end of their passionate friendship; what took its place was a cooler feeling, more wary, less exclusive, less demanding. When they began to meet again, intermittently, throughout the 1850s, they chose neutral ground, the opulent and convivial Paris salon of Madame Sabatier. Perhaps we catch the comic echo of Du Camp's domineering virtuosity in *Madame Bovary*; many of the man's less endearing qualities have been transposed into the ludicrous, eager monologues of Monsieur Homais, scientist, entrepreneur, journalist and master of all things modern.

M*ADAME BOVARY* is a large fact of our cultural history, and therein lies an interesting biographical problem. Flaubert's endless difficulty in writing his first great novel – he managed five words an hour, according to the scurrilous estimate of the de Goncourt brothers – is so well documented and so widely admired that it has acquired the status of a modern legend. Under a confetti of quotation from his letters, Flaubert is drawn into the light as the tormented hero of a parable entitled: *How to be Irreproachably Modern*. One of his favourite mock-heroic phrases, 'the pangs of art' (*les affres de l'Art*), is often taken entirely seriously. The exemplary slenderness of Flaubert's collected works – only four novels, three short stories and one stubbornly amphibious oddity (a novel pretending to be a play) – is held up as a reproach to the obesity of the ideal thirty-, forty-, fifty-, sixty-volume *opus maximus*, the standard by which his contemporaries habitually but mistakenly took the measure of literary achievement.

Dickens and Victor Hugo beware. After Flaubert, abundance such as yours will be regarded as the badge of mediocrity. Real Novels, written under Flaubert's austere patronage, are henceforth required to be ironic, allusive, impersonal. We may allow a devious, redeeming touch of the erotic, to catch the eye of authority. In this odd version of things, both the author and the book that he once thought he was writing disappear from view. The biographical problem is this: how to look at *Madame Bovary* as if it were not yet that large cultural fact, as if indeed it were still being written. We may begin the investigation by paying a visit to a small country graveyard.

T*HESE* days the quiet little country village of Ry is only a fifteen-minute drive away from the busy centre of Rouen. There, in the rich, damp Normandy earth, only a few feet from the door of the church, the best position in the graveyard, lies the body of the young woman who was, so they say, the original Madame Bovary. Here she is. If an imaginary woman can have a real grave, this must be it. Her name is Delphine Delamare. She died in 1848, at the age of twenty-seven, her name wrapped in a little poison cloud of local scandal. People said that Delphine Delamare killed herself. But Delphine's headstone looks new. It can't possibly be nearly 150 years old. The helpful official leaflet tells us that in 1990 she acquired a new tombstone, paid for by the local literary society and the chamber of commerce. The neat black lettering on the yellow slab leaves no room for doubt: *Delphine Delamare née Couturier*. Then, carved below the the real name, there are just the words '*Madame Bovary*'.

The audacity of it all. The village that once gossiped Delphine Delamare into an early grave now earns a good living from cultivating her memory. Ry is where the film crews shoot the outdoor scenes for meticulously authentic TV adaptations of the novel. There's a thriving florist's shop called *Emma's Garden*. A few doors away, housed in a big old barn, there's the Museum of Automata. For ten francs you can see the great scenes of the novel brought to life: the schoolroom, the wedding, the ballroom, the seduction, the amputation, the deathbed, the funeral. You hadn't realised that there were so many crowd scenes in the novel. It's all there. So blazingly, so blatantly literal. Hundreds of doll-sized figures in miniature crinolines and frock coats, moustaches inked on for the boys, pink cheeks ditto for the girls. How Flaubert would have loved such a sweetly lucrative confusion of art and life.

Like Emma Bovary, Delphine Delamare was the unhappy wife of a none-too-successful village doctor. Like Emma, she had expensive tastes, a gullible, adoring husband, a procession of lovers, and a secret, festering pile of debts. Like Emma she met an early and ignominious death, probably at her own hand. Unlike Emma, Delphine Delamare was nothing special. According to Du Camp, she was plump and pale and rather plain, with dull blonde hair and a blotchy complexion. But she oozed sex. Delphine Delamare had a sliding, sinuous walk, a caressing voice and wonderful beseeching eyes that seemed to change colour with the light. Were they grey, green or blue? Emma's eyes change colour too. But it's impossible to sort out the real Delphine. Everyone has embellished her story to make it fit the novel. Delphine Delamare now lies buried beneath a great mound of cultural fantasy. The real source, the elusively plural, miscellaneous, intangible sources must surely lie elsewhere.

ALL through the summer and the autumn of 1851 Flaubert was aware that his thirtieth birthday would soon be upon him. He did not need Du Camp to remind him that he had so far published nothing. He was not yet, in any real sense, an author. He was a man of modest private means who had spent the days of his youth producing voluminous manuscripts of dubious literary value. He had a cupboardful of *juvenilia* but he did not have an audience, and his most recent endeavours had been pronounced a disaster by his closest friends. It was now supremely important to make the right choice of subject, to find the tone, the colour, the milieu. Above all, it had to be something that was not *Saint Antoine* in disguise. It had to be something temperamentally uncongenial, something low, modern and prosaic, something indisputably mired in the real.

It was Louis Bouilhet, as far as we can tell, who set Flaubert the task of treating the sordid story of Delphine Delamare in the manner of Balzac. We don't know precisely when the subject was 'set'; we know that Flaubert was still undecided in July and that he finally began work, one Friday evening in September 1851, a few days before his excursion to London in the company of his mother. By the end of the first day of writing, he already had a sharply prescient sense of the stylistic difficulty of the enterprise: 'I'm afraid of lapsing into Paul de Kock or doing a Chateaubriand-ified Balzac.* The sense of terrifying initial difficulty, familiar to all writers, did not subside. If anything it was exacerbated; it became the perpetual gloomy condition of his writing.

In November he told Louise Colet that he was 'progressing painfully [. . .] spoiling considerable quantities of paper'. He also mentioned the fact, most alarming to Louise, that Caroline's new governess had recently arrived in Croisset. 'Her *physique*', he told her, 'does not impress me for all that. I have never been less venereal.' Ignoring her reproaches, he announced that he was coming to Paris. He had 'something important' to tell her. Perplexed by his mysterious manner, Louise Colet lay awake tormenting herself with the suspicion that Flaubert *was* interested in the new governess and that he had come to break the news to her. At some point, according to her journal, she conceived the idea of killing him. Rather that than see him in the arms of another woman. She put on her velvet dress and concealed her weapon, a dagger.

* De Kock – the evocative name is actually Dutch – was the contemporary author of hugely popular, discreetly pornographic novels.

When she received him at nine in the evening he told her that he had made his solemn decision: he wasn't going to publish *Saint Antoine*.

He returned several times over the next few days. As they walked together through the Bois de Boulogne in the pale November sunlight Flaubert seemed to be overwhelmed by weariness and distress. Then, to her surprise, he poured out all the bitterness that lay upon his heart, 'disturbed the dregs [. . .] that life leaves in all of us, the stuff we're meant to leave alone'. The smell was truly foul, she thought, yet she responded magnanimously, with 'deep words of tenderness which moved him'. 'If you are not resolved to die,' she told him, 'then have the strength to live and to overcome your suffering and to spare those who love you.' This was a new intensity, a new sympathy, a possible exception to Flaubert's tragi-comic vision of human egocentricity. Warmed by her words, he was oddly ceremonious in his gratitude. 'Oh, dear Louise, if you knew what blessings I call upon you before God!' They spent a passionate, animated final evening together and he promised to send her the manuscript of *Novembre*. When it arrived a week later she thought it feeble, apart from the inset story told in the woman's voice.

Driven from Croisset by the all-invading damp of the Normandy winter, Flaubert returned to Paris some weeks later, in the company of his mother. He was just in time to witness the coup d'état that began in the early hours of 2 December, decorating the boulevards with fresh blood, republican, socialist and patriotic. Flaubert described the coup itself in exuberantly facetious tones: 'I was nearly knocked out several times, not to mention almost being slashed, shot at or blown to bits, there being something for every taste [. . .]. But I had a perfect view: it was just the price of a good ticket. Providence, knowing how much I love the picturesque, has always contrived to send me to the first-night performances when they are worth the bother. This time I was not disappointed; it was superb.'

Flaubert had no tears to spare for the failed political experiment of the Second Republic; his mind was fixed on that supremely uncomfortable moment in every man's sentimental history, the thirtieth birthday, 'that fatal thirtieth year [. . .] the age at which you settle down; you take a wife, you find a job [. . .] very few people [. . .] do not become bourgeois at the age of thirty.'

The fall of the Republic coincided with a unique 'six weeks of intimacy' between the epistolary couple, an odd coincidence of the sentimental and historical that Flaubert would draw upon in *L'Education sentimentale*. It was precious, but it was scarcely perfect, as Louise Colet realised even at the time. 'Gustave loves me [. . .] in a deeply selfish way, to gratify his senses and read me his works.' His physical passion could not make up for his lack of tenderness. His vulnerable, confidential habit did not survive many days and nights; their intimacy soon decayed in mutual reproaches. 'You have hurt yourself on the secrets of my heart,' Flaubert said. He was surprised at his own audacity in exposing his sorrows. He had shown himself, 'so naked, so stripped bare, so weak'. The leper, he observed, may feel angry towards the kind soul who dresses his sores.

When Flaubert left Paris, to return to his 'long habitual existence' in Croisset, he promised to give Louise Colet his Egyptian ring and to write her a letter that would explain his feelings. He failed in both of these promises; instead he sent her the bulky manuscript of *L'Education sentimentale* (1846) and a number of 'admirable pages on the subject of art'. He didn't return to Paris for nearly three months.

CHAPTER SEVENTEEN

The Pangs of Art

CROISSET was horribly damp. On the ground floor the moisture ran down the walls. Damp houses, damp souls. This became one of his favourite images, woven almost invisibly into the writing of *Madame Bovary*, so perfectly did it evoke the sepulchral, buried-alive quality of long-stifled sorrow.

They lit fires in every room of the house and then it was several days before he could make a new start on *Madame Bovary*. We have to imagine the smell of the place, a rich, warm, damp blend of riverbank, garden leaf-mould, ancient staircase, leather-bound folio, authorial pipe smoke and *cuisine bourgeoise*. We also have to remember what a plaintive and lugubrious company of family ghosts, the living and the dead, was forever hovering just beyond the spacious charmed circle of Flaubert's writing table. The father and the sister, both vividly present in effigy; the little orphan girl, that classic nineteenth-century figure, now nearly six years old; Hamard, her useless father, steadily drinking himself to death; and Madame Flaubert, ageing in body and mind, exhausted by insomnia, anxiously watching over her precious widow's capital as it trickled away, month by month.

Apart from his late-night letters to Louise Colet, apart from reading Shakespeare and Goethe in the evenings, the only authentic relaxation came on Sundays when Flaubert tasted the pleasures of masculine conversation with his weekend house guest, Bouilhet. And Louis Bouilhet had published. He was launched on a brilliant career. 'Only me, still

with a non-position, a thoughtless schoolboy as if I were still 18.' On a
bad day it felt as if his life had stopped, as if only the writing and his
mysterious malady were real. 'I am', he told Louise Colet self-
disparagingly, 'a creature of the quill. I feel through it, because of it, in
relation to it and much more with it.'

After two major failures, *L'Education sentimentale* (1846) and *La
Tentation de Saint Antoine*, this would be his third try. 'Time to pull it
off,' he told himself, 'either that or throw myself out of the window.' He
was dismayed by Louise Colet's 'excessive enthusiasm' for parts of
L'Education sentimentale. That was not him, not any longer. 'What I'd
like to do,' he told her teasingly,

is a book about nothing, a book with no external attachment, one which
would hold together by the internal strength of its style, as the earth floats in
the air unsupported, a book that would have no subject at all or at least one
in which the subject would be almost invisible, if that were possible [. . .].
There are no beautiful or sordid subjects and one could almost
establish it as an axiom that, from the point of view of pure Art there is no
such thing as a subject, style being solely itself an absolute way of seeing
things.

Much quoted for its agreeable proto-modernist emphasis on the
absolute power of writing, the whole passage arises, in fact, from an
awkward early stage in the writing of *Madame Bovary*. It's not a manifesto, not a polemical preface of the kind so favoured by the previous
generation of French Romantics. It's a clandestine declaration of artistic independence issued at a time when the French state was breathing
heavily upon its writers. It's also a symptom of the impatience, the
revulsion that Flaubert felt towards the *low* subject that he had taken
on. His evolving scenarios for the novel show that the subject, in all its
lowness, was all too intrusive. Only the fastidious magic of style could
transform such rubbish.

Three months into the writing, Flaubert announced that with
Bouilhet's approval he had found the right tone: 'No lyricism, no
digressions, personality of author absent.' He had also slowed down to
five or six pages a week. He was writing tirelessly, hardly needing any
sleep, so energised that he could be found at 1.30 in the morning reciting Ronsard at the top of his voice. He was exploring Emma Bovary's
early life, 'trying to enter into the world of young girls' dreams', reading
books from his own childhood, 'tales of shipwreck and piracy', with

the engravings that he had coloured in when he was seven years old, feeling once again 'the terrors that came to me as a little boy'.

Madame Bovary, as we can already see, was never 'a book about nothing'. It was nourished from so many sources, both intimate and remote, that it appeared not to be imprinted with the literary personality of its author. This impersonality, a simple name for a complex attitude, was not mere self-effacement; it was a dynamic form of self-multiplication. Writing to Louise Colet, a woman rarely to be caught in the act of self-effacement, he explained its advantages succinctly: 'Disperse yourself into everything and your characters will come alive, and instead of the eternal declamatory personality [. . .] your work will be crowded with human faces.' The Flaubertian artist is to be everywhere and nowhere, the invisible power, the immanent deity, manifest only in his creation. Like Shakespeare, but unlike Byron, he should 'somehow manage to make posterity think he never existed'.

Be that as it may, these sublimities could never be achieved by sleight of hand; they were the consummation of the heroically messy *physiological* labour of writing. Making books was a bodily process: 'You have to drink up an ocean and then piss it all out again.' Publishing one's books was most unnatural, a crime against elementary physical modesty, like letting someone see your bum. Ideally, said Flaubert, he wanted to be buried in an enormous tomb along with all his never-published manuscripts, like a savage buried alongside his horse.

L OUISE COLET's reaction to her lover's fantasy of perfect silence is not known. She was busy organising a Parisian literary soirée for Louis Bouilhet. He had finally published his long poem and now it was to be recited before a select audience, including Flaubert, by the actress Edma Roger des Genettes. It was a brilliant occasion, a triumph; Bouilhet fell for the actress and wrote her an ardent sonnet that was only slightly spoilt by his mistake over the colour of his muse's eyes. Flaubert, back in Paris for the occasion, took Bouilhet off to the Café des Anglais to celebrate. There they sat up through the night, talking art and love, until six in the morning. Then they went to the Place de la Concorde to watch the dawn.

This was the literary life, the metropolitan glamour that Bouilhet and Flaubert had once imagined as provincial schoolboys in the 1830s. It was Bouilhet's first taste of success, his first step along the bright, pleasant path that quickly led down into the boisterous, commercial-literary underworld of nineteenth-century Paris. No place for the squeamish, this hustling, backstabbing, entrepreneurial world of journalism and the theatre. No place for Flaubert. The subsequent Parisian career of his best friend, waiting around in editorial offices, courting influential critics, turning out dramatic verse by the yard, scraping a meagre, genteel living from endless mental labour, stood as an awful warning. It confirmed Flaubert's suspicion that he was better off at home, polishing his syntax in the leisurely isolation of Croisset. The grim spectacle of Bouilhet's servitude would always give Flaubert a sharper sense of his own artistic liberty.

In 1862 Flaubert wrote, praising Louis Bouilhet's fortitiude:

The life of a man of letters is now [. . .] a painful business [. . .]. Innumerable obstacles impede this career in which one is assailed by calumny and slandered by stupidity as one is obliged to trample over those Lilliputian vanities that writhe in the dust! [. . .] once the task is completed nothing is achieved. Then one is subject to indifference, to rejection, to disdain, to insult, to the promiscuity of banal applause or to the sarcasm of the malicious [. . .]. –

For the moment, 'the promiscuity of banal applause' might suffice.

BACK in Croisset, Flaubert was subject once again to the pangs of art; he was now endeavouring, he said, to 'walk on a hair across the double abyss of lyricism and vulgarity (which I want to blend in a narrative analysis)'. He was working his way towards the ballroom scene, the dramatic climax of the first part of his novel; for want of more recent experience, he was drawing on his own exquisitely vivid memories of a grand country-house ball he had once attended as a schoolboy. The scene he was composing involved such a quantity of 'banal dialogue' that it left him lying on his divan for five hours in a state of 'imbecile inertia.' His concentration was ever more fragile and he announced (to Louise) that he needed a 'completely immobile existence' to be able to write at all. 'I think best lying on my back with my eyes closed.'

Just when the spark had almost disappeared, everything caught fire again and Flaubert entered a state of glorious creative exaltation, 'a permanent state of fury which sometimes turns to impotent tears [. . .] a frenzied perverted love [. . .].' How intimately, in his letters, do we witness the high romantic drama of his writing. He sprawls on his couch in despair, hating the insane pride that sends him chasing after shadows. Fifteen minutes later his heart is beating for joy. 'I had to go and get my handkerchief. The tears were running down my face. I had

205

written myself into a state, and it was immensely enjoyable [. . .] a state of the soul so far above ordinary life, a state in which fame counts for nothing and even happiness is irrelevant.' To such a man, subject to such ecstasies of the imagination, shielding theories of impersonality were psychologically indispensable.

When Flaubert is in full flight, expounding the glory and the misery of art, celebrating the high spiritual vocation of the artist, it is easy to forget, as we are drawn into his passion, that the whole performance is confined, discursively, to a series of private letters. It is all taking place out of sight, offstage, far away from the contemporary printed page. And then we see that there is good reason for Flaubert's public silence on the subject of his art. He knew that there had been all too much eloquent talk, ever since 1830, about art and artists. He realised, some time in the late 1840s, that the grandiose cultural fantasy of the artist was discredited. Such stuff could be healthily and invisibly ventilated in letters to friends, so as to keep it out of the real writing. Sober authorial reticence was to be the new rule. Accordingly, after the unpublished juvenilia, not only are there no 'opinions' on view, there are no artists playing the leading roles. They have been banished and they are only allowed back, in very mediocre guise, on the pages of L'Education sentimentale.

The creative excitement of the ball scene also engendered the idea of another book, known only from an undated three-page outline as La Spirale. Prompted by reading Dante's Inferno, he envisaged 'a large fantastical metaphysical loudmouth novel' that would prove that 'happiness is in the imagination'. In his real life the hero would be reviled, imprisoned, and ultimately thrown into a lunatic asylum; but in his imagined life he would achieve a triumphant serenity. La Spirale evolved over many years in the background as 'a novel about madness, or rather about the way in which you go mad'. But it remained unwritten, for good reason: 'because it is a subject that frightens me, for health reasons, I shall have to wait until I am far enough away from those experiences to be able to induce them in myself artificially, ideally, and therefore without risk to myself or to my work'.

LOUISE COLET, the original recipient of all the above, took no comfort from Flaubert's heartfelt passion for the imaginary woman he was creating at his writing table. Immaterial rivals were the worst kind. 'If Gustave loved me better,' she wrote in her journal, 'how I would open my heart to him [. . .].' She had learnt to hold back, learnt not to pester him with her affections and her sentimental enthusiasms. Flaubert had assured her that some time soon, in a year or so, he intended to live part of the year in Paris. Things would be different. Meanwhile he could just manage 3 June, at the hotel in Mantes.

Connoisseur of the triangular-erotic, Flaubert suddenly found himself, in the summer of 1852, in an unexpected position. Louise Colet informed him, with aggravating detail, that he now had a rival in the unlikely, debauched figure of Alfred de Musset. This news had a splendid effect. Flaubert the cool, teasing sensualist suddenly discovered that he was tempestuously, ridiculously jealous. His imagination was thrown to a fine romantic frenzy and he began to devise fantastic scenes of vengeance.

The tragi-comedy of jealousy had its origin in Louise Colet's growing dismay at the behaviour of her absentee lover. She resented his stubborn, calculating preference for *coitus interruptus*; she resented the fact that he never took up the opportunity to give her the money she always needed; she resented the lengthy serial monologue on 'Art' that made up the bulk of his letters. She had had enough, she said, of that 'jealous selfishness that delights in perpetual ruminations on its own personality'. One night together in a hotel in Mantes every six weeks, *if the book were going well*, was not what she meant by love. It was an insult.

When Alfred de Musset entered the scene, Louise Colet was more than usually in need of admiration. She was in the audience on the day of Musset's reception into the Académie Française. She praised Musset's speech in her next letter to Croisset and Flaubert responded with a long, loud denunciation of Musset, speeches and public honours. 'These things', he said, 'make me feel ill'. At this point Flaubert knew only that de Musset was interested in Louise Colet. He was not sure what she would make of it.*

Musset was an easy target for the fusillade of youthful disdain. Louise Colet had first met Musset in 1836, the year she arrived in Paris, when he was still the golden boy of French Romanticism. By 1852 Alfred de Musset was in his early forties and his best work already lay far behind him. Several decades of hectic dissipation had left their mark on that once-poetic countenance. Gaunt, ailing, and half-impotent,

---

* There may be much of de Musset in the love-talk that Rodolphe Boulanger, the local squire, uses to seduce Emma Bovary. Rodolphe's professional speciality is exalted second-hand romantic sentiment masking commonplace cynicism.

a dishevelled figure in his threadbare clothes, de Musset stank perpetually of absinthe.* Trading relentlessly on what remained of his genius, ever more petulant and tearful in his narcissism, he had less than five years left to live.

By the end of June, with no prospect of another meeting in Mantes until the beginning of August, Louise Colet's tentative flirtation with de Musset was beginning to warm up. Her aim was to persuade him to recite her prize poem at the next meeting of the Academy; her strategy was to work him into a desperate passion by teasing him with her disdain. He arrived on her doorstep, 'breathless, coughing, spitting, apparently drunk', demanding a glass of wine. Louise's journal records the following exchange: 'He said, "Since you preoccupy me so, it won't be long before I write to you saying: will you or will you not?" I said that we had other matters to see to and I asked him again, "Will you read my poem?" He replied, "We shall see. I'm going to the Jardin des Plantes to look at the lions, come with me and we can decide standing by the lion's cage." '

They gazed at the great lion and Louise reached impulsively through the bars of the cage to stroke its neck. The lion tried to bite off her hand. Louise fainted. De Musset, pale with fear, had to rescue her. To commemorate this incident both parties subsequently wrote sonnets of the decorously emblematic kind. Then they went to look at the bears, a sight that may have reminded Louise Colet of Flaubert. De Musset remarked fastidiously on how they stank. 'It's because they eat carrion and they're saturated in it.' 'Quite so,' replied Louise. 'People always smell of the things they consume.' De Musset took this, not unreasonably, as a reference to the effects of his drinking. His face darkened. There were no more little gallantries. She was puzzled. He drank a glass of absinthe and his speech became slurred. He announced that he did not intend to read her poem, and she then abandoned him outside the Café de la Régence, though trailing an invitation to call on her again.

Louise Colet recorded all these details in her journal and immediately posted a copy off to Flaubert. Reading her narrative, along with de Musset's recent letters to her (also enclosed) he found that it had 'a strange effect' on him. This was no doubt what she had intended.

* Absinthe, the undoing of Verlaine and many lesser nineteenth-century Parisian poets, was a pungent yellow-green liqueur that turned to an opalescent, cloudy white when mixed with water. An evil brew of wormwood, liquorice, fennel and aniseed, absinthe was so toxic it caused hallucinations and eventual psychoses.

Flaubert for once commended her prose as a fine piece of writing – 'It's gripping!' – and entered vividly into the drama of her flirtation by mocking de Musset's extravagant claims to sexual prowess and casting doubt on his ability to read Classical Greek. He advised her to play de Musset along and then dismiss him at the last minute, once he had read her poem. Flaubert even invented some stinging farewell lines for her to speak. For the moment at least his jealousy was under control.

Events in Paris soon pushed him towards the edge. Unknown to Flaubert, Louise Colet and de Musset had become lovers and their affair now lurched towards its brisk unhappy finale. One evening early in July they were returning from the Bois de Boulogne together in a carriage. De Musset had been drinking heavily and he began to rant and mock when Louise Colet refused to let him spend the night with her. Enraged and humiliated, she jumped from the moving carriage, landing on her back in the road and injuring her knees. The carriage stopped. The driver came to see if she was hurt. 'Tell him you couldn't find me,' she said, and began limping home through the empty moonlit streets, swearing that she would never see him again.

Before her knees had time to heal, Louise Colet sent Flaubert a full account of the scene in the carriage along with two of de Musset's begging letters. Even though she did not tell him the full story – 'I omitted my momentary lapse' – Flaubert's ironic poise collapsed. Temporarily unable to work on *Madame Bovary*, he poured out his jealous passion into a rapid series of letters to Louise. 'You have truly made me suffer strangely this morning [. . .] that man will one day have to pay me back, one way or another [. . .]. I would thrash him with great pleasure [. . .]. I saw you for a moment as you lay dying in the road, with the wheel passing over your stomach, the horse's hoof in your face, and you, in the gutter [. . .].' This was almost what Louise wanted to hear. She had shaken him, but still he had not relented of his selfish refusal to allow her nearer. 'Not a word', she lamented, 'on the subject of [. . .] Croisset and his mother. He keeps so much inaccessible; why should I give my heart over to him?'

Adopting her best tone of heroic indignation, Louise Colet wrote to tell Alfred de Musset that 'good relations are henceforth impossible between us [. . .]. I bear no grudge against you, but I ask you not to write to me again and not to visit me.' Two days later she invited him to supper, an indication of how much she was enjoying this drama of insult and ultimatum. In a mood of cold fury, following all these events closely, Flaubert confessed to something he still refused to call jealousy. It was a feeling of powerlessness, of scandal, of personal outrage. But then, with a wonderful gesture, the jealous lover gave way to the artist and Flaubert magically changed places.

I said to myself: indeed I spend so little time with her. So seldom. And after all I am not what might be described as a pleasant man. (If I were a woman I certainly would not want me for a lover. A flirtation, yes, but intimacy, no.) So on one of her empty days another man came along, a famous man, pleading like a little boy [. . .]. Would she do better to give me up? Wouldn't he make her happier?

Acting upon these thoughts, Flaubert promised somewhat unconvincingly to be with her 'in about four weeks' time' and then offered for the first time to lend her half of what was left from his inheritance.

Flaubert reported that an 'Olympian thirty-six hours' of writing had left him with a serene feeling of immense power. It was a joyful, physical affair of the voice, the authorial voice conferring life on the written word: 'Don't know why my chest hasn't caved in, I've been bellowing four hours without stopping. Must be that my lungs are bound in triple layers of brass [. . .].' Flaubert doesn't often mention the triumphs of writing. If he dwells upon the torment it may be because he wished to avoid sounding too promiscuously bardic, like Victor Hugo.

By the end of July Flaubert had finished the first part of *Madame Bovary*. The story moved too slowly, he could see that from reading it through. But it was 'impossible', he said, 'to give psychological analysis the rapidity, the clarity, the passion of a purely dramatic narrative'. And the writing was flawed. There was something wrong, something that would need changing, in almost every sentence. He spent a 'laborious, arid and humiliating' week going through it. This, he complained, was what came of writing books on subjects for which he had no real aptitude. After reading it aloud to Louis Bouilhet, he took the train to Paris and arrived with his nerves thoroughly on edge.

There in his hotel, late one night, Flaubert had an epileptic attack. Louise Colet, the only terrified witness, wrote the following account of the incident in her journal: 'He begs me not to call for help; his convulsions, the noises in his throat, the foam coming out of his mouth, the marks his nails left in my arm. He came round after about ten minutes, vomiting. I assured him that his attack had lasted only a few seconds and that he hadn't foamed at the mouth. Profound compassion and tenderness that I feel for him [. . .].'

She remembered the weeks that followed as the best they had ever known together. Released from his writing, piqued by his jealousy, Flaubert allowed Louise – however briefly – to mother him. He was 'more loving, more passionate than ever', more conventionally attentive, more willing to brave his mother's disapproval. He was also more often there. He gave her an amber bracelet, lent her 500 francs and promised to buy copies of her books. On their last evening, 'He said: in a year's time we'll be together. Patience, cheerfulness, pride. I shall follow his advice.'

IT was not to be. Once he was back in Croisset Flaubert seemed to turn against Louise Colet with an equal and opposite force. He wrote vehemently critical letters, taking her to task for small literary indiscretions. Chastened and feeling betrayed, she hastily repaid a significant portion of his recent loan. Plainly he would not be back in Paris for some time. 'Don't keep telling me that you want me,' he wrote to her. 'What's the use? Since things cannot be any other way, since I cannot work in any other way.' She must see that work came before everything else.

Labouring furiously at his vocation, intoxicated by solitude, Flaubert honoured and deplored Art (capital 'A') in equal measure. Art was a temple, a mystery, a priesthood, a thing beyond price. Art was also a powerful device for sucking out all the deep subterranean shit that lay hidden in the nineteenth-century soul, a sewage pump for a repressed bourgeois culture. Art was beauty and truth: sweet intimations of infinity and a bitter tincture of satiric realism, swirled up together in a copious solution of comedy. Strong medicine indeed.

This new mood, this 'aesthetic mysticism', served many purposes. It dignified – but also exaggerated – his isolation; it consecrated his apparently gratuitous literary activity; it was a refuge from Louise, from the intimacy she demanded; it was an escape from the busy pleasures of Paris, the kind that held Du Camp enthralled; it was also a mildly defiant way of 'cultivating one's garden' at a moment when infamy, in the plumply farcical person of Napoléon III, sat enthroned in the borrowed costume of France's national hero.

Flaubert was bitterly amused, as he embarked on the second part of

Madame Bovary, to observe the new emperor of the French busily consolidating his power while the liberal opposition, self-important but impotent, denounced him as loudly as they dared. The French nation, said Flaubert, seemed to be sinking into pious, reactionary conformity. Serious art would soon be impossible. The state would be eager to get its hands on the arts. Look out, he predicted, for masterpieces designed to raise public morale, expurgated editions of the classics, bland official résumés and rewrites. It didn't take long. In August 1854 the members of the Rouen Academy assembled for the public recitation of a verse dialogue in praise of private property, generously larded with allusions to the Emperor.

Henceforth, it was Art against Empire. Croisset, whatever the domestic reality of the place, could now signify an idea of Art. Flaubert's art, as Louise Colet was probably the first to point out, is not in any sense progressive, populist, or democratic-indignant. It is primarily a tragic-satiric vision of desire and destiny, and it draws its secret force from the argument in every bourgeois heart between the lawyer and the poet.

'Let the Empire march on,' Flaubert told Louise Colet in November 1852, the day after a plebiscite had endorsed Napoléon III. 'Close your door, climb to the very top of the ivory tower, the last step, the one nearest to heaven [. . .]. You can see the stars shining bright and you can't hear the racket that the turkeys are making.' Ivory towers are a familiar feature of the modern landscape, so familiar we forget that Flaubert's ivory tower offered a splendid view of the turkey-farm below.

He realised what was required. 'What the modern world needs is [. . .] an Aristophanes, but he would be stoned to death in public.'* Something more devious might do the job better. One month into the Second Empire, prompted by 'an atrocious urge to shower insults all over the human race', Flaubert announced the revival of a long-cherished project, the *Dictionnaire des idées reçues*. 'You would find there,' Flaubert explained,

in alphabetical order, on all possible topics, everything you ought to say if you want to be taken for a decent and a likeable person [. . .] once you had read it

---

* Flaubert was delighted to discover Aristophanes in September 1847: 'It's splendid, witty, and passionate. But it isn't decent, it isn't moral, it isn't even polite; it's utterly sublime.' It was the wild, festive impropriety of ancient drama that most appealed to him: 'In Aristophanes,' he said, 'they shit on the stage.'

you wouldn't dare speak a word for fear that one of its phrases would find its way spontaneously into your mouth [. . .]. The preface I find particularly exciting, and as I imagine it (a whole book in itself) no law could touch me even though I would be attacking everything. It would be the historic justification of everything respectable. I would demonstrate that majorities have always been in the right, minorities always in the wrong. I would sacrifice the great men to all the imbeciles [. . .] and it would all be done in an outrageous style [. . .] ironic and raucous from beginning to end.

All through the next three years, while Flaubert was principally occupied with *Madame Bovary*, both the Dictionary and its preface were bubbling away in the background. The whole project was a relief, an escape from the severe constraints imposed by a book 'so perfectly [. . .] laced up and corseted tight enough to strangle you.' In the Dictionary, as in his letters, he could vent the indignation that might otherwise poison his mind. He worked quickly. Within a few months he had the Preface sketched out, he had 'done the plan, put it down in writing.'

Though this sketch has not survived, we may guess at its tone and colour from a letter written some weeks later in which Flaubert launches a fearsome, thundering tirade against the nineteenth century and its foolish passions. Flaubert's catalogue of his favourite stupidities includes table-turning, popular remedies (tie a leg of lamb to the tail of a kite and send it up into the clouds to be devoured by the cholera), sea-serpents, giant cabbages, magic snails, and patented razors. More seriously, what is to become of a nation that inscribes the motto *Liberty, Equality, Fraternity* above its prisons and hospitals? Flaubert plays the angry giant in the grip of an epic theme. He fulminates ('splendid verb') prodigiously. He discharges his elemental *private* bolt of comic energy. Is he joking? We cannot tell. But *he* knows what he's doing and where it comes from. 'I'm talking a load of nonsense,' he writes, 'but even so the only lesson to be drawn from the current regime (based on the pretty motto *vox populi vox Dei*) is that the notion of the People is just as clapped out as that of the king.'

Much of the energetic comic spirit of the Dictionary was immediately deflected into a character who now made his debut, Yonville's pharmacist, Monsieur Homais. Though Homais scarcely figures in Flaubert's meticulous scenarios, he dominates Part Two of *Madame Bovary*. Talker, busybody, village polymath, reader of newspapers, encyclopaedic man of science, maker of chocolate and mixer of potions, Homais sprang from nowhere, from the deepest place of the imagination, a gigantic, joyful afterthought. 'I stink of my Homais,' said his creator.

Progressing at five hundred *irreproachable* words a week, it took Flaubert four and a half years to finish *Madame Bovary*. For all but the final year of the writing, Flaubert's letters to Louise Colet offer an intimate week-by-week diary of artistic difficulty. The scene of creation, the bright, spacious, silent room in which the book was written, the goose-quills in the brass bowl on the table, the neat stack of manuscript pages, the green morocco divan, the white bearskin in front of the fire – they are all so indelibly *there*, pencilled into the margins of a novel that otherwise parades its impersonality.

By the middle of the year 1853 Flaubert had arrived at the most difficult, the most lyrically erotic episodes of his story. The writing seemed to go ever more slowly as he struggled to transform his commonplace theme of adultery into the quixotic prose-poem that would seduce every reader by its psychological finesse. Before he could finally throw himself into the deep fires of passion he had to overcome an imaginative blankness, an inner resistance that disguised itself in various forms, of which abject despair was only the most obvious. Flaubert portrays himself 'sprawling in every possible position all over my room in search of what to say [. . .] nothing in this book originates from within me; never before has my personality been so useless to me.' Sometimes he disappeared so successfully into his creation that he lost the way out: 'My nerves were so on edge that my mother, who came into my room at ten o'clock to say goodnight, made me give an appalling cry of terror, which frightened her as well. For a good while my heart was racing because of it all and I needed about a quarter of an hour to recover. That is how absorbed I am when I'm working.'

Flaubert insisted, in the face of self-doubt, that all his endless preliminaries, all the extended expositions of character, landscape, and place, as well as the novel's lengthy and mournful conclusion, were in the service of a curious human truth: 'People carry a slumbering passion for twenty years then it breaks out and dies in a single day.' Is that the definition of bourgeois tragedy? Or is it a throwaway single-sentence autobiography? Whichever it may be, to portray both of these phases, both the long slumber and the day of the awakening, required an audaciously sustained inwardness in the construction of character.

There was also the risk that plot-hungry readers might leave before passion erupted.

He reached the high point, the explosion, towards the end of the year, on the night of 23 December 1853. The Big Fuck (*La Baisade*), as Flaubert mischievously referred to it, takes place in a forest on an autumn afternoon. It's a triumph of erotic evocation: 'no crude details, no licentious images; the lasciviousness has to be in the emotions'. True to his intentions, oceanic post-coital reverie has never been depicted so vividly:

The evening shadows were falling, the sun on the horizon, passing through the branches, dazzled her eyes. Here and there, all around her, among the leaves or on the earth, patches of light were trembling, just as if hummingbirds, in flight, had scattered their feathers. Silence everywhere; strange tenderness coming from the trees; she felt her heart, as it began to beat again, and the blood flowing in her body like a river of milk. And she heard in the distance, beyond the wood, on the far hills, a vague and lingering cry, a murmuring voice, and she listened to it in silence, melting like music into the last fading vibrations of her tingling nerves. Rodolphe, a cigar between his teeth, was mending one of the two broken reins with his little knife.

Flaubert recorded his own ferocious imaginative excitement in the letter that he wrote at two in the morning, after twelve hours of writing:

I've reached the Big Fuck, I'm right in the middle of it. We are in a sweat and our heart is nearly in our mouth. This has been one of the rare days of my life which I have spent in a state of complete Enchantment, from beginning to end. Just now, around six o'clock, at the moment when I wrote the phrase 'nervous attack', I was so carried away, I was making such a racket, and feeling so intensely what my little woman was feeling that I began to fear I was about to have one myself. I stood up from my writing table and I opened the window to calm myself down. My head was spinning [. . .]. I am like a man who has just come too much (if you will forgive me the expression) I mean a sort of lassitude which is full of exhilaration. [. . .] It is a delectable thing, writing, not having to be yourself, being able to circulate in amongst the whole creation that you are describing. Today [. . .] as a man and as a woman, as lover and mistress both, I have been out riding in a forest on an autumn afternoon, and it was the horses, the leaves, the wind, the words that they spoke to each other and the red sunlight that made them half-close their eyes, eyes that were brimming with love.

The fact that Flaubert so nearly lost his head whilst writing this scene adds a certain weight to his famously evasive remark, 'Madame Bovary, c'est moi.' Emma's imminent nervous attack disappears from the published text of the novel, but in the draft version we find: 'It was not the walk or the weight of her coat that made her pant, but a strange anxiety, an anguish of her whole being, as if she were about to have a nervous attack.' Flaubert often suggested, fancifully, that there might be a physiology of style. 'Just as the pearl is the oyster's affliction, so style is perhaps the discharge from a deeper wound.' He never explored the idea. Was he aware that this was a metaphor best left alone, tightly folded upon itself?

IT is a simple, unpleasant, seldom acknowledged fact that a man in the middle of writing his book is not always easy to be with. (Though perhaps a man in the middle of *not* writing his book is considerably worse.) Consider, in the light of this fact, the scene that unfolded between Flaubert and Louise Colet in November 1852. They were together again in Mantes, neutral ground, for six days. They had not seen each other since the passionate intimacies of August – a gap, as she would remind him, of eleven smouldering, unhappy weeks. They were on their way, probably in a hired carriage, to visit the chateau at Roche-Guyon, a few miles downstream from Mantes. Flaubert, though sitting beside her, seemed to be elsewhere, perfectly indifferent. He was aware of her voice, but not her words. 'It happens to me,' he explained some days later, 'particularly when I am in the presence of nature and my mind is blank; I go into a speechless, witless stupor [. . .]. I was in that state on the way to Roche-Guyon and your voice talking to me all the time and especially the way you touched me on the shoulder to attract my attention, it caused me real pain. How I had to restrain myself from brutally sending you packing.' It was not her fault. It was, he explained, a symptom of his affliction. 'Sometimes I curl up so tightly that I disappear into my shell, and everything that people do to make me come out again feels painful.'

Whatever the explanation, this disheartening scene pointed towards the distant moment at which Flaubert, like Rodolphe – his fictional counterpart in this respect – would indeed 'brutally send her packing'. His self-withholding, and especially his perpetually broken promises on the subject of her meeting his mother, all amounted, said Louise Colet, to 'a savage obstinacy'. It was a sentimental impasse. It might not change for year and years. Their love was now a tissue of elaborate letters, brief passions, promises renewed, recriminations repeated, apologies and more apologies, indignantly sarcastic or falteringly authentic. In the autumn of 1853 Louise Colet wrote wearily on the envelope of a letter from Croisset: 'Yet another year! I can see it plainly. You will always put art before feeling [. . .].' Except that something was about to change.

It began on the morning of 17 October 1853 when Flaubert said farewell to Louis Bouilhet. Eight years of Sunday conversations were at an end. Bouilhet was going to Paris, hoping to make his name. He would undoubtedly be calling upon the help of Louise Colet; indeed, he had been conducting a quaintly flirtatious correspondence with her for several years. It was innocuous, pedantic stuff, along the lines of: 'If poor old Saint Antony had been tempted by a devil as lovely as you I very much doubt whether he would have made it into heaven.' Louis Bouilhet addressed her as 'Dear Sister', to signal the official limits of his desire.

But the letters that passed between Bouilhet and Louise Colet were also mildy conspiratorial. Inevitably, confidentially, they had talked about Flaubert. The effects of Bouilhet's visiting Louise Colet were rather more dramatic. As soon as he arrived in Paris Bouilhet began to play the go-between with malevolent enthusiasm. He showed Flaubert Louise Colet's letters, in which she complained about him. He passed on her remarks, which Flaubert found 'upsetting'. Disconcerted and feeling 'desiccated' by his solitude, Flaubert spent the evening talking to his mother about Louise Colet. Madame Flaubert disapproved of her son's conduct. He was turning 'hard, quarrelsome and malicious', she said. 'People don't make enough allowance for my nerves,' he insisted. Sometimes, to escape, he had to 'roll up in a ball, like a hedgehog showing all its prickles'.

'You think that I don't love you,' Flaubert wrote to Louise. As proof of his affections, after careful consultation with his mother, he offered a new contract: 'I'll come and see you more often. One week every two months, without missing a single week. Except this time, when you won't see me again until the end of January [. . .].' By this stage in their unhappy history Louise Colet had an expert ear for every perfidious nuance of Flaubert's promises. Such inconsistency was laughable; indeed it was an unconscious insult. She teased him for it, telling him that his letters reminded her of Penelope's web. Astonished, or pretending to be so, he laid the blame on her, only to be further confounded by her generously affectionate response.

With susceptibilities thus inflamed on both sides, with Bouilhet feeding each of them malign speculations about the other, their next meeting, which took place in Paris, was predictably unhappy. Flaubert saw it all too clearly, but too late: 'though our bodies came together our hearts hardly had time to embrace'. Money – Louise Colet's lack of it – was the main source of their troubles. On the one evening they spent alone together Flaubert talked himself into offering her a loan, but subsequently decided that he couldn't afford it. 'Ever since then', Louise grumbled, 'you keep on telling me that you haven't any money.'

Madame Flaubert was the other issue that came between them. 'The day before you left,' Louise reminded him, 'when I tried to talk to you on the subject [of your mother], you sent me packing [. . .].' After a memorably wretched farewell, exhausted by her own tears, Louise Colet wondered aloud, into the pages of her journal, at the nature of her feelings for Louis Bouilhet. 'If I hadn't loved Gustave, would I have taken up with him? I have no idea! It's not very clear, in my mind.'

Flaubert, back in Croisset, was writing his lyrical forest scene, 'La Baisade'. A conspicuous divergence of Art and Life, it vindicated his aesthetic doctrine of impersonality. 'I sense that she is utterly weary of me,' he told Bouilhet. 'And for the sake of her private peace of mind, it is to be hoped that she drops me.' For motives that remain obscure, Bouilhet now gave their fading passion the coup de grâce. As the trusted confidant of both parties he knew exactly where to strike.* Bouilhet informed Louise Colet that Madame Flaubert had just left Paris. Then to Flaubert he reported helpfully:

Just had a series of impossible and hopelessly tedious conversations with her. 'You're an egoist, you're a monster, you're all sorts of things.' [. . .] I think that her intentions are neither frank nor impartial [. . .]. Do you want me to tell you my sense of it all? [. . .] She wants to be your *wife* and she believes she will [. . .]. I thought as much, without daring to admit it to myself, then someone simply spoke the word, not her in person, but positively attributed to her.

Wife! the word alone, whether spoken by Louise Colet or merely attributed to her, was enough to excite Flaubert's ancient fear of female entanglement. He wrote her a letter that demolished, in the name of art, the ruins of their love. Along with forty pages of notes – both 'acerbic and *abusive*' – dissecting her latest composition, *La Servante*, Flaubert

---

* We might squeeze something significant from the fact that Bouilhet, on a visit to Mantes, had made a point of sleeping at the same inn in the same bed.

denounced her for a piece she had written attacking de Musset. 'You have made art into a receptacle for your passions, a kind of chamberpot into which something rather unpleasant has flowed. It smells nasty. It smells of hatred.' He warned that de Musset could well retaliate and cover her in ridicule. Had she learnt nothing since the old scandal surrounding her botched attempt to stab the journalist who had insulted her?

It was a calculated humiliation, to remind her of that. Surprisingly, she sent a soothing, self-abnegating reply. Again he explained his position, his money and his mother, but he pushed her ever more insistently towards the ending he envisaged. 'I shall never reform. I have already scratched and corrected and erased or gagged so many aspects of myself that I am weary of it.' When they met again, for the very last time, in Paris, Flaubert was 'surly and disagreeable'. They quarrelled in all the old ways. 'On our last evening', he reminded her, 'you poured scorn, just like some bourgeoise, on my poor fifteen-year-old dream, criticising it yet again for *not being intelligent*!' She was forever mocking him, he thought, with her constant reassurances about the 800 francs she owed him. The occasion left almost no trace except for an odd glimpse of Flaubert, nursing a bad cold, uncomfortable in his tight, metropolitan trousers, sitting by her fire, writing an article for Louise Colet's new fashion-journal, *Les Modes parisiennes*. The article was a description of a children's fancy-dress party. Journalism? Why was Flaubert doing the thing he had sworn he would never do?

JANUARY 1854. The river is frozen over, the roads are blocked by snow and the house at Croisset is cut off from the town. Gangs of starving paupers wander the country lanes at night. A gendarme has been murdered in the next village. Respectable peasants are shaking in their shoes. A man from St-Malo has been found with a copy of Victor Hugo's throne-rattling poetic thunderbolt, *Les Châtiments*, hidden in the lining of his jacket. He is sentenced to three years in prison. The face of suicidal despair can be closely inspected in Rouen's morgue: it takes the harrowing form of a man who drowned himself with two small children tied to his belt.

Flaubert is writing *Madame Bovary*. He relays this collection of 'pleasant anecdotes' to Louise Colet and then portrays himself taking his fill of the melancholy pleasures of winter, gazing into the fire and savouring the rich, deep silence of the winter night that opens up such long perspectives into the past. Reading Herodotus he spends the evening dreaming about 'the many-coloured walls of Ecbatan'. Compared to those who have to earn a living, '[...] I always look like a dull bourgeois and a scoundrel. I sit here in what could (just about) be called a chateau, peacefully warming my feet by a big fire, wearing my silk dressing gown [...].'

Flaubert never saw Louise Colet again. There was no grand finale. His last letters to her are reproachful and inconclusive. They imply, amongst other, lesser matters, that she still wanted to have a child with him and that he had refused yet again. Some time between 16 and 21 March she became the lover of Alfred de Vigny. Aristocrat, soldier, romantic poet, novelist, dramatist and academician, de Vigny was a sombre, illustrious, dignified figure; he had influence with official literary committees and a rich invalid wife; thirteen years older than Louise Colet, Monsieur le Comte de Vigny idealised his new muse with all proper ceremony.

When Flaubert next went to Paris in the summer of 1854 he was keen to keep his visit a secret from Louise Colet, 'for fear of being pursued'. Louise Colet did indeed pursue Flaubert, somewhat scurrilously, in her published fiction for several years thereafter.*

Louise Colet also laid claim to one final vision of her impossible lover. In November 1869 she was sailing up the River Nile, on board the steamer *Gyzeh*, to cover the opening of the Suez Canal for a Parisian newspaper. Privately she intended to track down Kuchuk-Hanem, that dancing girl, hoping to find her former rival now reduced to corpse-like decrepitude. Lying awake in her cabin, pestered by cockroaches, Louise Colet was 'subject to a strange hallucination'. A ghostly image of Flaubert sprang into view, a giant of a man, 'domineering and brutal', reaching out as if to seize hold of her.

IT may be the supreme achievement of medical-Gothic. The botched operation on the village ostler's club foot is the episode that most readers of *Madame Bovary* remember with a shudder of disgust. The iron contraption, the trickling gangrene it conceals, the scream that announces the thigh amputation – they darken the mood of the story by pointing down towards a nineteenth-century underworld of inconceivable physical pain. The victim, Hippolyte, is an invention, one part

---

* *Histoire d'un soldat* (Feb. 1856) and *Lui* (Aug.–Sept. 1859).

Quasimodo and two parts Flaubertian simpleton; yet the club-foot operation itself was carefully researched. Flaubert interviewed his brother, Achille, a practising surgeon, as well as reading a medical treatise by Duval, a former pupil of his father's. Duval mentioned Dr Flaubert's failure to cure a deformed foot. He is said to have 'kept his young patient in bed for nine months with an iron splint fastened to her leg – but there was no improvement and the parents took the girl home again'. Was the disastrous operation performed on Hippolyte a mischievous transposition of his father's professional failure? The evidence points both ways.*

More importantly, what are we to make of the episode? Is it black comedy? A childhood memory? A satire on medical incompetence? A confused impulse, both sadistic and compassionate? Flaubert sometimes endorsed the simplest of these possibilities. 'Exhibitions of human misery', he told Louise Colet, 'give off something so raw that it excites the mind to cannibalistic desires [. . .]. I have a real affinity for it, the unwholesome.'

But this was not the whole truth. Mortal pain is an insistent feature of Flaubert's realism. It was also a disagreeable fact of mid-nineteenth-century life, intensified in Flaubert's case by the daily spectacle of the Hôtel-Dieu. Having lived 'behind the scenes in the theatre of Esculapeus', Flaubert had to make something of what he had witnessed there. In passive, compassionate mood he could become the patient, the victim, the destitute pauper, the object of 'the medical gaze', as when he himself suffered an epileptic attack. Otherwise, in his active mood, he could become the surgeon, the quill his scalpel, anatomising the very Romanticism that he cherished. From this intimate double attitude, he forged an aesthetic doctrine of the hideous. 'With any bourgeois subject', he explained in 1853, 'the *hideous* has to replace the *tragic* (which is quite incompatible).' Hideous human misery was all around him, the merely hideous, unredeemed by tragedy. It had been all around him from his earliest years, filling the air.

Simpler than the tragic, the hideous was deeply imprinted upon his imagination. During the writing of *Madame Bovary*, it was also taking

---

* Jean Bruneau has established that Dr Flaubert was prudently following traditional methods and that all such deformities were treated thus conservatively until the 1830s. The first operation on the tendon was performed only in 1846, some time after the period in which *Madame Bovary* is set. For his novel Flaubert chose a relatively simple operation that failed.

possession of his body. The evidence suggests that Flaubert already had syphilis and that the bacterium had begun its greedy, unpredictable, corkscrew progress through his innards. In December 1853 he told Bouilhet of a dream in which his body was covered in pimples that grew into green snakes, 'waving about attached to my body like seaweed on a rock'. His premonitions of disease were soon fulfilled. In August 1854 Flaubert suffered a severe physical crisis. For a whole week, his tongue was too big to fit into his mouth, swollen to 'nearly the size of an ox's tongue'. Salivating uncontrollably, unable to eat or speak or sleep, he dribbled and sweated feverishly. He endured various remedies – leeches, ice, bleedings – then he took huge doses of mercury, which turned his penis the colour of slate. He met this indignity with comic fortitude, lamenting facetiously: 'Ah why did I not give myself exclusively to the solitary pleasures!' Flaubert hoped to arrange a consultation with Dr Ricord, the famous Parisian syphilis specialist of the day. In the event he couldn't afford the fees and was relieved to find that his symptoms had subsided.*

Flaubert had long known all the colours of human affliction, and his epilepsy had given him a special affinity for the wretched of the earth. Syphilis now added its subtle portion of horror. We see it bodied forth in the malign figure of the blind beggar who appears at the moment of Emma Bovary's death, singing of sexual pleasure. A grotesque distraction from the tragic, devised in close consultation with Louis Bouilhet, the beggar is a potent individual variation on a familiar Romantic theme. 'Stationed in the eternal darkness like a monster', he elicits from Emma 'an atrocious, frantic desperate laugh'.

WITH Louise Colet consigned to oblivion, Flaubert began to enjoy Paris. On 1 November 1854, accompanied by his mother and his niece, he settled there for the winter, in the rue de Londres, one of the prosperous new streets in the quartier de l'Europe, much favoured by bankers and retired politicians. Since July of that same year he had been pursuing a complicated but essentially frivolous affair with Béatrix Person, a Parisian actress in her late twenties. None of Béatrix Person's letters to Flaubert have survived, but we catch a vivid glimpse of her, backstage one Friday night at the Théâtre du Cirque, the half-naked

---

* Flaubert's *Dictionnaire des idées reçues*, that cryptic repository of popular wisdom, offers the following entries: 'Syphilis: Everyone, more or less, is affected by it.' 'Mercury: Finishes off the patient along with the disease.'

heroine of a genre scene appreciatively observed by a frock-coated lorgnette-wielding Flaubert who was finding his tight trousers increasingly uncomfortable. The dancers are on stage, the orchestra is playing. Behind the scenes the actresses are sweating in the heat from the oil lamps as they change costumes. The theatre smell is delectable. The hairdresser is almost too drunk to change the wigs. Bottles of wine, sticks of make-up and pots of cold cream are strewn everywhere. Flaubert pictured himself with Béatrix, much to his own amusement, playing the part of a rich and lecherous old banker from a Balzac novel. A *cocotte*, a bit of skirt, made a pleasant change from the tempestuous Louise.

At this point, with the passing of Louise Colet, some portion of Flaubert's inner life disappears from view. The letters that she elicited from him were a succulent combination of emotional intimacy, epistolary performance, and high intellectual comedy. A new, unexpected, public figure now enters the scene: a metropolitan Flaubert in top hat, grey gloves and black frock coat, a man of the salon and the boulevard, master of intrigue, expert in 'the art of shaking hands', an author indeed. In this new role Flaubert acquired (or assumed) a somewhat military air. According to Bouilhet, he looked like 'an army officer out of uniform'. 'When I'm in my frock coat,' he said, 'I'm not the same man. I'm definitely wearing a disguise.' The other characters still existed: the man sitting by the fire in his silk dressing gown, the man walking along under the trees in his white burnous. The youthful Parisian character, relinquished in 1844 at the time of his first attack, was now brought back into active service.

Flaubert went back to Croisset for the summer, then spent a second consecutive winter in Paris, this time in his own set of rooms at 42 boulevard du Temple. He had long been observing, with a malicious eye, the brilliant career of his old friend Du Camp. He sent Du Camp the briefest thanks for the copies of his books and was mildly dismayed to find that he had been erased from the record of Du Camp's travels. 'It's a bit of petty malice on his part. He would prefer it if I did not exist.' Du Camp, he said, 'is one of the people I don't want to think about. I still love him essentially, but he has so angered and spurned and repudiated me, and played such filthy tricks on me that it's "as though he were already dead" [. . .].' Flaubert was equally critical of the editorial politics of Du Camp's journal, the *Revue de Paris*. 'We are their enemies in the realm of ideas,' he told Louis Bouilhet. 'They are steering towards the old Socialism of 1833 [. . .] hatred of art for art's sake, denunciations of Form [. . .]. Down with the dreamers! Get to work! Do our bit for social regeneration!'

These antagonisms subsided as Flaubert approached the end of *Madame Bovary*. Once he had something to show for himself, he could meet Du Camp again on equal terms. Du Camp, for his part, was tenacious in friendship. He kept in touch, intermittently, waiting for Flaubert to resume the conversation. There was no formal rapprochement, but the evidence suggests that the two men came together again, some time in the winter of 1855–6, as members of the circle that gathered in the Paris salon of the Aglaé Sabatier.

'Gathered' is probably too decorous a word to describe it. The gentlemen talked about art, certainly, but the principal entertainment was an extravagant, hilarious and inexhaustibly erotic game of *be-my-slave*. Madame Sabatier, known as La Présidente, presided over a serial comedy of masculine abjection. She was the queen, the empress, and they were her infatuated, helpless, adoring subjects. Her qualifications for this fantasy role were impressive, even by contemporary Parisian standards. Born in 1822, she was the illegitimate daughter of a laundry woman and the local prefect. After training as a singer, she became the lover of an English millionaire, who left her with a large pension. Whilst in her early twenties she achieved a certain centrefold fame as the model for a sculpture, *Woman Stung by a Serpent*, which, as everyone could see, celebrated the splendours of the female orgasm. Obedient to the ravenous imperatives of celebrity, Aglaé Sabatier then moved on to become the mistress of a wealthy but ideally acquiescent Belgian industrialist. Under his ample wing she presided over this Sunday evening salon, which met regularly throughout the 1850s.

Most of the guests were friends of Gautier's. At Madame Sabatier's Du Camp, Flaubert, and Bouilhet could have met Baudelaire, Berlioz and Delacroix, as well as many lesser figures. In his memoirs Du Camp left an appreciative account of the salon. The atmosphere, he said, was relaxed and playful. The conversation could be serious or frivolous. While Flaubert, Gautier and Bouilhet joyfully rode their hobbyhorse – art for art's sake – Du Camp stood aside. He was the cheerful unbeliever, the renegade, the barbarian, the bureaucrat (worst insult of all).

Since his conversion to the ideas of Saint-Simon, Du Camp held the view that literature must 'live in its time and for its time'. He was, in his own estimation, the man who could read the direction of history. He had recently published a book of poems, *Les Chants modernes*, equipped with a preface that spelt out the author's position. 'Three great movements, the humanitarian movement, the scientific movement and the industrial movement [. . .] are carrying our age into the future.'

Fortified by his progressive convictions, Du Camp listened in smiling silence to the assembled aesthetes and then wrote a briskly mischievous summary of their articles of faith. It went as follows:

No writer allowed to unveil his feelings; if a novel allows the author's opinions to show through then the novel deserves to be thrown on the fire. Impersonal and impervious, the writer stands in for his characters, thinks and acts like them [. . .]. Nothing that emerges from the imagination is excessive [. . .] the subject of a work of art [. . .] is as nothing, the execution is all that matters; describe a slug crawling up a cabbage, describe Apollo gazing at Venus, it makes no great difference.

As a satire on Flaubert's artistic opinions this is highly effective.

In the interludes of talking art and literature, the guests played charades and gave each other nicknames. Flaubert was 'le sire de Vaufrilard'. On special occasions they came in fancy dress. True to his fantasies of exotic ancestry, Flaubert arrived as a Red Indian chief with feathers in his hair, waving a kitchen sieve as a tomahawk. Madame Sabatier's presentation copy of *Madame Bovary* eventually arrived with an extravagant dedication from the author: 'To the delightful host, to the ravishingly beautiful woman, to the excellent friend, to our beautiful, kind, impervious Présidente [. . .] this meagre tribute comes from Gustave Flaubert.'

FLAUBERT'S tribulations with *Madame Bovary* were not yet at an end. The publication of the novel was to be an ordeal of another kind. Amused by the strange idea of earning money from his writing, Flaubert concluded an agreement with the editors of the *Revue de Paris*. He was to receive two thousand francs and *Madame Bovary* was to be published in six fortnightly instalments, beginning in July. Back in Croisset for the summer, Flaubert spent the month of May 1856 cutting his manuscript, probably at Maxime Du Camp's suggestion. Thirty pages were pruned away: 'three big speeches by Homais, a complete landscape, much of the bourgeois conversation in the ball scene, an article by Homais [. . .]'. He conceded that the book now moved more evenly but soon began to worry that Maxime Du Camp would merely insist on further cuts.

He was right. Du Camp wrote proposing a little surgical-editorial operation on his text. 'Be brave, close your eyes and trust in our [. . .] experience in these matters [. . .]. You have buried your novel under a pile of stuff which is nicely done but quite superfluous.' Flaubert went to Paris to argue it out with the editors and came away believing he had won. 'It has been officially agreed that I change nothing.' This was not quite the case. Publication was deferred. Promises were made. There was evidently fierce disagreement among the editors. Du Camp defended his friend's work as a masterpiece – so he claimed, long after the event – and was mocked for his partiality. Publication was announced in the August issue of the review. Was there any significance in the fact that the author's name had been corrupted to *Faubert*? The author himself, superstitiously alert in such matters, regarded it as an evil omen. They'd given him the name of a famous Parisian grocer.

Back in Croisset, with *Madame Bovary* off his hands, Flaubert was hard at work. All through the hot August afternoons, with the shutters and the curtains closed, shirtless, 'dressed like a carpenter' he was 'bellowing and sweating' his way through *Saint Antoine*. He wanted to make it flow, make it more readable. He was developing the main character, rewriting the whole thing. He intended to publish it some time in the new year. 'I shall only feel happy once this detestable thing is off my back, though it could well get me prosecuted and will certainly make people think I'm a madman.'

Away from his writing, Flaubert entertained himself by gazing across the dining table at the ample bosom of the new governess.* 'What a pretty comparison could be drawn between the slopes of that chest and the embankment of a fortress. Cupids go tumbling down as they press forward to the attack. As the sheik might say: "I know exactly which artillery-piece I'd like to use on it." ' The summer flirtation intensified. They read *Macbeth* together and Flaubert confessed to great difficulty in restraining himself when following the governess up the stairs.

Publication was on his mind. Flaubert predicted that the editors of the review would insist on more cuts. Then Du Camp wrote to say that *Madame Bovary* was delayed yet again. It would be held over until the October issue. Louis Bouilhet meanwhile was enjoying a smoother ride.

---

* According to Hermia Oliver, the new governess was probably Juliet Herbert.

His play had been accepted at the Théâtre de l'Odéon and he was soon going to be a famous man. Correcting the proofs of *Madame Bovary*, Du Camp teased the author for his fascination with boots. 'They come up at least five or six times. It's an obsession.' But he refrained from correcting one or two of Flaubert's incomprehensible Normandy idioms. 'I'm frightened you might have me strangled in my sleep.' It speaks for the resilience of their friendship to discover that Du Camp was also negotiating terms with a publisher on Flaubert's behalf.

O N 1 October 1856 the first of six instalments of *Madame Bovary* appeared in the *Revue de Paris*. It was a most disagreeable moment for the author. Flaubert was 'totally stupefied' by the sight of his work in print. He thought it flat and clumsy; the voice of his conscience seemed to be crying 'failure!'.

Some of his readers were unhappy too. According to Du Camp, '[. . .] the subscribers were up in arms; complaining of scandal and immorality. We received letters that were far from polite, accusing us of calumny upon the French nation [. . .]. I showed these letters to Flaubert and he said, "These people are all mad!"' Flaubert now wrote to the chief editor of the review, Pichat. Assuming his most urbane Parisian persona, Flaubert managed to be both graciously compliant and stubbornly principled. He even offered Pichat a surprisingly authentic account of his artistic intentions. Conceding the lowness of his subject, Flaubert reaches spontaneously for a surgical analogy: '[. . .] aesthetically I wanted to open it up, once and only once, down to the bone. And so I approached it heroically, I mean minutely, accepting everything, saying everything, portraying everything (an ambitious notion).' This, he said, was the reason for his resistance to all editorial criticism, 'however judicious'.

Flaubert did not realise that his troubles had only just begun. The clumsy machinery of repression was already grinding into action. (Curiously, it was persistent editorial censorship and Flaubert's subsequent public protest that attracted official attention and led to prosecution.) Back in Paris Flaubert was spending his afternoons at the theatre, keeping an eye on the rehearsals of Bouilhet's play. We may picture him there, in a state of high excitement, striding around the stage, taking the cast through the big speeches over and over again, doing all the gestures, calling everyone by their first names. He seemed to fill the whole auditorium.

Paris theatre was the dream of his youth. He was in his element. Bouilhet seemed stupefied by it all. He followed Flaubert around, like a shadow, looking gloomy, bursting into tears, timidly convinced that it would all be a failure. But Bouilhet's first night was a great success. A delegation of forty citizens, fired with local patriotism, came specially from Rouen. The applause lasted twenty minutes. It was like one of the great Romantic theatrical successes of the 1830s. After the performance the Rouen delegation presented the author with a little gold crown inscribed '*Cornelio redivivo*'. The reviews were good and a celebratory banquet was organised. Meanwhile, the early instalments of *Madame Bovary* made a considerable impression in literary circles. Amusingly, a publisher made Flaubert an offer.

But then, according to Maxime Du Camp, it all went wrong: '[. . .] early in November, one of my friends, a man with contacts as they say "at the highest level", came to tell me that we were going to be prosecuted.' The *Revue de Paris* had been under scrutiny for some time. Though it never dabbled in politics it had often published work by writers associated with the Second Republic, ex-ministers and officials, marked men. Under the heavy laws now controlling the press any such association was enough to get the review into trouble. The government of Napoléon was still exceptionally sensitive to criticism and times were hard for writers with any pretensions to independence. 'They had exiled many eloquent men and suppressed many of the newspapers. The watchword was "silence". France was like a sick-room. Everyone spoke in a whisper.' After three warnings a publication could be suspended and then suppressed. But it was a chaotic system. Any petty official who took offence could request that action be taken. Explicitly literary journals had been created, to avoid censorship, but they had suffered along with the rest because 'allusions to the emperor' could be detected in almost anything.

Hoping to forestall official action, the editors of the review decided to go through the remainder of the text, in collaboration with Flaubert, and remove anything that might look provocative. The first chapter of Part Three, in which Léon and Madame Bovary make love in a closed carriage travelling around the streets of Rouen, was felt to be scandalously suggestive. 'Your carriage scene is impossible,' Du Camp informed Flaubert, '[. . .] not for me as the one who signs the issue, but for the magistrates who would convict us out of hand [. . .] we have had two warnings, they're watching us closely and they won't waste the opportunity.' Flaubert reluctantly consented to the suppression of the passage in question, pointing out to his editors that 'in suppressing the cab scene you have not removed the source of scandal'. Indeed the cut made the episode seem even more bizarrely lubricious than before. Further cuts would not make any difference. 'You are attacking little details,' Flaubert pointed out, 'but it's the whole thing that is the problem. The brutal element is deep down, not on the surface.' Helpless to stop them mutilating his work, Flaubert insisted that his readers should at least be informed that something was missing.*

The final *Bovary* number of the *Revue de Paris*, published on 15 December 1856, did indeed make further cuts to the ending of the novel.† Feeling indignant, Flaubert made contact with a lawyer, Maître Sénard, 'regarding an unpleasant business in which I do not wish to make a fool of myself'. Sénard probably negotiated a compromise with the editors of the review. Flaubert then decided to have the whole book printed privately. His lawyer agreed to this and Flaubert drafted a preface that said, 'I'm accused on the evidence of phrases taken here and there from my book; my only defence must be my book.' Printing was almost complete when there came an order forbidding it.

Flaubert now signed a contract to publish *Madame Bovary* with the publisher Michel Lévy. Under the terms of that contract he was paid 800 francs over five years – 'well within conventional rates for an unknown author'. There was also a bonus of 500 francs paid in August 1857. A few days later, Du Camp told Flaubert that there was to be a prosecution. He advised him to keep it quiet and to start pulling strings.

Author, publisher and printer were summoned to appear on 31 January 1857 in courtroom number six.‡

* Du Camp tells a different story. In his version of events Flaubert truculently refused to cut a single word: 'Whatever I said to him he came back with "I don't care. If my novel upsets the bourgeois, I don't care. If we end up in court, I don't care. If they suppress the *Revue de Paris*, I don't care. You had only to reject *Bovary*. You took it on, so much the worse for you. You'll have to publish it as it is."'

† The scene of extreme unction was cut, as well as parts of the conversation between Homais and his clerical antagonist Bournisien.

‡ Once again, Du Camp's version of these events strays significantly from the available evidence. Here is Du Camp's story, in summary form. Acting on an angry impulse, Flaubert searched through the back numbers of the *Revue de Paris* and compiled a little dossier of choice phrases and 'delicate situations', intended to vindicate his own writing. Somewhat imprudently Flaubert showed his dossier to a journalist. The journalist wrote a tendentious article, quoting passages from the dossier. The article was noticed in high places and a prosecution was initiated.

Far away from all this hectic Parisian intrigue, in the sombre provincial town of Angers, Mademoiselle Leroyer de Chantepie, a pale, sulky, badly dressed woman in her mid-fifties, an unmarried heiress with a modest income from inherited property, was writing an appreciative and admiring letter, the first of many, to the author of the novel she had been reading with such perfect, greedy pleasure in the six recent numbers of the *Revue de Paris*. 'Yes,' she wrote,

this is exactly how it is in the provinces where I was born and have spent my life. [. . .] How I understood the sadness, the boredom and the sufferings of that poor lady [. . .]. From the beginning I recognised her and I loved her as though she were a friend. I so identified with her experiences that it was just as though she was me. No, this story cannot be fictional, it must be true, this is an actual woman, you must have witnessed her life, her death and her sufferings. [. . .] Where have you acquired your perfect knowledge of human nature, it's a scalpel applied to the heart, to the soul, it is alas the world in all its hideousness [. . .].

This letter, dated 18 December 1856, three days after the publication of the final instalment of the novel, is fascinating testimony to the powerful effect that *Madame Bovary* had upon its first women readers. Mademoiselle Leroyer de Chantepie had responded just as Flaubert had imagined. 'If my book is any good,' he wrote in September 1852, 'it will gently tickle many a feminine wound. One or two will smile when they recognise themselves. I will have known your sufferings, poor obscure souls, damp from your stifled sorrows, like your provincial back-yards, where the moss grows on the walls.'

Gratified to learn that he had chronicled the secrets of the female soul with such imaginative authority, Flaubert responded most graciously. Within the week he received a large parcel from Angers. The parcel contained a portrait of Mademoiselle Leroyer de Chantepie, three volumes of her unpublished writings, and a letter that further explained her deep moral affinity with Emma Bovary. She 'loved her like a sister' and had wept three days, she said, over Emma's death. 'Excessive sensibility and an ardent imagination have always led me to desire the impossible [. . .]. The love of art and literature are my only consolation.'

Since the death of her mother, whom she had nursed for twenty years, Mademoiselle Leroyer had acquired a houseful of blissfully idle dependants, an unemployed Polish refugee, an elderly Latin master and an assortment of destitute friends and relations, fourteen people in all. Harassed by her greedy, quarrelsome household, estranged from her gossiping provincial neighbours, unable to go to confession, Mademoiselle Leroyer suffered from all the symptoms of neurotic guilt: migraine, hallucinations and thoughts of suicide. The theatre was her only pleasure. Yet she had never been to Paris, such was her fear of imaginary dangers. Her letter ends with an impassioned plea for Flaubert's sympathy: 'Console me, advise me.'

Flaubert accepted, stepping into the priestly therapeutic role with remarkable enthusiasm. 'I love you', Flaubert wrote to her in 1863, 'for your ideas, your feelings and your sufferings.' In return, she idealised him from a safe distance, listening in mute adoration to the shadowy, heroic tale of his inner life as he began to unfold it to her. Mademoiselle Leroyer de Chantepie was the most virginal, the most wretched and the least sophisticated of the three female readers who sought the friendship of the author of *Madame Bovary*.* The love of such women was to count high among the intangible rewards of authorship.

F LAUBERT spent the month of January 1857 in a state of anxious excitement. He was waiting for his trial, wondering what was happening behind the scenes of the miniature legal-political drama in which he had now been assigned a leading role. 'My trial is *political* because they want at all costs to eradicate the *Revue de Paris* which is a thorn in their side.' He was not, he told a friend, attacking religion or condoning adultery, 'since like every good author I show the punishment of misconduct'. A conviction would be disastrous. 'If I am found guilty it will be impossible henceforth for me to write another line. I'll be carefully watched and the least transgression will land me in prison for five years.' If he could pull through then the book would sell extremely well. It was his low subject that had landed him in such trouble, but influential people would testify that he wrote for educated readers, not for 'hysterical kitchen-maids'.

Flaubert had great faith in the power of the family name. The mere fact of being a Flaubert would have considerable influence. The letters he wrote to his elder brother, Achille, now the senior member of the family, expound these hopes somewhat fancifully. 'They have to realise in the Ministry that we are what they call *a family* in Rouen, in other

* The other two arrived later: Amélie Bosquet and Edma Roger des Genettes.

words that we have deep local roots.' A guilty verdict might even prejudice the voters of Rouen in future elections. More tangibly, a letter
from the local prefect, arranged by Achille, would help his case. He had
female supporters too, *bovarystes enragées*, in high places. Princesses,
he said, were busy lobbying the Empress on his behalf.

At one point it looked as though the prosecution had been called off,
for shame. Then Sénard informed his client that the case would proceed. Why should it be stopped and then started again? The plot was
thickening. 'There is *something* behind it all,' Flaubert insisted, 'somebody invisible and relentless.' This was a flattering notion, probably
mistaken.* More sensibly, Flaubert gathered his defences in the days
immediately preceding the trial. The Empress, he confided to Achille,
had spoken on his behalf.

Flaubert was also busy preparing something for his own defence, a
dossier of choice quotations from classic authors, but Du Camp
advised him against it. He might well harm his own cause. It would be
better to leave tactics to Sénard. 'These fellows are naive,' said Du
Camp, 'your book has shocked them [. . .]. Your book is brutal [. . .]
and they take brutality for immorality [. . .].' A posture of dignified
defiance seemed most appropriate. Flaubert told one of his allies, 'I pity
the people who are bringing this prosecution. This book, which they
are attempting to destroy, will in later years simply flourish all the
more, wearing all these scars with honour.'

On 25 January Flaubert went by invitation to see Lamartine, the
elder statesman of French Romanticism, now in his sixties. Lamartine
welcomed his visitor with great warmth. 'You've written the best book
I've read in twenty years,' he said, and recited several pages from memory. They spent an hour in conversation. Lamartine had only one
criticism of *Madame Bovary*. The scene of Emma's death was too much
for him, the poet of consolation, the man so often bereaved. 'It caused
me pain,' he said. 'Literally made me suffer. The expiation is out of
proportion to the crime [. . .]. Certainly the woman who soils the conjugal bed should expect to make amends, but this is horrible, it's a
torture [. . .]. You've taken it too far [. . .]. Such powers of description
applied to a deathbed left me unspeakably distressed.'

Flaubert told Lamartine that he was about to be prosecuted. 'My

---

* Jean Bruneau, the most recent editor of Flaubert's letters, suggests that the affair was much
simpler than Flaubert wanted to believe.

dear boy, it's not possible. There is no court in France that would condemn you. It is most regrettable that anyone should have so mis-understood your work and ordered a prosecution. But it is inconceiv-able, for the honour of our country and our epoch, that any court would condemn you.' Lamartine then promised a letter of support, a promise that he never kept, though his high opinion of *Madame Bovary* was subsequently quoted in court.*

Lamartine's faltering public endorsement was probably less signifi-cant than the words spoken behind the scenes in the days before the trial. Prompted by Flaubert, Gautier solicited the support of Charles Abbatucci, the son of the Minister of Justice, who was already 'extremely biased' in Flaubert's favour; Abbatucci then used his influ-ence with his father to push the case in the right direction. A compli-mentary copy of *Madame Bovary*, along with a gracious note from the author, may well have made its way, eventually, on to the minister's desk.

I N one of his lighter moments, a few days before the trial, Flaubert imagined himself in chains, languishing on a pile of damp straw in some obscure dungeon. He toyed pleasantly with the idea of buying a bale of straw and a set of chains and having his portrait painted, thus romantically posed, like one of Byron's delinquent heroes. The reality of the trial was, of course, grindingly prosaic. At best, an episode from Molière. At worst, like being back at school.

Palais de Justice, 29 January 1857, ten in the morning. The three defendants were charged with 'offending public morality, religion and decency'. The courtroom was crowded, in anticipation of something special, some choice specimen of legal eloquence. The presiding judge, Monsieur Dubarle, was a man of literary tastes, more accustomed to the trivial misdeeds of pickpockets, streetwalkers, pimps and swindlers than the grandiose transgressions of novelists. Monsieur Dubarle regarded this case as a rare treat; he smiled his discreet complicity and was so evidently well disposed towards the three defendants – the author, his editor and their printer – that he did nothing to suppress the laughter provoked by the clumsy solemnities of the imperial prosecutor.

* Details of the encounter with Lamartine are drawn from Sénard's speech in court – Pléaide *Oeuvres* 1: 642–3 – and from Flaubert's letters.

Ernest Pinard, the prosecutor, stood up to speak. Pinard was young, the same age as Flaubert. An ambitious, diminutive man, he had recently arrived in Paris from a successful provincial legal career. Rumoured – many years later – to be the author of a collection of pornographic verses, Pinard, from the evidence of his indictment, already had a keen eye for the erotic. 'The offence against public morality', he declared, 'is in the lascivious scenes which I shall put before your eyes, the offence against religious morality is in the voluptuous images which are mixed up with things sacred.' Under a tendentious new title, 'The Adulteries of a Provincial Wife', Pinard proposed to tell the story of Emma Bovary from beginning to end, without quotation, and then read out the most incriminating passages verbatim.

By way of introduction, though, he would pick out various choice details. Consider Emma's adolescent confession: 'The metaphors of the betrother, the spouse, the celestial lover and the eternal marriage, such as recur in sermons, excited a strange sweetness deep in her soul.' Evidently lascivious. Consider the tone of the passage describing the morning after the wedding night: 'Next morning, however, he seemed a different man. He was the one you would think had just lost his virginity, whereas the bride gave not the slightest sign of anything to anybody.' Equivocal. Consider the description of Charles's sexual contentment: 'ruminating over his happiness, like a man who, after a meal, still relishes the taste of the truffles'. Pinard also objected to various lesser details: the slander against Marie Antoinette in the ballroom chapter, Justin's fascination with Emma's underwear, and Charles's lingering appreciation of the smell of Emma's skin. 'The beauty of Madame Bovary', he declared, 'is the beauty of provocation.'

Ernest Pinard, however ludicrous his official role as the scourge of modern art, deserves some recognition as a singularly discerning early reader of Flaubert. He notices the details: Rodolphe's interest in the shape of Emma's body under her dress. Emma's unrepentant 'glorification of adultery' when she returns from her assignation in the forest. Emma's laughter when the champagne flows over her fingers in the hotel bedroom with Léon. The sheet laid over the corpse, moulding itself to the shape of her breasts and her knees.

'What the author is showing you is the poetry of adultery and I ask you once again if these lascivious pages are not profoundly immoral.' Pinard objects particularly (responds powerfully?) to Emma's glorious confusion of religion and sexuality, her dangerous mingling of the sacred and the profane. 'Voluptuous one day, religious the next, no woman, even in other countries, even beneath the skies of Spain or Italy, would murmur to God the adulterous caresses she has given to her lover.'

Summing up, Pinard denounces realism. '[. . .] the genre that Monsieur Flaubert cultivates, without the restraints of art but with all the resources of art, is the descriptive genre, the realist painting.' Pinard takes issue, intelligently enough, with the defence argument that Emma is horribly punished. 'I tell you, gentlemen, that lascivious details cannot be covered over by a moral conclusion, otherwise a writer could portray all the orgiastic deeds imaginable, describe all the depravities of a woman of the streets, as long as she dies in misery in the poorhouse. We would be allowed to study and display all her lascivious poses? That would be to go against the rules of common sense, to place poison where anyone might reach for it [. . .].'

Who, asks Pinard, will be reading *Madame Bovary*?

Will they be men who concern themselves with social and political economy? No! The irresponsible pages of *Madame Bovary* will fall into the hands of the irresponsible, into the hands of young girls and married women. Well, then! Once the imagination has been seduced, once this seduction has worked its way down to the heart, once the heart has whispered to the senses, do you think that cold reason will prevail against this seduction of the senses and the feelings?

Even men of virtue have base instincts, and only a very painful effort keeps them out of danger. Emma, he argues, is never effectively condemned. 'Madame Bovary obviously dies of poison. She has indeed suffered greatly. But she dies at the hour and on the day of her choice. She dies not because she is an adulteress but because she wants to die. She dies in all the glamour of her youth and her beauty [. . .].' Flaubert's impersonality, says Pinard, is an abnegation of artistic responsibility. The book affirms no principle in the name of which Emma might be condemned. Not conjugal honour, because Charles is perpetually besotted. Not public opinion, because Homais, the voice of reason, is a mere grotesque. Not religion, because Bournisien, the parish priest, is almost as grotesque as Homais. And not authorial conscience, because the author affects a quiet scepticism about the promise of the afterlife. 'Is there', wonders Pinard, getting to the point, 'a single character in the book who can control this woman? There is not. The only character in control is Madame Bovary.' Christian morality condemns adultery because it is 'a crime against the family'. Christian morality also condemns realist literature because it knows no limits. 'Art without rules is no longer art; it is like a woman who takes off all her clothes.'

PINARD'S speech for the prosecution had lasted for about an hour and a half. The defence lawyer, Maître Jules Sénard, now rose to make his reply. Sénard was in his late fifties, an accomplished orator, an old friend of the Flaubert family, and a powerful figure in national politics. He 'spoke for four hours without a pause'. His exonerating theme was 'incitement to virtue through the horror of vice'. He opened his defence with a brief family history, designed to establish Flaubert's impeccable moral character and high social position. The defendant's father, said Sénard, was an old friend of his. The defendant himself was a close friend of his family. The name of Flaubert was well known and Gustave Flaubert was the worthy son of a great father. He was a highly educated man of serious intellectual ambition, a grave and a serious character, not a frivolous scribbler of pornography.

Gustave Flaubert does not belong to any 'school'. Or rather he belongs in some sense to them all, the realist, the psychological and the romantic. But his main aim is scientific: 'to constitute various true types from the middle class and to arrive at a useful result'. His book is not a glorification of adultery. It is 'The Story of a Provincial Education', the tale of a woman who has been educated above her station in life and is disturbed by 'strange aspirations'. Distracted from her real duties Emma Bovary escapes into 'endless daydreams'.

At this point Sénard invokes Flaubert's readers, the many wives and mothers, intelligent, pure-minded women, who have already, he says, written grateful, appreciative letters to the author. Alongside these nameless women there is also the testimony of Lamartine, a man who can be trusted, a school-prize author, a writer of impeccable purity.

Sénard affirms that it was the cut in the published text of the cab scene that provoked the prosecution. The suppression led people to imagine things that weren't there. When the censors saw the cut and the accompanying note they became interested. They said, 'Better keep an eye on this,' and they went through the next issue with eager curiosity.

Sénard ends with a tendentious account of the early part of the book, trying to prove the heroine's innocence. A farmer's daughter, he says, shouldn't be given a fancy convent education. Young girls, he says, 'sensualise religion' with their taste for relics and medallions, their mysticism, their little ceremonies and their poetical daydreams. Flaubert has simply described this process. He doesn't endorse it. He's giving a useful warning. Sénard vindicates the scene of extreme unction in great detail and argues that the deathbed scene, with its bawdy song coming up from the street, is in the great tradition. Shakespeare and Goethe both treat death in this way, with a touch of irreverence.

Sénard's speech was a triumph. According to Flaubert, the Imperial prosecutor Pinard was 'crushed [. . .] writhing in his seat', and he offered no reply. The defendants now had to wait another week for the judge to deliver his verdict. This delay may well have worked in Flaubert's favour. It allowed time for the whispering effects of 'influence'.

Flaubert was optimistic. He felt drawn into the high drama of the whole episode. 'My cause,' he wrote to Champfleury, a sympathetic journalist, 'was that of contemporary literature. It was not just my novel but all novels that were under attack [. . .].' Realist art, defined by its refusal to idealise or soften its 'unpleasant' subject matter, was the enemy of all decorous contentment with things as they are. Plucked from the obscurity of Croisset, Flaubert was the exemplary realist, a heroic role that he soon began to find irksome. He was a public figure, a man with a reputation, an audience, an income. Women wrote to him. Men sent him their books. The managers of theatres and the editors of newspapers were eager to cultivate him.

His acquittal came on 7 February, delivered along with a stern, schoolmasterly reprimand, a brief, amateurish critique of realism, and a reminder that 'the mission of literature ought to be to enrich and refresh the mind by elevating the understanding and refining morals'.*

Once the excitement of the trial and the acquittal died away Flaubert felt sad and weary. He was also keenly anxious about his artistic future. Though acquitted, he remained 'suspect'. He had been hoping to publish *Saint Antoine*. But that was now quite impossible because such a book would, he realised, land him in court once again. For the same reasons he now postponed further work on his story about Saint Julian.

---

* The *Revue de Paris* was finally suppressed by the government in January 1858, the week after an attempt to assassinate Napoléon III.

He was looking forward to being back in Croisset, 'far from human-kind, as they say in the best tragedies'.

He complained that even his most worldly-wise supporters (probably Lamartine and Du Camp) were pressing him to make 'a few little corrections' to his text in the interests of prudence and good taste. Lamartine, his supposed ally, was praising *Madame Bovary* but deploring its cynicism. The prosecution might launch an appeal against the recent verdict. His publisher was nagging at him to publish quickly. From where he lay, ruminating upon his couch, coughing and spitting and nursing a filthy cold, it was evident that social hypocrisy reigned supreme.

In spite of his acquittal, the trial weighed heavily upon him. What could he possibly write that would be 'more inoffensive' than *Madame Bovary*? Someone must be working against him. 'All the people I've met personally were full of goodwill and yet somewhere underneath all that there was an incomprehensible ferocity.' Disgusted with the world and with himself, Flaubert told his publisher to 'stop everything' and retreated to his bed.

Within a week, under pressure from his mother and from Louis Bouilhet, he changed his mind. *Madame Bovary* was published in April 1857: two small yellow-green volumes priced at two francs each, part of the *Collection Michel Lévy*, a new series recently launched and already highly successful. Flaubert had joined 'the elite of contemporary authors'. The first batch of six thousand copies sold quickly and there were two further impressions in the course of the same year. In August Flaubert received a bonus payment of 500 francs.

THE reviews were mixed. There were thistles, said Flaubert, woven into his laurels.

Sainte-Beuve, the foremost critic of the day, was equivocal. He praised the early crowd scenes: the wedding, the ball and the agricultural show. But then he objected strongly to the cruel and painful tone of the final chapters of the book. It was all too much, he said. The deathbed, the refusal to ennoble the husband, the absence of simple human goodness. His review ended with a famous salutation. He acknowledged that this book was the voice of a new generation. Committed to science and observation, they had already achieved a slightly hard maturity. 'The son and the brother of eminent doctors, Gustave Flaubert wields the pen like a scalpel. Anatomists and physiologists, you are everywhere!' A cartoon image of Flaubert with Emma's dripping heart impaled on his scalpel-pen was soon in circulation.*

Local opinion was more openly, more ignorantly hostile. A superior young man from Rouen, when asked for his opinion of *Madame Bovary*, exclaimed: 'You Parisians think well of *this*? [. . .] Well personally I do not! The author is a sort of eccentric, a thing not greatly to our taste in Rouen [. . .]. He was *deliberately* drawing attention to himself. He didn't want to do his bit in the National Guard [. . .] and then, all of a sudden – *without a word* – off he went to Africa [. . .]. We *don't like* that sort, not in Rouen.' Flaubert, for his part, singled out this anecdote as being 'absolutely correct'.

ONCE acquitted, Flaubert found himself transformed into the successful author of *Madame Bovary*. He was inevitably a public figure, the reluctant but legitimate object of curiosity, envy and admiration. It was not a pleasant sensation. 'All this uproar around my first book seems so irrelevant to Art that it sickens me, it dazes me. How I miss the fish-like silence in which I had persisted until now.' Dismayed by the uproar, Flaubert longed to disappear. In defiance of the Romantic cult of genius, his work would have no bellicose preface, no princely portrait; it would beget no newspaper morsels of gossip, no weighty pronouncements. This artist – unlike Lord Byron and Victor Hugo – would silently but majestically vanish into his work.

Faithful to this principle, all of Flaubert's subsequent 'explanations' of *Madame Bovary* were remarkable mainly for their energetic self-contradiction. Mademoiselle Leroyer de Chantepie was told that the story was 'totally invented'. Amelie Bosquet was told, enigmatically, '*Madame Bovary, c'est moi.*' The de Goncourt brothers were told, ridiculously, that only Charles's father was based on a real person.

In each case we may assume that Flaubert was covering his tracks. Flaubert's secret, his nervous affliction, was too dark and too repugnant a thing to be housed within the conventional forms of celebrity. In the months following the publication of *Madame Bovary*, the salient features of Flaubert's contemporary reputation came into focus. A *succès de scandale*, the book was 'selling superbly'. Flaubert was simultaneously maligned as a mere imitator of Balzac and acclaimed as his illustrious heir. Flaubert had entered the arena, said the reviewers, like a

* Magnified into an accusation of heartless sadism, the image of the artist-as-anatomist came back to trouble Flaubert five years later, at the time of the publication of *Salammbô*.

gladiator showing off his muscles. The brutality of the physiological perspective was to be deplored.

Most gratifying of all was the hostility of the local priest. In the little church over the hill, just behind Croisset, the man had denounced *Madame Bovary* and forbidden his parishioners to read it. Flaubert rejoiced in the news. 'I have been attacked by the government, by the priests and by the newspapers. My triumph is complete.' There was talk of a stage adaptation, an idea that Flaubert initially found amusing. Let them go ahead, he declared. Let them do it any way they like. 'The thing seems impossible to me.' There was also to be an English translation, prepared under his supervision by the family's resident governess, Juliet Hebert. 'A masterpiece', it subsequently vanished without trace, remaining as a source of vexation between Flaubert and his publisher.

Perceptive responses to *Madame Bovary* appeared more slowly. In October 1857 George Sand published an essay on realism – one of the infinitely contentious topics of the day – making favourable reference to *Madame Bovary*. Her judgement was generously nuanced. 'On reflection,' she wrote, 'we realised that it was more Balzac [. . .]. A Balzac purged of every concession to benevolence, a Balzac sour and sombre, Balzac distilled, as it were. [. . .] People have worried, mistakenly, in my opinion, about the morality of the book. On the contrary [. . .] reading it would be good for all the budding Madame Bovarys that are engendered by similar circumstances in the provinces.'

Baudelaire's review of *Madame Bovary* also appeared in October. It was a gesture of profound mutual recognition. As a writer of the same generation, schooled in the same ideals, subjected like Flaubert to the recent indignity of prosecution, Baudelaire responded with passionate authenticity to 'this essentially suggestive book'. He fastened upon Emma Bovary's secret masculinity, the psychosexual paradox at the heart of the book. 'This bizarre androgyne', he wrote, anticipating many later expositions of the gender theme, 'has retained all the seductions of a virile soul in a charming feminine body.' In her imaginative mingling of the sacred and the profane, Emma is 'a poet-hysteric'.

Within a few days Flaubert wrote to congratulate Baudelaire: 'You have found your way into the secret places of the book as though my brain were your own.' Such close artistic affinity might one day be problematic, but for the moment at least it was a pleasant exception.*

---

* The theme of androgyny was by no means peculiar to Flaubert. It was a major Romantic preoccupation, especially evident in the work of Chateaubriand, Stendhal and Balzac.

Baudelaire's review was many years ahead of its time. Infinitely more representative was the miniature biography of Flaubert published around the same time in the *Gazette de Paris*. When Flaubert read it he was delighted by the sharpness of the comic image that told him just how he might appear to others.

He dresses as a man of the world, correct and elegant though without dandified affectation. He is tall. His expression is serious, almost severe; his smile is lacking in benevolence and his gaze is searching. He has a large forehead, balding at the temples [. . .]. He has an active imagination and a robust temperament. He has struggled with boredom, the malady of the underemployed. If he had been poor he would have worked. Rich and independent he has led the life of a provincial playboy. [. . .] One fine day he left for the Orient [. . .] he camped in amongst the ruins and smoked his cigar, gazing at the desert [. . .]. Monsieur Flaubert, on his return, settled down to his books. He said to himself, 'I shall produce a work of some substance [. . .].'

If there must be a portrait of the artist then it had best be innocuously comic. Flaubert was not consistently at his ease in the public sphere. Not yet. Soon after the article in the *Gazette de Paris* Flaubert refused *Le Gaulois* permission to publish a similar caricature portrait and biography. As he put it later the same year, 'Do not put your portrait at the beginning of your book. Leave that little trick to the scribblers. The artist *ought not to exist!*' Flaubert had decided to ignore those who were advising him to exploit his success.

Perhaps it was already too late to remain invisible. Paris theatres were eager to stage *Madame Bovary*. Henri Monnier, a famous actor of the day, had written to ask if he could play Homais. Le Théâtre de La Porte-Saint-Martin was offering Flaubert 'extremely advantageous' terms. Would he merely allow the theatre to use the title of the novel? They would hire a man to write the adaptation and Flaubert would get a generous share of the takings, probably about thirty thousand francs. Short of cash, Flaubert was tempted. But Bouilhet talked him out of it.*

By December 1857 there were already two unofficial versions of Madame Bovary on the Paris variety stage. One of them sang comic

---

* Flaubert wrote to Louis Bouilhet saying, 'I'm eternally grateful to you for having stopped me from giving my permission to turn *Bovary* into a play.' It was unseemly, Bouilhet argued, this juggling with art and cash. Flaubert accepted the argument and turned down the contract, though he preferred to dignify a reluctant decision as a noble gesture of principle. 'I refused it all point blank,' he said, 'and went back into my lair.'

songs and the other one gossiped about her love affairs. Flaubert saw them both – and was not amused. 'Two turpitudes', he said, 'are quite enough.' His next novel would offer its readers none of those easy pleasures. 'It will be Art, pure Art and nothing but.'

CHAPTER EIGHTEEN

Barbarians at the Gates

NOBODY these days reads *Salammbô*. In the nineteenth century everyone read it. Michelet, Gautier, Berlioz, the Empress Eugénie, Oscar Wilde, Joris Huysmans, Algernon Charles Swinburne – they all declared their influential admiration. Flaubert's sumptuously perverse fancy-dress eroticism was the magic ingredient. Romantic realism, always a pleasantly freakish compound, could reach no further. The naked priestess of the moon lasciviously entwined with a large serpent was the image that ensured the book a certain dubious success. *Salammbô* was surprisingly congenial to the educated taste of the day, already accustomed to a rich diet of grand opera and history painting. It became a cult book, the bible of fin-de-siècle decadence. In 1890, after long delay, the novel was staged as an opera; the opera then inspired a short-lived Salammbô school of paintings and statues portraying women with snakes.*

EVER since his wild schoolboy fantasies of painted barbarians howling at the gates of Rouen, Flaubert had been enthralled by the fierce elemental poetry of the ancient world. After five years of *Madame Bovary*, five years in the company of pusillanimous mediocrity, he was now eager for action of a more spacious and decisive kind. 'I feel a need for immense epics,' he announced, even before he had finished with Yonville-l'Abbaye. He wanted to write 'novels with a grandiose setting [...] luxurious and tragic all at the same time [...]'. Reading Herodotus, for the sake of the history lessons he gave to his niece Caroline, he found himself carried away by the account of the battle at

---

* Bram Dijkstra, in his book *Idols of Perversity* (1986), hacks at the roots of these 'fantasies of feminine evil in fin-de-siècle culture'.

Thermopolyae, as if he were still twelve years old. The subject for his next novel lay somewhere in that direction, anywhere out of this world of frock coats and flannel vests.

What kind of subject? 'A good subject for a novel', he wrote later, when he was nearly at the end of *Salammbô*, 'is the kind that comes to you all at once, all in one go. It's the matrix from which all the rest will flow. We are certainly not free to write any old thing. We do not really choose our subjects [. . .]. And that is the secret of any masterpiece: the concord between the subject and the temperament of the author.' And yet the subject of *Salammbô* did not come to Flaubert in this ideally instantaneous form. The first year of writing was marked by hesitation and doubt.

ALL through the summer of 1857, confined to Croisset by lack of funds, Flaubert conscientiously 'gobbled up' nearly a hundred books on Carthage. He had chosen his subject: an obscure and very bloody episode from the first Punic War between Rome and Carthage. The book was to be set in the middle of the third century BC when Carthage's unpaid mercenary soldiers banded together against their employer in the aftermath of the city's first defeat at the hands of Rome. After some initial success, the rebel army had been massacred. The story was to be found in the pages of Polybius, the Greek historian who had chronicled the early triumph of Rome. Its peculiar imaginative appeal lay in the ingenious atrocities that had been committed by both sides, as well as in the notorious savagery of Carthaginian religious beliefs that sanctioned the sacrifice of children to the god Baal. Ancient Carthage allowed the novelist considerable freedom of invention because almost nothing of the pre-Roman city had survived, only a few evocative fragments. Into this loose historical fabric Flaubert planned to weave a tragic love story centred on an invented heroine, Salammbô, the daughter of a great Carthaginian general, who conceives a fatal passion for Matho, the leader of the rebel mercenaries.

Flaubert set to work from the outside, immersing himself for several months in the finer points of Carthaginian siege warfare and temple architecture. He kept postponing the writing of his opening chapter, in the hope that the religious and psychological dimensions of his subject would eventually come alive in his hands. For the moment, though, his subject remained stubbornly inert. His table was stacked with books, but nothing was moving. 'Sometimes', he complained, 'Carthage scares me (its emptiness) so much that I'm tempted to give it up.' But he was not to be deterred, he said, from this 'truculent little pleasantry', which 'ought to be done in a broad and *lively* style'.

Procrastinating horribly, by August Flaubert was 'in a labyrinth' and it was too late to turn back. The 'psychological element' was the problem that no amount of archaeological reading could resolve. There was a great danger of falling in love with trinkets, all the little material details. He would give his whole stack of notes, he said, in exchange for 'being *truly* moved if only for three seconds by the passions of my heroes.'

When Flaubert finally wrote the opening of *Salammbô*, after six months of groping about in the labyrinth, he was dismayed by the 'deplorable academic style' of what he had done. He covered his heroine in precious stones for her first appearance, but then began to worry that an excess of detail was deadening the effect. Where was the simple, vivid image that he needed?

He wrote nothing for a whole month. He was stuck. Sitting gazing into the fire, he reflected that this was a punishment for having started a new novel 'without having carried it in my belly for long enough'. Demoralised, he withdrew from a lucrative agreement to publish *Salammbô* in serial form in *La Presse*. It was folly, he said, 'trying to resuscitate an entire civilisation about which we know nothing'. His writing was veering between the wildly extravagant and the inertly academic. The dialogue was especially dreadful because it kept falling into violent melodrama. 'I feel as if I'm on the wrong track [. . .] my characters didn't actually speak like that [. . .]. I can sense the truth but it doesn't take me, the emotion is missing.'

To supply whatever was still missing, Flaubert decided that he must go to North Africa. He could visit the site of Carthage, absorb the landscape, and pursue his elusive ghosts by daylight. It would be delightful, travelling on horseback, sleeping in a tent once again. 'Living in a house', he wrote, ' is one of the sad features of civilisation. I believe that we were made to sleep on our backs looking up at the stars.'

FLAUBERT was away for three months. Travelling alone, he left Paris on 12 April 1858. In the train to Marseille, ignoring his fellow passengers, he feasted on the sweet melancholy of travel, smoking endlessly, gazing out at the splendid starry night and mulling over all his 'favourite old ideas'. Marseille was pleasantly familiar. Flaubert spent two days there, wandering the sloping streets above the old harbour, rejoicing in the sight of the blue sea, stuffing himself with bouillabaisse, 'smoking in back-street taverns, surrounded by sailors'. Twice he returned to the Hôtel de la Darse where Madame Foucaud had visited his bedroom eighteen years previously, a bedroom that was now a barber's shop. Twice Flaubert went there for a shave, assailed by 'Chateaubriandesque reflections on the passage of time'. He realised that he hadn't spoken to anyone for nearly a week.

The sea crossing on board the steamship *Hermus* took forty-eight hours. Sailing overnight along the African coast towards Tunis, Flaubert was kept awake by his impatience to see Carthage. The moonlit deck was covered in sleeping bodies, lulled by the ship's engines, barefoot men in white robes, pilgrims on their way to Mecca. Flaubert filled the pages of his notebook with comic miniature portraits of his fellow passengers: a clock-maker with a club foot, a diminutive cavalry officer, a sylph-like chambermaid. Leaving home, Flaubert could leave behind him the burden of his indignation. Like a boy released, the man could begin to observe the world anew, with a fresh, delighted, omnivorous curiosity.

Flaubert spent six weeks in Tunisia. This was not Egypt, but it was familiar. 'I can smell it once again, carried on the warm breeze, the old smell of the Orient.' He worked purposefully, often spending twelve or fourteen hours in the saddle, exploring Carthage, Constantine and the principal archaeological sites. Armed with ministerial letters of introduction, he sought the company of the congenial elite of the expatriates. He conversed with engineers, postmasters, army officers, consular officials, archaeologists, adventurers and their lady companions. Le Colonel Caligaris, Miss Nelly Rosemberg, le Comte de Saint-Foix, Baron Alexandre de Krafft, their sonorous names alone evoke a long-lost world of elegant riding-boots, monogrammed porcelain and *louche* masculine anecdote. Conscientiously, every evening, Flaubert wrote up his notes. He was gathering impressions rather than recording artefacts or telling the story of his journey. He wanted colour and atmosphere, landscapes, ruins, sunsets, and the play of light on the mountains.

Certain moments stood out. He remembered a misty day in a quiet rose garden by the sea. There he saw an exquisite Roman mosaic with three women, a sea monster and a horse. The gardener filled a watering can and watered the mosaic, suddenly bringing all its colours to life. He remembered dining with a postmaster and three other 'gentlemen' and discovering that they had all read *Madame Bovary*. He remembered evenings in Tunis, sitting in a Moorish tavern, listening to the Jewish singers. 'I'm not thinking about my novel at all,' he wrote. 'I look at the landscape, that's all, and I enjoy myself enormously.'

Back in Croisset, exhausted from his journey, Flaubert slept almost continuously for four days. He was dazed by the sudden calm and the silence of the place. 'I feel as though I had just come home from a two-month masked ball.' He was now in excellent spirits, full of hope and energy, swimming in the river every day, 'just like some sea god'. This time, with *Salammbô*, he would be writing to please himself. There would be no concessions. 'I shall write horrors, I'll put in male brothels and serpent stew.' In a mood of playful triumph, Flaubert ended his African travel journal with a prayer for inspiration: 'All the energies of nature that I have soaked up, may they invigorate me and pass through into my book. Come to me, you powers of sympathetic emotion. Come to me, come to me, resurrection of the past [. . .]. Take pity on me, God of Souls, give me Strength – and Hope!' Within a week Flaubert had made his decision. 'Carthage', he announced, in surprisingly cheerful tones, 'will have to be completely reworked, remade in fact. *I'm demolishing everything*. It was absurd! Impossible! False!'

FLAUBERT began *Salammbô* again. He spent three months writing 'a chapter of explanations', a lengthy description of the city of Carthage and the Carthaginian people, 'including clothing, government, religion, finance, commerce, etcetera'. Beyond the details, Flaubert's Carthage comes into sharp political focus as a 'monstrous oligarchy' dedicated to commerce, tyrannising the local tribes and controlling the neighbouring cities. For all its material wealth, Carthage is a culture without a soul, selfish, greedy and blind. It has no vision, no indigenous traditions, no artists of its own to teach it sublimity. Interestingly, there is only one individual figure in this new chapter. He is a nameless wandering poet, a visionary tramp who represents, impotently, everything that is missing from the all-conquering city-state: 'wrinkled as a mummy, pale as a ghost, crowned in seaweed, completely naked [. . .] chanting prayers to the four winds, conjuring spirits, hurling curses [. . .]'.

The new chapter came to nothing. Flaubert soon decided, perhaps at Bouilhet's insistence, that this great block of material had better be absorbed invisibly into the narrative. The explanatory chapter was discarded and Flaubert lapsed once again into self-lacerating uncertainty. It was '*la maladie noire*', his old friend, the black sickness. 'I've had it once before,' he explained, 'in the great days of my youth, for a whole eighteen months and it almost did for me; it went away then, it will go away again, let us hope.'

It took the form of intense self-disgust. 'When I take a look into it, my heart gives off a sickening smell. Sometimes I feel sad enough to drop dead.' The symptoms were physically overwhelming: aching limbs, twinges in the cerebellum and stomach pains so intense that he took to his bed.

By December 1858 he was recovering, working on *Salammbô* with a feverish intensity. He portrayed himself alone at Croisset, working until four in the morning, sleeping into the afternoon, walking from room to room, shouting and singing, in a slightly crazy mood, hardly ever seeing daylight, hardly aware of the day of the week. The wintry isolation of the place was intoxicating: '[. . .] nothing happening, no sound. Complete objective nothingness.' The long December nights brought endless rain. Sitting in the lamplight, smoking his cigar, he could gaze into the fire, listening to the wind in the trees, dreaming about his heroine, the daughter of Hamilcar. To the bourgeois eye this might look like wasting time. The *Dictionnaire des idées reçues* puts it succinctly. 'ARTISTS: All hoaxers [. . .]. What artists do can scarcely be called work.' But for Flaubert it was of the essence. These hours of slow-drifting reverie were indispensable, a form of primary imaginative labour that fed into the other secondary labour of writing. 'For me,' he wrote, 'a book has always only been a *way of living* in some particular milieu. That is what explains my hesitations, my anguish and my slowness.'

The psychological subject matter of *Salammbô* was undoubtedly part of the problem. On the surface it was a gleefully sadistic extravaganza. This aspect of the book was most prominent when Flaubert described his intentions to Gautier in January 1859: 'My characters don't talk, they bellow. It's the colour of blood from beginning to end. There are male brothels, cannibalism, elephants and scenes of torture. But it may well be that the whole thing is profoundly stupid and perfectly tedious.' Beneath this masculine *badinage*, the psychosexual subject of *Salammbô* was perilously close to home. 'I am convinced', he confided to Mademoiselle Leroyer de Chantepie, that the most furious material appetites are expressed *unknowingly* by flights of idealism, just as the most sordidly extravagant sexual acts are engendered by a pure desire for the impossible, an ethereal aspiration after sovereign joy. I do not know (nobody knows) the meaning of the words body and soul, where the one ends and the other begins. We feel *the play of energy* and that is all. [. . .] The anatomy of the human heart has not yet been done. [. . .] recently I have come back to those psycho-medical studies which I found so fascinating ten years ago when I was writing my *Saint Antoine*. In my *Salammbô* I am dealing with hysteria and mental illness. There are treasures yet to be found in all of this.

Furious, sordid and joyful, body and soul and *the play of energy* between them: Freud and De Sade alike might have endorsed this dynamically disruptive formulation. It confirms Flaubert's modernity. It also suggests that his malady and his most profound psychological theme were all of a piece. His self-tormenting saints and his doomed visionary heroines were all cut from the same gloriously bright cloth.

B Y the autumn of 1859, after two years of work, Flaubert had finally begun to 'see' his characters. They were now more than just dolls with names. But this was not a comfortable condition. Bouilhet was worried by the mysterious reappearance of his friend's 'deep endless sadness'. Flaubert was exhausted. The emotional demands of this strange creation, exacerbated by unspecified 'domestic worries and upsets', pitched him into a new series of epileptic attacks. On the evening of 18 September 1859, returning to Rouen from a weekend in the *pays de Caux*, Flaubert almost fell under a train. 'It would have been a great loss to literature,' he joked. '[. . .] but [. . .] it would have spared me all the corrections I still have to make.'*

Resuscitating Carthage, that city of the dead, inflicted an inconceivable sadness. Yet Flaubert pushed on, undeterred by periods of physical illness and deep melancholy. He had been this way before. He knew the path. He could even envisage writing about the experience. 'For years', he told a close friend, 'I have been pondering a novel about madness, or rather about *the way* in which you go mad.' One of his many unwritten novels, *La Spirale*, was a shadowy possibility, never abandoned, but never pursued beyond the merest outline.

* Jean Bruneau, the editor of Flaubert's letters, suggests that this fall may have been due to an epileptic attack. Flaubert himself blamed it on having recently looked over his notes from the Orient.

On 15 January 1860, walking along a Paris street, Flaubert fell on his face, causing serious injuries to his nose and eyebrow. Mildly exasperated by his younger brother's bad habits, Achille wrote to Dr Jules Cloquet for advice. 'Is it really the case that the epileptiform accidents can have started again? That would be wretched after such a long apparent cure. Gustave, however, does all he can, by the way he lives, to bring them on again: stays up all night, overworks, perpetual overexcitement. [. . .] once he has recovered give him a thorough lecture on this subject; he likes you and he [. . .] trusts you. Perhaps he will listen to you [. . .].' Frightened by the severity of his injuries (and perhaps by Cloquet's lecture), Flaubert spent ten days in bed. He was soon well enough to 'visit Paphos' again, embarking on a heroic sexual binge with women referred to only as '*mes cocottes*', a normal feature of Flaubert's winters in Paris.

There was no lasting cure for the sadness and the self-disgust. It had to be drained off and deposited prophylactically between the lines of *Salammbô*. When Flaubert pictured himself writing, that year, he saw another Job, sitting on his dunghill scratching at his sores. By October 1860 he had reached the climactic chapters of the book, 'Le Serpent' and 'Sous la tente', in which the priestess of the moon sacrifices her virginity to the barbarian warrior Matho. This was the great test of Flaubert's powers. 'It has to be simultaneously obscene and chaste, mystical and realist.' Having read everything ever written about Carthage, he was out on his own, striving for an audacious blend of the archaeologically exact and the archetypically suggestive. Flaubert was the very pattern of the erudite bourgeois Orientalist, sitting by his fire in a room full of books, 'dreaming about hairless cunts beneath a cloudless sky.'

IN May 1861, to celebrate his work-in-progress, Flaubert summoned close friends to his Paris apartment for a private reading of excerpts from *Salammbô*. To mark the occasion, a special Oriental dinner was to be served. The menu included 'human flesh, brain of bourgeois and tigress clitorises sautéed in rhinoceros butter'. The reading proceeded intermittently for ten hours, from four in the afternoon until two in the morning. The de Goncourt brothers, Jules and Edmond, were among the guests; they recorded their impressions of Flaubert's vocal performance, which was remarkable even by the histrionic standards of the day: ' fierce, resonant, roaring [. . .] droning out dramatically like the voice of an actor'. Reading aloud was a vital dimension of Flaubert's artistic personality. He had told the de Goncourts how he loved to act and declaim furiously from his novel as he wrote it, shouting himself so hoarse that he needed to drink water by the jugful, intoxicated by the noise he was making. Delicately and snobbishly fastidious, the de Goncourts found Flaubert slightly menacing, as though he were some large wild animal that had found its way into their drawing room. In their journals, Flaubert has a voice like a bull, he howls, 'his eyes bulging, his face turning red, his arms in the air [. . .] like a lion roaring'.

Recitation, both solitary and convivial, was a well-established Romantic ritual. In his youth, Flaubert used to recite poetry aloud to himself: 'When I am on my own out in the country I walk to the rhythm and it keeps me company along the way as if I were singing.' He could recite whole pages of Chateaubriand from memory. Du Camp recalled – it was merely another of his friend's oddities – that Flaubert would read aloud what he had just written 'quite compulsively' to the first visitor who turned up, giving every word a special intonation, 'as if to inflate its meaning and increase its sonority'.

Composition was a performance too. Caroline, Flaubert's niece, remembered sitting at her sewing with him in the evenings while he wrote at the big circular table in his study. He would groan aloud over difficult passages; then, when he found the right phrasing, his voice would sink to a gentle whisper, rising in volume as he repeated the words over to himself. Then he would stride around the room triumphantly chanting the syllables in time to his footsteps. When he reached the end of the chapter he was writing, he would take a day off to read it aloud to her, so as to 'see the effect'. She recalled that 'his style of reading was unique, lilting, emphatic in a way that felt exaggerated to begin with but was eventually very pleasing'. Such enthusiasm was contagious. 'You quivered along with him.'

The champion of impersonality needed a good pair of lungs, romantically *bellowing*, to bring the realist novel into the world.

It was the 'moral colouring' of Carthage, not the material detail, that Flaubert sought to render. The moral colouring of his novel's final chapters was so very dark and bloody that Flaubert began to waver. Every conceivable atrocity was to be described in lingering detail: death in battle, with the victor sucking the blood from his victim's neck; death by hunger, with men driven to cannibalism and suicide; human sacrifice, with children being roasted alive; then, as a finale, the chaotic, jubilant vengeance of the Carthaginian people on the captive body of Matho, the barbarian leader. Flaubert liked to project his artistic purpose in the most aggressive terms. He could imagine his reader: 'Drown the bourgeois in the hard stuff, make it 11,000 degrees proof, and let his mouth burn from it until he bellows aloud in pain. That'll be the way to rouse him. No point making concessions, pruning down, sweetening up [. . .].' Was this meant to be poison? Or was it just exceptionally strong medicine? A satiric-exotic vision of human extremity, somewhere in between *Candide* and *Justine*?

Salammbô, whatever its lineage, was intended to be 'instructively' outrageous. But what if it were just 'deadly boring'? Flaubert was suddenly 'full of doubts' about the whole thing. 'I think there are too many soldiers.' The book was going to 'revolt the sensitive [. . .] irritate the archaeologists [. . .] and win me a reputation as a pederast and a cannibal'. Because it gives off 'an immense disdain for the human race [. . .] the reader will be vaguely offended [. . .] and will hold it against me'. It was also Flaubert's singular misfortune to find himself up against Victor Hugo's massive new *humanitarian* novel *Les Misérables*. The first instalment of this gigantic rival to *Salammbô* was published on 19 April 1862, the day before Flaubert finished his last chapter.

CHAPTER NINETEEN

Dining Out

WHAT would we see if we could conjure up Flaubert at this point, around the year of his fortieth birthday? 'Very tall, very broad, large bulging eyes, swollen eyelids, heavy cheeks, untidy drooping moustache, battered complexion with red blotches.' Tinged with professional malice, that was how the de Goncourt brothers, Jules and Edmond, saw their new acquaintance, Gustave Flaubert, in May 1859. They had recently met through Gautier, in the editorial offices of *L'Artiste*, and their friendship flourished over the next ten years. They met regularly; they conversed exuberantly and confidentially. The de Goncourts, indulging their mildly treacherous habit, also made notes at the end of the evening. Thanks to their efforts, we can listen in to the literary gossip that flowed so copiously across the café tables, through the opulent salons and along the gas-lit theatre corridors of the 1860s. We hear Flaubert talking among his friends, holding forth, unbuttoned. This is Flaubert the nineteenth-century man of letters, slightly larger than life, easily identified.

The de Goncourt 'portrait' of Flaubert is like an album of sketches, an intimate, episodic impression of a subject on the move. The sequence begins in the late 1850s and extends to the very last months of Flaubert's life. The portrait itself is often sharply critical. His voice, his size, his jokes, his moustache – and possibly his talent – were all somehow *excessive*. What was it about him? Something not quite to their taste. Flaubert was a fascinating, preposterous specimen, a coarse, declamatory provincial whose salient feature was mere tenacity. He could toil like an ox but he lacked true finesse. Flaubert, for his part, soon had the measure of his new friends. He referred to them teasingly as *les bichons*, the lapdogs, the little darlings. When in their company he liked to exaggerate. He became both more cynical and more opinionated.

Dining with them for the first time, in November 1858, Flaubert launched recklessly upon one of his favourite and most provocative topics, the Marquis de Sade. Flaubert, the de Goncourts decided, had 'a mind haunted by de Sade, to which he keeps returning, as though to a mystery that he finds alluring. Essentially fond of depravity, seeking it out [. . .] and constantly acclaiming de Sade: "It's the most wonderfully amusing thing I've ever seen!"' That name came up once again, about a year later, in the course of a Sunday evening of masculine conversation. 'Stories about teachers at the Collège de Rouen. Then some talk of De Sade, to which Flaubert is always returning, as if fascinated. "It's the last word of Catholicism," he says [. . .]. "It's the spirit of the Inquisition, the spirit of torture, the spirit of the medieval Church, the horror of anything natural. There isn't a single tree or an animal in de Sade."'

What was the nature of Flaubert's fascination for de Sade? Why did he place de Sade alongside Rabelais and Byron as one of the great comic truth-tellers? Beyond any fleeting male-adolescent taste for the disgustingly cruel, Flaubert responded profoundly to something in de Sade's strange visions of the flesh. Drawing on the miscellaneous Romantic fascination with pain and disaster, *Salammbô* pushes beyond de Sade, expels the sadists from their candlelit dungeons and pushes them out into the street, on to the battlefield, where they occupy positions of the highest authority. *Salammbô* invites us to imagine a whole society run *like that*. (Several twentieth-century examples come to mind.) In that sense *Salammbô* belongs alongside Voltaire's *Candide*. It's a nineteenth-century *conte philosophique* pretending to be a historical novel.

Such niceties may have been lost on many of *Salammbô's* earliest readers. They were more interested in newspaper gossip about the size of Flaubert's advance. Flaubert, arguing that *Salammbô* would sell and sell, demanded 30,000 francs. His publisher, Michel Lévy, calculating that *Madame Bovary* would be a difficult book to follow, drove a hard bargain. Thirty thousand, said Lévy, was much more, than Victor Hugo or George Sand would get. *Madame Bovary* had only made eight thousand, and that was a huge success. How many copies had actually been sold? Lévy refused to say. *Salammbô* was scarcely commercial. And this time there would have to be an illustrated edition.

Flaubert was adamant on the subject of illustrations. They violated all the special effects of writing. 'The finest literary description is swallowed up', he said, 'by the most mediocre drawing. As soon as a character is fixed by the illustrator's pencil it loses its generality [. . .]. A picture of a woman looks like one woman, and that's all. The idea is closed up, complete, and all further words are useless. But a woman in writing makes the reader dream of a thousand women.' Lévy backed down on the illustrations and offered his author 10,000 francs, on condition that he have an option on Flaubert's next novel, which must be set in modern times. Flaubert accepted. *Salammbô* was to be published in November 1862, by which time public interest in *Les Misérables* would be subsiding.

Meanwhile, in between books, Flaubert felt gloomy and exhausted. He spent the summer at Croisset, reading and sleeping and not knowing what to do with himself or where his next subject was to be found. 'The future is a worry. What am I going to do? I'm full of doubts and fears and dreams. A novel, whatever its subject, is like a long journey; I hesitate and my heart aches before I set off.' He tried his hand at writing a pantomime, but his collaborators deserted him. He wrote an Academy speech in praise of Louis Bouilhet, that illustrious local author. He read Victor Hugo's *Les Misérables* and was predictably dismissive. Hugo had allowed his populist enthusiasm to blur his vision. His style was 'deliberately low and incorrect [. . .] a way of pleasing the masses'. The characters were mere puppets. Very eloquent, but they all sounded the same. 'It's not allowed', Flaubert observed, 'to paint a false portrait of society when Balzac and Dickens are your contemporaries.' Flaubert's next novel, *L'Education sentimentale*, would be – amongst many other things – a subtle riposte to *Les Misérables*.

In September, after spending three dutiful weeks in Vichy with his mother, Flaubert settled in Paris for the winter. He was still no further forward. 'I'm thinking vaguely about another book, but I still need to do a great deal before I even make a plan. I have a great desire, or rather a great need to be writing.' He wanted to avoid the mistake he had made with *Salammbô*. There were to be no false starts, no wasted months of writing. He would take his time, look around and wait for the right subject. In the event, Flaubert's state of indecision lasted for nearly two and a half years. Not until the late summer of 1864 did the ingredients of his great Parisian novel finally come together in the correct combination.

What was Flaubert looking for? Why did he take so long to find it? There is no simple answer to such questions, but the problem went back, I suggest, to the year 1844 when Flaubert had been obliged to abandon his less-than-brilliant Parisian legal career. In those years, 1862–4, we may see a man in his early forties unconsciously retracing his steps along a path he had followed once before. He is trying to do it all over again, allowing himself now some belated portion of the metropolitan success that was so abruptly denied to him – by illness? by incompetence? – in his early twenties. This time, even though he is rather too old to figure plausibly as the hero of a fairy tale, he will boldly make his way into the palace, win the heart of the princess, amuse the queen and carry off a richly symbolic medal. In the 1860s, the final hectic decade of the Second Empire, Flaubert enjoyed considerable worldly success. He had the time of his life. *L'Education sentimentale*, the novel that he now wrote after such long hesitation, is thus a record of the *two* distinct Parisian chapters of his life.

THIS new and pleasant conjunction of art and life was marked out by Flaubert's presence in the Latin quarter *Restaurant Magny* on the night of 6 December 1862. Flaubert was there, at the invitation of Jules and Edmond de Goncourt, for the second of the Magny Dinners, the title adopted by an informal dining club, recently founded by Sainte-Beuve and his friends. Composed loosely of writers and artists, the club met every other Saturday in one of Morel Magny's private dining rooms. The food was excellent, the company was sympathetic and the conversation was notoriously uninhibited. Over the next few years the Magny Dinners brought Flaubert into contact with a large circle that included Sainte-Beuve, Taine, Renan, Turgenev and George Sand.

Salammbô had been published just a few weeks earlier and Flaubert was now working energetically to promote his new novel. He was in his element; his expertise in the dark arts of influence disconcerted even the de Goncourt brothers. 'He quietly pushes himself forward, establishes relations with important people, creates a network of useful acquaint-ances, all the time pretending to be independent, lazy, and fond of solitude.' Copies of *Salammbô* had gone out to an illustrious company of friends and allies that included three countesses and a government minister. Immediate reactions were mostly favourable. Berlioz was enthusiastic: 'It scared me, I've been dreaming about it for the last few nights.' Champfleury thought that it reflected a stale romantic taste for history and 'should have been printed in an edition of a hundred copies like a volume of poems.' Victor Hugo, ever oracular, congratulated the author on 'having resurrected a vanished world'. Michelet thought it a thing of astonishing splendour, like a meteorite. There was one small dissenting voice: 'It's an atrocious book, utterly sadistic from beginning to end.'

Flaubert's principal purpose on this December evening was to cultivate the good opinion of Sainte-Beuve, the most influential literary journalist of the day. Aware of his objections to *Salammbô*, fearing a strongly hostile review, Flaubert immediately cornered Sainte-Beuve and 'with a wealth of gestures' tried to 'convince him of the excellence of his work'. He thought he had succeeded. 'Old Sainte-Beuve has come round a great deal,' he told the de Goncourts after the dinner. 'He's going to do three articles on me and apologise in the last one.'

Flaubert must have realised his mistake when he read the first of Sainte-Beuve's articles in the Monday edition of *Le Constitutionnel*. Putting their friendship aside, Sainte-Beuve intended to pay Flaubert the supreme compliment of 'an attentive and impartial judgement'. There followed, over the next three weeks, Sainte-Beuve's judicious sigh of disappointment that Flaubert had not fulfilled the expectations aroused by *Madame Bovary*. He criticised the moral tone of *Salammbô*. Such lengthy and impassive descriptions of torture and mutilation betrayed 'a slightly sadistic imagination'. Sainte-Beuve offered a cultural diagnosis of this condition. It was the old desire to shock. 'For fear of sounding like a squeamish whimpering bourgeois he has deliberately pursued the opposite vice: he cultivates the atrocious.' Sainte-Beuve concluded with the observation that historical novels cannot be nourished by mere erudition. They require of the author a deep affinity with their subject, an affinity such as Walter Scott enjoyed. Without this there can be no true 'resurrection' of the past, only a laborious restoration of surface detail. Salammbô, the heroine, is simply uninteresting; merely a bizarre mask with nothing beneath, nothing that engages our human sympathies.

Undaunted, Flaubert wrote an energetic letter of self-justification, privately explaining his artistic intentions, a luxury he never allowed himself in public. The main problem, he told Sainte-Beuve, was this: 'You simply dislike the very object of my book, this whole barbarian, oriental moloch-ish world.' His aim had not been to emulate Scott. He had endeavoured, he said, 'to pin down a mirage by applying to Antiquity the techniques of the modern novel [. . .]'. As for his heroine, he drew a veil over the question of her authenticity. 'I do not know how real she is. For neither you nor I nor anyone, ancient or modern, can understand the woman of the Orient, simply because it is not possible to be on visiting terms with her.' It's a joke: the supreme enigma is both feminine and oriental, an object of reverie, not to be prosaically *visited*.

More seriously, Flaubert took issue with Sainte-Beuve's moral allegations.

I must tell you quite frankly, *cher Maître*, that your phrase about the 'sadistic tendency' of my imagination was rather wounding. Everything you write is taken seriously. Now any such phrase of yours, once it is in print, becomes almost a mark of dishonour. Have you forgotten that I once sat on the criminal bench in a courtroom, accused of offending public decency, and that the stupid and the vicious will use anything to attack me? So do not be surprised if one of these days in *Le Figaro* you read something to this effect: 'Monsieur Flaubert is a disciple of de Sade. His friend, his sponsor, a master critic, has said as much quite clearly [. . .].' What would I say to that? What would I do?

Flaubert deleted the next paragraph of his letter. It is of great interest as his most lucidly critical appraisal of de Sade.

In my bloody excesses I am quite opposed to the great Marquis. He hated Nature, whereas I adore it. I defy you to find in all of de Sade either a tree or an animal or even a description of a naked woman. Descriptions of sexual organs, that's all there is. At every turn, it must be said. But never a man or a woman. [. . .] this supremely insincere [*archifaux*] metaphysical intelligence always went straight to the point, continually preaching, never even trying to portray his subject.

I N spite of Sainte-Beuve, in spite of church sermons denouncing its paganism, in spite of pedantic objections from scholarly antiquarians, in spite of infuriating personal slanders in *Le Figaro*, *Salammbô* flourished. It was the great event of the season. Berlioz praised it in his weekly column in *Le Moniteur universel*, claiming that he had already read it three times. The new director of the Opéra invited Flaubert to discuss the possible staging of *Salammbô*, with a libretto by Gautier and music by Verdi.* George Sand published an appreciative review and invited Flaubert to pay her a visit. The Empress Eugénie, wife of Napoléon III, was fashionably delighted by *Salammbô*. Such was its reputation that a third edition of the novel was required within a few months of its publication.

Prosecuted for *Madame Bovary*, Flaubert was cultivated for *Salammbô*. Here was an irony of the most obvious, the most awkward kind. But what was to be done? Flaubert put aside his hermit's gown, invested in some expensive trousers and welcomed his new celebrity without excessive moral embarrassment. In January 1863 he received an invitation to Princess Mathilde Bonaparte's Wednesday evening reception. Princess Mathilde presided over a mildly dissident liberal salon where selected artists and writers could taste imperial splendour without permanently compromising their principles. A friend told Flaubert that the Emperor and the Empress *would be there*. 'They have expressed a desire to see you.'

Flaubert arrived at nine in the company of the de Goncourt brothers. The modest imperial mansion on the rue de Courcelles was lit up. In the entrance hall stood a uniformed guard; the women wore their diamonds; the men had their medals. 'We were almost the only three people there without decorations.' The Empress Eugénie asked Flaubert if she could have one of Salammbô's costumes copied as a ballgown. Flaubert obligingly commissioned a fashionable artist to prepare a set of drawings. A few days later he was disappointed to learn that the Empress had changed her mind. The bodice of the authentic Salammbô costume would have been too indecently tight for Her Catholic Majesty.

What was Gustave Flaubert, *bourgeoisophobus* and hermit of Croisset, doing here in the Paris salon of La Princesse Mathilde Bonaparte? Simply enjoying the company of a plump, imperious, bejewelled, bare-shouldered woman of his own age? Admiring her watercolours and her taste in soft furnishings? No, that will not do. Let us take her seriously for a moment. Flaubert himself took her seriously enough to write more than a hundred and fifty letters to her.† Princess Mathilde presided, so it is always said, over one of the great salons of the

---

* They agreed, interestingly, that there might be a problem 'finding a tightly consecutive dramatic action' in the novel. Gautier then procrastinated for many years over the libretto for *Salammbô*.

† Mathilde's letters to Flaubert were all destroyed, probably by his niece.

nineteenth century. Her regular guests included Gautier, Dumas, Sainte-Beuve and the de Goncourt brothers. An ardent Bonapartist ever since childhood, she liked it to be known that if her uncle, the first Napoléon, had not made himself emperor, she would probably be selling oranges on the quayside at Ajaccio. She had once been married, briefly and miserably, to an incontinently sadistic Russian mining millionaire, Anatole Demidov. Her political loyalty to her cousin, Louis Napoléon, was generously rewarded in 1852 when he blustered his way on to the imperial throne. Mathilde was given a title, *Sa Altesse Impériale*, an official residence on the rue de Courcelles, and an allowance of 200,000 francs per year, later increased to 500,000. To add to her allure, she also had a summer villa with a lake, an hour away from Paris, at St-Gratien. Her nickname was *Notre Dame des Arts*, an affectionately mocking reference to her immense powers of cultural patronage. Flaubert evidently regarded her with a wary fascination, inextricably political and erotic. Imaginatively, a princess is still a princess, however dubious the legitimacy of the regime on which she depends. The princess used to send out her commissionaire, bristling with medals, to deliver invitations to dinner; a gesture that always made a great impression on Flaubert's Parisian concierge.

IT is in this new setting that we see Flaubert, late one night in February 1863, after a dinner with Princess Mathilde. He is waiting for a cab in the rue de Courcelles, talking to the de Goncourts 'about his modern novel'. He was planning, he said, to put everything into it: 'the movement of 1830 – in relation to the love affairs of a Parisian woman – and the physiognomy of 1840, and 1848, and the Empire'. It would be just like 'fitting the ocean into a carafe'. This is already close to *L'Education sentimentale*. Like *Les Misérables* it would have everything in it; unlike *Les Misérables* it would not be oceanic.

But Flaubert was not as single-minded as he may have seemed. Back in Croisset for the summer, he was hesitating. He spent his days reading Goethe and Theocritus and spent his evenings 'working simultaneously on my two plans', quite unable to decide between them.

I'm slaving away at my Parisian novel which is not coming on at all. [. . .] I can't see any central scene. It doesn't grip me. [. . .] I'm really drawn to the story of my two old cockroaches. That's the one, I'm quite sure. In spite of dreadful difficulties in varying the monotony of the effect. But I'll be hounded from France and from Europe if I write that book! Though it might be better than botching another one. And it's more my sort of thing, *stories of the heart* not being my strong point, I do believe.

L'Education sentimentale, though it still lacked a title, was soon 'beginning to take shape'. Yet doubts persisted. The thing was still just 'a series of analyses and mediocre gossip'. He might still go back to *Bouvard et Pécuchet* – 'It's an old idea that I've had for years [. . .]. I'd rather write a passionate book. But we don't choose our subjects, we submit to them.' Du Camp recognised his friend's symptoms. 'You're like a fish out of water when you haven't got a good subject to be immersed in.' He advised him to stop trying so hard and just let it condense by itself.

After 'three very distressing months in Croisset, writing nothing', Flaubert accompanied his mother to Vichy. Charles Lambert, his old acquaintance from Cairo, was staying there too, but even his 'philosophical companionship' had no effect on Flaubert's mood. He sat in the Hôtel Britannique, reading and eating, too dejected even to seek distraction in the local brothels. 'I am not cheerful enough, or not young enough to pay homage to the common Venus of the masses.' The summer heat was most uncomfortable. A Rabelaisean torpor engulfed him. 'I feel as limp as a dog's dick after coitus, I'm red, breathless and moist, wilting and incapable of any new spurt, any valiant spattering forth.'

The decisive impulse came to Flaubert in unexpected form at the end of the summer. It was a paragraph in a letter from Maxime Du Camp, a man always in touch with the gossip of the day. This is what it said: 'Mère Schlésinger is mad, melancholy to the last degree and locked up as such in an asylum somewhere [. . .]. They are keeping it all very quiet, but I heard it from her doctor himself.' Elisa Schlésinger, the idol of his youth, the great love of his life. It was a bitterly sad dénouement. And there was more to come. 'Mère Schlésinger', wrote Maxime Du Camp a few weeks later, 'is out of the asylum and back in Baden-Baden. I saw her recently walking along the avenue [. . .] on the arm of her son: she was superb; thin, pale, dark complexion, hair completely white and a wild look in her big blue eyes [. . .].' Here, in the image of Elisa Schlésinger's tragically tarnished beauty, was the precise imaginative focus for the *ending* of his novel. The work of creation might happily begin from this.

CHAPTER TWENTY

Tuesday's Child

IN March 1863, the week of her seventeenth birthday, Caroline Hamard inherited 200,000 francs. This pleasantly large sum of money, which came to her from her grandfather, Dr Achille-Cléophas Flaubert, would yield her an annual income of 15,000 francs. Caroline Hamard's inheritance would also bring down upon her, before very long, the catastrophe of a most unhappy marriage, a marriage that her devoted uncle, Gustave Flaubert, was jointly responsible for arranging. Art is evidently more spacious than life. How otherwise could the author of *Madame Bovary*, a chronicle of the secret sufferings of women, so collude in the emotional betrayal of his beloved niece? In a moment of moral crisis, Flaubert played the bully bourgeois. He allowed the family name, that dense and soporific cloud of received ideas, to prevail over all else. What ensued was a tragi-comic fable of filial obedience, quiet desperation and forbidden love that rivalled the plot of any Balzac novel.

CAROLINE, Flaubert's sister's child, had long afforded him all the fierce and sweet emotions of fatherhood. She arrived in his life ideally detached. A child, but without the dreaded encumbrance of a wife. He had supervised the more interesting parts of her education, teaching her history and geography and imparting, by his own example, high notions of intellectual ambition. She called him 'Nounou'. 'We were', she recalled, 'infinitely fond of each other.' She habitually turned to him for affection, throwing herself eagerly into his strong arms. Her grandmother, Madame Flaubert, true to her glacial temperament, disapproved of such extravagant behaviour. She used to scold them for it. '*C'est ridicule, Gustave!* You're spoiling that child.'

Caroline, perhaps in protest, was given to volcanic infant rages; her 'nervous attacks' (as they were ominously called) might be linked to those of her uncle. Beyond the comfortingly immense presence of her *Nounou*, Caroline's emotional life was centred upon her own privately improvised version of Catholicism. She made barefoot pilgrimages among the fruit trees in the garden. She constructed a little chapel in her bedroom, decorated with dozens of tiny candles. Her uncle, though he was no believer, never mocked these devotions. Unlike Uncle Achille, with his sarcastic jokes about her orthodox Friday omelette, *Nounou* respected the tender spiritual poetry of her girlhood.

In the summer of 1857, when Caroline was eleven years old, a professional artist was employed to teach her to draw. A few years younger than her uncle, Johanny Maisiat was a flower-painter, an intelligent, imaginative man, 'a charming fellow'. He had agreed to teach Flaubert's niece privately, as a special favour to a friend. Generous and patient, Maisiat was ideally qualified to expound to Mademoiselle Hamard the subtle glories of the Louvre or the play of light and shadow in the landscape at Croisset. Maisiat was also the first man who took Mademoiselle Hamard seriously 'as a woman'. Her private lessons were her 'greatest pleasure' and all her ardent girlish affections were soon attached to the image of her teacher.

Her guardians had other plans. The talented but impecunious Maisiat was not a suitable match for a girl with Caroline Hamard's expensive worldly tastes. Maisiat was an artist, a bohemian, an unreliable type. She would do better with a young man in a social position equivalent to her own. Ernest Commanville, that prosperous young timber merchant, for example. He had had his eye on Caroline ever since she was fourteen, having met her briefly at her cousin's wedding back in 1860. Commanville would do very nicely for Caroline. He was not merely a decent fellow. He was, in the words of Madame Flaubert, 'an industrialist in a splendid financial position. He has a mechanical sawmill with a steam engine in Dieppe which yields excellent profits.' How could any girl say no to 'a rich man who loves her and will take her without a penny'.

Caroline hated the whole idea. She wept with rage. The prospect of marriage to that *Monsieur C* was 'like being thrown off the summit of Mount Parnassus', where she had dwelt so pleasantly and for so long, savouring her ideal passion for Johanny Maisiat. Madame Flaubert, faced with a storm, fell ill and sought shelter in her bed. The task of persuading the wretched girl now fell to her uncle.

From his bachelor apartment on the boulevard du Temple, Flaubert mustered his *savoir-vivre* and wrote a kindly but decisive letter to his niece on 23 December 1863. He conceded that the imminent formal meeting with Ernest Commanville might well leave her 'as unsure as ever'. He urged her, nonetheless, to do her duty.

Look and consider and scrutinise your whole being (heart and soul) and see if the gentleman entails any possibility of happiness. Human life is not made up of poetical ideas and noble sentiments. But if a bourgeois existence makes you die of boredom, then what are you to do? Your poor old grandmother wants to have you married, for fear of leaving you all alone, and I too, my dear Caro, would like to see you united to some decent fellow who would make you as happy as possible. When I saw you the other evening, weeping so copiously, your desolation broke my heart. We love you dearly, my bibi, and the day of your marriage will not be ever so cheerful for your two old companions. [. . .] I don't have any real advice to offer you. The thing that counts in Monsieur C's favour is his whole manner. What is more, we know his character, his origins and his friendships, things almost impossible to ascertain with a Parisian. Perhaps you could find somebody more brilliant, here in Paris. But wit and *charm* fall almost exclusively to bohemian types. It's such an atrocious idea, my dear niece married to a man with no money, that I cannot entertain it for even one moment. Yes, my darling, I do declare that I would rather see you married to some millionaire grocer than to some penniless genius. The genius, apart from his poverty, would be so brutal and tyrannical in his behaviour that you would be driven mad [. . .]. You will have difficulty in finding a husband who is above you in intelligence and education [. . .]. You are therefore obliged to take a decent fellow who is your inferior. But will you be able to love a man over whom you sit in judgement? Will you be able to live happily with him? That is the question that has to be answered.

Caroline replied on the evening of the next day. Yes, the meeting with Commanville had taken place and she was still undecided. 'This [. . .] cannot go on, it seems that people are beginning to talk about it in Rouen; and I am frightened to think that I shall have to say yes or no only a few days from now [. . .]. Certainly Monsieur C (since that is how you refer to him) has many qualities, we played music together yesterday, he's a good musician [. . .].' She had been making inquiries

17 The Rich Friend: Maxime Du Camp
18 The Other Friend: Louis Bouilhet
19 The Big House: Croisset

20 *Cupid and Psyche* by Canova
21 *The Temptation of Saint Antony* by Callot

22 Sailing the Nile: *cange* on the Nile at Luxor, *c.*1838
23 Maternal Love: *Madonna and Child* by Murillo
24 High Society: Princesse Mathilde Bonaparte

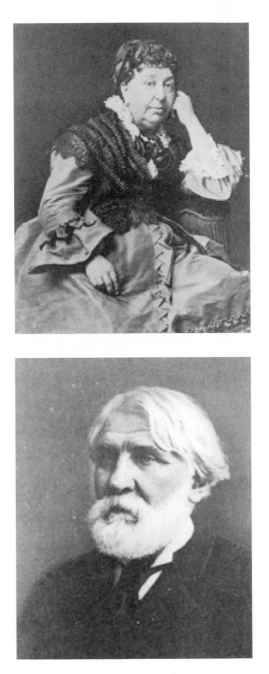

25 George Sand
26 Ivan Turgenev

27 Flaubert's Niece: Caroline Commanville, *née* Hamard

28 The Mother: Madame Flaubert, *c.*1870

29 The Public Face: Gustave Flaubert, *c.*1865

30 The Public Face: Gustave Flaubert, *c.*1880

about him. Even the family lawyer had been consulted, such was her perilous moral isolation. 'I feel ridiculous [. . .] but I am so frightened, so frightened of making a mistake.'

Caroline's indecisive reply, and the fact that his mother had retreated from the field, prompted Flaubert to take the situation in hand. He cancelled all his Parisian arrangements and returned to Rouen to talk some sense into his niece, an operation that took only a few days. 'I've broken the ice,' he wrote. 'I don't think there will be any need to resort to exceptional methods. Everything will be respectably sorted out, I hope. Though there were some tears.' Confident of victory, Flaubert returned to Paris in time for Princess Mathilde's Sunday reception.

There was still the potentially awkward matter of Caroline's father. Madame Flaubert instructed her Parisian lawyer to inform Hamard of the impending marriage. Persuade him, she said, to accept it as a *fait accompli*. And tell him to keep out of the way. Everything seemed to be proceeding smoothly. In the middle of January, Caroline summoned her uncle back to Croisset. He was to be present when the engagement was officially announced. He was delighted. 'I shall see you in the true state of "a young lady with a young man".'

It was generally thought to be a good match. Commanville had money and the young couple would be able to live in style. Caroline thought him handsome enough: 'tall and well built, with an easy manner and a correct bearing [. . .]'. Only Commanville's cold blue eyes and his peculiar low forehead told against him.

And yet all was not quite resolved. There were further 'scenes' at Croisset. In a novelettish episode – as when the unspeakable long-lost relative returns, drawn in by the smell of an inheritance – Caroline's paternal guardian, her disagreeable great-uncle Achille Dupont, professional house guest and ladies' man, appeared in Croisset and 'made a scene', greatly upsetting Madame Flaubert. It may have been a question of money, perhaps a belated objection to the terms of Caroline's dowry.

Many years later, recalling the days immediately before her marriage, Caroline felt that she had been bullied – and even tricked – into accepting Commanville. 'The dreams of my imagination were criticised as foolishness by the two beings whom I respected and loved the most.' Once she had said *yes* she was caught up in the mysterious pleasures of premarital shopping. 'Suddenly I became an important person.' And it was intoxicating, being so important. There were bouquets of white flowers from the most fashionable Parisian florist. There were cashmere shawls and gowns of watered silk so thick that they stood up on their own.

There was also a *significant* conversation with Madame Flaubert. Caroline had decided, she said, that she did not want to have children. Would her grandmother please inform Monsieur Commanville of this fact? Grandmother appeared to accept. 'She smiled at what she no doubt considered a girlish absurdity, but promised to carry out this strange errand. A few days later I asked her if it had been agreed. "Don't worry," she said. "Everything will be fine." '

A few hours after the April wedding, just before the couple left for Italy, Commanville walked his bride out to the summer house at the end of the garden. They sat on the sofa and he took her by the hand. This was their first moment alone together. 'So,' she said tentatively, 'you didn't mind marrying me, even though . . . ' She couldn't finish her sentence. He had no idea what she meant. Madame Flaubert had told him nothing.

Caroline Hamard saw that she had been 'sacrificed'. The conversation with Monsieur Commanville that now ensued was 'difficult and painful'. Their honeymoon in Italy was going to be a sad business, but the bride resolved to say nothing to her grandmother and her uncle of the cruel disillusionment that had now seized upon man and wife. Between Caroline and her new husband 'the abyss' soon opened up. Forty years later, writing her memoirs, she remembered the very moment. They were crossing the Alps, on their way down to Venice. In St Gothard they encountered a small band of itinerant musicians. Caroline was delighted, for she shared her uncle's love of vivid human oddity. Commanville, educated in a different school, merely snarled with contempt. 'Filthy ragamuffins.' He had betrayed his secret. There lived a priggish bourgeois just behind those cold blue eyes.

In Croisset, life continued more quietly without the daughter of the house. A lady companion was employed to distract Madame Flaubert from her ever-anxious imaginings. Mother and companion both came to sit with Flaubert in his study in the evening. Mother soon fell asleep and the companion sat on in a stiffly dutiful silence. 'Fortunately,' Flaubert told Caroline, 'I am working away on the plan of my big Parisian novel.' After two days without a letter Madame Flaubert was worrying about her granddaughter. She may have fallen ill. But then there came an insistently cheerful letter from Venice, reassuring them all.

Flaubert wrote back to his niece. So glad to hear that 'you are having a good time with your companion and are getting on well. Keep that up for another fifty years and you will have done your duty.' Do we hear a rather odd note there? A joke?

On her return to Rouen Caroline Commanville entered into the busy social life of the town. She moved in the best provincial circles, 'rich merchants, military men and civil servants'; she was warmly received by all the grander bourgeois families who had known and admired her grandfather. She was a good housekeeper, 'cold and orderly' like her grandmother. Her husband seemed to be happy enough. Business was good and Commanville always took his young wife with him whenever he had to go to Scandinavia.

Less than a year after the wedding, in February 1865, at a ball given in the local prefecture, Caroline met the man who immediately stole her heart: 'the handsome Baron Ernest Leroy, the very model of a Second Empire prefect'. Though not especially intelligent, Baron Leroy had exquisite manners. He was 'tall, slender and elegant [. . .] his gaze was ardent, and he had *that fatal look*, as they say in novels'. Baron Leroy also just old enough to be her grandfather.

Perfectly fascinated by the melancholy young Madame Commanville, Baron Leroy turned all his formidable energies to the task of seducing her. Having read all the best novels of adultery, this was a part he could play with great style. He pencilled enigmatic messages on her garden door. He hid bunches of violets in her church pew. He crouched in a little boat moored on the Seine among the reeds, watching her window. He even followed her to her villa in Dieppe and sent her fiery love letters that she preserved until the year of her death.

Baron Leroy was splendid. He deployed 'all the passionate romantic stratagems of the heroes in George Sand's novels'. The whole thing was immediately obvious to Flaubert. He began to tease his niece gently on the subject of her frivolous social life. 'The aforesaid prefect seems to be enchanted by your presence.' Caroline, familiar with the script, played her own part with triumphantly calculated passion. 'I committed every indiscretion,' she wrote, rather discreetly, 'but I did not fall [. . .]. The thought of inflicting despair on the three people to whom I felt I belonged – my husband, my uncle and my grandmother – deterred me from eloping with the man I loved.'*

* Caroline Hamard told the story of her first marriage in *Heures d'autrefois*, a fragmentary forty-page memoir written when she was in her early sixties, the ultra-respectable *grande dame* of the Villa Tanit, a kind of shrine – in Antibes – dedicated to the memory of her celebrated uncle. Unexpectedly, Caroline put her younger self (rather than her uncle) at the centre of her story.

CHAPTER TWENTY-ONE

Troubadours

'I CAN only compare you', Flaubert wrote, ' to one of the great rivers of America. A Gentle Immensity.' This was a splendid compliment, especially from such a passionate connoisseur of rivers. Flaubert was writing to George Sand in December 1866. It was a moment of delighted mutual appreciation, towards the end of the first year of their amorous friendship. She was in her early sixties and he was in his mid-forties, a difference of age that was just enough to set them fascinatingly apart. Over the next ten years, the last years of her life, Flaubert and George Sand enjoyed a warm autumnal intimacy in which the erotic, the creative and the openly combative were fruitfully confused.

In many ways it would be difficult to imagine a more unlikely conjunction. On all questions political, sexual and literary, they held quite contrary views. She was an old libertarian, 1830-vintage. He was one of the generation of 1848, defensively sceptical. She had been a utopian socialist in the 1840s, active during the revolution of 1848, retreating into her own obliquely political version of pastoral after the defeat of the Republic. Flaubert, for his part, felt only disdain for those who presumed to speak in the name of the people; he greeted all forms of humanitarian art with exasperated mockery. George Sand was one of the pioneers of Romantic feminism. Emancipation had been the great theme of her early life and writings. Flaubert's public notions of women were emphatically conservative: an orthodox mixture of gallantry and misogyny that he shared with most of the men of his circle. Her writing was miraculously fluent and copious. She drew a large part of her income from the theatre and she had recently written a sprawling, evocative autobiography. His writing was a torment to him. He was a stubborn perfectionist, wedded to an austere idealisation of art.

269

She loved flowers and young children. He preferred books and paintings.

On what ground did they meet? Perhaps such manifest differences of temperament and principle imposed their own subtle discipline of sympathy. Across that deep-echoing divide, each could be an object of passionate curiosity to the other. Explaining himself to her, 'the most comprehending of his confidants', Flaubert was undoubtedly granted a clearer and a larger vision of his own possibilities. In their letters they argued about art and literature, love and revolution. It was one of the great private moral conversations of the nineteenth century, inspired by a fierce political antagonism and an equally sturdy emotional sympathy. Though their friendship broke down, eventually, in the wake of the bitterly divisive events of the Paris Commune of 1870, it prompted Flaubert to define and reconsider his most cherished artistic principles. Flaubert's conversations with George Sand nourished the great works of his later years, *L'Education sentimentale* and *Un Coeur simple*.

THE first chapter of their friendship was courteous and tentative. In 1863 Sand published a sympathetic review of *Salammbô* and Flaubert was most grateful for her support at a time of public hostility towards his new work. He wrote to thank her and she invited him to visit her in Nohant. 'Do come and see me when you have time [. . .]. But I'm an old woman – don't wait until I'm in my dotage.' Equivocating cheerfully, Flaubert asked her to send him a portrait 'to hang on the wall of my study in the country'. They met again several times over the next few years, in the theatres and restaurants of Paris. For the moment, nothing more would come of all this. Sand was caught in the melancholy task of nursing her ailing lover, Alexandre Manceau. Only after Manceau's death, in the summer of 1865, did she begin to draw closer to Flaubert.

That moment arrived in February 1866 when George Sand attended the Magny Dinner for the first time. It was a unique occasion for all concerned: Sand was the only woman ever to enter this sanctum of masculinity on equal terms. 'I was greeted with open arms – they have been inviting me for the past three years,' she remarked. But she went alone, 'unescorted', to avoid comment. 'Everyone pays ten francs, the dinner is mediocre. There's a lot of smoking and loud talk and you leave when you like.'

She evidently found Flaubert the most agreeable man in the room.

'She looked shyly at the assembled company and whispered to Flaubert: 'You are the only person here who doesn't frighten me.' In her diary she wrote, 'Flaubert impassioned and more sympathetic to me than the others. Why? I'm still not sure.' Unlike the others, Flaubert didn't talk about himself – a restraint that was quite uncharacteristic.

We may picture the restraining face that Flaubert saw across the table that evening from the evidence of a near-contemporary portrait photograph of George Sand taken by Nadar. At sixty years old her short, thick, dark hair is beginning to turn grey. Her face is unlined, her features are 'delicately defined' and the look in her eyes is 'sweet, gentle and serene'. Her habitual manner is grave and dignified, her voice is level and slightly monotonous. With her 'wonderfully delicate hands almost entirely hidden in lace cuffs' she rolls her own cigarettes from Turkish tobacco, constantly relighting them with little wax matches. For a woman, smoking was still a small social gesture of emancipation.

Flaubert and George Sand coincided socially, at Magny's and elsewhere, six or seven times over the next few months. 'Mme Sand', the de Goncourts observed sullenly, 'makes her entrance in a peach-flower dress, a love-dress, which I suspect was intended to rape Flaubert.' Their friendship had progressed, though not in the direction imagined by Edmond de Goncourt. They played games, writing joke letters to each other in the rough, grouchy voice of Goulard, a down-at-heel comic character invented by Sand. Here was a woman who could throw herself wholeheartedly into elaborate comic fantasies. It was like having a big sister, a robustly mischievous companion, something he had never known. She could do other characters too. After her Goulard, Sand invented Marengo l'Hirondelle, an impoverished tightrope artiste. Marengo wrote to Flaubert, a clumsy half-plausible letter fabricated by George Sand and Bouilhet, inviting him to write the story of her 'Unfortunat Existance'.

There were serious moments too. He read her recent work and she urged him to 'bring me your criticisms of my book', reassuring him that 'it doesn't mean that you change one another, on the contrary, it generally makes you even more stubborn in yourself. But by stubbornly being yourself you simply become more complete, explain yourself better, develop more fully, and that is why friendship is a good thing, even in literature [. . .].' As a consecration of their friendship she dedicated her next novel, *Le Dernier Amour*, to him. Pointing delicately to the position he now held in her heart, the dedication would, of course, be 'the source of the most good-natured pleasantries'. The theme of *Le Dernier Amour* may also have spoken to him. It describes adultery, free from immorality and guilt.

THE growth of this mutual sympathy was furthered by George Sand's two visits to Croisset, first in August and then again in November 1866. A thing unprecedented in Flaubert's dealings with women, the mere fact of her visiting him *there*, tells an interesting story. He could see quite clearly that this was something different. 'I don't know what it is,' he wrote, 'the feeling I have for you. But I feel a special affection for you, such as I have never felt for anyone until now.'

Her first visit lasted only a few days. Characteristically, George Sand found everything delightful. Her diary recorded it all:

Tuesday, 28 August. Flaubert's mother is a charming old lady. A quiet place; the house comfortable, pretty and well arranged [. . .] I'm in clover. In the evening Flaubert read me a superb *Tentation de Saint Antoine*. We chatted in his study until two in the morning. Wednesday, 29 August. At eleven o'clock we took the steamboat to La Bouille [. . .] terrible weather: wind and rain. But I stayed on deck to watch the water and the river banks – all superb [. . .] came back with the bore, the tide [. . .] back by one, lit a fire, dried ourselves and had some tea. Went out with Flaubert again to look around [. . .] the view down over the Seine, the orchard, on a height and very sheltered, the arid white land above. Dressed for dinner, a very good one. I played cards with the two old ladies, then talked with Flaubert and went to bed at two.

They both wanted more. Delighted by each other, they exchanged a swift sequence of letters. Taking the initiative, she ventured into the teasingly familiar: 'You are a splendid kind boy, great man though you are, and I love you with all my heart.' How fondly he recalled 'the final farewell look you gave me' and declared: 'We have done nothing but talk about you since you left [. . .] nobody can hold out against the irresistible and spontaneous seduction of your person.' Sand asked for three leaves from the tulip tree under his window and promised to send him the seventy-five volumes of her complete works. 'There's lots of it. Just put it all away on some shelves in a corner and dip into it when you feel like it.' He responded eagerly. 'That is a present – a royal present which moves me deeply. And don't forget the portrait so that I may have your dear and lovely face ever before my eyes.'

The great box of books arrived from Paris and the seventy-five volumes were laid out. Within the week Flaubert had read all ten volumes of Sand's autobiography, *Histoire de ma vie*. He was greatly taken with the chapters describing her convent education, perhaps because they chimed with his own imaginings of Emma Bovary's adolescence. He was keen to discuss that portion of her life with her. She wrote back, to 'my Benedictine [. . .] all alone in your ravishing monastery, working without pause', and wondered appreciatively at the prodigious range of the imagination that could describe Emma Bovary as well as portraying a battle between a sphinx and a chimera.

'You are,' she wrote,

a very mysterious, a very exceptional being, though gentle as a lamb for all that. I had a number of questions I was longing to ask you but I was restrained by the excessive respect I feel for you [. . .] [the disasters] a great mind must have suffered to be able to produce anything, I regard them as sacred things that are not to be touched roughly or frivolously. Sainte-Beuve [. . .] claims that you are frightfully dissolute. But perhaps he looks with a jaundiced eye [. . .].

Flaubert, though evidently gratified, responded to her astute compliment with an abruptly satirical self-portrait. 'Me! A mysterious being! *Chère maître*, really! I find myself revoltingly banal and am often very bored by the bourgeois who lives under my skin.' He would expand upon this at their next meeting. 'If you want my confession, I'll make you a full one.' He was particularly eager to correct her impression that he had led a most dissolute life. 'I have dreamed much and done very little.' She was reassured. Her next visit to Croisset would last for a whole week. 'If the weather's fine I'll make you run about. If it keeps raining then we'll toast our shins by the fire and swap stories about our love problems. The great river will run black or grey under the window saying "Quick, quick!" and carry away our thoughts and our days and nights [. . .].'

She sent him her portrait, along with her pleasantly fanciful reflections on identity and change. 'I do so much dreaming and so little living that sometimes I'm only three years old. Next day, if the dream has been sad, I'm three hundred. Don't you find it the same? [. . .] as if you were starting out in life without knowing a thing and then as if you were carrying the burden of thousands of centuries like a dim and painful memory.'

Flaubert responded emphatically:

Unlike you, I don't ever have that sense of a life just beginning [. . .]. I feel as if I've existed for ever. I possess Memories that go back to the Pharoahs. I can see myself very clearly at different moments in history, following different trades, according to my luck. My present self is the outcome of all my extinct selves. I was a boatman on the Nile, a pimp in Rome at the time of the Punic Wars, then a Greek orator in Suburra where I was devoured by bed-bugs. I died during the Crusades from eating too many grapes on a beach in Syria. I have been a pirate and a monk, an acrobat and a coachman. Emperor of the Orient too perhaps?

This is a strong new note. Her affection releases in him once again the exuberant, free-flowing, imaginative energy of earlier days. Desire might find ample expression in such autobiographical games.

O N 3 November 1866 George Sand and Flaubert travelled to Croisset together for the week. This was her second visit to the house. 'She worked all day and at night we chattered like magpies until three in the morning.' They took the steamboat into Rouen and visited the Saint-Romain Fair where the customary attractions were on display: 'Superb animals as tame as dogs. Foetuses, a bearded lady, a puppet-show.' In the evenings they both read to each other from their work-in-progress. Flaubert read to her 'the beginning' of *L'Education sentimentale* and though the story had not yet reached 1848, George Sand was already keenly engaged by the political themes of the book. In Flaubert's account of it, 'she has insights that evince very keen good sense, as long as she isn't on her socialist hobbyhorse. Very reserved concerning herself, she talks readily about the men of '48 and stresses their goodwill rather than their intelligence.' Her reminiscences of 1848, though impossible to identify, were to be woven into *L'Education sentimentale*.*

Their nocturnal, fireside conversations reached ever deeper into the personal past. On her initiative, they began to tell their life stories, prompting one another with a tender and respectful curiosity. It ended all too soon. 'We parted', wrote Flaubert, 'at a moment when many things were about to pass our lips. All the doors between us are not yet open. You inspire a great respect in me and I do not dare to ask you questions.'

She shared Flaubert's pleasure in their new emotional intimacy:

We're lucky, don't you think, to be able to tell our life stories like that? It's much less complicated than the bourgeois think it is, and the mysteries you can

---

* When George Sand reviewed *L'Education sentimentale* in December 1869 she didn't mention Flaubert's account of 1848 – though her conclusion implies a reproach for having merely satirised the past without offering any vision of the future.

reveal to a friend are always the opposite of what people imagine. I was very happy in the week I spent with you. No worries, a warm nest, a fine landscape, affectionate hearts, and your handsome open face which has a certain fatherly quality. Age has nothing to do with it. I feel an infinitely kind protectiveness in you, and one evening when you called your mother 'my girl' it brought tears into my eyes. I didn't want to leave, but I was keeping you from your work [. . .]. From a distance I can tell you how much I love you without fear of overdoing it. You are one of the rare kind, still impressionable, sincere, in love with art, uncorrupted by ambition, not intoxicated by success. You will always be 25 years old, by virtue of all kinds of ideas that are, according to the senile young people of today, quite out of fashion.

The only sour note came after George Sand's departure. Having read of her visit in the local newspaper, Flaubert's Croisset neighbours were indignant that he had kept such a celebrity all to himself.

KEPT apart by a combination of illness and hard work, Flaubert and George Sand did not meet again for another eighteen months. The conversation continued by letter, taking on a new and yet deeper tone as Sand stepped into another of her personae, signing herself now as 'your old troubadour'. A mysterious thread of half-private allusion, their old troubadour was many things. At the simplest level, it started life as a quotation from a poem about an emblematic figure painted on a clock case in a country inn. This troubadour, according to Sand, 'sings of perfect love and always will'. As the champion of *perfect* love the troubadour stands for George Sand's serene chastity, her decision – perhaps since the death of Manceau – to renounce all further sexual adventures. More than a simple figure of renunciation, though, the troubadour is also the colourful, restless, bohemian aspect of the Romantic artist, a gypsy, a beggar, a sentimental wandering creature, as well as 'merely' an elderly woman in her sixties. Finally, 'the troubadour' was perhaps simply the picturesque aspect of herself, the silhouette that George Sand wanted Flaubert to see. She had always excelled at this kind of liberating make-believe, this fashioning and refashioning of an image.

Flaubert knew what the troubadour stood for. 'You ask [your friend] if he sometimes thinks of his "old troubadour on the clock". I should say so. And he misses her as well. They were very fine, our nocturnal chats. There were moments when I had to restrain myself from giving you little kisses as though you were a big child.' The troubadour was the emblem of the delicacy of their understanding. Under this auspicious sign they could explore ideas and images of love and art and revolution, weaving sentiment and intellect into a single rich fabric of discourse.

They began light-heartedly. A young friend of George Sand's, a man in his early twenties, had embarked on a four-year-long engagement. 'He's in love,' she wrote, 'and engaged, and has to wait and work for four years to be in a position to marry, and he's made a *vow*.' It was amusing to compare this with their own histories.

SHE: 'I don't think young people nowadays have the energy to cope with science and debauchery, tarts and fiancées all at the same time.'

HE: 'In my day we made no such vows. We made love! And boldly! [. . .] We were Romantics, in short. Red Romantics, utterly ridiculous, but in full efflorescence. The little good left in me comes from those days.'

SHE: 'You are not in favour of chastity, my lordship, that's your business. Personally, I think "there's plenty to be said for it".'

HE: 'Great Temperaments [. . .] are supremely prodigal and do not scrutinise their every little action. We need laughter and tears, love and labour, joy and pain, we need to quiver in every fibre of our being. That's what it is to be fully human.'

Why the gap, she wondered, between Flaubert's riotous theory and his fastidious practice? That very simple question was unavoidable.

'It always surprises me,' she wrote, 'the difficulty you say you have in writing. Are you just being bashful? [. . .] let the wind blow through your strings a bit. I really do think that you go to more trouble than you need to.' She never sent the letter. Perhaps it was too direct, too facetious.

Next day she wrote to Flaubert again, on the same theme, but in a gentler tone:

Great artists are often invalids and many of them have been impotent [. . .]. I don't believe in those Don Juans who are also Byrons.* [. . .] One day try to write a novel with an artist, a genuine artist for a hero and you'll see what an immense but delicate and restrained life-energy flows through him [. . .]. The artist is such an excellent subject that I have never really dared to take it on. That would be aiming too high for a mere woman. But it might well tempt you one day, and it would be well worth doing. [. . .] Be less cruel towards

* Was George Sand thinking of Musset and Chopin? Both men had been her lovers. Both of them had fallen ill and been nursed by her.

yourself [. . .]. What you do seems so spontaneous and so abundant, it's a perpetual brimming-over. I do not understand your anguish at all.

'My literary anxieties!' he replied. 'I don't understand them myself. However, they do exist and they are violent.' As for the possibility of an artist novel, Flaubert gave a briskly predictable rejoinder: 'Contrary to your opinion I don't think that there is anything worth doing with the character of the Ideal Artist. He would be a monster. Art is not for portraying exceptions.' This disagreement about the Artist is highly significant. Suddenly we see the effects of the great divide of 1848. Those who came after 1848 no longer spoke the same language. The high Romantic conjunction of Art and Liberty, so powerfully present in the imaginings of the 1840s, was a mere mockery to these post-Romantics. Flaubert's work in progress, *L'Education sentimentale*, would try to show how this mockery had come about.

CHAPTER TWENTY-TWO

Chevalier Flaubert

AROUND this time, troubled by certain persistent symptoms, Flaubert sought a consultation with his eminent Parisian friend Dr Jules Cloquet. After he had confidentially 'displayed his member' Flaubert was diagnosed as having syphilis. Dr Cloquet prescribed iodide of mercury, to be taken in the form of a syrup. There was no great cause for alarm. According to the medical wisdom of the day, syphilis was now much less virulent than it had been in the past. Until around 1870 the traditional mercury cure was thought to be largely effective.

Syphilis was nevertheless a considerable social embarrassment. Flaubert wrote to Maxime Du Camp in October 1863 lamenting the venereal aches and pains that confined him to Croisset. He had sores around his eyes, pains in his knees, and an ulcer on his pubis. 'Venus is no doubt partly to blame, but I think it's mainly because of our ultra-nervous temperaments.' Adopting the traditional pose of highminded disdain, Flaubert was hiding himself away. Mercury-blackened lips were such a pathetically obvious sign.

Though his nervous ailment seemed to be in remission, the sad truth is that Flaubert's general health was inexorably declining. He was putting on weight and taking less exercise. He kept contracting hideous boils, and he suffered from increasingly long bouts of flu. Winter was the worst time. In 1865 it was 'rheumatism, neuralgia, and an abominable state of melancholy'. In 1866 it was boils of such dimensions – 'as big as a little hen's egg' – that he soon found it impossible to walk or even to stand up. 'My only entertainment is to sit at my table and watch the traffic on the boulevard.' These chronic physical afflictions, aggravated by the mental toil of literary composition, pushed Flaubert slowly and intermittently towards an exhausted state of misanthropic rage.

His 'Homeric' rages were often sparked by some minor vexation, such as being disturbed by a servant too early in the morning. Flaubert's 'extreme excitability' began to dismay and perplex his friends. It frightened him too. Was it possible to die of rage? Did such epic furies suggest that he might be drifting into madness? By the late 1860s he began to wonder.

Consider Flaubert's own account of one extraordinary day in May 1868, as relayed to the de Goncourt brothers:

Returning to my room in Paris on Sunday at half past eleven in the evening, I go to bed, promising myself a good night's sleep, and I blow out my candle. Three minutes later, a blast of trombones and a beating of drums! There was a wedding party just across the road at Bonvalet's. The windows of the aforesaid pot-house were wide open (it being a hot night) so I caught every single quadrille and every shout. [. . .]

At six in the morning, the builders start up again. At seven I move out and make my way to the Grand Hôtel.

There I have three-quarters of an hour wandering about before I find a room.

Scarcely settled (in the room) when someone next door begins hammering nails into a packing case. Further wanderings around the same hotel in search of a resting place. Eventually, at nine, I leave and go to the Hôtel du Helder, where I find a dismal little closet, as dark as a tomb. Except that the silence of the grave was impaired by the loud voices of departing guests, carriages rumbling along the street, clattering of tin pails in the yard.

From one o'clock until three, I pack my things and I leave the boulevard du Temple.

From four until six, tried to get some sleep at Du Camp's, rue du Rocher. But I had not reckoned with another gang of workmen who are building a wall down the edge of his garden.

At six, I am transported to a bath-house, rue Saint-Lazare. There, children playing in the yard, plus piano.

At eight, back to the rue du Helder, where my man had laid out on my bed everything I needed for the evening ball at the Tuileries. But I had not yet dined and, thinking that perhaps hunger was weakening my nerves, I go to the Café de l'Opéra.

I had just sat down when the gentleman at the next table begins to vomit.

At nine, I'm back in the Hôtel du Helder. The idea of dressing for the ball finishes me off [. . .]. With a groan I decide to make my escape as fast as I can. My man packs my trunk.

But there is more to come. Final instalment: my trunk rolls down from the roof of the carriage and lands on my shoulder. I still have the bruises.

Scène de la vie parisienne: between the lines of the comic anecdote we can feel the chaotic energy of the great city. It's Baudelaire's 'swarming city, city full of dreams', a labyrinth of noisy little rooms haunted by some malevolent comic spirit. Flaubert fled from the accursed place, back to the deep, pastoral silences of Croisset where he spent two days 'in a violent fever', nursing his bruise and waiting for 'the quiverings' of his 'wretched brain' to subside. It took some time. Flaubert was most disconcerted, a few weeks later, to find that he had lost his way whilst walking the streets of Rouen. Something was wrong. He announced half-mockingly to Princess Mathilde that he was now a fossilised romantic, an anachronism: 'capable of violent feeling [. . .] great suffering and great intoxication [. . .] the least thing troubles me and agitates me'. This uncomfortable condition persisted. He found himself, towards the end of the writing of *L'Education sentimentale*, plagued by headaches and hardly sleeping more than a few hours a night, 'becoming more and more irritable and unsociable'.

By a triumph of the comic spirit, Flaubert's *Dictionnaire des idées reçues* offers a gloriously mocking perspective on all the miscellaneous tribulations of the flesh. How gleefully he recites the alphabet of human discomfort. A small selection of the physiological entries from the dictionary will show us this Flaubertian body – not to be confused with Flaubert's body – in all its macabre glory.

BALDNESS: Always premature, caused by youthful indiscretions or the gestation of great thoughts.

CONSTIPATION: Influence on political convictions. All men of letters are constipated.

DEBAUCHERY: Source of all ailments suffered by elderly bachelors.

ECZEMA: Sign of good health.

HAEMORRHOIDS: Come from sitting on stone benches and on hot stoves. Do not attempt to treat them.

HERNIA: Everyone has one, without realising.

LAXATIVES: Taken in secret.

MASTURBATION: Self-pollution that thwarts the intentions of nature, usually with the very direst consequences.

MERCURY: Finishes off the patient along with the disease.

NERVOUS AILMENTS: Always a sham.

ORCHITIS: Gentleman's ailment.

PIMPLES: On the face or elsewhere, sign of healthy, strong blood. Never squeeze them.

SECRETIONS: Be delighted when they appear and express amazement that the human body can contain such quantities of fluid.
SYPHILIS: Everyone, more or less, is affected by it.

This is not a portrait of the artist in disguise. It is something more slippery: an impeccably ridiculous portrait of the body, male, human, nineteenth-century, ageing, aching, and caught up in a fine web of words.

FLAUBERT's new Parisian social life was embarrassingly expensive. As the confidant of princes and princesses he had a stylish part to play and it was a part that required fashionable clothes, a modest amount of dining in expensive restaurants and the hire of carriages to preserve one's fashionable clothes from the mud. Flaubert knew that he was living well beyond his means. He had always lived somewhere vaguely beyond his means. How could it be otherwise? As the imaginative son of a very rich man he had predictably expensive tastes. Couldn't they see that he was actually behaving with great restraint? His mother, who still controlled the money (and had moreover watched her husband earning it), was not impressed by these ingenious arguments. Her younger son was notoriously incompetent with money.

In February 1865 the precise depths of his incompetence were exposed to her pitiless gaze. Two years of *la vie mondaine* had been Flaubert's undoing. It all came out: unpaid bills accumulating invisibly in the account books of fashionable Parisian suppliers. There was 500 francs for gloves; 2000 francs for tailoring; 3000 francs for furnishings and 'redecorating my study in Croisset'. He needed 7000 francs to pay them all off. It wasn't very much. Could *Maman* possibly see her way . . . ? No, she could not.

At this point the family's Parisian lawyer, Maître Fovard, was called in to deal with this spendthrift son. Things had gone too far. On 10 February Madame Flaubert wrote to Fovard. Magisterial in her indignation, she laments the fact that Gustave has been unable to live within his annual income of 7000 francs, even though he has spent the greater part of the year in Croisset. She is most reluctant to sell off any of the family property. There *is* a farm near Nogent called Courtavant, but if that were sold and if Gustave were given the money he would simply spend it all in no time. She had often sacrificed her comforts for him in the past, but this time she would suffer real hardship if she were to hand over that sort of money.

Madame Flaubert instructed Maître Fovard to give her son a stiff lecture on how to live within his income, 'so that he may conduct himself more prudently and more in keeping with his situation.' Gustave must gather up all his unpaid bills and send them to Fovard. Then she and Fovard will look them over and see if they can be talked down. With terrible maternal acuity Madame Flaubert lays bare her son's deplorable little habits. 'I don't believe that he owes as much as he says he does, I think he has asked for 7000 francs in order to lay his hands on some cash. I tell you I won't pay out anything until I've seen the shopkeeper's bills.'

Flaubert complied reluctantly, for he had no real choice. It was dreadful, he told Fovard confidentially, having to ask his mother for money all the time. 'Try to persuade her that I do not go in for wild debauchery [. . .] and since she has decided to pay my debts let her do it [. . .] without too many recriminations.' All this fretting over money. It was very bad for his nerves.

It was decided that the farm, Courtavent, was to be sold off, though this transaction might well take several years to go through. Meanwhile Flaubert's financial problems rumbled on, like distant thunder, whilst he was writing *L'Education sentimentale*. In 1866 he was trying to negotiate a secret loan. 'If I were to go to my brother,' he confided to a friend, 'I could have the money immediately. But that is precisely what I do not want to do. I am anxious to keep all this from my family.' Without the loan he would have to stay in Croisset 'indefinitely' until his debts were paid off from his regular income. Flaubert's rising anger over money began to leak out in sour anti-Semitic exclamations directed against his tight-fisted publisher Michel Lévy.

The sale of the old family farm eventually went through in February 1867. Flaubert received around 15,000 francs from the transaction, the equivalent of two years' regular income. But he then took the fatal step of arranging for Ernest Commanville, his niece's husband, to become his unofficial banker.* Flaubert would become ever more entangled with Commanville, and the collapse of Commanville's fortunes would eventually plunge Flaubert into great misery. He now handed to Commanville all of his 15,000 francs with instructions to pay off

---

* This might suggest that Flaubert knew enough not to trust himself with money. Jules Cloquet had similarly been his banker at an earlier stage of his life.

current debts of 5000. Commanville must keep the whole transaction a secret from Madame Flaubert. 'She'd think I was on the road to ruin and that would distress her.'

Flaubert was still living beyond his means, but he was now contriving to conceal the fact from his mother. He had always hidden significant portions of his life from her, but these subterfuges marked a new kind of quiet estrangement. An elusive feeling of doomed extravagance seeped into the deepest layers of Flaubert's current writing. Money, like a capriciously tragi-comic force of destiny, drives the plot of *L'Education sentimentale*. The young hero, Frederic, is stuck at home in a provincial town with his widowed mother, idly waiting for something to turn up. He inherits lots of money and returns to Paris. There he spends his money, impulsively, pointlessly, foolishly, drawn down ever deeper into the metropolitan world of alluringly false values. As a satirical anatomy of the modern, *L'Education sentimentale* is mainly about money, money in all its more sinister disembodied forms, money in the turbulent new age of railways, industrial cartels, and the stock exchange. Love and Art, ever the source of deeper precapitalist values, don't stand a chance.

DEBT and syphilis were a kind of punishment. Reality's sharp revenge upon the unruly impulses of the imagination. The other threads of Flaubert's life were being woven into patterns much more agreeable. The years just after the publication of *Salammbô* were, according to Du Camp, 'the high point of Flaubert's existence'. His malady was in remission. Perhaps he had thrown it off for good. He could emerge from his long confinement.

Through Princess Mathilde's salon Flaubert came into contact with some of the most celebrated figures of the age. And celebrity was wonderfully contagious. Flaubert himself was suddenly an influential person, chatting to the powerful, presented to Frau von Metternich and the Czar. Old friends began to ask him for little favours.

Having been admitted to this charmed circle, Flaubert was quickly taken up, making splendid progress through the various antechambers, reception rooms and private apartments that symbolised the intimate architecture of power. Elegantly dressed and copiously perfumed, cackling at his own image in the mirror, joking that he looked like Almanzor, the worst of de Sade's old aristos, Flaubert conquered every salon into which he was invited. Du Camp, who observed him at close quarters, left a scurrilously amused account of his friend's fondness for *les grandeurs*.

He was always noticed. Whatever feelings he inspired, everyone could not but be struck by his presence, his size, his wholehearted sincerity [. . .]. Eager to please, he flirted with the women who were all intrigued by his strangeness. The young men, the aspiring writers, he treated with a sort of gentle paternalism. His fame gave him a certain stature and he was entirely at his ease in this world [. . .] for in spite of his oddities he was always well liked by those who met him; it was as if he took hold of their souls and made them his own.

In November 1863, only his second *saison mondaine*, Flaubert was puzzled and amused to receive an invitation to the Palais-Royal from Prince Jérome Napoléon (Mathilde's brother). The prince was a weighty loose cannon in the imperial entourage, forever quarrelling with his indulgent cousin the Emperor. With all the powers of his ruth-lessly sarcastic eloquence Prince Napoléon was currently campaigning for a liberal and democratic Empire. He would, of course, place himself at its head, playing some brilliant historical role worthy of his great ancestor. Meanwhile, proud of his reputation as a freethinker, the Prince habitually gathered writers, artists and intellectuals around him.* Affectionate and charming, but also fatally impetuous, the Prince was given to making intemperate remarks. Consequently, by the year 1863, he languished in an ever more grandiose political isolation, 'convinced that he could save everything'. Such was the man who now welcomed Flaubert into his retinue.

Plon-Plon – for this was the Prince's nickname, a comic corruption of Na*poléon* – was soon addressing Flaubert as 'my dear friend' and send-ing him copies of his recent political speeches. Whether or not Flaubert read them – and it may have been difficult to avoid doing so – he had clearly been 'taken up' by their author. In February 1864 Flaubert attended the Saturday ball at the Opéra in the company of Plon-Plon and the ambassador from Turin. They all sat together in the grand imperial box until five in the morning. Wishing to appear unbedazzled, Flaubert reported the occasion to his niece, carefully emphasising that it was a kind of social research. 'In the midst of all this I think continuously about my novel; on Saturday I even found myself in a situation belonging to my hero. For this book I am as ever making use

---

* Among the Prince's close friends were Renan, Maxime Du Camp, George Sand, Sainte-Beuve, and Emile de Girardin.

of everything that I see and feel.' A few weeks after the ball, Flaubert took a daring initiative. He wrote to the Prince with 'a humble request' on behalf of a friend, thus opening a new chapter in his career as a master of intrigue. There may have been more of the scheming Homais in Flaubert than could ever decently be acknowledged. Flaubert merely preferred to work on a more spacious canvas.

In April 1864, the month in which he finally sketched out the idea for *L'Education sentimentale*, Flaubert was invited by the Emperor to a reception at the Tuileries. The invitation stipulated *in uniform*, a minor problem for a 'mere civilian' who lacked even a decoration. We may surmise, from the fact that he was invited back, that Flaubert did not disgrace himself.

In November 1864 the author of *Salammbô* was to be found at the Palais de Compiègne, room number 85, on the second floor. Having silently pardoned the incompetent persecutors of *Madame Bovary*, Flaubert was there for the week at the invitation of the Emperor. Artists and intellectuals such as Flaubert added a certain lustre to the regime as well as lightening the burden of after-dinner conversation. Mérimée, Delacroix, Verdi, Gautier, and Sainte-Beuve had all, in their time, made the same richly symbolic journey. Compiègne imposed on them all, *arriviste* or artist, the same ritual. The chosen ones, summoned in weekly batches of a hundred, would set off from the Gare du Nord for the fifty-mile journey into Picardy. They travelled in the special chartered imperial train, eyeing one another nervously along the way. Profound boredom, exquisite social anxiety, pompous allegorical murals and freezing cold corridors soon enveloped the Emperor's guests. Beneath all the outward elegance there was, in the words of an English visitor, 'an absolute egotism, the unscrupulous hostility of each [. . .] towards his neighbour, like himself in pursuit of a favour, a possibly profitable transaction, or an intrigue.' The Château de Compiègne was clearly a wonderful place. For those who had eyes to see, it functioned as a kind of moral-industrial furnace, a large and expensive device of many nozzles through which one might extract and study the toxic residues of the age in their purest form. To the novelist about to embark on a study of the curious passions of modernity Compiègne offered a uniquely instructive spectacle.

This imperial country-house hotel – we may call it simply *The Grand* – had begun life as a Louis XV chateau set in 36,000 acres of forest. Napoléon I had moved in, with indecent haste, after the

revolution and *The Grand* was now the gilded apotheosis of the Napoleonic Idea. Dinner was served on the first evening to the accompani-
ment of a military band in a room dominated by an immense white
marble statue of the real Napoléon. A mural portrayed the rich fruits of
empire: 'Peace distributing Olive Branches to the Spirits of Agriculture
and Industry'. There was the Empress Eugénie, with gold dust sprinkled
in her wonderful red hair. After dinner there were decorous quadrilles to
a mechanical piano. On wet days one resorted to photograph albums,
pinball machines, charades and quizzes. The Emperor, a keen amateur
archaeologist, may have asked Flaubert questions about Egypt.

The small sharp details of Flaubert's visit to Compiègne are lost,
though we may catch brief glimpses of him. Through the eyes of La
Comtesse Stephanie de Tascher de la Pagerie, from the other side as it
were, we see 'Gustave Flaubert [. . .] strutting about in our midst. He
has a searching, penetrating gaze but his high colour makes him look
like a man who has taken too much wine.' We also have a deliciously
flustered letter from Flaubert to a friend in Paris. He asks him to buy a
bouquet of white camelias from Madame Prevost's in the passage de
l'Opéra and have it sent out to the chateau. 'Only the best blooms,
I want it to be ultra-chic [. . .]. For God's sake, don't forget.' The
camelias were a little gift for the Empress herself. 'You have to create
a good impression,' Flaubert declared, 'when you belong to the lower
ranks of the social order.'

There is heartening evidence that the Compiègne Flaubert was never
perfectly house-trained. This comes through in a story told by Maxime
Du Camp:

In this compliant and straightlaced world he more than anyone else kept up a
spirit of literary independence. One evening, in the circle around the Empress,
someone was talking mockingly about Victor Hugo. [. . .] Flaubert intervened
boldly: 'Stop just there! That man is our supreme master. He may only be
mentioned with proper respect.' The other speaker retorted: 'But you must
agree, sir, that the man who wrote *Les Châtiments* . . . ' Flaubert rolled his eyes
impressively and shouted: '*Les Châtiments!* Magnificent stuff! I shall recite
some of it to you if you want!' [. . .] the conversation was deflected along a
different track.*

* The force of the story lies in the fact that Victor Hugo was a most illustrious and eloquent
critic of the Second Empire. Hugo had gone into exile in protest against Napoléon III's seizure
of power in 1851. *Les Châtiments* (*Chastisements*) was his superb poetic denunciation of the
imperial regime.

Flaubert returned to Paris on 16 November. He was tired, worn down by the requirements of ceremonial court etiquette, the strict timetable and all the changes of costume. 'I expected to be bored, but in fact I had a good time,' he told his niece. 'The bourgeois citizens of Rouen would be more amazed than ever if they only knew what a success I was in Compiègne.' In private, Flaubert practised his latest turn: 'a classic impersonation of the Emperor in his dressing gown, dragging his feet, putting one hand behind his back, twisting his moustache and uttering idiotic phrases of his own invention'.

Flaubert's winter season of 1864–5 included further successes. At the Prince's February ball in the Palais-Royal there was the author of *Salammbô*, strolling triumphantly through all twenty-three of the large and lavishly decorated apartments, astonishing Louis Bouilhet by the number of people he knew. 'I spoke to about two hundred people.' Avoiding a dull quartet of worthies from Rouen, Flaubert sat on the steps leading up to the throne, chatting to Princess Charlotte Bonaparte and flirting decorously with her cousins Mathilde and Clotilde. When the Princess sent him her album, for his 'high thoughts', Flaubert wrote on its lustrous pages only the enigmatic line: 'Women will never know just how timid men are.'

Flaubert now begins to play a bizarre comic role. Could the fearless author of *Salammbô* also be the farcically timid admirer of Imperial females? Three anecdotes, variously convincing, attest to the fact that he probably was. The most reliable of these tales concerns the Empress Eugénie. She was a great admirer of *Salammbô* and it was widely known in Flaubert's circle that he had conceived a passion for her. We have it in his own hand: 'I love Her,' he wrote in May 1865 with a certain defensive irony.

Princess Mathilde also figures dramatically in two semi-amorous episodes from around this time. The first episode is undated, possibly a mischievous invention. The scene is Saint-Gratien, the Princess's opulent suburban villa. She sits at her easel painting a little watercolour. The door opens. Enter Flaubert, very quietly, like a schoolboy. He gazes ardently at the Princess Mathilde. After a long silence, suddenly irritated, she says, 'Well! What do you want to tell me that's so confidential and so urgent? We're alone, as you requested, and I am ready to hear whatever you wish to say.' She is amazed to see his cheeks turning red then turning pale. Fear and anguish, terror and despair are racing across his face. He stammers a few incoherent words and rushes out through the door.

The second episode, from April 1865, was observed by the de Goncourts. The scene is the Princess's Parisian mansion on the rue de Courcelles. 'The Princess [. . .] only has eyes for him, only finds room for him next to her, thinks only of Flaubert, who told me after we left that she had walked him twice round the garden, alone, through the shadows, in the dark [. . .]. Would she like to take Flaubert as her lover?' Flattering themselves obliquely, they conclude that she must be playing a game, trying to shield herself from damaging rumours that she gives her favours to the de Goncourts.*

By 1866 Flaubert was known as a man with friends in high places. Petitions began to arrive. Could he influence the outcome of a court case? Or could he possibly, wrote a friend of a friend, put in a word with the Emperor to get her husband promoted to *chef de bataillon*? Reluctantly he agreed to do what he could. 'All this is infinitely flattering,' he told his niece, 'but I really don't have the power they think I have.' Flaubert may have had more influence than he realised. In the event he found that he had 'done a great deal' on behalf of the would-be *chef de bataillon*. Dispensing patronage was one of the novel pleasures of his social position.

The crowning moment arrived on 15 August 1866, when Flaubert received a letter from the Minister of Education. He had been made *chevalier de la Légion d'honneur*. The coveted red ribbon, at last. 'If only you could be given it at eighteen!' he exclaimed. Flaubert was being honoured specifically as the author of *Salammbô*. It was Sainte-Beuve's doing, in league with Princess Mathilde, and Sainte-Beuve's letter of recommendation made much of the fact that Flaubert had been so warmly received by the Emperor at Compiègne.

Did the ribbon signify Flaubert's reconciliation with the Empire? When asked this tactless question by Amélie Bosquet, Flaubert tried to sound defiant: 'As for forgetting about my trial and forgiving them for it, not at all! I take impressions like clay and preserve them like bronze. Nothing is ever erased; it all mounts up.' Perhaps he was thinking of *L'Education sentimentale* as a sophisticated gesture of revenge.

---

* Jean Bruneau, the editor of Flaubert's letters, describes these supposed *amours* as 'a delicate problem'. The problem is compounded by the fact that none of Princess Mathilde's letters to Flaubert have been found.

Flaubert had only one complaint. Why did he have to share the honour with that non-entity Ponson du Terrail? It was humiliating. But then Maxime Du Camp offered the consoling thought that Ponson du Terrail was probably even more dismayed to be sharing it with him.

The last word on the subject of Flaubert's medal should come from the *Dictionnaire des idées reçues*: 'LEGION OF HONOUR, MEDAL OF THE: To be sneered at, even though you rather covet one. When you eventually get it, always say that it came quite unsolicited.'

CHAPTER TWENTY-THREE

L'Education sentimentale

'It's the feeling of *Modernity*, that's what I like about it.'

TWO years after finishing *Salammbô*, Flaubert began his new novel in May 1864. He worked at it first with Louis Bouilhet, sketching out possibilities, bringing his main idea into clearer focus. The writing proper could wait until the end of the summer. He needed to be reading, exploring the political ideas of the 1840s. It was a daunting project, this 'big Parisian novel'. Like *Salammbô*, though unlike *Madame Bovary*, it would require sustained historical research. 'I'm beginning to understand it, but never before have I taxed my brain like this [. . .]. I need to spend a good month in Paris, looking through collections of newspapers.'

Returning to Croisset for the summer, Flaubert worked his way through volumes of Saint-Simon and Fourier, Lacordaire and Lamennais. None of it was 'hugely amusing', though Flaubert spent his evenings more agreeably, rereading bits of de Sade. Utopian socialists were not to his taste. They came in many different colours but they were not very pleasant company. A vaguely satirical theme was already forming itself in his mind. 'What despots they are! And what louts! Modern socialism stinks of petty authoritarianism.'

Flaubert began writing at the end of August 1864. Progress with the opening chapter was slow and difficult. He fumbled his way along, timidly, as if he had lost the habit of writing. 'I have written fifteen pages in the last seven weeks,' he reported, 'and they are not up to much.' Deep dejection was perfectly normal for Flaubert, almost the sign of a healthy start. But this was different, this vague discontent with his chosen subject. He explained the problem very

290

clearly to his faithful correspondent in Angers, Mademoiselle Leroyer de Chantepie:

Since last month I am harnessed to a novel about modern life which will be set in Paris. I want to do the moral history of the men of my generation; 'sentimental' history, to be more precise. It is a book about love, about passion; but passion in the form it is allowed to take these days, that is to say the inactive kind. The subject, as I conceive of it, is profoundly true, but, for that very reason, probably not very entertaining. Dramatic deeds are somewhat lacking; and the action is spread over too great a tract of time. In a word it is causing me a lot of trouble and I am thoroughly uneasy about it.

As the winter deepened so Flaubert's writing came more quickly. He was alone in the old house. There was thick fog outside and silence on the river, a perfect emptiness all around him:

It's like being inside an enormous milk-white tomb. The only sound in here is the ticking of the clock and the crackling of the fire. I work by lamplight for about ten hours in every twenty-four, and time passes by. But I waste so much of it! What a daydreamer I am, in spite of myself. [. . .] What distresses me most of all is my conviction that what I am doing is useless, I mean contrary to the purpose of art, which is vague exaltation.

He was, he told the de Goncourts, 'living the life of an oyster'. 'I go to bed at four in the morning and begin to gather my wits at about four in the afternoon.'

By February Flaubert was back in Paris, gathering his historical material, working it up, mainly from printed sources but also seeking out some oral testimony. 'Yesterday', he told his niece, 'I spent the whole afternoon with workers from the faubourg Saint-Antoine and the barrière du Trone. In the morning I had a visit from a cab driver.' Predictably, we don't hear these proletarian voices in Flaubert's novel. We wouldn't expect it. In their absence, we may try to imagine such scenes of earnest nineteenth-century urban investigation. I see waistcoated gentlemen with interestingly expensive watches buying rounds of drinks and filling their notebooks with colourful phrases still warm from the lips of the People. Reading newspapers in public libraries was an altogether less strenuous mode of social inquiry.

IN the summer of 1866, far from Croisset, somewhere on the vast alluvial plains of Central Europe, half a million soldiers wearing the bright archaic insignia of Hohenzollern or Hapsburg were gathering for a battle. They met and they fought on 3 July in eastern Bohemia, near the village of Sadowa. It was the biggest battle ever seen in Europe. The Prussian soldiers, mobilised by railway, possessed one startling technical advantage over their opponents. With their breech-loading bolt-action rifles they could fire six rounds for every one discharged from the Austrians' muzzle-loaders. Six to one: enough to shift the course of history. It spelt the end of old-style close-formation battles and romantic cavalry charges. It ensured Prussian hegemony over Austria, destroying in a few months a balance of power that had lasted fifty years. Napoléon III, to judge from his quixotic behaviour, had not grasped the implications of Prussia's victory at Sadowa. This was a misunderstanding that would soon have the most grievous practical consequences for the residents of Croisset.

The Second Empire could slumber on, however unquietly, for another few years. Luckily for Flaubert, Napoléon III survived just long enough to allow him to finish writing *L'Education sentimentale*. Yet the public world of those last years of Empire, the fancy-dress Compiègne vision of ruthless *arrivisme*, pervaded Flaubert's writing so deeply that his novel acquired a double layer of historical reference. *L'Education sentimentale* is officially and authentically set in the Paris of the 1840s. Unofficially, all along the way, it evokes the Paris of the 1860s. For readers of Flaubert's generation, those who had witnessed Haussmann's restyling of the fabric of their city, *L'Education sentimentale* was a precociously nostalgic experience.

Meanwhile, as the diplomats assimilated the dangerous new fact of Sadowa, Flaubert struggled with the stuff of an earlier history. Princess Mathilde wanted to take him to her villa on Lake Maggiore for the month of September. It was always awkward, refusing her invitations, but he insisted on returning to Croisset to resume work on *L'Education sentimentale*, aware that he had left it quite long enough.

The difficulty of the whole thing depressed him. Why reinvent the novel? Why toil so conscientiously? He deplored his own absurd artistic audacity. There was not only the pervasive familiar difficulty of composition itself. There was some peculiar difficulty with this novel that ominously still lacked a title. 'It'll be mediocre,' he wrote,

perhaps because the conception is faulty? I want to portray a psychological state – true in my opinion – which has not yet been described. But the setting in which my characters move is so copious and so swarming that with every line they are almost swallowed up by it. I am thus obliged to push into the background the things which are precisely the most interesting. I merely touch on lots of things that readers will want to see treated in depth. My aim is complex – bad aesthetic method [. . .].

The fear of some essential defect remained with Flaubert.

In November 1866, two years into the writing, Flaubert's thoughts turned to the events of 1848. His recent nocturnal conversations with George Sand were a rich source of contrary ideas. 'When you have nothing else to do,' he wrote to her, 'scribble down on a bit of paper what you remember about '48. [. . .] just a few of your own recollections.' Maxime Du Camp also added to the mixture with his new novel, *Les Forces perdues*. Flaubert thought highly of it – 'obviously the best thing he has done' – and was struck by how much it had in common with his own work in progress. He described it to George Sand as '[. . .] a very naive book that gives an accurate idea of the men of our generation, real fossils to the youth of today. The reaction of '48 opened up an abyss between the two Frances.' George Sand, in her reply, confirmed his reading of the pattern of recent history. She was of the generation that had been shaped by revolution. 'I am among the last of that kind,' she wrote, 'and you who came after us are somewhere in between the illusions of my day and the dreadful disappointment of the new age.'*

Looking back on another winter of writing, Flaubert told Princess Mathilde that he felt like a road-mender. The shaping of sentences, though pursued indoors with a delicate quill, was very like breaking up stones with a great hammer. It was endless hard labour with no prospect of release.† Flaubert's doubts persisted: 'Damn me if I have any idea of the quality of the thing! That is what is so atrocious about this book of mine, I have to finish the whole thing to find out what holds good. No Big Scene, no splendid bits, no metaphors even, because the least touch of decoration would wreck the whole fabric.'

The year 1867 was a season of 'universal panic'. The months of April and May, from the evidence of Flaubert's letters, were especially

---

* In her review of *L'Education sentimentale* George Sand argues vigorously against Flaubert's reading of this history.
† There is a whole essay to be written on Flaubert's Images of Labour. A ghostly company of artisans and proletarians – blacksmiths, road-menders, and plantation slaves – they make brief emblematic appearances in his letters whenever he evokes the physical toil of composition.

anxious. The Emperor's ambitious plans of social reform had recently been published. The laws regulating the press, public meetings and trade unions were to be liberalised. Clichés were in the air. ' "The political horizon is darkening," everyone says, though nobody can say why.' When the tailors went on strike, *Society* itself was in danger. Flaubert informed his niece with obvious relish,

The bourgeois are frightened of everything. Frightened of war. Frightened of workers going on strike. Frightened of the (probable) death of the Prince Imperial. There's a universal state of panic. A level of stupidity unparalleled since 1848! I am currently reading lots of books about those years. The impression of stupidity that they give off, added to the stupidity of the present day, leaves me feeling as if I had mountains of cretinism weighing me down.

Not even the Magny Dinners were immune. Everyone wanted to talk about Bismarck and Flaubert swore to himself, in dismay, that he would never go there again.

Bourgeois conversation was so excruciatingly predictable: the prospect of war, the Paris Exhibition, the perfidious workers. Flaubert's exasperations found their way out in the form of a grandiose comic proclamation addressed to George Sand.

Maxim: hatred of the Bourgeois is the beginning of all virtue. In that word 'bourgeois' I personally include the bourgeois in overalls as well as the bourgeois in the frock coat. We (I mean the literati), we are the ones, the only ones, who are the People, or should I say the tradition of Humanity.

Yes I am given to disinterested anger and I love you the more for loving me on that account. Stupidity and injustice make me bellow. And *I let rip*, in my little corner, against all kinds of things 'which are none of my business'.

What did the politically literate George Sand make of these aggressive paradoxes? Did she scold the man in the name of fraternal love? Was she dismayed by the insult to her leftist principles? Her affectionate reply suggests that she recognised the familiar voice of *le Garçon*, the raucous-old-giant *persona* that allowed Flaubert such liberty in the art of bellowing, letting rip and generally playing rough.

As a romantic anarchist with a modest private income Flaubert was never to be drawn into organised political anything. He preferred the larger, wilder emotions, the more picturesque minorities. Witness his delight in gypsies, bandits and nomads. There were gypsies in Rouen during the anxious summer of 1867. Forty-three Zingaris, en route from Hindustan, camped out for a week on the Cours de la Reine.

Flaubert 'swooned with delight' over them, as he explained to George Sand:

This will be the third time I have seen them. And every time it brings me a new pleasure. The wonderful thing is the *Hatred* they provoke in the bourgeois, even though they are perfectly harmless. I put myself into everyone's bad books by giving them a few pennies. And I heard some splendidly fatuous remarks being made. That kind of hatred has its root in something deep and complex. You find it in all *right-thinking people*. It is the hatred they feel for the Bedouin, the Heretic, the Philosopher, the solitary, the poet. And there is fear in that hatred. It infuriates me, I who am always on the side of the minority. It is true that I find a lot of things infuriating. The day my indignation subsides I shall fall in a little heap like a puppet with broken strings.

The Zingaris so impudently installed on the Cours de la Reine might have stepped from the pages of Victor Hugo. Exotic strangers, they were easy to admire. The sad, grey lives of the contemporary urban poor were altogether more difficult to take into the imagination. Amélie Bosquet, one of Flaubert's Rouen acquaintances, a socialist-feminist à la George Sand, had just published a novel that tried to enter that elusive proletarian world. Amélie Bosquet's *Le Roman des ouvrières*, set in a working-class quarter of Rouen, portrayed the lives of factory workers. It had a melodramatic plot that turned on alcoholism and insurrection; it had a perfidious bourgeois hero in pursuit of a virtuous daughter of the people. When Flaubert read *Le Roman des ouvrières* he found it clumsy and conventional. 'You must look beyond the People [. . .],' he told Amélie Bosquet. 'It's too narrow and too transitory a thing.' Artless sincerity, he implied, did not make for a strong, hard prose style.

The mood of 1867 came into sharper focus for Flaubert during a brief visit to Paris. He had unexpectedly been invited to a grand ball at the Tuileries in honour of the miscellaneous royalty of Europe who were visiting Paris for the Universal Exhibition. Flaubert himself was to be one of exhibits. 'Their majesties being desirous of my presence as one of the most splendid curiosities in all of France [. . .].' The Czar of all the Russias was a slob, Flaubert reassured George Sand. 'I enjoyed myself enormously at the Tuileries. Gathered some very interesting material [. . .]. Your giant was most attentive towards the ladies [. . .] *without for one moment ceasing to be Literary.* I quickly stashed everything felt and seen into a corner of my memory, for later use.'

After the ball, enraged by the inexplicable loss of his best jacket, Flaubert slipped into a fanciful vision of the city of Paris as a modern Babylon. The obliviously cynical magnificence of the Imperial circle – it would all surely end in disaster. 'Paris is becoming colossal. It is sliding into crazy extravagance. Perhaps we are going back to the old Orient. I have a notion that idols are about to emerge from the ground. We are heading for a new Babylon. Why not? The Individual has been so thoroughly disparaged by Democracy that he will submit to being utterly obliterated, just as happened under the great theocratic tyrannies.' The outline of a Second Empire social novel is clearly visible in Flaubert's notebooks of the early 1870s. A loose sequel to *L'Education sentimentale*, it remained unwritten, consigned to that sealed chamber of the authorial imagination where glorious possibilities are laid out, immaculately preserved.

B Y the autumn of 1867 Flaubert had reached 1848. He was gathering material for the third and final part of *L'Education sentimentale*. He read pamphlets and newspapers, chronicles and memoirs; he asked old friends who had seen action on the streets to search their memories for the authenticating details that he needed. George Sand put Flaubert in touch with Armand Barbès, one of the grand old men of 1848.* Flaubert was deeply impressed by the primitive moral grandeur of Barbès. 'Since my record has scarcely been *patriotic,*' he explained to George Sand, 'since I was growling out my sentences in the silence of my study whilst he was out on the streets risking his life for the sake of liberty, I did not think I ought to tell him what a high opinion I have of him – I would have sounded like some kind of courtesan.' Flaubert admired Barbès' fortitude whilst under sentence of death. 'He read Lord Byron and he smoked his pipe. It's quite distinctive.' He particularly admired the exemplary reticence of Barbès. 'He loved Liberty [. . .] and he did it without *speechifying*, like someone from the pages of Plutarch. To my mind he was the one who was on *the right path*, whereas the rest of them (and almost all of our kind) had lost their way.'

This contrast, between Barbès and all the rest, shapes the deeper political argument of *L'Education sentimentale*. The simple purity of

---

* Barbès was a professional revolutionary: leader of a secret society in the 1830s, elected deputy in 1848 and imprisoned for his part in the rising. Notoriously, in 1841, Barbès had been dragged down the staircase of the prison on the Mont Saint-Michel, banging his head on every step. Pardoned in 1854, Barbès now lived in Belgium.

Barbès was superior to the fraudulent eloquence of the ideologues. In the final moment of the book's political action, this thesis is dramatised in the form of a murder. Dussardier, the heroic proletarian simpleton, is cut down on the street by the sword of Sénécal, the ex-revolutionary who has signed up with the police. It's the intellectuals, the ideas men, who betray the Revolution. All political discourses, bourgeois and radical alike, are the mere vapourings of human egotism. *Speechifying* is the problem. Equipped with this equitably reductive comic thesis, Flaubert proposed to offend Conservatives and Patriots in equal measure. Right and left would both be dismayed by their images in the mirror.

In March 1868 Flaubert finally began writing the contentious third section of *L'Education sentimentale*. It was especially difficult, composing a historical novel with a near-contemporary setting. Walter Scott and Victor Hugo were no help. There was so much testimony, so many documents, such an abundance of material that the real was always encroaching on the imagined. Flaubert told a friend,

I have serious problems, dovetailing my characters with the political events of '48. I am worried that the background will overwhelm the foreground. [. . .] The historical characters are more interesting than the fictional ones, especially when the latter are not especially passionate. I wonder if people will be less interested in Frédéric than in Lamartine? Besides, how do you choose from amongst the things that really happened? I'm perplexed. It's so hard.

On top of this perplexity, Flaubert was feeling the unpleasant effects of prolonged 'moral cohabitation with the bourgeois'. How much more congenial to be Maxime Du Camp, filling his notebooks for a project oddly parallel to Flaubert's. 'Du Camp spends all his time in markets and abattoirs, for the sake of his great work on the city of Paris. He dragged me along to Les Halles one night. But when it got to three in the morning I left him to it because I was frozen.'*

Reading through 'a great pile of mediocre stuff', Flaubert reported that he was 'discovering many things [. . .] that explain the current state of the world. [. . .] the Catholic influence has been immense and deplorable.' Here was a serious ideological theme. The Christian

---

* Du Camp's book, *Paris, ses organes, ses fonctions et sa vie dans la deuxième moitié du XIXe siècle*, was published in six volumes between 1869 and 1875. With his sharp journalistic intelligence, Du Camp was walking the same streets as Flaubert's protagonist Frederic Moreau.

anti-capitalists of the 1840s, men like Félicité de Lamennais, had preached the social virtues, expounding a democratic fraternal neo-Catholic vision of the future. They were largely to blame for muddling politics, Romanticism and religion. They should have followed Voltaire instead of Rousseau, should have kept to the 'high road' of critical freethinking.

George Sand, loyal to the muddlers, took issue with Flaubert's punitive thesis that all subsequent misfortunes had arisen 'exclusively' from their mistakes. She offered a sober, generous defence of the idealism of the men of '48. The vanquished, she argued, surely deserve our forgiveness rather than our scorn. They have all come a long way in the last twenty years. They smile at their old dreams. They see beyond the illusions of their youth. 'I rely on you', she told Flaubert, 'to practise magnanimity. With one word more or less you can use the lash without leaving a wound when the hand on the whip is strong and gentle. You are too good-natured to be cruel.'

In his reply, Flaubert protested that art was impartial:

Rich or poor, victors or vanquished, I make no allowance for any of them. I don't want love or hate, pity or anger. Sympathy is another matter. There is never enough of that. [. . .] since I have absolute confidence in your powers of mind, when my third part is finished I will read it to you and if there is anything in my work that you think *spiteful* I shall remove it. Though I am convinced in advance that you will have no objection.

Flaubert's novel was almost finished when it eventually acquired a title in April 1869. He wrote to George Sand with the news. 'Here is the one I've adopted, in desperation: *L'Education sentimentale, histoire d'un jeune homme*. I don't say it's good. But so far it's the title that best conveys the theme of the book. This difficulty in finding a good title makes me think that perhaps the idea (or rather the conception) of the work is not clear.' As promised, Flaubert read his manuscript to George Sand, a performance that lasted eight hours with an hour off for dinner. 'Prime example of beautiful painting,' she observed warily in her journal.

In his rooms on the boulevard du Temple, after twenty-one hours at his desk, at four minutes to five on a Sunday morning – the moment was ceremoniously recorded – Flaubert finished writing *L'Education sentimentale*. His head was 'splitting' and he was exhausted. Within the week, Princess Mathilde let it be known that she too would like to hear him read his novel. After three imperial requests, Flaubert read the first few chapters to her and was dismayed to learn that she was delighted with it. So delighted that she insisted on hearing the whole thing, a task that required four readings of four hours each.

In the event, Flaubert 'dazzled' himself with his own reading of the beginning of the final chapter.

This is the passage. It describes the emptiness of the hero's later life:

He travelled the world.

He tasted the melancholy of packet ships; the chill of waking under canvas; the boredom of landscapes and monuments; the bitterness of broken friendship.

He returned home.

He went into society, and he had affairs with other women. They were insipid, beside the endless memory of his first love. And then the vehemence of desire, the keen edge of sensation itself had left him. His intellectual ambitions were fading too. The years went by and he resigned himself to the stagnation of his mind and the apathy that lived in his heart.

This is Flaubert's homage to Chateaubriand and to the melancholia of all his beautifully blighted young men. But it also looks forward to another kind of writing. In this wonderful prose poem Flaubert is showing his successors how to smuggle their old Romantic contraband into a modern realist novel.

Having finished *L'Education sentimentale*, Flaubert began the next chapter of his Parisian life. Within a couple of weeks he had signed a lease for a new apartment in a new block on a new street, 4 rue Murillo. Situated in the 17th arondissement, between the rue de Courcelles and the avenue Ruysdael, the rue Murillo was one of *les beaux quartiers*, a quiet spacious street that still speaks of tranquil metropolitan affluence. From his rooms on the fourth floor Flaubert enjoyed a view of the Parc Monceau, a formal garden with enormous gilded iron gates, antique colonnades and artificial grottoes. No great surprise to discover the rhetorical *bourgeoisophobus*, author of *Salammbô*, comfortably installed here in the plush new-bourgeois heart of nineteenth-century Paris. His old quarters on the boulevard du Temple were costing him too much in cab fares; he wanted to be nearer to his niece Caroline in her new residence on the rue de Clichy. We may imagine Flaubert's new neighbours, bankers and industrialists, murmuring to each other, in the style of the *Dictionnaire des idées reçues*, over the new arrival: 'Artists!

Amazing that they dress like everyone else. Always being invited out to dinner. Earn insane sums of money, but it all slips through their fingers. Literature? An occupation for idlers.'*Yet Monsieur Flaubert, as everyone knew, had been to Compiègne in '66.

FLAUBERT didn't realise that his best friend was dying. Bouilhet had been so miserable, ever since moving to Rouen in the summer of 1867, so lugubriously miserable, that Flaubert had made a habit of teasing him about it. 'He was not the same man [. . .],' said Flaubert belatedly. 'Strange things are happening in my body,' Bouilhet complained, 'but I've decided not to take any notice.' By the beginning of July 1869 Bouilhet could hardly walk. He took to his bed, still refusing to acknowledge that he was fatally ill. His two dreadful pious unmarried sisters arrived at the bedside, intending to harangue him in the name of religion and hoping to carry off some of his furniture. But Bouilhet was 'splendid and *inflexible*'. He received them, said Flaubert, 'in the antique manner', and 'died like a *philosophe* [. . .]' without calling for the priest. In the last hours of his delirium Bouilhet was enthusiastically dictating a scenario for a play about the Inquisition. He called out to Flaubert, his trusty collaborator, to come and admire his work. But Flaubert was in Paris. He had left the day before, in the mistaken belief that his friend was recovering.

Flaubert returned to Rouen and took charge of the funeral. Two thousand mourners assembled to pay homage to their famous local dramatist . 'Would you believe', wrote Flaubert, 'that as I was following his coffin I was vividly savouring the grotesquerie of the whole ceremony? I could hear the comments he was making about it to me. I could hear his voice in my head. It was as though he was there beside me and we were both following someone else's funeral procession. It was dreadfully hot, thundery weather. I was soaked in sweat and the climb up to the Cimetière Monumentale finished me off.' Standing near his father's grave, Flaubert fainted as the speeches were about to begin. His brother Achille led him away.

Flaubert had known Louis Bouilhet for thirty-seven years, ever since school. They had worked alongside each other for twenty-three years. Bouilhet had edited *Madame Bovary*. Flaubert had helped Bouilhet with his poems and his plays. Without Bouilhet he was diminished. 'I

* *Dictionnaire des idées reçues*, entries for 'ARTISTS' and 'LITERATURE'.

say to myself, what is the use of writing now, since he's gone. It's over, the wonderful reading aloud, the shared enthusiasms, the future projects we dreamt about together.' 'It feels like a major amputation. A large part of me has disappeared [. . .] my literary conscience, my judgement, my compass.'

As an executor, Flaubert quickly took possession of all Bouilhet's papers and letters and entered upon the unrewarding task of promoting his friend's literary reputation. There would be a volume of verse to see through the press, an unfinished play to polish up and take to market, a modest public monument to be campaigned for. Flaubert laboured energetically but fruitlessly for many years on behalf of Louis Bouilhet. He wrote a preface for the poems and bullied Michel Lévy into publishing them. He talked the Théâtre de l'Odéon into staging the play and he chaired the Bouilhet monument committee. There would be something quixotic about these loyal exertions, as though to atone for some unacknowledged act of neglect.

Du CAMP was reading the manuscript of *L'Education sentimentale* and his observations were not very encouraging. 'You have managed a kind of tour de force writing a book like this, a book with a non-existent subject, no plot at all and featureless characters. It's interesting.' Du Camp objected to the slowness of Part One, the excessive detail of the masked ball and the ridiculous behaviour of the duellists. He also objected to the title: 'it's completely useless because the theme is missing [. . .]. If I were you [. . .] to avoid being trounced for the flabbiness of all the characters, the intentional flabbiness, I would call my book: *Mediocrities*.' Whatever their truth, Flaubert found Du Camp's observations 'annoying'. He didn't know whether to accept them or ignore them completely. Flaubert's publisher, Michel Lévy, announced that he didn't like the title either. At this point authorial morale was perilously fragile. Two days before publication, George Sand sent him a friendly warning. The subject of his novel was so intensely topical that it would certainly cause 'fireworks'. 'The real progressives and the true democrats will applaud you. The idiots will rage [. . .].'

L'Education sentimentale was published on 17 November 1869, the very day of the ceremonial opening of the Suez canal. Extracts from the new novel by the author of *Salammbô* appeared in 'about thirty newspapers', and Flaubert, his customary zeal unimpaired, sent out a hundred copies to friends and allies.

He received some astutely appreciative replies.

This is our generation. We have all experienced the feelings, the passions, the influences, the inward and the outward disappointments that you have described, all spoken the words you have written down [. . .].

Never has irony been wielded with such a constant, even, and implacable power; never has any society been lashed so ferociously. How harsh you are!

Do you know [. . .] the great catchphrase of the day? It comes from your book. You say: 'THE LAST PAGE OF L'EDUCATION SENTIMENTALE!' And you cover your face with your hands.

It felt as if the account of the events of 1848 had originally been much longer and that this was an abridged version.

Your characters are so vivid that I felt as if I were under their skin, living their lives, thinking their thoughts. They are so accurate that I could put real names to all of them, because I know them, these are indeed my contemporaries.

[. . .] an evocation of the generation that emerged from the daydreams of Chateaubriand and Lamartine, a spineless cowering half-baked generation that has produced nothing.

Not all of the early reviews were hostile. Emile Zola, the youthful author of *Thérèse Raquin*, was delightfully enthusiastic. He acclaimed *L'Education sentimentale* as 'the only truly historical novel that I know'. Théodore Banville, a fellow spirit and a contemporary, wrote to Flaubert: 'you need to have been young in 1840 to grasp how powerfully evocative it is, your portrait of that time of transition with all its failings and its thwarted aspirations'. Banville later praised the novel's distinctive renunciation of conventional plot. *L'Education sentimentale* was 'sad, indecisive and mysterious like life itself [. . .] making do [. . .] with endings all the more terrible in that they are not materially dramatic.' A perceptive review appeared in the *Journal de Rouen*, praising the descriptions but arguing that 'the repetition of the same technique seems slightly contrived [. . .]'. Flaubert wrote to congratulate the reviewer: 'You are the only reader [. . .] who has found the major flaw in the book.'

It was not enough. One or two favourable notices made no real difference. Hostile reviews began to appear and Flaubert was unpleasantly surprised by 'such hatred and such bad faith'. One of his old enemies, Francisque Sarcey, was comparing him to de Sade: 'Such mysticism in the language, such brutality in the actions [. . .] the author stays cold while he describes nights of debauchery.' Barbey d'Aurevilly, the mischievous high-Catholic dandy, declared the novel disagreeably 'dry' and overdone. Flaubert, he said, 'stays on the surface, knows no feeling, no passion, no enthusiasm, no ideal, no insight, no reflections, no depths [. . .]'. *L'Education sentimentale* was 'a robust piece in the same vein as Courbet's *Les Baigneuses*, women who pollute the stream in which they bathe'. Maliciously perceptive, Barbey mocked Flaubert's cult of perfectionism, inviting his readers to imagine a crowd that 'goes down on its knees – like the three kings at the crib of the Infant Jesus – before the box that contains Flaubert's manuscript. Because Flaubert has devised a box for his manuscript' – an idea of great genius – 'and will henceforth be known as "the man with the box".'

Amélie Bosquet, an old acquaintance, reviewed *L'Education sentimentale* in more earnestly political terms in *Le Droit des Femmes*. As a woman who had spoken at public meetings in 1848, Amélie Bosquet took exception to Flaubert's humiliating portrayal of the socialist-feminist La Vatnaz, best described as a scrawny hack. She spoke out against Flaubert's impartiality: 'disdainful impartiality [. . .] which dwells upon the ridiculous and the ignoble [. . .] and makes out that all opinions and their representatives are equally stupid, base and criminal'. Flaubert, she declared, had wilfully 'sterilised his talent'. 'Not very kind', her review marked the end of their friendship, even though Amélie Bosquet had written to Flaubert, apologising for having attacked him in print. It would be treachery to publish, she said, but cowardice to keep quiet. Flaubert thought her ungrateful, and regarded her review as 'violent abuse'.

He was losing his nerve, even though he had predicted that *L'Education sentimentale* would make everyone angry. He wrote to George Sand: 'I know that the Rouen bourgeois are furious with me, because of Père Roque and the scene in the cellar of the Tuileries. They think that "people should be prevented from publishing such books" (I quote), that I'm being nice to the reds, that I'm guilty of inflaming revolutionary passions and so on. [. . .] All the newspapers are quoting the final brothel episode, completely out of context, as proof of my baseness.' Would she please step in with an article in his defence? Nearly all the people who had been sent copies of the novel were keeping quiet: 'For fear of compromising themselves or out of pity for me. The most sympathetic think that what I've written is just a series of tableaux, completely lacking composition and form.' George Sand set to work and her vindication of *L'Education sentimentale* was ready within a couple of days.

'You seem surprised by all this malice,' she wrote. 'You are too innocent. You have no idea just how original your novel is and how its power will inevitably upset important people. [. . .] I have emphasised the shape of your book. That is its least understood and its most impressive feature.'

Sensing his need for distraction, she wrote again a few days later, inviting Flaubert to spend Christmas with her and her numerous family in Nohant. 'Come and shake off this persecution [. . .] ours is a happy, foolish house.'

'A hundred thousand leagues away from Paris and all things literary', Nohant was the perfect refuge. Flaubert's brief but highly satisfactory visit to George Sand in December 1869 was the belated fulfilment of several broken promises. George Sand had taken to teasing him for his reluctance. *Cul de plomb*, why would he never drag himself away from his desk? Was his seclusion a private form of ecstasy? 'Perhaps you're being rather coy, to make us feel sorry for you and love you even more.' To refuse her latest invitation, now that his novel was finished, would have been unpardonable. Besides, it had been teasingly decreed that he could wear his dressing gown and slippers 'all the time'.

And so he made the long winter journey towards the blessed maternal warmth of Nohant, carrying the manuscript of his magic-play, *Le Château des coeurs*, along with two small dolls, his Christmas gifts for George Sand's grandchildren. Seven hours in a train, another hour in a carriage, and Flaubert reached Nohant on the evening of 23 December 1869. He found a spacious eighteenth-century country house, the main staircase decorated with murals, the high windows looking out on to walled gardens and the blank pastoral expanses beyond. After the melancholia of Croisset and the solitude of the rue Murillo, Nohant was bubbling with life, a family house with children all wildly excited by the idea of Christmas. There were numerous local visitors too, 'my young men', as she called them. Here, in the mansion inherited from her grandmother nearly fifty years ago, George Sand presided over a sumptuously domestic world. She would spend the winter days 'making dresses for her daughter-in-law and costumes for puppets, cutting out stage sets [. . .] and spending hours with little Aurore', her granddaughter, currently 'the jeune premier' in her life.

As with most nineteenth-century house parties, the time was highly organised. The first evening was decorously playful. 'We met, dined, talked, played Arab tunes on the serpent. Flaubert told stories. We parted at one.' The next day, Christmas Eve, Flaubert 'enjoyed himself like a schoolboy'. His dolls were a great success. 'All the young men came and stayed to dinner. Afterwards the puppets and the tombola in a fairy-tale decor.'* On Christmas Day, 'from three to six Flaubert read us his great magic-play, which is very delightful but not likely to succeed. Everyone enjoyed it and discussed it at length. [. . .] Great merriment this evening. Flaubert had us rolling about with his version of *The Prodigal Son*.' On Sunday 'we went out into the garden – even Flaubert, who wanted to see the farm. [. . .] introduced him to Gustave the ram. Then some quiet conversation in the drawing room.' On Monday, 'Flaubert dressed up as a woman and danced the chahucha [. . .] it was grotesque, everyone went wild.'

Flaubert left Nohant, as agreed, early the next day, 28 December. He would not be staying until the New Year. Urgent theatre business drew him back to Paris. It was over, this 'winter escapade' that had been, he told his host, the only convivial moment in a very dark year.

Back in the rue Murillo, Flaubert sank into his melancholy. Profound intellectual solitude, punctuated by the ominous, envious squeakings of reviewers, now closed upon him. George Sand quickly did her best to cheer him up. Tactfully encouraging, she wrote: 'They're still attacking your book [. . .]. It didn't come at the right moment, apparently; or rather it was all too timely. It exposed all the confusions of the hour. It touched an open wound. Everyone saw themselves in it only too clearly.' The younger generation of readers were not ready for it. She reported that 'her young men' had found *L'Education sentimentale* 'depressing'. 'This man who is so kind, so friendly, so cheerful, so simple, so congenial, why does he want to discourage us from living?'

George Sand also sent Flaubert the gift of a magically comforting verbal portrait of himself as seen through the eyes of his admiring

---

* George Sand's son, Maurice Sand, had trained as a pupil of Delacroix. Maurice's puppet theatre was a gloriously elaborate venture, which absorbed most of his time and energy. Twice a week he staged performances lasting several hours, satirical cartoon-style epics playing on contemporary political themes.

friends in Nohant. 'He is larger and greater than ordinary beings,' she wrote.

His mind, likewise, is beyond the common measure. In that department he is at least as much like Victor Hugo as he is like Balzac but he has the taste and the discernment that Hugo lacks, and he is an artist, which Balzac was not. Do you mean that he is greater than either of them? *Chi lo sa*. He hasn't yet had his say. The immensity of his brain troubles him. He doesn't know if he's going to be a poet or a realist. Being both, he finds it awkward. He has to untangle his visions. He sees everything and he wants to take hold of it all at once. He is too much for the public who prefer little morsels and choke on anything large. But the public will eventually take to him, once it has understood. It will take to him quite soon if the author can allow himself down to the level of their understanding. Though he might have to make a few concessions to their intellectual indolence.

Flaubert was in no mood to be admired. 'Your friendship blinds you to the truth,' he wrote in reply. 'I do not belong to the family you describe.' Nor was he considering any concessions to the indolent. 'I'm quite determined to write for my own personal pleasure, totally unconstrained.' Without Bouilhet to advise him, Flaubert didn't know what to do next. 'When I lost my dear Bouilhet I lost my *midwife*, the man who could see more clearly into my thoughts than I can.' He now embarked on a defiantly ambitious rewriting of *La Tentation de Saint Antoine*, a task that would require several months of preliminary reading.

Winter was miserable. By the end of February Flaubert was 'physically broken, shattered', disfigured by a boil below his eye and so weakened by flu that he was unable to climb stairs. Jules Duplan, his closest friend after Bouilhet – 'a dear old confidant who was devoted to me like a dog'– died on 1 March. Intellectual work was an escape from grief: 'I gobbled up too many books one after the other,' he confided, 'but I did it to deaden my sorrows.' 'I'm entering the cantankerous misanthropic phase,' he told George Sand. 'Everything and everyone vexes and irritates me. I can feel old age coming on. I never see people I can talk to.'

There was always Turgenev. Turgenev was a delightful companion, a fellow spirit, an urbane colossus, the only man in Paris with a taste for talking about art and poetry. Everyone else was more interested in plebiscites, socialism, and the International. Flaubert and Turgenev had ceremoniously exchanged portraits, the nineteenth-century sign of intellectual intimacy, and Turgenev had recently spent a day at

Croisset. Infinitely congenial, Turgenev was all too elusive. He so often cancelled a visit at the last minute, rushing off to Karlsruhe or Baden-Baden, governed by the whims of his opera singer Pauline Viardot. Flaubert loved Turgenev's company. 'I could talk to you for weeks at a time,' he wrote. 'We are like moles both tunnelling in the same direction.' But it was embarrassing, being so obviously eager for his company.

Flaubert decided to 'allow himself' ten solitary days of dark depression. Then it was down to work again, reading Plotinus to keep back the tears. Increasingly, he confided his grief to George Sand. 'Though I keep hold of myself in public, I sometimes burst into great floods of tears and I feel like I might be going to die.' By April it was better, and yet it was not. 'I've been reading enormously and overworking and now I'm almost back on my feet. Except for the dark gloomy tangle around my heart, which is slightly worse.'

Flaubert's extended stay in Paris had emptied his purse. Back in Croisset for the summer, still 'suppressing a perpetual sob', 'frightened of turning into a hypochondriac', he now had to endure his ageing mother's peevishness. 'When I leave my study I sit down to eat with my mother, who is as deaf as a post and is only interested in talking about her health.' His niece Caroline had 'exiled' herself for a second summer to a spa town up in the Pyrenees, in search of a cure for her mysterious infirmities. Deprived of her company, Flaubert wrote affectionately complaining letters, 'from that old bloke your uncle'.

It had been 'an accursed year', he told George Sand. Though he was still making 'prodigious efforts to be stoical.' On hot afternoons he went swimming 'furiously' in the Seine. Late at night he sat reading. Autumnal wisdom from *Eckermann's Conversations With Goethe*, then the busy pomposities of the hour, the printed election addresses of candidates for the local council. It was a splendidly cheerful conjunction.

On 20 June Flaubert completed the first draft of his only published critical essay, a preface to Bouilhet's *Dernières Chansons*. Minimally biographical, the preface concentrates on Bouilhet's poetry and on the literary doctrines that the two writers had shared. His dead friend was still with him. 'Here in Croisset,' Flaubert wrote, 'his ghost pursues me everywhere. I meet him behind the bushes in the garden, on the sofa in my study, even in my clothes, in the dressing gowns of mine he used to wear.'

There were already new friendships to mitigate the loss of the old. Men in their twenties and thirties had begun to seek out the author of *L'Education sentimentale*. Close to home, there was 'the terrible Raoul-Duval', Rouen lawyer, candidate in the regional elections and bright exception to the dreary bourgeois norm. Raoul-Duval had 'conceived a passion' for Flaubert and was soon visiting Croisset, filling the garden 'with his three horses, his four dogs and his two daughters.'

On 14 July 1870, in Berlin, Chancellor Bismarck was waiting to see if Louis Napoléon Bonaparte would fall into the clever trap he had set for him. The so-called Ems telegram, as secretly doctored by Bismarck, was a diplomatic insult intended to push the French into reckless political adventure.

In Croisset Flaubert spent the day working on the third and final version of *La Tentation de Saint Antoine*. At two in the morning he wrote to his niece, 'The moon is coming through the tulip tree; the boats cast dark shadows on the drowsy Seine, the trees are reflected on the water, the rhythmical sound of oars breaks the silence: it is utterly exquisite [. . .].'

In Paris, on that same summer evening, a woman draped in the *tricolore* stood on the stage of the Opéra and sang the 'Marseillaise'. Her audience rose to its feet and joined in the chorus. *Marchons, marchons*, declaimed with self-consciously historical bravado. The bellicose revolutionary anthem had been banned ever since 1850. The Emperor had given his special permission to have it sung tonight, because there was going to be a war with Prussia. France had been insulted. France would strike back. France had over a million new rifles ready for use. Out on the boulevards, groups of friends were making facetious arrangements to meet up again, 'in Berlin'. 'At last,' roared the sober *Paris Journal*, 'we are going to know the delights of massacre. Let the blood of the Prussians flow in torrents [. . .]. Let the wretch who dares to utter the word *peace* be shot like a dog and flung into the sewer.'

CHAPTER TWENTY-FOUR

Into the Dark

'The war with Prussia felt like a sort of great natural disaster, like one of those cataclysms that happen every six thousand years.'

ON 19 July 1870 France declared war on Prussia. 'I am disgusted,' Flaubert told George Sand, 'I am heartbroken by the stupidity of my compatriots. [. . .] The good Frenchman wants to fight: 1 Because he thinks Prussia has issued a challenge; 2 because savagery is the natural state of man; 3 because war contains something mystical which intoxicates the masses.' Within a month, Flaubert would begin to feel that same mystical intoxication. For the moment he was still sober.

People are going crazy, he told his niece. Their Croisset neighbour has hallucinations in which Prussian soldiers are raping his wife. Then he wants to strangle his wife because he thinks she's a Prussian. Flaubert was 'floundering in the deepest melancholy, in spite of work, in spite of good old Saint Antoine who ought to distract me.' Roused by the war, monstrous fantasies were stirring in his own mind. 'I feel that we are entering into darkness [. . .]. Perhaps race wars are going to begin again? Over the next hundred years we shall see several million men killing each other at a single sitting. All of the Orient against all of Europe, the old world against the new. Why not!' In her reply George Sand was more prosaically compassionate. She had seen peasants weeping as their sons were marched away.

The war was going badly for France. After pouncing on an insignificant border town and declaring a famous victory, the French army had lost its way. They had the wrong maps, insufficient rations, no consistent strategy. Swaggering military incompetence, helped along by rousing choruses of the 'Marseillaise', was no match for impeccable Prussian logistics.

By 17 August, with defeat in the air, Flaubert was no longer floundering. He had enrolled as a nurse in the Hôtel-Dieu and with the help of Raoul-Duval he was organising a batallion of the National Guard. Flaubert was eager to see some action. If Paris were to come under siege he would join the fighting. 'My rifle is all ready,' he told George Sand. Meanwhile, his niece's husband, Ernest Commanville, had won a war contract, making biscuit tins at a rate of a thousand a day. A crowd of Nogent cousins, fleeing the Prussian advance, arrived in Croisset. 'The house is packed out.'

The Empire had only a few days left, 'yet we are supposed to defend it to the very end'. No matter. His mood had changed: 'My sadness has turned into an eager belligerence. Yes, I'm stupidly keen for a fight [. . .].' 'Is it', he wondered, 'the blood of my ancestors, the Natchez, coming to the surface? No, it's just the shit-awful nature of existence breaking out.' In Paris, faced with imminent Prussian victory, a committee of scientists was devising fiendish modern tricks for the defence of the city.

Princess Mathilde was preparing to flee the country and she sent Flaubert several boxes of her Napoleonic silverware, to be hidden away until better days returned. On the quayside in Dieppe an angry crowd forced the Princess to open her bags, in the reasonable belief that she was making off with millions in gold. Flaubert made a special journey to Dieppe to 'quash this idiotic slander'.

Defeat at Sedan brought down the Empire. The Third Republic was declared in the week Flaubert was appointed lieutenant of a company of National Guard. 'Splendidly energetic' in his new role, Lieutenant Flaubert had his portrait painted in uniform, drilled his men conscientiously and signed up for 'lessons in the art of war'. Newspapers were soon carrying a story – not utterly implausible – in which Flaubert harangued his household: 'Anyone who feels afraid had better leave, because I declare that if a Prussian ever dares to cross the threshold of this house I shall blow his head off.' The joke was taken seriously and Flaubert found he was being congratulated on his bravery.

He was still eager, he said, to get at those 'compatriots of Hegel'. It would be an escape from his relations. 'What a houseful I have here! Fourteen people all whining and getting on my nerves.' Beneath his belligerence he felt sad, 'rivers and oceans of sadness all surging through me [. . .]. I regard myself as finished. My brain will never be the same again [. . .]. My heart feels parched and dry. I am turning stupid and vicious.'

The everyday order of things was crumbling. 50,000 soldiers passed through Rouen in two days. Achille made plans to hide the family silver. Caroline Flaubert left for England, at her husband's insistence. A neighbour barricaded his garden gate with planks. Just outside the house, paupers were gathering down on the riverbank, asking for food. Within a week they turned nasty. Gangs of twenty or thirty began to hang around all day, shouting threats and shaking the big iron gates to the garden. Flaubert put aside 50 francs to buy a revolver. Class hatred was in the air. 'My militia begins its patrolling next week,' he announced, 'and I am not inclined to be merciful.'

Flaubert was proud of his first local night patrol. He wrote to his niece with the news: 'I have just delivered a paternal speech to "my men" in which I announced that I would stick my sword in the belly of the first man to turn tail and then I had them promise to shoot me down if they saw me running away. Your old windbag of an uncle has *achieved* the epic note [. . .]. Would you believe that I am feeling almost cheerful.'

With Paris under siege, Rouen council voted a million francs to buy rifles. Balloons and carrier pigeons were employed to carry the post. In the village of Mantes, they said, a peasant had strangled a Prussian and pulled him to pieces with his teeth. Flaubert shared the general impulse to moralise on the causes of the national disaster. 'We are paying,' he wrote to Du Camp, 'paying for the great lie that we lived by. For it was all a fake: fake army, fake politics, fake literature, fake credit and even fake whores. To have told the truth would have been an act of immorality.'

By the middle of October the Prussians were about thirty miles away. Flaubert said that it was like being back in the fourth century when the barbarians overran Italy. Winter was closing in and 400 paupers had called at the house in one day. 'They shout threats at us and we have to keep the shutters closed [. . .]. My militia is so undisciplined that I just have resigned my commission.'

Flaubert had long ago stopped writing. He now lived in a state of lethargic anguish, waiting for the Prussians. He read Walter Scott. He went into Rouen, walking along the quayside, sitting in the café. He remembered the 'paradise on earth' of Princess Mathilde's weekly receptions at the Imperial mansion on the rue de Courcelles. 'Every kind of elegance is finished for many years.' He could foresee only an austere, shabby, parsimonious, ultra-Catholic world to come.

Flaubert felt about eighty years old. He waited all through November, sitting alone in front of the fire, brooding on the past, watching the first snow falling, convinced he could hear cannon-fire in the distance. 'I spent my nights groaning on my bed like someone in their death-agony.' Prussian troops would be billeted in Croisset. He would flee the house rather than look after them. 'Why do they detest us so violently?' he wrote to George Sand. 'Do you not feel crushed by the hatred of forty million men?' '[. . .] if only I could escape to a country where you never see uniforms, never hear the sound of the drum, hear no talk of massacre, feel no obligation to play the citizen!'

PRUSSIAN soldiers arrived on 5 December and commandeered the house. 'What a night it was, the night before we moved out [. . .].' He burnt many of his papers, 'buried a large box full of letters', then moved into Rouen, to live at his niece's house on the quai du Havre. The first week of the occupation was the worst. 'I spent whole nights', Flaubert recalled, 'weeping like a little child. I was not far from killing myself. I felt madness taking hold of me, and I had the first symptoms, the first signs of a cancer.' All through December and January snow lay on the ground and the Seine was frozen. Locked in by the frost, bursting with soldiers, Rouen was like a city under siege, like a prison. Anyone found carrying a newspaper would be severely punished. It was rumoured that Achille had been killed by an angry crowd.

Prussian troops were soon billeted in Croisset: seven soldiers, three officers and six horses, with Flaubert in attendance. They were surprisingly well behaved, but there were so many of them. They filled every room, burnt extravagant quantities of firewood, left his books all over the house and ran up very large wine bills. Then there was the sound of their snoring in the next room, the sight of their helmets on his old bed and all the humiliation of having to run errands for them. 'Yesterday I spent three hours searching out hay and straw for their horses.' Every night, for the first time in his life, Flaubert had to clear the table after they had eaten.

Flaubert began to worry about his own moral state. 'I can feel my intelligence weakening,' he wrote, 'my heart crumbling away. Yes I'm turning nasty as I become mindless. As if all those Prussian boots had trampled across my brain.' His mother kept waking him in the night, weeping and calling for Caroline, convinced that they were hiding something dreadful from her.

Things got worse as the siege of Paris dragged on. On 25 January 1871 the Grand Duke of Mecklemburg-Schwerin entered Rouen with a fresh contingent of Prussian soldiers. They were much more threatening than their predecessors.

On 28 January an armistice was declared and Paris surrendered the next day. Achille wanted to jump off a bridge and Flaubert fell into an 'indescribable' state of rage. 'I'm angry that all of Paris has not been burnt to the ground, so as to leave just a dark stain on the earth [. . .]. I hope that the civil war kills lots of people. May I be included among their number!' Never again would he wear the red ribbon of the Légion d'honneur. 'I'm going to ask Turgenev. . . how to become a Russian.' The Prussians had left Croisset, after forty-five days. Flaubert would only visit the house once it had been cleaned. 'That poor dear house I used to love, I tremble at the thought of going back again [. . .]. If it belonged to me I would certainly have it demolished.'

Flaubert didn't go back to Croisset. He went to stay with his niece Caroline in Dieppe for a month. Even there, away from the scene of his humiliation, he found it impossible to write. He spent the days dreaming about the past and it was as though the war had already lasted for fifty years. Caroline found him greatly altered. At her gentle insistence he soon resumed work on *La Tentation de Saint Antoine*. 'I was completely off my head [. . .]. But thanks to you, your sweet company and the hospitality of your house, I gradually pulled myself together [. . .].' Ernest Commanville, Caroline's husband and Flaubert's banker, was in great distress. Perhaps his business was going badly?*

Then Flaubert was in Paris, feeling shabby and watching preparations for Kaiser Wilhelm's triumphal entry into the city. He saw stacks of Prussian rifles gleaming in the sunlight, and 'heard the sound of their music, their horrible music, under the Arc de Triomphe.' 'What barbarism!' he wrote to George Sand. 'The bitterness is choking me. These white-gloved officers who smash mirrors, who read Sanskrit and guzzle

---

* The details of the disaster emerged painfully and slowly over the next few years. Commanville had recently bought vast tracts of Scandinavian forest, in the belief that timber prices would rise. Prices crashed because of the war and Commanville was forced to sell at a heavy loss. He struggled on, trying to avoid bankruptcy, observed by his wife and her uncle, whose capital was tied up in Commanville's business.

champagne, who steal your pocket-watch and then send you their visiting card [. . .].'*

In Rouen there were scenes of great agitation. When Crown Prince Friedrich Wilhelm Hohenzollern arrived to review his troops he was greeted by black flags on every house. Knives and sabres drew blood on both sides. The conquerors were 'behaving abominably' as Flaubert left to spend a few days with Princess Mathilde, comfortably exiled in Brussels.

The conquered were worse. Some Parisians simply wouldn't lie down. With three generations of revolutionary tradition behind them, they repelled the two French regiments sent to retrieve the cannons positioned on the heights of Montmartre. To make their message clearer, they also executed a few generals. Prussia had vanquished Napoléon III. Now it was Red Paris against the Third Republic. The official government of France retired to Versailles and prepared to fight a civil war against the unofficial government of Paris. Flaubert observed the initial manoeuvres from his hotel in the West End of London. Commanville had a lucky escape from 'our brothers' in Paris. A few days later an old friend of Achille's was 'shot by the insurgents'.

Flaubert was back in Croisset on 1 April, 'trying to work so as to forget about France', somewhat astonished to find himself there again. The carpenters had gone. The old house was clean and tidy. 'Contrary to expectation I'm delighted to be back [. . .]. The Prussians did not plunder my house. They *pilfered* a few little things of no real importance [. . .] but all in all they did no damage.' Sunday visitors could be received once again. There was the beautiful Léonie Brainne, widow, journalist and generously receptive object of desire. There was General Valazé, soldier-politician and teller of superlatively lewd stories. There was Guy de Maupassant, now in his early twenties, fresh from the ordeal of military service, with mannerisms reminiscent of his uncle, Alfred Le Poittevin.

Rouen was returning to normal. The harbour was full of shipping, the Prussians were about to leave and the town council was secretly preparing 'formidable defences' against any local socialist insurrection. Writing was an agreeable escape from 'the putrescence of the present'. Shaping sentences was very like turning serviette rings, 'just as innocent and as useful'.

---

* These are probably Parisian witticisms rather than personal experiences.

This was Flaubert's third and final revision of *La Tentation de Saint Antoine*, 'my whole life's work,' he said in June 1872, 'because the idea first came to me in 1845 in Genoa, looking at a painting by Breughel, and since that moment I have never stopped thinking about it and reading books to do with it.' It was a good moment to try again. The everyday life around him was sliding into horror and madness. The Prussian invasion of France, the occupation of Croisset, the social convulsions of the Paris Commune and the cruelty of its aftermath, such were the events that pressed so imperiously upon his imagination. Projecting himself into the mind of a fourth-century desert hermit allowed him to 'deaden his sorrows' and 'forget about France'. 'This extravagant book,' he said, 'keeps my thoughts away from the horrors happening in Paris.'

La Tentation de Saint Antoine also allowed him to reach back into his own artistic past, to take stock in this his fiftieth year of the aspirations he had once valued so highly. More surreptitiously, perhaps it was a way of continuing an ideal posthumous conversation with the spirit of his dead friend, Alfred Le Poittevin. Flaubert's exceptional reluctance to decide on the ending of *La Tentation de Saint Antoine* suggests an impulse so chaotically complex that it could scarcely find expression in an achieved work of art.

A LETTER from George Sand – the first in many weeks – arrived at the end of April, initiating a political conversation that unfolded all through the summer of that year. George Sand detested the Paris Commune. It was an 'ignoble experiment' that filled her with 'bitter despair'. And yet she struggled to preserve her generosity of feeling. Flaubert relished her confusion. 'She realises', he told Princess Mathilde, 'that her old idol was hollow.' Gleefully scenting victory, Flaubert wrote her a 'disillusioning letter', a real tirade against the follies of democracy and the chronic childishness of the masses. 'Our salvation', he informed her, 'lies in a *legitimate aristocracy* [. . .] a government of mandarins'. Prostitution, he argued, was the key to the inglorious history of the Second Empire. 'It was all false: false realism, false army, false credit, and even false whores. They were called 'duchesses', and great ladies casually called each other 'little slut' [. . .]'. Had he gone too far? George Sand was not a woman to be silenced by raucous club-land misogyny. Flaubert heard himself and paused. 'Once I begin to lash out at my contemporaries,' he explained, 'I find it difficult to stop.' But he sent the letter anyway.*

No reply from George Sand. After six uncomfortable weeks of silence Flaubert wrote to her again. 'I've just returned from Paris and I don't know who to talk to. I'm choking. I'm overwhelmed by it, disgusted rather.' The Commune had fallen. Flaubert had found smouldering ruins, a city ravaged by petrol bombs and firing squads, a people exhausted by arson and massacre. 'It's sinister and marvellous [. . .]. You'd have to stroll about and take notes for a couple of weeks.'

The smell of corpses sickened me less than the miasma of egotism breathing from every mouth. The sight of the ruins is nothing compared to the immense stupidity of Paris. With few exceptions *everyone* looked barking mad. Half the population wants to strangle the other half, and vice versa. You can see it clearly in the eyes of people on the streets. [. . .] I have collected a mass of horrible and little-known details, which I shall spare you.

George Sand responded soothingly. She had not had the heart to answer his previous letter, overwhelmed by her own indignation and disgust at 'the infamous Commune'. She felt as if she were 'waking from a dream to find a whole generation divided between cretinism and *delirium tremens*.' Nevertheless, she promised, friendship would prevail over politics. 'We parted in such good spirits eighteen months ago, and so many dreadful things have come between us. To see each other again, once it's over, will be our *just* reward.'

At the end of July, as the surviving communards were brought to trial, George Sand wrote to Flaubert once again, dismissing the communards as 'scum' and welcoming their defeat as a sharp lesson in political realism for the proletariat. Flaubert was gratified, a month later, to see George Sand's penitential opinions in print: 'For the first time in her life she calls the rabble by its true name.' This was the moment to affirm his position. '*Chère maître*,' he wrote to her, 'if only you could hate! That is where you are lacking: hatred. For all your great sphinx eyes, you have seen the world through a golden mist.' Recent events had vindicated Flaubert's original darker vision of the world. 'The human race', he explained, 'is not doing anything unexpected. Ever since my youth its hopeless miseries have filled me

---

* Flaubert drew his later social ideas from an essay by Renan. 'Do your best', wrote Renan in 1868, 'to create upper classes inspired by a liberal spirit: otherwise you build on sand.' The education of the masses could best be achieved from above. It was the by-product of the advanced culture of their superiors.

with bitterness. Therefore I feel no disillusion at all. I believe that the crowd, the herd, will always be odious. The only important thing is a small group of thinkers, always the same, who pass the torch on to each other.' Free elementary education and universal suffrage, as currently proposed by Republicans, were a serious political mistake.

Exasperated by her fellow troubadour's jubilant pessimism, George Sand composed a lengthy reply and published it as a newspaper article. Writing as if to a friend, George Sand took issue with the belief that 'progress is only a dream'. Flaubert didn't much like the character he saw reflected in the friend, 'not a very pleasant bloke, a real egoist'. George Sand's article had brought a humanitarian tear to his eye: 'Though I was not converted, I should say. I was moved, that was all. But not persuaded.' His position was clear and simple. 'I believe that the poor hate the rich and the rich fear the poor. And it will be like that for ever.'*

Faced with such anxious intransigence, George Sand very sensibly changed the subject. She was only answering his rational public arguments. Of course she knew that his heart was more generous than his head. 'Our real discussions', she said, 'remain between ourselves, like the caresses that lovers give and receive. More gentle even than that, because friendship has its mysteries too [. . .].'

FLAUBERT was exhausted. His friends were dying, slipping away from him, one by one, like the despairing survivors of a shipwreck struggling to cling to their raft.† In this year of perpetual calamity he had witnessed war, invasion, defeat, occupation, insurrection and massacre. Add the depressing fact that *L'Education sentimentale* had not yet sold its first impression and we may understand why he felt like 'an old elephant stuck in a swamp'. Keeping still was best. 'I have achieved a state of calm constitutional despair from which I do not wish to be dislodged in case my despair should turn shrill and wild again.' Yet keeping still clashed with the writing of *La Tentation de Saint Antoine*, writing that induced 'a terrifying state of exaltation'. Perhaps some other activity would restore authorial morale.

* The biographer would like to point out to his subject, in the relative privacy of a footnote, that the heroic compassion of Achille-Cléophas Flaubert might be a significant exception to the rule he has just expounded.
† Flaubert prized this heroic analogy. He and his circle, he told Princess Mathilde in February 1869, were like the little band of survivors in Géricault's *Raft of the 'Medusa'*.

An opportunity soon arose.

In December 1871 Rouen Municipal Council rejected Flaubert's proposals for a public memorial to Louis Bouilhet. *The New Corneille* would have to wait for his monument. Indignant on behalf of his friend, proud of his record as a great tactician, Flaubert conceived a plan. *La Tentation de Saint Antoine* would be put to one side and Flaubert would *bombard* the town council from all directions. It would be a splendid campaign. He could deploy everything: the Paris première of Bouilhet's play, the publication of Bouilhet's poems (with laudatory preface), and a protest from the ex-pupils of the college.

Flaubert was soon prodigiously busy. He spent every afternoon at the Théâtre de l'Odéon, scene of his youthful dreams of fame, negotiating contracts, reading Bouilhet's script to the actors, researching designs for costumes, arguing with the prompter, deciding on the decor, finding the best props, directing rehearsals, placing free tickets and coaxing promises from the reviewers. In whatever time remained, Flaubert still laboured for Bouilhet, rewriting his Preface, choosing the paper for the book, hiring an engraver for the frontispiece and correcting proofs. 'I feel as if I were handling his corpse all day long!' He would certainly not be going to Nohant for Christmas.

After a splendid première, with Sarah Bernhardt playing the leading role, hostile reviews emptied the theatre. Bouilhet's *Mademoiselle Aisse* was taken off after only a month. Here was yet another failure, the reward for three months of constant activity. Simultaneously disgusted and exhilarated, Flaubert felt so weary that he often burst into tears at the end of the day.

He also felt indestructible and eager to do battle with Bouilhet's detractors. In the name of Louis Bouilhet Flaubert would risk appearing 'in person'. He would write prefaces. He would write letters to newspapers. On 26 January 1872 *La Presse* accordingly published Flaubert's lengthy open letter to Rouen Municipal Council. 'A little piece which will endear me to our stinking compatriots', it was a thundering polemic directed at bourgeois stupidity, local and national. In his letter Flaubert spoke directly against his own kind:

In itself this business [Bouilhet's memorial] is of little importance. But one can take it as a sign of the times – as a characteristic feature of your class – and I am no longer merely addressing you, gentlemen, but all the bourgeois. I therefore say to them:

Conservatives who conserve nothing, it is time for a change of direction –

and since there is talk of regeneration [. . .] time for fresh thinking! Take some initiative, finally!

The French nobility disappeared because, for two centuries, it had the mind of a menial. The downfall of the bourgeoisie has begun, because it shares the feelings of the rabble. I cannot see that it reads different newspapers, that it enjoys different music, that its pleasures are any more dignified. In both cases, there is the same love of money, the same reverence for the *fait accompli*, the same need for idols to overturn, the same hatred of anything superior, the same spirit of denigration, the same crass ignorance!

To win the respect of those below you, show some respect for those above you!

Before you send the populace to school, go there yourselves!

You are the intelligent classes. Use your intelligence!

Because of your contempt for intelligence you think yourselves *full of common sense, realistic, practical*. But people are only truly practical on condition that they are a little more than that [. . .]. You would not be enjoying all the benefits of industry if the only ideal of your eighteenth-century ancestors had been material usefulness. [. . .]

You practical! What nonsense! You have no skill with the pen or the rifle. You allow yourselves to be plundered, imprisoned and slaughtered by a crowd of convicts. You no longer have even the brute instinct of self-defence; and, when it is a question not merely of saving your skin but your purse as well (which should be the more precious to you), then you do not even have the energy to walk as far as the ballot box. With all your capital and your cleverness you cannot even organise the equivalent of the *International*.

Your only intellectual effort consists in shuddering at the thought of what the future holds.

Use your imaginations! Quickly though! Or else France will sink ever lower, caught between a hideous demagogy and a stupid bourgeoisie.

For three days Flaubert's letter caused a great stir. The local newspaper, *La Nouvelliste de Rouen*, wouldn't risk publishing it. Once he saw his own anger in print Flaubert had second thoughts. 'It is rather brutal and lacking in subtlety.' What would his brother say? 'It may have been a mistake. [. . .] What the hell! I have spat out my bile. It's a relief.' '. . . now they are afraid of me in Rouen, and I pass for a *serious man* because I've quoted some figures.'

Affectionately dismayed by this evidence of her friend's 'hyper-choleric' temperament, George Sand took the risk of offering him some good advice. 'At your age,' she wrote, 'I would prefer to see you less irritated, less preoccupied by the stupidity of others. [. . .] perhaps this chronic indignation arises from your constitution.' Could he not cultivate 'a disdainful serenity'?

APRIL 1872: Madame Flaubert, the indestructible, was dying. Nearly eighty, the great survivor was slipping away from her son. It was gruesome, her obsessive eating, 'to fortify herself'. The Prussian soldiers had turned her house upside down. The war had aged her by ten years. Now she could no longer walk on her own and she was 'terribly frail.' 'So sad,' wrote Flaubert, 'to witness the decay of those you love, to see their strength declining, their intelligence disappearing.' Commanville had recently taken over as the family's banker and accountant, now that she could no longer manage the remains of the family fortune.

Flaubert hardly dared to leave her alone, however frail, imperious and irritating she became. He had hurried back to her from Paris, dutifully but reluctantly, in the summer of 1871. 'At my age,' he grumbled, 'I think I have the right to do what I please at least once a year.' Mealtimes with *Maman* were exhausting. She was now so very deaf that one had to shout very loud. She wanted to have people to dinner every night, thus procuring an audience for her ailments. 'Mother's health was always a dangerous topic. I'm afraid of saying too much or not enough.' Twice a day Flaubert walked her round the garden, in the intervals of writing about his saint, currently being made to watch devilishly lovely prostitutes performing in the city of Babylon.

Madame Flaubert died, 'after thirty-three hours of agony', early in the morning of 6 April 1872. Shrewdly aware of her son's financial habits, she had left Croisset to her niece, Caroline Commanville, on condition that Gustave be allowed to live there. Brought together by death, niece and uncle spent many days compiling the inventory of the house. Caroline stayed with him for three weeks, three good weeks in which they talked their way back towards each other. 'I think', he wrote cautiously, 'that we did each other some good. Your old uncle understands you, doesn't he?'

The day after she left Croisset Caroline wrote him a long letter, a 'stupid' letter, which she tore up. The time for further confidences had not yet arrived. Once she had left, the big house seemed so calm and so silent. The memory of his mother was floating all around him, 'like a mist'. He ate alone at the big table, weeping into his dessert every evening, tears followed by yawning. 'I'm like an old man,' he told Caroline. 'The past overwhelms me. I wallow in memories and I lose my way.' He wondered if he would have the strength to live there all on his own. More to the point, would he have the money? This was an expensive house to keep up and it was already looking shabby. The carpets were worn. The wallpaper in the bedrooms was torn and dirty.

'I have realised', Flaubert wrote to George Sand, two weeks after the death, 'that my poor dear mother was the person I have loved most. It feels as though a piece of my guts has been torn out.' 'More than ever,' he wrote to her again, 'I'd like to have you here at Croisset, to have you sleeping near to me, in my mother's room.'

CHAPTER TWENTY-FIVE

Ghost Love

Having shared out the family silver and finished *La Tentation de Saint Antoine*, Flaubert was ready for something new. It had been three years since he had completed *L'Education sentimentale*. He was ready, he told George Sand on 1 July, to embark on 'a modern novel, the counterpart to *La Tentation de Saint Antoine*, which will have pretentions to being comic'. 'It's the story of those two old copy-clerks,' he explained. 'A kind of critical encyclopaedia in the form of a farce.' His first subject would be Medicine, a choice of some significance for the son of Achille-Cléophas Flaubert. After that he would work his way through the whole library of nineteenth-century knowledge, from agriculture to zoology.

It was superlative intellectual folly, an exorbitant deed worthy of the great Gargantua. 'I gobble up a pile of books and I take notes. I shall do so for another two or three years, after which I shall begin writing.' But whereas Rabelais's giant had merely pissed all over his fellow citizens, in sport, from the highest tower of Notre-Dame, Flaubert had in mind a darker comic purpose: 'to vent upon my contemporaries the disgust they inspire in me. I shall at last unveil my thoughts, exhale my resentment, vomit my hatred, expectorate my bile, ejaculate my anger, purge my indignation.' His note-taking arm would soon ache gigantically.

Meanwhile, Flaubert needed to get out of Croisset. With his niece, but without her husband Commanville, he was to spend the month of July in Luchon, a fashionable resort high in the Pyrenees, just near the border with Spain. He ordered a stylish new suit from his Parisian tailor, 'so that my beautiful niece need not feel ashamed to be seen with me'. An old man with a young woman, he would 'play the duenna', a joke that veiled the pleasant fact of their *rapprochement*.

Their month together began badly. Caroline was 'ill and unhappy'. Flaubert was 'very gloomy' and unsociable. The cheerful banality of the faces in the street, the noise from the room above – they were quite enough to infuriate him, such was his 'nervous susceptibility'. After a few days they moved to another hotel, the Maison Bonnette, where one could lie pleasantly in bed and listen to the roaring of the lion in the neighbouring menagerie.

Luchon in July was excessively hot. Flaubert slept long hours, drank the waters and read *The Pickwick Papers* rather than doing the serious writing he had planned. He couldn't work properly. He was in ' "a state of dryness", as the mystics say'. Then, by a glorious creative accident, the kindly, quixotic bachelor comedy of *The Pickwick Papers* precipitated a new idea. Flaubert now sketched out the first scenario of his novel. Dickens, along with Cervantes, presided over its conception. First of all, he needed a pair of names. He began with *Dumolard . . . Dubolard et Becuchet*. Changed it to *Bolard et Manichet*. Then it came to him: *Bouvard et Pécuchet*. A four-page scenario. He thought it *'superb*, but [. . .] quite *terrifying*'.

In Luchon there also unfolded one of the great scenes of Flaubert's later life. Secluded together in the anonymity of that modest provincial hotel where the long July days were governed by the monotonous routine of their rest cure, uncle and niece found their way back to the intimacy they had once known. Their reconciliation was a small miracle of moral energy. (Such feats of mutual intelligence are almost unknown in Flaubert's novels.) Caroline's account of those conversations is decorously vague: 'He knew my hurt, I poured out my heart to him and he saw how little happiness I had found with Monsieur C and how little that man cared for what was in my heart or my mind. So it was from my uncle that I continued to draw the intellectual nourishment which I needed.' Their alliance, broken in the year of her marriage, was renewed and Caroline was installed hereafter as Flaubert's confidante.

There was much more than Caroline Commanville could bear to put in writing. She delivered the rest of the story to her confidante, Lucie Chevaley-Sabatier, during the long twilight years of her life in the villa in Antibes. It was all there: her resentment at the imposed marriage; her anger at Madame Flaubert's broken promise; her husband's incomprehension; her delight in Baron Leroy; the recent sorrow of his death. 'These revelations', we are told, 'came as no surprise to her uncle.'

FLAUBERT'S greyhound was called Julio. He acquired this serene and beautiful companion on his return to Croisset. He fondled it and talked to it, and then it lay asleep on the bearskin in his study while he was writing.* Alone in the house, Flaubert wrote elegantly sorrowful letters to the women of his acquaintance. He portrayed himself as an old man, walking alone with his dog in the autumn sunlight, bright images of the past crowding into his mind. Pleased with this image, he worked himself into a passion of reminiscence, à la Chateaubriand: 'For me the future holds no more dreams, and I picture all the days gone by as if they were bathed in a golden haze. Upon this bright ground I see ghostly beloved figures who reach out their arms to me [. . .].' The rich autumnal harmonies of *Un Coeur simple* (1877) arise from here, from this compound maternal ghost, a hazy incorporeal figure of love that brings together Madame Flaubert, Elisa Schlésinger, George Sand and his ancient nursemaid, Julie.

Unconscious reconciliation with the feminine was slower but slightly easier than the real thing. Exasperated by Flaubert's stubborn refusal to visit Nohant, George Sand offered him a few home truths. 'You avoid your friends,' she wrote, 'and you bury yourself in work and you don't make any time for loving or being loved.' 'You're making a prison for your exuberant nature. You have a kind affectionate heart and you are turning yourself into a crusty misanthropist [. . .].' She told him that he ought to find himself a wife.

Greatly provoked by this suggestion, Flaubert confided to Princess Mathilde that George Sand's 'perpetually *pious* tone' got on his nerves. He might retaliate, he said, by sending her a few political insults. He took the more sober course of explaining himself. Her suggestion was 'fantastical'. 'The feminine', he confessed, 'has never fitted into my existence. And then I am not rich enough, and then, and then [. . .] I am too old [. . .]. And then I am too sensitive to inflict my person on anyone in perpetuity. There is something in me that is profoundly ecclesiastical, something that nobody knows about.'

It was nearly a month before George Sand replied. 'Sad or cheerful, I love you and I am still hoping to see you, even though you never mention coming to see us and you immediately turn down every

* The name *Julio* may signify. *Juliet* Herbert was Flaubert's English woman. *Julie* was Flaubert's nursemaid. *Djali* was the name of Esmeralda's goat – in *Notre Dame de Paris* – and also the name of Emma Bovary's greyhound.

opportunity; everyone here still likes you though I know that we are not literary enough for you [. . .].' Flaubert admitted, in his reply, that he was passing through another 'gloomy phase'.

I didn't say that I scorned 'feminine sentiment' but that women, physically speaking, had never been part of my daily life, which is quite a different thing. *I've loved* more than anybody – a presumptuous phrase [. . .]. I've known every kind of love. 'The storms of passion' have 'rained' upon me. And then, by chance and force of circumstance, this solitude has gradually grown upon me and now I am alone, absolutely alone. My income is not enought for me to have a wife of my own, nor even for me to live in Paris for six months of the year.

Mollified by his pathos, she offered some brisk but affectionate moral wisdom. 'You ought to be more in harmony with yourself [. . .]. Your momentary rages are good. They come from a generous temperament [. . .] they are neither vicious nor spiteful [. . .]. But your sadness, your weeks of depression, I don't understand them and I don't like them. [. . .] Why do you keep saying you'd rather be dead?' His reply was disarmingly sober. 'Don't take the melodrama of my wrath too seriously.'

It was a dark winter, his first winter alone. 'I read difficult books, I watch the rain falling and I make conversation with my dog.' In a new twist of self-mockery he signed one of his letters 'Géant Aplati'. The old giant was down on the floor, brought low by a great army of tiny vexations. He hated having to ask his niece for money every month. When she urged him to economise he delivered a mighty rebuke. 'There is no need to rub my nose in my poverty. I think about it quite enough. Were you hoping that your remarks would make me change my ways? Do you think I have it in me to *keep an eye on how my servant spends the housekeeping*? Suicide is a sweet prospect in comparison.' He caught flu and couldn't shake it off for several months. He joked at the exhausting violence of his moods. 'I go from exasperation to a state of collapse, then I recover and go from prostration to Fury, so that my average state is one of being annoyed.'

By March 1873, approaching the first anniversary of his mother's death, he had begun to feel better. 'What has been wrong with me for the past four months [. . .] I don't know. What is quite certain is that I have been very ill with something or other.'

APRIL 1873: it was nearly four years since Flaubert had been in Nohant. When he arrived with Turgenev, George Sand saw that her long-awaited guest had aged conspicuously. He had lost weight. He was soon short of breath. 'He shows his age much more than I do.' He seemed uncomfortable in their midst: 'We deafened him with our noise.' On the afternoon of the third day he read his work to them – the final chapters of *Saint Antoine* – for six hours. By the end of the week, her disappointment had turned to irritation: '[. . .] we jumped about, danced, sang, shouted, and generally bored Flaubert stiff – he never wants to do anything but talk about literature. It was all too much for him.' Next day, 'Flaubert talked and was very lively and funny but he monopolised the conversation, and Turgenev, who's much more interesting, could hardly get a word in. This evening the onslaught lasted until one o'clock.' George Sand was glad to see him go. 'I love him dearly and he's an excellent man, but his personality is too excitable. He wears us out.' Turgenev, the urbane professional house guest, made a much happier impression. The old troubadour had turned into *Cruchard* – the *Old Crock*.

The unfavourable impression was confirmed, some weeks later, when George Sand met Flaubert in Paris. She wrote to her son:

I've just dined with Flaubert, and his conduct was odder than ever [. . .] said he was exhausted, at the end of his tether, been reading a play [. . .] from two until five in the morning [. . .] he couldn't talk about anything else, and wouldn't let Turgenev get a word in [. . .]. I made my escape at ten o'clock. I'll be seeing him tomorrow, but I shall say I'm leaving on Monday. I've had enough of my young friend. I'm very fond of him but he gives me a splitting headache. He doesn't like noise, but he doesn't mind the din he makes himself.

IN between books, Flaubert suddenly found himself writing 'a big political comedy' for the stage. *Le Candidat* came to him at high speed. Sketched out in July 1873, it was finished by the end of November. 'It amuses me *enormously*,' he said, composing his play in the evenings as a relaxation after a hard day of making notes for *Bouvard et Pécuchet*. Success in the theatre, the dream of his youth, could earn him very large amounts of money; it would be a triumphant solution to the problem of having to ask his niece for every penny. Flaubert was also surprisingly well qualified to write a topical comedy about politics. He had the right connections. Two of his friends, Charles d'Osmoy and General Valazé, were deputies. Thus we find Flaubert very happily installed one October evening in the Café Riche among a friendly group of left deputies, talking politics until one in the morning.*

Carvalho, manager of the Vaudeville theatre, scenting a potential success, travelled to Croisset for the weekend to negotiate with the author. But this author turned out to be bewilderingly stubborn. Did Monsieur Flaubert not see that theatre demanded endless artistic compromise? Could he not work in one or two big provocative monologues on topical subjects? Flaubert refused, 'because it's facile, vulgar and anti-aesthetic'. To Carvalho such intransigence was simply unprofessional. He probably thought, said Flaubert, that he was dealing with a lunatic. A few days later a telegram arrived in Croisset. It was from Carvalho, summoning Flaubert to Paris. Rehearsals of *Le Candidat* were to begin immediately.

On 11 December, the day before his fifty-second birthday, Flaubert stepped on to the stage of the Vaudeville theatre. For the first time, the script that he had in his hand was not the work of Louis Bouilhet. He told his niece:

I began reading, calm as a god [. . .] *on* stage, by the light of two oil-lamps in front of my 26 actors [. . .]. So as to mellow his tone, Monsieur had lubricated his valves with a dozen oysters, a nice beefsteak, half a bottle of Chambertin, a glass of whisky and a Chartreuse [. . .]. By page two, laughter from the auditorium [. . .]. I read [. . .] like an angel. No hoarseness, no emotion [. . .] and 'the ladies adore me' . . . they're all saying that it will be a great success.

Mollified by the happy prospect before him, Flaubert worked most obligingly with Carvalho, cutting and changing as required. 'No indignation! No explosions! [. . .] gentle as a lamb, and even easy-going.' But Carvalho was being increasingly unpleasant. He kept demanding script changes, kept talking Flaubert down in front of the actors. He seemed impossible to please. 'I left the theatre', Flaubert reported, 'in the state of a man who had been beaten over the head with a stick.'

The week before the first night, everything began to unravel. The leading actor came down with flu and the première had to be delayed.

---

* For the plot of *Le Candidat* Flaubert took his favourite triangular theme and gave it a comic treatment. Julien, an exaggerated young poet, is stuck in the provinces, working as a journalist and dreaming of Paris. Julien adores Madame Rousselin – a manipulative older woman – and works for her husband, who is a candidate in the forthcoming elections. Shamelessly unprincipled, everyone in this world is for sale. The best scene in the play shows Monsieur Rousselin rehearsing a speech for his first election meeting, playing every part required of him.

Then Flaubert learnt that the Russian translation of *Saint Antoine* had been banned by the Imperial Censor in Moscow on the grounds that it was 'detrimental to religion'. Here was further proof of the fact that Art was always hateful to Authority.

Crushed by this further evidence of his bad luck, Flaubert sank into a mood of deep melancholy. 'Sitting by my fire,' he wrote to George Sand,

coughing and spitting, I brood upon the years of my youth. I think of all the dead that I have loved and I wallow in the Blackness. Is it the result of overexerting myself for the last eight months, or is it the complete absence of the feminine element in my life, but never before have I felt so bereft, so empty and so battered. What you told me in your last letter about your little grandchildren moved me to the depths of my heart. Why don't I have my share of that? I was born with tender feelings! But we don't choose our destiny. We submit to it. I was cowardly in my youth. *I was afraid* of life. It all comes home in the end.

The first night of *Le Candidat* was a disaster. The audience whistled, mocked and jeered. They were expecting something different. Something light and sharp and amusingly scurrilous. Behind the scenes the leading actor was in despair. Flaubert was trying very hard to look undismayed. A friend suggested that the second night might go better. Flaubert exploded. First-night audiences were always detestably frivolous. 'All fops and speculators who simply don't understand what words mean. They make a joke of the poetic bits.' The author consoled himself after the performance with a substantial second supper. He put away two dozen oysters, a bottle of iced champagne, three slices of roast beef and a truffle salad. When he read the first reviews Flaubert was relieved to find that they were at least polite.

The second night was as bad as the first. Flaubert saw the principal actor coming off the stage with tears in his eyes. 'I felt like a criminal and I said to myself "that's quite enough!"' He declared impulsively that he wanted the play to be taken off immediately. His friends and the theatre manager talked him out of it. But the reviews next day were openly hostile. The audience had been 'bored to death'. None of the characters were in the least sympathetic. Six lines of *Bovary*, any six lines, would be worth more than the whole of *Le Candidat*. Was it worth carrying on? Worth enduring all the abuse? Critics he had wooed so carefully were writing treacherous little articles making fun of his slippers and his dog.

After only four performances, Flaubert withdrew the play. Edmond de Goncourt, who rather savoured the spectacle of his friend's humiliation, made a note of the intimate details. Flaubert, he wrote, is 'quite philosophical on the surface, but the corners of his mouth are drooping and his great thundering voice is lowered [. . .]. With intense bitterness he blurted out "My dear Edmond, there's nothing to be said, it's an utterly stinking flop." '

Something had to be done to cheer Flaubert up. In April 1874, The Five (so-called) met up for the first time in the Café Riche. Zola, Turgenev, Goncourt, Daudet and Flaubert had all had their work whistled off the stage. They were all failed dramatists, 'men of talent who have a high opinion of each other's work'. 'We began with a long discussion on the special aptitudes of writers suffering from constipation and diarrhoea; and we went on to talk about the mechanics of the French language.'

LA TENTATION DE SAINT ANTOINE was published in May 1874, bringing down upon its author an 'avalanche of stupidity'. Flaubert's old enemy, the journalist Barbey d'Aurevilley, mocked it for being 'relentlessly boring', boring with 'a German boredom, the boredom of Goethe's second Faust'. Distressingly hostile or merely bewildered, the reviews added to Flaubert's sense of artistic failure. 'Beneath it all,' he wrote, 'I sense a personal hatred of me [. . .] I annoy people, less by what I write than by my character, my isolation (natural and systematic) being a sign of disdain.'

Back in Croisset, Flaubert devised a new and cheerfully practical research syllabus for *Bouvard et Pécuchet*. Open up a few corpses ('that is how far my love of literature takes me'). Wander the lanes of Normandy in search of the ideal location. Walk around Croisset's kitchen garden by candlelight. He soon gave himself a headache, reading about the cultivation of fruit trees.

It was time to begin writing. First he needed an excursion, an adventure, 'to get some air, clear my head, and *de-neuropathicate* myself'. Flaubert's strange choice of destination suggests that he was following medical advice. How else can we explain the lonely and improbable month that he now spent in Kaltbad Rigi, in the the Swiss Alps near Lake Lucerne. The magic mountain was detestable. Flaubert filled the days with eating, sleeping, and smoking. He felt morose and emptyheaded, he spoke to nobody, and kept being woken up from his afternoon nap by the sound of little electric bells. The clumsy playing of

Chopin on the hotel piano and then the Germans with their fancy walking sticks and their little telescopes – they were so infuriating that he had to restrain himself from 'insulting the imbeciles'. The beauties of the Alps left him cold. 'You would need to be twenty-five years old and [. . .] with your darling girl.' He wanted to be in Venice looking at pictures but instead he forced himself to go for walks. He was a grotesque spectacle, 'sweating like a pig, puffing like a seal, groaning like a donkey, and stopping every twenty paces'. 'I was tempted', he wrote, 'to kiss three calves I came across in a meadow, out of simple humanity and the need to express my feelings.' There were little refreshment rooms everywhere, with crowds of waiters impeccably dressed in black. 'You begin to think you are being waited on by a tribe of solicitors or a crowd of funeral guests. It puts you in mind of your own exit. Most uplifting.'

When he returned home, he was ready to begin writing *Bouvard et Pécuchet*. Beginnings were always dreadful. 'I tremble at the thought, as if I were about to set off on a journey around the world.' He sorted his papers and arranged all his quills and then, 'after an entire afternoon's torment', at four o'clock on 1 August 1874, he found his opening sentence. He then sat on it for four days, 'floundering, rewriting it, in desperation'. Suffering from severe stomach ache, he finally sent the sentence off to his niece as he had promised. In a gentle mockery of his own religion of style the sentence arrived with a warning that it was not 'The True Sentence' and must not be accorded the ceremonies due to an authentic relic.*

By late September, after two months of writing, Flaubert was once again struggling with the blackness. His thoughts seemed to be 'the colour of ebony'. Living from hand to mouth he kept worrying about money. 'When you have an exasperated sensibility', he explained, 'and a deplorable imagination you are beset by gloomy speculations.' *Bouvard et Pécuchet* was impossible, like 'trying to put the ocean in a bottle'.

George Sand responded affectionately to his complaints. 'I worry about your way of life, excessive intellectual work and being stuck too long indoors [. . .] and nobody to remind you to eat and drink and sleep [. . .].' She was generous, even when he refused her invitation to Nohant. 'The unhappier you are the more I love you,' she wrote. 'All

---

* The first sentence of *Bouvard et Pécuchet* reads: 'With the temperature at 33 degrees centigrade, the boulevard Bourdon was absolutely deserted.'

that you are complaining about is life [. . .]. You love literature too much. It will kill you and you will not kill human stupidity. Poor dear stupidity, which I do not hate. I look at it with maternal eyes. Because it's a sort of childhood and all childhood is sacred.'

'Don't tell me', he protested, 'that "Stupidity is sacred like all things childish." Stupidity doesn't germinate anything.' Undaunted, she urged him to make something of his suffering: 'describe your martyrdom, there is a fine book to be written there'. Martyrdom, ancient and modern, impersonally fictionalised, would indeed be the theme of his next work, *Les Trois contes*.

By February 1875 Flaubert had reached a state of 'physical and moral prostration'. He sat by the fire unable to work, overwhelmed by memories of his childhood, 'a sign of decrepitude'. He took potassium bromide, which calmed his nerves but also gave him eczema, so that he looked hideous, 'like a leper', he warned a friend. He couldn't describe the disaster that was waiting for him. 'Something abnormal is happening inside me,' he told George Sand. 'My state of depression must have some hidden cause. I feel old, stale, and disgusted with everything. [. . .] I expect nothing more from life than sheet upon sheet of paper to be darkened with my scribble.'

FLAUBERT's fears of ruin were well founded. On 9 May 1875 there was a crisis meeting of all the family in Caroline's apartment on the rue de Clichy. Here, among the monogrammed porcelain and the rich brocade, it emerged that Commanville's trading debts were now impossible to meet. The honour of the family was at risk. How could they escape the bourgeois hell, the ignominious descent into poverty that began with the auctioning of assets and ended in the malodorous confines of the Hôtel-Dieu? At the very least there would have to be economies. Flaubert would have to change his way of life, give up his expensive rooms on the rue Murillo and move – along with the Commanvilles – to a smaller and cheaper apartment at a less prestigious address on the rue du Faubourg Saint-Honoré.

Flaubert travelled back to Croisset with his brother Achille. There was not much to be said. In the train the two men slept most of the way. Then Flaubert took the steamboat back to Croisset and went to bed very early. He lay listening to the mournful howling of his dog Julio. 'The sound was inexpressibly sweet and musical: almost like a large flute [. . .] it was heart-breaking.'

Next day, when he woke in the big house, there was 'a dead calm on the river and an immense silence all around me'. Flaubert felt 'roving twinges of gout, pains everywhere, an invincible melancholia, a sense of "universal futility" and serious doubts about the book that I'm writing [. . .]. Add to all that worries about money and a perpetual longing to bite the dust along with lugubrious excursions into the past [. . .].'

For the moment it was impossible to work. Flaubert felt only an immense need for sleep. 'I'm bone-weary,' he wrote, 'sad as death, worn out, knackered'. After a long barren month he took himself in hand. He would stop work on *Bouvard et Pécuchet*. 'I had embarked on an absurd project, as I now realise. And I'm afraid of getting stuck with it.' He also decided that his 'cerebral exhaustion' required a 'heroic remedy'. Leaving all his books and papers behind, he would go to the seaside for two months, with his friend Georges Pouchet.

Yet he felt so fragile. One evening a summer storm brought rainwater in through the ceilings upstairs. 'At one point I thought the house was going to collapse around me and I was in a splendid state.' Upset by the storm he slept badly and had terrible dreams that followed him all through the next day. The old house was 'full of sacred memories'. Losing that house was not merely a bad dream. It had become a real possibility.

All the sacrifices that Caroline envisaged were too much to bear. He protested to her: 'I have spent my life depriving my heart of its rightful fodder. My existence has been industrious and austere. And now I just cannot keep it up any longer.'

At best we shall have hardly enough to live on [. . .]. As for earning money, how exactly am I to do that? I am not a novelist, or a playwright, or a journalist. I am a writer, and style, style as such, does not make money. [. . .] I have sacrificed everything in my life for the sake of my intellectual freedom! And it's being taken from me by this misfortune. It is that in particular that drives me to despair.

By the end of July it was quite clear that Commanville was ruined. He had been 'somewhat imprudent and had had very bad luck'. His debts amounted to one and a half million francs. 'Dark days are coming: lack of money, humiliation, life turned upside down.' There was some hope that Croisset would not have to be sold.

In August, 'at a most advantageous price', Flaubert sold his 'last patch of land', the farm at Deauville, the only property he had inherited from his mother. An honourable but a foolish gesture, it was intended to 'save my poor nephew'. The sale didn't cover Commanville's liabilities but merely delayed the inevitable bankruptcy. Flaubert also began to draw two of his 'real friends' down into this hell with him, persuading them to give their signatures to complicated documents.

Behind the scenes, treading softly, Flaubert's old friends were trying to procure an official pension for him. When he first heard of the scheme, Flaubert sent a dignified letter of refusal. Details of the pension would be made public and then he would be attacked in the press and the courts. Others might enjoy their pensions unmolested, but he would never be allowed to get away with it.

E ARLY in September 1875, believing that family honour might still be saved, Flaubert set off for six weeks by the sea. Perhaps a new and inspiring subject would come to him, away from all the ominous legal documents that he could not bear to read. Flaubert spent two days with Caroline in Dieppe, making a great effort to behave with dignity. He kept choking and bursting into tears, 'three-quarters dead with misery'. Then he set off on the long, complicated journey down the coast. Trouville, Lisieux, Le Mans, Brest – these places revived pleasant memories of the summer of 1840. And travelling brought moments of serenity. 'I spent Wednesday night watching the moon. It was travelling at the same speed as the carriage, just behind the trees that line the road.' The Breton women still wore their big white bonnets and their pleated collars.

On 15 September, tired and hungry, Flaubert arrived in Concarneau. The Hôtel Sergent was 'a good old-fashioned inn' and Flaubert had 'a pretty room with a view of the harbour'. Breton cuisine was lavish, seven or eight courses at every meal. Flaubert's hands were trembling so much that he could hardly write; he had to form each letter separately. He kept sobbing, amazed and humiliated by the signs of his nervous weakness. He went swimming in the sea every day, then every night he dreamt vividly and endlessly about Croisset. Waking in the morning was a bitter moment. The disgusting harbour smell of sardines mingled with thoughts of Commanville's 'liquidation' that was now in progress.

Flaubert sat in his room, trying to write, looking out at the old town, the seventeenth-century ramparts, the drawbridge, the little fishing boats, listening to the sound of children in clogs playing marbles under his window. His companion, an expert biologist, was somewhere out on the shore, contentedly dissecting a new fish. Flaubert felt 'rootless, drifting along like a piece of dead seaweed', yet he forced himself to write a half-page plan for a tale about Saint Julien.

After two weeks a letter arrived with the news that the liquidation had been concluded. This was an immense relief and it released energy and emotion for the writing of letters to all his close friends. 'A man weeping over his money', he told George Sand cheerfully, 'is of no interest at all. [. . .] I'd become used to a great independence of mind and a complete insouciance with regard to material life.' He had decided, in spite of everything, that he would not attempt to earn any money. 'The idea of accepting a position,' he wrote to Commanville, 'of no longer being independent, I find *extremely* repugnant.'

Friends came forward, to console and assist. George Sand applauded his decision to abandon *Bouvard et Pécuchet*. She thought he should 'do something more down-to-earth that will appeal to everyone'. Could she possibly buy Croisset, so that he could stay living in it? Moved to tears by her generosity, Flaubert explained that the house was worth 100,000 francs and would be too expensive for him to maintain.

O N 1 November 1875 Flaubert was back in Paris, 'three-quarters ruined'. He settled into his modest new rooms at 240 rue du Faubourg-Saint-Honoré and was surprised to find that his life had not greatly changed.* He still saw the same people. Guy de Maupassant came to lunch every week and Flaubert received the regular Sunday circle of friends, Turgenev, Zola, Daudet and de Goncourt. *La Légende de saint Julien*, 'my little religio-poetic, rococo-medievalesque story-ette', was progressing slowly. 'I will have finished it I think by the end of February.' Flaubert was keeping up appearances, insisting proudly that he was the same man as before. 'There have been such rumours circulat-ing about my ruination that people are really quite surprised, I can tell, to see that I am not going about in rags. My manner forbids their pity, and we talk of other matters.' Zola and Daudet were pressing Flaubert to try for a seat in the Academy, but he stood firm. Such stupidities, he reminded them forcibly, had always been against his principles.

Writing to George Sand, Flaubert disowned these friends who

---

* The rue du Faubourg-Saint-Honoré is at the top end of a long narrow road that runs two kilometres north-west to south-east – roughly parallel to the Seine. It was one of the oldest roads in the city, a complete contrast to the rue Murillo.

claimed to share his artistic principles. 'They value everything that I despise,' he said, 'and they care very little for the things that obsess me. Technical detail and authentic local colour, indeed the whole precise historical business, I regard as very secondary. Beauty is the object of all my efforts, a thing my companions scarcely give a thought to. I see them looking on unmoved at things that leave me convulsed with admiration or horror.'

George Sand met his declarations of austerity with her habitual sympathy. 'One aspect of your life', she wrote, 'is all affection, protection of others, graceful and simple kindness [. . .] but as soon as you're dealing with literature you insist for some reason or other on being a different person, one who has to disappear or even annihilate himself – one who doesn't exist.' She offered him her explanation for the failure of *L'Education sentimentale*. Artistic intransigence!

I kept telling you, but you wouldn't listen. It needed either a short preface, or some expression of disapproval, if only a significant word here and there, to condemn evil, call weakness by its right name, and draw attention to endeavour. All the characters in the book are weak and come to nothing except those whose instincts are evil; that's the criticism people make, because they haven't understood that your intention was precisely to depict a deplorable society which encourages bad instincts and ruins noble efforts. But when we are misunderstood it is always our own fault.

She held this letter back for three days, then she relented. 'I've been on the point of throwing it on the fire [. . .]. I fear you will understand me now no better than before. [. . .] You could do with a success, after some bad luck which has affected you deeply. [. . .] Let there be some decent and strong men among the madmen and idiots you like making fun of.'

It was three weeks before Flaubert replied, espousing an intransigence that went beyond what he felt. There was, he told her, 'an essential difference' between them:

You always [. . .] begin by soaring up into the sky and then from there you make your way back down to earth.. You start from [. . .] the ideal. That is the source of your habitual forbearance, your serenity [. . .] your greatness. I poor devil find my feet stuck to the ground, as if I had lead in my boots; everything moves me, lacerates me, devastates me, though I do try to leave the ground [. . .]. It is all very well you lecturing me, I cannot do anything about the temperament with which I find myself, nor the aesthetic that springs from it. [. . .] And remember that I detest what they call *realism*, even though I am regarded as its pope.

In the aftermath of this conversation, Flaubert sketched out a plan for his next tale, *Un Coeur simple*. This new tale was to be his real answer to George Sand. He wrote to her on 29 May, 'You will see from *Un Coeur simple* (in which you will recognise your own direct influence) that I am not as obstinate as you think. I believe you will like the moral tendency, or rather the underlying humanity of this little work.'

CHAPTER TWENTY-SIX

Alchemist with Parrot

FLAUBERT'S tribute to George Sand, *Un Coeur simple*, was too late. George Sand died on 8 June 1876, before her tale was finished. Flaubert took the night train to Nohant for her funeral. 'I wept buckets', he wrote, 'when I embraced her granddaughter Aurore who looks so like her [. . .] her eyes that day looked so like her mother's that it was like a resurrection.' 'In the little country cemetery the mud was ankle-deep. A gentle rain was falling [. . .]. A crowd of good country people were mumbling prayers and telling their rosary beads. It was just like a chapter from one of her novels.'

Flaubert rushed away soon after the ceremony, a strange discourtesy that required some explanation. 'If I did not stay on longer,' he wrote to Maurice Sand, 'it was because my companions dragged me away. It seemed as if I were burying my mother a second time!' Some months after the funeral, in a letter to Maurice Sand, Flaubert acknowledged the extent of her creative moral influence upon him. 'Being able to settle down to work again I owe partly to your mother's good advice. She found the way to restore my self-respect.'

Returning to Croisset, Flaubert drank a great flagon of cider and shook off the misery of recent months. Weeping buckets, ostensibly for George Sand, had done him good. There he was, simply drinking cold cider, back in his old house. Everything was there, mysteriously restored, all his old things, the silver soup tureen, the sugar bowl, the little chair that Caroline had used as a child. 'To tell the truth I'm delighted to find myself back here, like a petit bourgeois, sitting in *my* chairs, surrounded by *my* books, in *my* study with a view of *my* garden. The sun is shining, the birds are cooing amorously, the sailing boats are skimming silently over the smooth

337

waters and my tale is rolling along. In two months I shall probably finish it.'

He had a clear sense of what he wanted it to be:

The Story of a Simple Heart is quite simply the tale of the obscure life of a poor country girl, devout but not given to mysticism, devoted in a quiet sober way and soft as newly baked bread. One after the other she loves a man, her mistress's children, a nephew, an old man she nurses, then her parrot; when the parrot dies she has it stuffed, and when she is on her deathbed she takes the parrot for the Holy Ghost. It is in no way ironic (though you might suppose it to be so) but on the contrary very serious and very sad. I want to move my readers to pity, I want to make sensitive souls weep, being one myself.

Flaubert now acquired a stuffed parrot. 'At the moment,' he told his niece, 'I'm writing with an "Amazon" standing on my writing table, his beak askew, gazing at me with his glass eyes.' 'The sight of the thing is beginning to annoy me. But I'm keeping him there, to fill my mind with the idea of parrothood.' The parrot in Flaubert's story would be called Loulou, a name that undoubtedly had a certain resonance for the author. Caroline's pet name was Loulou, and Caroline was a first name that went back three generations. Loulou meant love and affection, happy domesticity, the unbroken maternal line.

Flaubert's parrot has overshadowed the other figure who contributed significantly to *Un Coeur simple*. Julie, Flaubert's nursemaid, was still in service with the family after nearly fifty years. It's interesting, though it may be mere coincidence, that Julie arrived in Croisset in the same week as the more famous parrot. 'I'm going to bring Julie out here tomorrow,' Flaubert wrote on 22 July, with the parrot recently installed on his desk. We catch sight of Julie in Flaubert's letters. Thin and frail, but delighted to be in Croisset 'for the country air', Julie was now almost blind. A child had to lead her around the garden.

Gladdened by the extraordinary August heat, Flaubert worked on *Un Coeur simple* with a singular passion. On his table, alongside the stuffed parrot, he had laid out the raw materials for his story's ending: a medical treatise on pneumonia, a breviary and a collection of prayer books. He had entered a realm of mysterious intellectual exaltation. 'Before dinner, around seven, I frolic in the bourgeois waters of the Seine', 'like a young man'. He was turning phrases while he was swimming and they still came to him in his sleep. 'In the night the sentences go rolling through my mind, like the chariots of some Roman emperor, and they wake me with a start by their jolting and their endless rumbling.' He was often writing all through the night, with the windows open, in his shirtsleeves, 'bellowing like a fiend, in the silence of my study', until his lungs were hurting and he saw the dawn. 'One day', he joked, 'I shall explode like an artillery shell and all my bits will be found on the writing table.' 'I think', he told his niece, 'I've been seriously and secretly ill without realising ever since the death of our poor dear mother. If I'm wrong about that, why have all the clouds lifted for me recently? It's like a mist clearing. And I feel physically restored.'

As proof of his new powers he offered up a mock-heroic portrait of himself, swimming playfully around the wooded islands in the river, like some splendidly lithe sea god in a Renaissance tapestry. Fortified by a substantial supper he would retire to his library and toil through the night, working the language, like some old alchemist heating precious metals at his secret forge.

On 17 August 1876 Flaubert wrote to his niece with the news: 'Yesterday at one in the morning I finished *Un Coeur simple* [...]. *Hérodias* is coming and I can see (as clearly as I can see the Seine) the surface of the Dead Sea sparkling in the sun. Herod and his wife are on the balcony with a view of the gilded roof of the Temple. I'm longing to get started and hack away at it this autumn.'

I WOULD happily relinquish Flaubert here, in the full splendour of his achievement, sporting himself in the river Seine with the heat of the August sun on his back and pictures of gilded temples still forming in his mind. And yet a stern biographical convention requires us to see it through to the very day of the funeral, to the moment when we must lay down the corpulent personage whom we have carried so lightly in our imaginations.

Though he lived for another three and a half years, Flaubert never recovered the wonderful creative exuberance that carried him through *Un Coeur simple*. Adversity, financial and medical, was piled upon his head as he laboured at the writing of *Bouvard et Pécuchet*. His book soon acquired the resounding sub-title, 'an encyclopaedia of human stupidity'. A laborious, cheerless task, the making of *Bouvard et Pécuchet* induced days and weeks of dark depression. By the end he had 'absorbed' 1500 books and accumulated a stack of notes eight inches high.

Flaubert savoured the details of his own undoing with a lucid comic anguish. He had been falling apart and yet holding himself together ever since his first nervous attack in January 1844. Lavish affliction was his old speciality. The months now unfolded in an ever-darkening pattern of poverty, isolation and decrepitude. Writing was rather like roadmending, relentless toil, breaking stones with a big hammer, day after day. The 'abominable book' left him feeling 'like an old cab-horse, weary but ever willing'. Money-problems were getting steadily worse. 'I who detest such preoccupations, I live like an anxious little shopkeeper. What an atrocious irony of fate.' 'Sometimes,' he told Caroline two weeks before the end, 'I think I'm liquefying like an old Camembert, I feel so weary.'

There were one or two consolations still to be found. Turgenev was an exquisite intellectual companion, though he could never be persuaded to stay for more than twenty-four hours because he had to hurry back to his hotel-hopping *ménage à trois*. Guy de Maupassant, champion oarsman and story-teller, was an amusing, boisterous character who might yet do great things if he could avoid shagging himself into an early grave. Emile Zola advertised his sincere admiration for the subtlety of Flaubert's achievement whilst buying himself a splendid country house on the proceeds of Naturalism.

Now that his best friends were dead, Flaubert found a companion close to home in the person of Julie, the loyal half-blind servant who had been with the family for over fifty years. On winter evenings, to satisfy a mutual need for affection, they sat together after supper, master and servant, enjoying the simple equality of old age. 'Talking about the old days she reminded me of all kinds of things, portraits and images, which gladdened my heart. It was like a breath of fresh air.' Julie, the witness of Flaubert's childhood, was like a second mother. The maternal likeness was enhanced by the fact that Julie now wore garments that had once belonged to Madame Flaubert. 'I gaze at her,' said Flaubert, 'in the old black dress that maman used to wear. Then I remember the dear old thing until the tears rise up in me.'* Ancestral memories were conjured up to fill the big empty house. Flaubert retrieved a collection of mouldering family portraits from the attic and hung them in a corridor. A miniature of his maternal grandfather,

---

* In the final chapter of *Madame Bovary* the house-maid, Felicité, is to be found wearing the dresses that had once belonged to her dead mistress. Charles Bovary is enchanted by her illusory resemblance to his wife.

Fleuriot, was soon installed in pride of place on the mantelpiece of his study.

Sexual scandal – ingredients by De Sade, but sweetened with a generous measure of Rabelais – remained a rich source of lonely but sardonic amusement. One of the milder examples deserves to be mentioned, for the light it throws into this odd corner of Flaubert's imagination. In December 1876 a prominent politician, one Monsieur Germiny, was arrested for indecency. Flaubert was indecently delighted. 'A gentleman being wanked off in a urinal', he told Edmond de Goncourt, 'has monopolised the capital of the civilised world for two weeks . . . A little bourgeois ejaculation has silenced discussion of the Eastern Question.'

TROIS CONTES, published in April 1877, was surprisingly well received. Here was recognition at last, though it had come several years too late to assuage Flaubert's bitter sense of having been disregarded, ever since *Salammbô*. Here was a conspiracy of approval, gratifying of course, but also slightly embarrassing to an author who had been so resolutely misunderstood for the last ten years. *Un Coeur simple*, wholesome and profoundly moving, was something for the common reader. *La Légende de Saint Julien l'hospitalier* offered all the darker pleasures of the *conte fantastique*. *Hérodias* was the grand finale, a *conte orientale*, something for the connoisseur, cruel and magnificent, like a Delacroix. Achille Flaubert, not the most reliable judge of literary merit, told his brother that *Trois contes* was the best thing he'd ever written.

The eloquent diversity of *Trois contes* was something new, a vindication of Flaubert's laborious cult of style, but also, paradoxically, a reminder of the importance of improvisation. Here was a magisterially assured letting-go, a letting-through of the deepest creative powers of the mind. Broken into three parts, projected into three different worlds, here was the great psycho-mythological novel that had always been too dangerous for Flaubert to attempt. *Saint Antoine* and *Salammbô* were grandiose rehearsals for this. Ancient or modern, sublime or ludicrous, Flaubert's finest characters are visionaries. They are not quite of this world, though the mud clings thick and heavy to their boots. Like their creator they are pestered, isolated, tormented and bewildered by their visions. They travel towards the dark places of the mind, and their fate prompts our pity, fear and laughter.

341

Trois contes ends with the severed head of the prophet John the Baptist. There it is, 'a lugubrious object, on its dish, among the remains of the feast'. The spirit of the prophet may have 'gone down among the dead to proclaim the coming of Christ' but the prophet's head poses a stubbornly practical problem to his disciples. They set off with it, in the direction of Galilee. 'As it was very heavy,' says the last line of the story, 'they each carried it in turn.' A conclusion so inscrutably prosaic that it leaves us yearning for the poetry of the sacred, for the very thing that is so delicately withheld.

THE precise cause of Flaubert's death remains unknown. In the absence of verifiable fact, speculation has flourished. Discreet whisperings were already to be heard among the mourners circulating in the gardens at Croisset on the day of Flaubert's funeral. Was it a cerebral haemorrhage? Was it an epileptic fit? Or was it a heart attack, brought on perhaps by *imprudent* sexual exertions with Suzanne, the young housemaid?

Here is the official family version of his death, as told by Caroline Commanville in a memoir published a few years after the event, when the primary witnesses were still alive:

Death took him whilst he was in good health [. . .] He was preparing to leave for Paris where he was to stay with me. It was the day before he left, he got out of the bath, went up to his room; the maid was about to serve his breakfast when she heard him calling. She ran upstairs. His fists were already clenched and he could not open the bottle of smelling salts he was holding in his hand. He uttered an incomprehensible string of words in which she could only make out 'Eylau . . . go . . . find . . . avenue . . . I know him.'

My letter that morning had informed him that Victor Hugo was going to move into the avenue Eylau; his last words no doubt were a memory of this piece of news . . . The last glimmer of his mind evoked the great poet who had so inspired him.

Then he fell down unconscious. A few moments later his breathing stopped. A massive apoplexy had finished him.

There is a more circumstantial though less uplifting account of the same events in a letter that Guy de Maupassant wrote to Turgenev on 25 May 1880, only a few weeks after Flaubert's death.

At Croisset we found him on his bed, looking almost unchanged, except that his neck was black and swollen from the apoplexy [. . .] He had been feeling well for the last few days, happy to be nearing the end of his novel [. . .] he looked forward to enjoying himself, having, he said, 'hidden a nest egg in pot'. It wasn't a very large nest egg and he had earned it by his writing. He had eaten a very good dinner on Friday and spent the evening reciting Corneille with his doctor and neighbour, Monsieur Fortin, slept until eight the next morning, taken a long bath, dressed and read his letters. Then, feeling a little unwell, he called his maid; she was slow in coming, and he called to her out of the window to fetch Monsieur Fortin, but as it happened he had just left for Rouen on the boat. When the maid arrived she found him standing, quite dizzy but not at all alarmed. He said, 'I think I am going to have a kind of fainting fit; it's fortunate that it should happen today; it would have been troublesome tomorrow in the train.' He opened a bottle of eau de Cologne and rubbed some on his forehead, and let himself down quietly on a large divan, murmuring, 'Rouen, we aren't far from Rouen – Hellot – I know the Hellots . . . ' and then he fell back, his hands clenched, his face darkened and swollen with blood, stricken by the death which he had not for a second suspected.

It would be fair to say that Maupassant's account of the death is designed to confirm the official story. Maupassant was almost 'one of the family' by 1880. But there are several other accounts of Flaubert's final hours, written by old friends who were undoubtedly hostile to Flaubert's niece. They all tell more or less the same story and they all contradict the authorised version, arguing that Flaubert's sickening financial worries brought about a fatal recurrence of his epilepsy.

Edmond de Goncourt was told the secret on the morning of Flaubert's funeral:

This morning Pouchet took me down a deserted path and said: 'He didn't die from a stroke, he died from an epileptic fit . . . In his youth, you know, he had had several fits . . . His travels in the Middle East had so to speak cured him . . . He didn't have any more for sixteen years. But the worry over his niece's affairs brought the trouble back . . . And on Saturday he died from an epileptic fit . . . Yes, with all the symptoms, foam on his lips, and so on . . . And then his niece wanted to have a cast taken of his hand, but it couldn't be done, the hand was so tightly clenched . . . Perhaps if I'd been there to give him half an hour's artificial respiration, I could have saved him . . . I must say it made an impression on me, going into that study of his, with his handkerchief on the table next to his papers, his pipe with the tobacco-ash on the mantelpiece, and the Corneille from which he had read a few passages the day before sticking out from the shelves of the bookcase.'

According to another friend, Charles Lapierre, Flaubert had told

Suzanne, the maid, that he was 'seeing yellow'. This was always a premonition of an epileptic attack.*

Maxime Du Camp was in Paris when Flaubert died, and he was far too ill to be present at Flaubert's funeral. Yet Du Camp wrote a detailed account of Flaubert's death, a vivid, intimate, macabre invention drawing on authentic memories of earlier attacks and embroidering on whatever first-hand testimony he had been able to collect.

On Saturday 8th May 1880, in the morning, he had a nervous attack which he endeavoured to control by inhaling ether. When he came round he could still see a yellow cloud – the thing he called his golden vision. His head was swimming, the blood rushed into his face. Groping his way, he reached his divan and lay down on his back. There was a whispering in his throat. He was breathing heavily and trying to speak. In the midst of the shadows that were gathering around him he no doubt realised that his last moment had arrived. Twice he called for his doctor, his friend, 'Hallot! Hallot!' His mouth twisted suddenly, he turned his head and died.

Beyond the faked-up death-bed, Du Camp had interestingly scurrilous things to say about Flaubert's last days. He blamed Flaubert's sudden death on the cruel vexations of the recent past. Du Camp hinted menacingly in his memoirs that he possessed a long accusatory letter from Flaubert, a memoir with supporting documents, into which Flaubert had poured all the bitterness he felt towards his niece and her husband. The implication was clear. They had treated him atrociously. Kept him poor. Made him ill with worry. Brought back his epilepsy.

THE moral and medical facts of Flaubert's death remain hidden inside this dark little cloud. Family and friends, Flaubert's first biographers, were already at each other's throats within a few days of his passing. His funeral took place on Tuesday, 11 May 1880. Led by Caroline Commanville, the procession made its way up the steep hill behind the house, then out along the ridge to the little village church at Canteleu. The hearse was handsomely decorated with a large floral wreath at each corner and a set of silver shields bearing the initials GF. Reporters from the Paris newspapers were intrusively busy, counting heads and writing the mourners' names in their notebooks.

---

* Zola also reported this crucial detail, 'seeing yellow', and attributed it to Maupassant. The testimonies of Lapierre and Zola, independently agreeing as they do, suggest that epilepsy was indeed the cause of Flaubert's death.

'No sign of Du Camp.' 'Where's Zola?' 'It's like Emma Bovary's funeral.'

Five miles from the church at Canteleu to the Cimetière monumentale high on the hill above the city of Rouen. Five warm slow miles of country lane, hawthorn hedge, poplar trees and rich green meadow. Edmond Goncourt remembered frivolous gourmet talk of *caneton à l'orange*. Emile Zola remembered a cow that peered over the hedge and gave a long sorrowful bellow. Flaubert's friends took turns at holding the tassels on his coffin. At the city gates the procession was met by a small body of soldiers, a meagre ceremonial tribute to Flaubert as a Chevalier of the Legion of Honour. Along the quayside, across the city, observed by a handful of indifferent spectators. It was an insult. At the time of his death, according to Zola, four fifths of the population of Rouen had never heard of Gustave Flaubert. The remainder all detested him.

At Flaubert's request there were no speeches at the graveside. Charles Lapierre, a friend and editor of a local newspaper, said a few words. Flaubert's coffin, too big to fit into the grave, had to be left stuck at an angle, headfirst, and only half way into the earth.

Endings

O^N 20 May 1880 Gustave Flaubert, '*propriétaire*, man of letters, chevalier de la Légion d'honneur', has been dead for twelve days. At eleven thirty in the morning Maître Lemoel, watched by his colleague Maître Denize, arrives in Croisset to remove the official seals from the doors and begin the task of compiling an inventory of the contents of the house. The document, running to seven extra-large folio pages, is a strangely cold mirror of the life that had unfolded in amongst this eloquent constellation of things.

In the bedroom on the first floor,
   panama hat,
   top hat,
   red silk cravat,
   5 pairs of gloves,
   19 shirts,
   2 dressing gowns,
   5 waistcoats,
   7 walking sticks,
   tobacco jar,
   two pairs of boots.

In the dining room,
   35 champagne glasses,
   48 porcelain dinner plates,
   a painting representing Napoléon 1,
   a pocket watch in a gold case engraved with initials 'GF',
   a gold watch chain,
   a gold signet ring with square stone,
   a silver spoon and two forks marked 'N Flaubert',
   5 oyster-knives with black handles and silver blades.

In the study on the first floor,
Engraving in oakwood frame representing *The temptation of Saint Antoine* by Callot,
Marble clock with bronze figurines, maker's name 'Destigny' engraved on dial,
Photographic reproduction of painting entitled *Visions,*
Array consisting of lances, javelins, arrows, mandolin, Basque drum, axe, oriental pipe, cardboard Chinese statuette,
Large round table in mahogany,
Green woolen tablecloth,
One tiger skin, one lynx skin, one bear skin, white,
Penholder in the shape of dragon,
Bronze inkwell,
Three paperknives, one with initials 'GF',
Two Egyptian lanterns,
Unfinished manuscript of work entitled *Bouvard et Pécuchet,*
Creuzer, *Religions of Antiquity* in 11 vols.,
Works of Saint Theresa in Migne edition,
Works of Walter Scott in 32 vols.

In the drawer of one of the small bookcases is found the sum of 2515 francs, which sum is deposited with Maître Bidault to cover funeral expenses, burial charges and other debts.

MAY 1881: Ernest Commanville has just sold the house at Croisset. It is sold again almost immediately in June 1881. The demolition of the house begins in August 1881 and is completed in less than a month. On 7 November 1885, *Le Figaro* prints the following account of the demolition:

It was the garden that they attacked first, a large rococo garden, in the gap between the hill that looks down on the Seine and the road that runs along its bank, a garden built almost entirely on a series of terraces, crowned with old yew trees. It took an army of woodcutters to do the job: for several years they had just raked the paths and planted the flowerbeds and the trees were densely overgrown. Next they set to work on the model farm that stood to the right of the house. They levelled the old buildings. They cut down the apple trees that make this bit of meadow so typical of Normandy. They felled the tall 100-year-old poplars. In less than a month everything had gone: the entrance gate with its porch and its lime trees where you waited for the boat to Rouen, the tall railings where you used to see Flaubert walking, the cluster of trees where he used to sit in the summer.

In Defence of *Madame Bovary*

Flaubert to Maître Sénard, January 1857

I stand accused of 'grossly offending against public morality, religion and decency'. My book is my justification. Here is that book. Once my judges have read it they will see the truth: far from having written an obscene and irreligious novel, I have composed a work which is eminently moral in its effect. Does the morality of a work of literary art reside in the mere absence of certain details which could incriminate if taken out of context? Should we not consider rather the impression of the whole, the indirect lesson which emerges. And if, for lack of talent, the artist has been unable to produce this effect except by crude and entirely superficial means, does this not mean that the apparently reprehensible passages are all the more instructive and useful? Has Juvenal ever been accused of immorality?

Though it may be arrogant to invoke the names of great men in connection with a book such as this, I ask you to recall, before you pass judgement upon me, Rabelais, Montaigne, Regnier, all of Molière, l'abbé Prévost, Lesage, Beaumarchais & Balzac. Sincere books may sometimes have a certain salutary pungency. Personally I deplore rather those sugary confections which readers swallow without realising that they are quietly poisoning themselves. It had always been my belief that the novelist, like the traveller, enjoyed the liberty to describe what he saw. Following the example of many others, I could have chosen a subject drawn from the 'exceptional' or ignoble ranks of society. I chose, on the contrary, from among the most prosaically ordinary. I grant you that the representation is unpleasant. I deny that it is criminal. Indeed I do not write for young girls, I write for men, for educated men. Readers in search of lascivious material, readers who may take harm, will never progress beyond the third page of what I have written. The serious tone will not be to their taste. People do not go to watch surgical operations in a spirit of lubricity.

I hereby accept, in advance, the verdict of my judges. Faced with the enormity of the accusations made against me, I plead my own naivety and ignorance. Puzzled as to the nature of my misdeed, I may perhaps take some consolation from my punishment.

Transcribed by Yvan Leclerc
Translated by Geoffrey Wall

Chronology

1803 Achille-Cléophas Flaubert, Gustave's father, arrives in Paris to study medicine.
1810 Achille-Cléophas Flaubert arrives in Rouen to work in the hospital.
1812 Achille-Cléophas Flaubert marries the adopted daughter of the head of the hospital.
1813 Birth of Achille Flaubert, Gustave's elder brother.
1819 Flaubert's father begins to buy parcels of land and property.
1821 Birth of Gustave Flaubert.
1824 Birth of Caroline Flaubert, Gustave's sister.
1825 The servant 'Julie' enters the service of the Flaubert family.
1832 Epidemic of cholera reaches Rouen.
     Flaubert enters the Collège de Rouen as a boarder.
1835 Summer holidays on the coast at Trouville.
1836 First encounter with Elisa Schlésinger.
1839 Elder brother qualifies in medicine and marries.
1840 Flaubert passes final school examinations.
     Voyage to Corsica with Dr Jules Cloquet.
     Amour de voyage, in Marseille, with Eulalie Foucaud.
1841 Flaubert registers as a law student in Paris, though continues to live at home.
1842 July: Flaubert moves to Paris.
     December: Flaubert passes first-year law exams.
1843 Writing *L'Education sentimentale* (first version).
     First meeting with Maxime Du Camp.
     August: Flaubert fails second-year law exams.
1844 January: Flaubert suffers first nervous attack.
     April: Flaubert's father buys a house at Croisset.
     June: Flaubert family moves to Croisset.
1845 March: Flaubert's sister Caroline marries Emile Hamard.

April–June: Flaubert family travelling in Italy.

November: Flaubert's father falls ill.

1846 January: Flaubert's father dies; Flaubert's sister Caroline gives birth to a daughter.

March: Caroline dies.

July: Flaubert begins liaison with Louise Colet.

August: Flaubert begins friendship with Louis Bouilhet.

1847 May–July: Flaubert walking in Brittany with Maxime Du Camp.

August: Flaubert breaks with Louise Colet.

December: Flaubert attends Reform Banquet in Rouen

1848 February: Flaubert arrives in Paris to see the street-fighting.

April: Death of Alfred Le Poittevin.

May: Flaubert begins work on the first version of *La Tentation de Saint Antoine*.

September: finishes *La Tentation de Saint Antoine*.

October: Flaubert embarks on eighteen-month tour of Egypt and the Orient.

1849 November: Flaubert in Alexandria.

December–January: Flaubert in Cairo.

1850 February: Voyage up the Nile.

March: Encounter with Kuchuk-Hanem; Flaubert reaches the Second Cataract of the Nile.

May: Excursion to the Red Sea.

August: Jerusalem.

November: Constantinople.

December: Athens.

1851 January–February: Greece.

March: Naples.

April: Rome.

July: Flaubert, back home in Croisset, resumes his liaison with Louise Colet.

September: Flaubert begins writing *Madame Bovary*.

1852 January: Maxime Du Camp awarded Légion d'honneur.

September: Maxime Du Camp becomes editor of the *Revue de Paris*.

1853 Death of Père Parain, a favourite uncle.

1854 Final break with Louise Colet.

1855 Flaubert takes rooms in Paris.

1856 April: Flaubert finishes *Madame Bovary*.

May: rewriting *La Tentation de Saint Antoine*.

October: first instalment of *Madame Bovary* published in *Revue de Paris*.

1857 January: Flaubert prosecuted for writing an immoral book.

February: trial ends in acquittal.

April: *Madame Bovary* published in book form.

October: Flaubert begins writing *Salammbô*.

1858 April–June: Flaubert visits Carthage and North Africa.

1862 February: finishes writing *Salammbô*.

November: *Salammbô* published.

1863 January: friendship with George Sand.

February: first meeting with Turgenev.

1864 January: Flaubert's niece Caroline engaged to Ernest Commanville.

May: Flaubert begins writing *L'Education sentimentale*.

November: Flaubert visits Compiègne as guest of the Emperor.

1866 August: Flaubert nominated Chevalier de la Légion d'honneur.

November: George Sand's first visit to Croisset.

1868 May: George Sand in Croisset.

1869 May: Flaubert finishes writing *L'Education sentimentale*.

July: death of Louis Bouilhet.

November: publication of *L'Education sentimentale*.

December: Flaubert spends Christmas with George Sand in Nohant.

1870 August: France declares war on Prussia.

December: victorious Prussian troops arrive in Rouen.

1871 January: armistice signed with Prussia.

May: socialist-led insurrection in Paris.

July: Prussian troops leave Rouen.

1872 April: death of Flaubert's mother.

June: Flaubert finishes final version of *La Tentation de Saint Antoine*.

1874 March: *La Tentation de Saint Antoine* published.

August: Flaubert begins writing *Bouvard et Pécuchet*.

1875 Bad health and serious financial problems.

September: Flaubert begins writing *La Légende de saint Julien*.

1876 Begins writing *Un Coeur simple*.

June: death of George Sand.

November: Flaubert begins writing *Hérodias*.

1877 April: publication of *Trois contes*.

1879 Flaubert awarded official pension.

1880 February: Maxime Du Camp elected to the Académie française.

May: death of Flaubert.

1884 Publication of first volume of Flaubert's letters, expurgated by Caroline Commanville.

The Flaubert Circle

BONAPARTE, PRINCESS MATHILDE (1820–1904) Imperious, influential cousin of Napoléon III, nickname 'Notre Dame des Arts', presided over a salon in the 1860s, friend and patron to Flaubert.

BOSQUET, AMÉLIE (1815–1904) Journalist and novelist, lived in Rouen. Ardent, flirtatious friendship with Flaubert began in 1859, cut short by her hostile review of *L'Education sentimentale*.

BOUILHET, LOUIS (1822–69) Minor poet and dramatist. Flaubert's close friend and editor from 1846–69. They shared literary values and an enthusiasm for Parisian actresses. Bouilhet and Flaubert looked so alike that Bouilhet was mischievously rumoured to be Flaubert's half-brother.

CHANTEPIE, MADEMOISELLE LEROYER DE (1800–89) A small-town admirer of the great man, author of several unpublished novels, she wrote to Flaubert in 1856 after reading *Madame Bovary* in the *Revue de Paris*. Much afflicted by religious doubts, a prisoner of neurotic anxiety. They corresponded voluminously but never met.

CHEVALIER, ERNEST Flaubert's childhood friend, one of the creators of *Le Garçon*. Left Rouen for Paris in 1839. Conventional, cheerful and energetic, he became a successful lawyer. This was the career Flaubert was supposed to have had.

CLOQUET, DR JULES (1790–1883) Pupil and colleague of Flaubert's father. Handsome, worldly, and congenial, he was Flaubert's guide and companion on the voyage to Corsica in 1840. Thereafter a trusted mentor.

COLET, LOUISE (1808–76) Socialist-feminist writer, intermittently Flaubert's mistress, victim of much misogynist ridicule, notoriously vain and spiteful. An impossible person.

COLLIER, GERTRUDE AND HENRIETTE Daughters of an English naval family who spent summers in Trouville. Henriette was the serious sister, Gertrude was the frivolous one. Flaubert was drawn to Henriette; Gertrude was drawn to Flaubert.

COMMANVILLE, ERNEST The eligible young man, he married Flaubert's niece Caroline in 1864. Went bankrupt in the early 1870s.

DU CAMP, MAXIME (1822–94) 'The Thin Man', Flaubert's close friend and travelling companion; a wealthy adventurer, man of letters, pioneer photographer, and literary editor. Notoriously tried to persuade Flaubert to cut *Madame Bovary*.

FOUCAUD, EULALIE Flaubert's adolescent *amour de voyage*, encountered in a hotel in Marseille. Long remembered, the first in a line of voluptuous older women.

HAMARD, EMILE Schoolfriend who married Flaubert's beloved sister Caroline and went slowly mad after her premature death.

LE POITTEVIN, ALFRED (1816–48) Refined, lethargic, precociously decadent pessimist and minor Romantic poet. The beloved companion of Flaubert's adolescence.

MIGNOT, PERE Rouen neighbour and adopted uncle, Ernest Chevalier's grandfather, read Flaubert stories from *Don Quixote*.

ORLOWSKI, ANTON Emigré Polish musician based in Rouen, Flaubert's drinking-companion in the early 1840s.

PRADIER, JAMES (1790–1852) Parisian sculptor, nicknamed 'Phidias', introduced Flaubert to Louise Colet and to Victor Hugo. His work was elegant, sensuous and smoothly conventional. Married to Louise Pradier.

PRADIER, LOUISE A childhood friend of the Flaubert children, nickname 'Ludovica', the recklessly extravagant estranged wife of James Pradier, one of the models for Emma Bovary.

SABATIER, AGLAÉ (1822–90) 'La Présidente', a banker's mistress, Flaubert frequented her salon and conducted a coolly ceremonious flirtation with her.

SCHLÉSINGER, ELISA (1810–88) The older woman, Flaubert's first love, the model for Madame Arnoux, the untouchable virtuous wife in *L'Education sentimentale*. First encountered in Trouville in 1836, then again in Paris 1841–4, then intermittently at long intervals.

SCHLÉSINGER, MAURICE Music publisher, impresario, patron of the arts, husband of Elisa Schlésinger, a warm, impetuous, flashy, predatory character, model for Jacques Arnoux in *L'Education sentimentale*.

SÉNARD, JULES (1800–85) Rouen lawyer and politician, an old family friend, successfully defended Flaubert against prosecution for immorality in 1857.

Acknowledgements

For simply keeping me at it, with a sustaining mix of shrewd advice, lavish encouragement, inspiring conversation and delicious cooking, I am variously indebted to Julian Atterton, John Barrell, John Birtwhistle, Daniela Bernardelle, Jacques Berthoud, Lee Brackstone, Richard Brown, Jean-Pierre Chaline, Jack Donovan, Paul Driver, David Ellis, Germain Galérant, David Gervais, James Harley, Angela Hurworth, Stephen Minta, David Moody, Sara Perren, Adam Phillips, Alan Raitt, Jon Riley and Graham Robb.

For their readiness to debate the finer points of nineteenth-century Parisian topography, I am indebted to Caroline Szylowicz, Larry Duffy, Dominique Poitelon, Sarah Capitanio, Mike Wetherill, Michael Berkvam, and Priscilla Ferguson.

For the copies of the Croisset probate inventory and of Flaubert's pre-trial notes, I am indebted to Yvan Leclerc.

For information about French railways in the 1840s I am indebted to Colin Divall.

For information about the town of Sens in the 1790s I am indebted to the local historians of the Société archéologique de Sens.

I would also like to acknowledge large but intangible debts to Richard Ellmann, who taught me to ask different questions, and to Richard Holmes, whose incomparable book *Footsteps* first tempted me down this new path.

GW

357

List of Illustrations

References

Abbreviations used in Reference Notes:

HH: Flaubert, G., *Oeuvres complètes*, 16 volumes. Club de l'Honnête homme, Paris (1971–5).
Intégrale: Flaubert, G., *Oeuvres complètes*, 2 volumes. Seuil, Paris (1964).
Pages: Baldick, R, *Pages from the Goncourt Journal*. OUP, London (1962).
PC: Bruneau, J., ed., *Flaubert: Correspondance*, 4 volumes. Gallimard, Paris (1973–98).
Oeuvres: Thibaudet, A. & Dumesnil, R., eds., *Oeuvres de Flaubert*, 2 volumes. Gallimard, Paris (1952).
SL: Wall, G., trans., *Flaubert: Selected Letters*. Penguin, London (1997).

References to the four major novels, *Madame Bovary*, *Salammbô*, *L'Education sentimentale* and *Bouvard et Pécuchet*, are given in the form of chapter references.

CHAPTER ONE: The Family Name

  3 Flaubert loved his father: Germain 1987, 25.
  – Flaubert liked to boast . . . Indian blood: Du Camp 1882, 1, 220.
  4 Achille-Cléophas simply excelled: Védie 1847, 5.
  6 Footnote: Twenty-five years later: Flaubert, A.-C. 1810, 35.
  – In mortal terror . . . suicide: Everyday Life in Jail Under the Great Terror', in *Chronicle of the French Revolution*, Longman, 1989, 431.
  – Though there was little to spare: Commanville 1886, xiv.
  7 Only Saint Stephen himself . . . hammer: Robertson 1997, 611.
  – You could look out . . . open countryside beyond: Information derived from a contemporary watercolour: *Vue du Collège et d'une partie des murailles de Sens (1823)*. Supplied by the Société archéologique de Sens.
  8 'morale et bonne conduite': *Affiche de Sens*, 21 October 1796.
  – Jacques-Barthelmy Salgues . . . many parts: Monceaux 1890, 578.
  – Now he had turned headmaster: Salgues 1829, 175–84.
  – 'whose only patrimony was his intelligence': Védie 1847, 7.
  – His library . . . the works of Buffon and Rousseau: Dubuc 1980, 40.
  9 Doctors . . . true benefactors of the human race: Kennedy 1989, 34.
 10 substitute to do your military service: Ramsey 1988, 109.
  – fierce competition with one another: Ackerknecht 1967, 36.

10 fees paid by the state: Védie 1847, 7.
- Most of them . . . rather than shoes: Galérant 1955, 26.
- textbooks . . . as prizes: Védie 1847, 7.
11 His mind . . . no specific utility: ibid., 23n.
- Anatomy and physiology . . . passions: ibid., 8.
- Open up a few corpses: Bichat 1803, xcix, quoted in Foucault 1973, 146.
12 Dupuytren . . . notoriously vindictive: *Dictionnaire de biographie française*, 11, 614–15. Entry for Dupuytren.
- journey to Rouen: Védie 1847, 9.
- 'with few possessions': ibid., 9.
13 'Opinionâtre en toutes choses': ibid., 8.
- At the bookshop of Vallée frères: *Journal de Rouen*, 4 December 1806.
- 'useful for fathers and teachers': ibid., 10 November 1806.
- grand opera on an oriental-imperial theme: ibid., 2 November 1806.
14 Monsieur Forioso's elder sister . . . tightrope: ibid., 14 November 1806.
- 'The high deeds which continue to distinguish: ibid., 28 November 1806.
- On the inside page: ibid., 11 November 1806.
- 'in gratitude to the Supreme Being': ibid., 14 November 1806.
16 Allow the patient, says Achille-Cléophas: Flaubert, A.-C. 1810, 16.
- The oversensitive types: ibid., 27.
17 the mind itself seems exhausted: ibid., 46.
- In the second phase: ibid., 50.
- After the operation: ibid., 22.
- Narcotics such as opium: ibid., 47.
- Sunlight . . . 'forces': ibid., 18.
- Humid air . . . mortality: ibid., 15.
- The doctor is advised to assume: ibid., 65.
18 Instead of staying a couple of months: Commanville 1886, xiv.

CHAPTER TWO: A Very Queer Place

21 'the doctor's little boy' . . . nineteenth-century child: PC 1, 660.
- 'I can remember': PC 4, 24.
22 'External reality': PC 2, 377.
- 'I remember a circle of lawn': PC 1, 574.
23 Then they had to be hugged six times: HH 15, 51.
- 'familiar to us from our earliest days': Bosquet 1845, vi.
- 'Early impressions . . . never fade': PC 1, 712.
24 Dr Achille-Cléophas paid 52,000 francs: Galérant 1955.
25 'Sancho Panza, you can see him': PC 2, 417.
- He made notes on Don Quixote: PC 1, 6.
- 'asking my nurse to say the letters': PC 2, 110.
- By the age of ten: Germain 1987, 13.
- 'So immersed in his reading': PC 3, 881.
26 'The regular movement lulled me': Intégrale 1, 246.
- They took it slowly: Commanville 1886, xx.
27 'the vines . . . and the white houses': PC 2, 430.
- Sailors disembarked: Chevreuil 1966.
- 'a splendid man': PC 2, 30.
28 '. . . all the tittle-tattle': PC 3, 109.

28 The Dutuit millions: Chaline 1982, 111–14.

CHAPTER THREE: Awakenings

30 Old soldiers who remembered Waterloo: Bouquet 1895, 31–7.
31 He was being lenient: Reddy 1977, 74–5.
 – 'Entertainments vented by his nascent muse': Bruneau 1962, 40.
32 'Constipation is a tightening': ibid., 41.
 – 'the hideousness of avarice': ibid., 41.
33 'People in rags': *Journal de Rouen*, 26 Feb. 1831.
 – 'the excitement and the energy': ibid.
 – Sensing that history was not yet: *Journal de Rouen*, 4 March 1831.
 – 'There have been grave disturbances': ibid, 15 March 1831; Labracherie 1957, 2–3.
34 Schoolboys lived in an atmosphere: Spitzer 1987, 37 & 41.
 – Flaubert especially admired: Brombert 1984, 74.
35 Footnote: In 1998 the dormitory: Labracherie 1957.
 – What did I dream of: Intégrale 1, 249.
 – And when the evening came: ibid., 249.
 – The punishments ordained for the young: PC 1, 857.
36 You wrote, shivering: Bouquet 1895, 11–13.
 – . . . it was winter: Intégrale 1, 253.
 – Four short pieces: PC 1, 6–7.
37 Here was animation: Rouen, Bibliothèque municipale. Dossier: Rue du Champ de Foire aux Boissons.
 – 'under the little avenue of poplars': PC 3, 90; PC 1, 105.
38 '. . . a green coat laced with gold': Ramsey 1988, 133.
 – The Schmidt Menagerie advertised: Steegmuller & Bray 1993, 33.
 – Most miraculous of all the engines: Pinkney 1986, 15.
 – Mechanised textile production . . . capital: ibid., 18.
39 including Guy de Maupassant: Chaline 1982, 110.
 – 'A simple wooden partition': PC 3, 173.
40 Doctors disagreed bitterly . . . angrily denounced: Briggs 1961, Sussman 1973 and *Encyclopaedia Britannica CD 1999*, 'Cholera'.
 – his name was there, in print: *Journal de Rouen*, 13 Aug. 1833; Bruneau 1962, 42.
 – They received crowns . . . outside their houses: Bouquet 1895, 28.
41 It was all a waste of money: PC 1, 12; *Journal de Rouen*, 7 & 10 September 1833.
 – Two transplanted female vultures: Biasi 1991, 23; *Journal de Rouen*, 15 September 1833.
 – I have a great respect: PC 3, 102.
 – Our dreams . . . were superbly extravagant: Raitt 1994, 24.
42 We lived in an ideal hothouse: PC 2, 41.
 – He admired the . . . Romantic taste: PC 1, 17.
43 'desperate attitudes, sombre glances': Kelly 1976, 57.
 – founded a literary . . . of his own: PC 1, 21.
 – chose a pen-name . . . Kocloth: ibid., 18.
 – Pierre-Adolphe Cheruel . . . a rich clear voice: Labracherie 1957, 5.
 – In my youth I loved immeasurably: PC 3, 61.
44 Devouring her breast . . . frenzy of passion: Intégrale 1, 236–8.
 – His thoughts . . . awake until dawn: ibid., 238–9.
45 Plumply maternal . . . aptly devised: Bart 1967, 192.

45 If we place . . . striking contrast: ibid., 178.

CHAPTER FOUR: Coming of Age

46 Flaubert felt '. . . selfish cruel': Germain 1987, 20–21.
– Only two more years . . . 'madhouse of a college': PC 1, 29.
– On top of this . . . disgust with the world: Bardèche 1988, 16 and 21.
– With his family . . . Chateau du Heron: Bruneau 1962, 494n.
– 'I spent the whole night': PC 1, 607; Biasi 1991, 290.
47 He makes the denouement too black: Intégrale 1, 113–23.
– He read it the very day before Easter: Commanville 1886, xxxix.
– 'found himself a couple of miles outside Rouen': Raitt 1998, 25.
48 'What a splendid trio': PC 1, 32.
– 'a nervous irritation . . . to myself': Intégrale 1, 233–4.
– 'neither instructive nor amusing . . . human heart': ibid., 230.
– 'My usual character': Germain 1987, 20–21.
49 'If ever I play an active part': PC 1, 38.
– 'I am incapable of imaginative work': ibid., 37.
– 'De Sade . . . is everywhere': ibid., 868.
– Footnote: Janin 'made his mark': France 1995, 408.
– 'I'd pay you their weight in gold': ibid., 48.
50 'the supreme science': ibid., 52.
– 'Montaigne . . . he's my man': ibid.
– 'You said . . . like children': ibid., 56.
– 'spoiling their future prospects': ibid., 57.
– 'Philosophy students . . . to its conclusion': ibid.
51 By Tuesday . . . including Flaubert: Labracherie 1957, 8–10.
– The price . . . Good Behaviour: PC 1, 56–8 & 874.
52 'Looking at each other and smiling': ibid., 60.
– 'a mass of witticisms . . . hold of you': ibid., 59–60.
– 'He gave up the flute . . . ruins of a poet': *Madame Bovary* 3, 6.
– At Easter . . . a few days: PC 1, 62.
– At Chateau-Gaillard . . . in the sunshine: ibid., 451.
– They went . . . singing a song: ibid., 146.
53 I was sitting outside: ibid., 63.
– 'I am now in a bizarre position': Germain 1987, 29–30.
– she played Andromaque, Camille and Emilie: PC 1, 864.
– She resurrects classical antiquity: Intégrale 1, 227–8.
54 'Rationally I want to go': PC 1, 65.
– They enjoyed . . . Flaubert's life: ibid., 562–7.
55 'I shall only feel less anxious': ibid., 66.
– 'Look, observe and take notes': ibid., 68.
– 'I announce my doubts': Germain 1987, 41.
– 'with as much veneration': Intégrale 2, 426.
– He dedicated several pages . . . of modernity: ibid., 426–7.
– dined with a field marshal: PC 1, 67.
– He wrote a letter . . . his tears: Germain 1987, 42.
56 'Yesterday I was in Spain': Intégrale 2, 431.
– 'For two days . . . antiquity': ibid., 438.
– Writing it up in his journal: ibid., 439.

56 'I had just woken up': Intégrale 2, 555.
 – 'half poet and half doctor': ibid., 441.
57 'a mixture of everything . . . by the fire': ibid., 441.
 – 'installed in fine comfortable rooms': PC 1, 73.
 – An illustrious liberal exile: *Journal du département de la Corse*, samedi 9 octobre 1830. No. 40.
58 'In Ajaccio I dared': PC 2, 316.
 – 'Make a little bouquet': PC 1, 73.
 – The sea has a scent more delicious: Intégrale 2, 443.
59 'It is impossible to travel': ibid., 444.
 – 'much larger . . . than ours': ibid., 445.
 – 'a fine country, still untouched': PC 1, 238.
 – 'This little man . . . antique tragedy': Intégrale 2, 445.
60 For Flaubert it was a rare: ibid., 448.
 – 'I stood for half an hour': Intégrale 2, 450.
61 'like one of those long-dead cities': ibid., 452.
 – Our guide was singing some *ballata*: ibid.

CHAPTER FIVE: Something the Matter

62 Under grey northern skies: ibid., 552.
 – It was over: ibid.
63 Sitting by his fire, Flaubert: PC 3, 871.
 – Went back to Marseilles: ibid.
64 How I have lived since then: Germain 1987, 39.
 – I'm pissed off at being back: PC 1, 75.
65 Better to choose a career: Intégrale 1, 254–5.
 – 'wearied by dreams': PC 1, 77.
66 She holds the little baby so tenderly: Intégrale 1, 257.
 – 'So that was it': ibid., 261.
67 I hope that heaven still has a few good days: Bruneau 1962, 317.
 – 'to link myself once again to my own past': PC 1, 78.
 – 'I'm becoming colossal': ibid., 83.
68 'turning gloomy as a result': ibid., 82.
 – He gave particular attention . . . pipes: ibid., 84.
 – His mother said to him: Intégrale 1, 278.

CHAPTER SIX: Mainly Parisian

69 I have reached a decisive moment: PC 1, 93–4.
70 'I've made a start on the *Code*': PC 1, 91.
 – 'Went to a masked ball': ibid., 96.
 – 'He spends his afternoons': ibid.
 – 'make a racket in the night': PC 1, 97.
 – It reminded him of antiquity: ibid., 100.
 – 'In the name of God': ibid., 104.
 – However extravagant his lamentations: Raitt 1998, 46.
71 Alfred Le Poittevin, meanwhile: PC 1, 892.
 – 'I hope that you are feeling more cheerful': ibid., 109.
 – 'I'm working like a navvy': ibid., 112.

71 'The law . . . leaves me in a state': ibid., 120.
- He used to stare at mutilated male statues: PC 2, 218.
- He resisted the 'mystic mania': Bruneau 1962, 381, n.96.
- 'I arrived, on foot': PC 2, 388.
- He soon adopted a gloriously indolent routine: PC 1, 123.
72 'superb lodgings': ibid., 161.
- 'a small sunny set of rooms': Du Camp 1881, 1, 222.
- 'In the summer, at night': PC 1, 285–6.
- 'I'm working like a wretch': ibid., 131.
- Or he would spend the afternoon: PC2, 73.
- 'I used to promise myself': PC 1, 402.
- 'simultaneously sombre, preoccupied': ibid., 128.
73 'atrocious spasms': ibid., 132.
- 'I want to be finished': ibid., 134.
- 'The walls of my room in the rue de l'Est': PC 1, 228.
- 'I cannot resist hurting you': ibid., 140.
- 'feeling like an imbecile': ibid., 141.
- Family meals, since his departure: ibid., 144.
- They make love to marquesses: ibid., 143.
74 ten kinds of mustard on the table: ibid., 923.
- Their 'exquisite hospitality': PC 2, 637.
- Beautiful naked women: Du Camp 1882, 1, 333–43.
- 'It's a place I like very much': PC 1, 196.
- 'a statue made flesh': Siler 1973, 72–3, quoting from Houssaye 1885, 1, 404–5.
75 One evening when we had eaten together: Du Camp 1881, 1, 226.
- The two friends spent the rest of that day: ibid., 130.
- 'It was . . . a kind of intellectual engagement': Du Camp 1882, 1, 254.
76 Flaubert was especially keen: Du Camp 1881, 1, 232.
- 'Our mutual affection is growing': PC 1, 165.
- He would copy out, quite mechanically: Du Camp 1881, 1, 237.
- 'I launch into silent monologues': PC 1, 153.
- 'Sometimes I want to beat the table': ibid., 158.
77 'Sometimes I start to twitch': ibid., 160.
- '14 or 16 hours at a stretch': ibid. 165.
- 'was so often humiliated': ibid., 349.
- 'You are a fool twice over': ibid., 184.
- 'I think I'll be pleased': ibid., 185–6.
- 'The conversation was all about punishment': ibid., 195–6.
78 Worst of all, Father has now decided: ibid., 197–200.
- 'I think this letter of mine is rather silly': ibid., 201.
- 'What a pleasure it would have been': ibid., 202.

CHAPTER SEVEN: The Fall

79 Epigraph: 'First an indeterminate anxiety: PC 3, 572.
80 It may be a measure of his fears: Bruneau 1962, 381n.
81 I've had a cerebral congestion: PC 1, 203.
- 'the skin all wrinkled like a mummy': ibid., 447–8.
82 Footnote: The accident must have: ibid., 202.
- Du Camp placed it . . . first attack: ibid., 944.

82 'every evening [. . .] in that position': Du Camp 1978, 40.
 – 'He would lie on his bed shouting': Du Camp 1882, 1, 248.
 – 'Not a day goes by . . . than the others': PC 1, 207.
 – He began to use his right hand again: ibid., 206.
 – 'My dear child . . . if I seem': Descharmes 1924, 187.
84 The workmen were busy renovating: PC 1, 208.
 – He'd read it . . . twenty times: ibid., 210.
 – 'One day soon I'm getting a little boat': ibid.
 – 'You are a surprising mixture': Du Camp 1978, 34.
 – 'You have to see things as far as possible': ibid.
85 'If ever you travel to the Orient': Du Camp 1978, 42.
 – 'How far have you got with it: ibid., 57–8.
 – 'Don't worry about reading your book': ibid., 77.
 – 'the life you dream of': ibid., 82–3.
86 You have imagined beauty: ibid., 84–5.
 – 'It was . . . like a silent prayer': ibid., 91.
87 He was . . . 'old Boun': PC 1, 216.
 – It was the first time . . . for over a year: ibid., 219.
 – 'I have seen him': ibid., 225.
 – 'I approved of her conduct': ibid., 221.
 – Flaubert remembered her: ibid., 223.
88 'I still see her with her head . . . as I read to her': ibid., 359.
 – 'Hardly had we left Rouen': ibid., 237.
 – Achille, left in charge at home: ibid.
 – 'It wasn't real travelling': Du Camp 1882, 1, 299.
 – 'If you knew all the thoughts': PC 1, 226.
 – Flaubert worried that his true feelings: ibid., 226.
 – 'Full of hope going down the . . . river': Intégrale 2, 458.
 – Their reunion . . . bitter and farcical: PC 1, 222–5.
89 'The Hotel Richelieu . . . I left her': Intégrale 2, 459.
 – 'They don't keep the Hôtel': PC 1, 224.
 – He began to remember all kinds of little details: Intégrale 2, 459.
 – 'My father . . . to extend it further': PC 1, 225–8.
 – When I go . . . in the world: ibid., 226.
90 'I kept on thinking about the ceilings': ibid., 226 & 228.
 – 'Naked woman lying down': Intégrale 1, 463.
91 'a different sort of fellow from me': PC 1, 230.
 – The only way of not being unhappy: ibid., 229.
92 'On our own, you and I': ibid., 228–30.
 – 'We are two Trappists': Descharmes 1924, 195.
 – Footnote: Maurice Bardèche suggests: HH 12, 147.
 – Footnote: Flaubert creates a character . . . author: ibid. 10, 388.
 – I didn't look at anything else: Intégrale 2, 468.
93 'I attract fools and animals': PC 1, 234.
 – One day we were alone together: ibid., 359–60.
 – 'What a fine story they make': HH 10, 386.
 – 'A singular thing it is': PC 1, 232–5.
94 Footnote: Flaubert's journal for that day: HH 10, 386–7.
 – Before he left Paris: ibid.
 – If I were to take it seriously: PC 1, 240–1.

94 'Back in my cave': ibid.
 – 'I'd rather like to buy a nice painting': ibid., 238.
 – 'I'm recovering, I'm on my way up': ibid.,236.
 – 'I often see you . . . passengers': Descharmes 1924, 201.
95 'I cut through the swell': PC 1, 369.
 – Flaubert was keen to read: ibid., 242.
 – Caroline was in Paris: ibid., 243–6.
 – 'I have nobody here to strangle': ibid., 245.
 – 'I have cast off the foolish pretension': ibid., 246.
 – 'It's boring but it could be useful': ibid., 247.
 – He soon decided that . . . 'pitiful': PC 2, 417.
 – Impersonality . . . Voltaire: Raitt 1998, 46.
 – 'My life . . . is still surprisingly chaste': PC 1, 249–50.
 – 'We can see each other every day': ibid., 247.

CHAPTER EIGHT: Under the Knife

98 'For ten weeks . . . neither the tender care': Védie 1847, 29.
 – The men who worked in the harbour: ibid., 30.
 – 'a man who practised virtue': *Madame Bovary*, 3.8.
 – 'The town . . . will pay for his tomb': PC 1, 255.
99 'I have taken command of the situation': ibid.
 – 'He went rapidly from a state of exaltation': Du Camp 1882, 1, 305.
 – Caroline is talking, smiling: PC 1, 257.
100 I was at her bedside: ibid., 431.
 – 'With a special feeling of regret': Dumesnil 1947, 163.
 – The Seine was brimming: PC 1, 258.
 – 'In the morning when everything had been done': ibid.
 – 'Not one of us really understood': ibid., 261.
101 'an old school friend who writes poetry': Du Camp 1882, 1, 320.
102 'In the midst of my weariness . . . perpetual edification': PC 1, 676.
 – 'My boils are going down': ibid., 264.
 – 'My courage wavers sometimes': ibid., 270.
 – 'I'm doing my best to live': ibid., 271.
103 'I worry about becoming desiccated': ibid., 264.
 – 'Are you quite sure, great man': ibid., 268.

CHAPTER NINE: Louise

104 'Twelve hours ago . . . together': SL, 43.
 – 'I think I love them as much': ibid., 52.
105 'your curls touching your white shoulders': ibid., 45 & 64.
 – 'buried a large box full of letters': PC 4, 313.
106 'shattered, dazed . . . working away avidly': SL, 44.
 – 'Now I feel within me': ibid., 50.
 – 'Do you realise . . . utter monstrosity': PC 1, 299–300; SL, 64.
 – 'I have no heart for work': SL, 58.
 – 'My mother was waiting for me': ibid., 53.
 – 'The two women I love the most': PC 1, 308.
 – 'Mother was in a terrible state': SL, 50.

106 'This winter . . . to see you': ibid., 52.
107 'Can I drop everything and go': ibid. 53.
  – 'I don't know what it was that pushed me': ibid., 52.
  – 'I began by displaying my sores': ibid., 56.
  – 'I did warn you': ibid., 63.
  – Everything about him is vile: ibid., 55.
  – He capitulates: ibid., 62.
108 'Destined to pickle myself here': PC 1, 293.
  – 'My mother has seen it': ibid., 302.
  – 'It is a picture I love greatly': ibid., 307
109 'You criticise me . . . for always analysing': ibid., 308.
  – 'I'm turning cold at the very idea': ibid., 311.
110 'They keep an eye on you . . . do they?': ibid., 329.
  – 'For your name, for your reputation': ibid., 330.
111 'My mother . . . so distressed': ibid., 332.
  – 'when you want to . . . put a stop to it': ibid., 335.
  – 'In the six weeks since I have known you': ibid., 336.
112 'We cannot live together': ibid., 338–9.
  – 'One might think it . . . that refrain': ibid., 340.
  – 'It would be better if you stayed in Rouen': ibid.
  – 'All the better if I have no offspring': ibid.
113 'I would like to have someone to talk to': ibid., 345.
  – 'I would like to have been there': ibid., 383–4.
  – 'I'm still afraid of writing': ibid., 375.
  – 'I'm awaiting a book': ibid., 378.
  – 'I am the obscure, tenacious pearl-diver': ibid., 378.
  – Bruneau suggests that the chapters: ibid., 989.
  – 'I'm rereading the *Aeneid*': ibid., 346.
  – 'Revision and declamation . . . own': ibid., 352.
  – 'One day . . . I shall unfold to you': ibid., 346.
114 'O bed! If you could speak': ibid., 376.
  – 'Uncomplainingly, Louise revised her poem': ibid., 348.
  – 'the old feminine rage': ibid.
  – 'We have spent three days with our maps': ibid., 353–6.
115 'Thus . . . we shall be totally free': ibid., 353.
  – 'If my mother dies': ibid., 261.
  – 'I simply have to stay here . . . I expected to get': ibid., 369–71.
  – 'Can it be possible . . . armchair': ibid., 371.
116 'You thought my letter was too fond': ibid., 378.
  – 'My mother is not at all well': ibid., 387.
117 'You are quite right . . . not loving me': ibid., 398.
  – 'Do I even know if it will happen?': ibid., 400.
  – 'Farewell, dear comrade': ibid.
  – 'Since my love is hateful to you': ibid., 401.
118 'Do you realise . . . looked like a torturer?': ibid., 404 & 406.
  – 'I'll bring *Novembre* for you': ibid., 406.
  – At some point . . . met Madame Flaubert: ibid., 1020n.
  – 'I was born . . . in a state of *ennui*': ibid., 410.
119 'I throw myself headlong': ibid., 414.
  – 'We spend our time in talk': ibid.

119 'It felt like a profanation': ibid., 417.
  – 'Why . . . have you tried': ibid., 419.
  – 'What does this thing mean?': ibid., 421.
  – 'His mockery . . . her love': ibid., 422.
  – 'as a woman of the lowest order': ibid., 423.
  – 'I find it impossible to continue': ibid., 422.
  – 'Personally . . . howling despair': ibid., 423.
  – 'If you could have been content': ibid., 424.
  – 'Why do you, poor darling': ibid.
120 'Du Camp . . . lift your morale': ibid., 428.
  – 'and I shall send it to you my poor dear': ibid., 829.
  – Footnote: 'I forgive Du Camp his treachery': ibid., 824.
  – 'Love . . . is not the first thing': ibid., 429.
  – 'You want me to roll around': ibid., 431.
  – 'May his son be a torment to him': ibid., 430.
121 Perhaps his secret intention: ibid., 1029.
  – The farm . . . realised almost 23,000 francs: ibid., 1090.
  – 'killed in bed . . . exploded': ibid., 440.
  – 'I was beginning to lose my head': ibid., 444.
  – 'Which I am sad to say . . . the two of you': ibid., 825.
122 'When he is deeply moved': ibid., 826.
  – 'If you had allowed yourself to be guided': ibid., 827.
  – 'He doesn't mention . . . his current reading': ibid., 827 & 828.
  – 'the very type of womanhood': ibid., 445.
  – 'My soul . . . has been through fire': ibid., 448.
123 Flaubert found him . . . into apathy: ibid., 452.
  – 'Poor lad, he has taken more wind': ibid.

CHAPTER TEN: On the Road

124 'How many times . . . best moment of our lives': Du Camp 1882, 1, 365.
  – 'alone, free and together': ibid., 1352.
125 'Never . . . was any party outfit chosen': Tooke 1987, 84.
  – Flaubert listed their equipment: ibid., 83–4.
  – 'Nobody . . . knew what we were': Du Camp 1882, 1, 356.
127 'Until another day': Tooke 1987, 82.
128 Though it was easy for Flaubert: PC 1, 439.
  – 'like a machine that grinds to a halt': ibid., 440.
129 'silent intimate streets': Tooke 1987, 669.
  – Contemplating the grass growing: ibid., 91.
  – Among these peaceful houses: ibid.
130 'We shall sound the depths': ibid., 93.
  – I feel an intense . . . hatred: Intégrale 2, 478.
  – 'unmoved in the midst': Tooke 1987, 97.
131 The young count . . . royalist nostalgia:Henri d'Artois, comte de Chambord', in
    Encyclopaedia Britannica, CD99.
  – '[. . .] the whole rabble of sham nobility': Tooke 1987, 101.
  – 'Emma dabbled in the remains': Madame Bovary I, 6.
  – 'hit the body like cannon-fire': Du Camp 1882, 1, 353.
132 'The weather is warm': Tooke 1987, 143.

132 There they drafted . . . weakest of the collection: PC 1, 263.
  - 'would have required six months': PC 1, 463.
  - They therefore . . . returned home: Du Camp 1882, 1, 363; Intégrale 2, 483.
134 'a slow heavy wail . . . being slaughtered': *Madame Bovary*, 2: 11.
  - At that instant I had the idea: Tooke 1988, 382.
135 'always a pleasure [. . .] to be out': Intégrale 2, 501.
  - She had gone for ever: ibid.
136 'That evening our heads': ibid., 503.
  - A few miles from the little village: Tooke 1987, 353–4.
137 'the invigorating, exciting, healing idol': ibid., 355.
  - 'It will be a farewell then': PC 1, 1455–6.
  - 'Yes I often think of you': PC 1, 456.
138 When I'm walking silently: ibid., 458–9.
  - 'Bare-chested, our shirts billowing out': ibid., 495–6.
  - 'administration, discipline, sheets of paper': ibid., 498.
  - 'Not very entertaining': ibid., 497.
139 'entered one of those establishments': Tooke 1987, 504.
  - What do you most regret: ibid., 506.
  - 'That idea of being engrossed': PC 1, 461.
  - 'We walked around the tomb': Tooke 1987, 591.
140 'Everywhere was silence': Chateaubriand 1951, 143–6.
  - 'Nothing . . . will convey [. . .] the shudderings': Intégrale 2, 546.
141 'Flaubert had tears in his eyes': Du Camp 1882, 1, 360.
  - Sometimes we walked together: Chateaubriand 1969, 1119.
142 'As the shadows fell upon the pages': Tooke 1987, 623.
  - 'Man . . . the time of your migration': Du Camp 1882, 1, 361.
  - 'more tears, more recriminations': PC 1, 463.
  - 'You think . . . that I didn't celebrate': PC 1, 465.
143 'A year ago I was in Paris': Tooke 1987, 231.

CHAPTER ELEVEN: French Revolutions

145 'The animal . . . base and bloody': PC 1, 469.
  - 'like a man with a perfect pitch': ibid., 473.
  - 'Next summer . . . *Saint Antoine*': ibid., 475.
  - 'pure fantasy and digression': ibid.
  - 'It gave me a great deal of trouble': PC 2, 66.
  - 'I hesitate, I worry': PC 1, 477.
  - 'the humiliations . . . relative pronoun': ibid., 478.
  - 'Art, what a great chasm!': ibid.
  - 'I dream of travelling': ibid., 489.
146 'At night I feel supremely calm': ibid., 478.
147 Surely . . . will finish it off: Du Camp 1876, 43–4.
148 'to watch the riot': ibid., 51.
  - 'Not while the *people* . . . the street': ibid., 51–4.
149 They spent . . . *Melaenis*: ibid., 54–6.
150 'Blood of the victims': ibid., 78.
151 *chapeau du piqueur*: ibid., 91.
152 'initiated by simpletons': Du Camp 1876, 110.

CHAPTER TWELVE: In Mourning

153 'It's all very amusing . . . favourable to Art': PC 1, 493.
  – I watched over him for two nights: ibid., 360.
154 '[. . .] the ground was slippery': ibid., 493–5.
  – May 1848. Stuck at home: ibid., 497.
155 A lovely but ridiculous idea: ibid., 498.
  – The writing of *Saint Antoine*: ibid., 500.
  – 'shame and sorrow': ibid., 1046.
  – He blamed it . . . of his writing: ibid., 502.
  – 'I don't give a damn': ibid., 503.
156 'It's hateful . . . with you': Du Camp 1882, 1, 405.
  – 'Yes . . . but we won't bathe': ibid., 409.
157 'When his grandmother died': PC 2, 257.
  – He told Flaubert . . . 200,000 francs: Du Camp 1978, 153.
  – 'Take a down-to-earth subject': Du Camp 1882, 1, 430.
  – 'I saw everything . . . What's the use?": PC 1, 678.

CHAPTER THIRTEEN: Oriental

158 It was no surprise . . . daughter instead: Biasi 1991, 119.
  – His slippers . . . beside his bed: ibid., 124n., quoting Du Camp.
  – 'Poor woman . . . lavish upon her': Pl. Corr., 1, 556.
159 There, in the company of Antonia: Biasi 1991, 121.
  – Supposed to be leaving . . . Saturday: ibid., 121–2.
  – At a station buffet . . . something to do: ibid., 123.
  – This was unlike anything . . . before: ibid., 125.
  – 'I shall never see my mother again': ibid., 124n.
160 'No! I'd be so ridiculous': ibid., 124.
  – He made her a promise: PC 1, 514–5.
  – Flaubert was . . . commercially useful: ibid., 1058.
  – 'refreshed, bedazzled and full of life': ibid., 516.
  – Chewing morosely at his cigar: Du Camp 1882, 1, 440–41.
  – After the meal . . . less than a week: Biasi 1991, 127.
161 'The senses . . . poor tormented nerves': ibid., 125.
  – 'No more separations': ibid., 128.
  – Saying farewell . . . capacity for feeling: PC 1, 518.
  – The sun was shining . . . full of hope': ibid.
  – 'Do you know . . . I was delighted': Biasi 1991, 139.
  – From this very place: PC 1, 520.
  – When she began to vomit: Biasi 1991, 140.
  – 'He had just wandered': ibid., 146.
162 It was raining when they arrived: ibid., 149.
  – He gave his guests useful letters: ibid., 155.
  – Flaubert went . . . which door it was: ibid., 156.
  – The singer gave a splendid performance: ibid., 157.
  – They were travelling first class: ibid., 157–8.
  – 'they bored us stiff': ibid., 158.
  – 'staggering along like a drunkard': Du Camp 1882, 1, 441.
  – Flaubert standing at the rail: ibid.
  – He then went below: Biasi 1991, 158.

162 Roux had a rich fund of sea-stories: ibid., 159.
163 'It's funny . . . the rough sort': PC 1, 527.
 - 'Everyone is on intimate terms': ibid., 524.
 - 'there was the most astounding racket': ibid., 528.
 - 'solemn and anxious impression': Biasi 1991, 168.
 - 'Scarcely had we set foot on land': PC 1, 540.
 - 'We go gently': ibid., 529.
164 Abbas-Pacha, they said: Du Camp 1882, 1, 450–51.
 - They felt the exiles' sudden eagerness: PC 1, 555.
 - 'Set your mind at rest': ibid., 530.
 - 'the name *Thomson of Sunderland*': Biasi 1991, 175.
 - It was as though his father: PC 1, 535.
165 'treated like princes': ibid., 530.
 - 'First night on the Nile': Biasi 1991, 185.
 - 'Blue in the distance': Du Camp 1860, 31.
 - They made their way to Ezbekiyya: Biasi 199, 186.
 - It had a pleasant promenade: Du Camp 1860, 33–4.
 - 'If it had been possible': Du Camp 1882, 1, 480.
166 'No; having come this far': ibid.
 - Now in his sixties: ibid., 456–8.
 - Out of favour with the new ruler: ibid., 451–3.
 - After only a few weeks in Cairo: PC 1, 549.
 - 'always and everywhere in search': Du Camp 1882, 1, 464.
 - 'He has a nose like a parrot's beak': PC 1, 638.
167 Du Camp simply did not understand: Du Camp 1882, 1, 464–67.
 - Flaubert . . . low life of the city: Du Camp 1860, 47.
 - the clowns . . . in the square: SL, 136.
 - the madame of the nearby brothel: ibid., 137.
 - antics of the snake-charmers: ibid., 138.
 - Flaubert was gathering material: Du Camp 1882, 1, 472–3.
 - Footnote: Flaubert made 63 pages of notes: PC 1, 1078.
 - Khalil-Effendi was so useful: ibid., 579.
 - 'Bigger and bigger it rose': Biasi 1991, 208.
168 'like an enormous mushroom': Du Camp 1860, 66.
 - 'like corpses in their shrouds': Biasi 1991, 209; PC 1, 551.
 - Sirius was rising: Biasi 1991, 209.
 - 'Once I got my breath back': PC 1, 549.
169 '29 December 1849': Biasi 1991, 235.
 - Du Camp's friendship with Charles Lambert: Du Camp 1882, 1, 468–74.
 - 'a formidable specimen': Biasi 1991, 445.
 - 'a charming man . . . intelligence': PC 1, 655.
 - 'This man is a French lord': Biasi 1991, 234.
 - 'I began to ask him questions': PC 1, 559.
170 'What shall I do when I return?': ibid., 561.
 - 'What can satisfy me': PC 1, 585.
 - 'What does this mean': PC 1, 592.

CHAPTER FOURTEEN: Sailing the Nile

171 The *cange* had a crew of nine: Du Camp 1860, 86; PC 1, 582; PC 1, 1079.
  – The wind dropped . . . sight of the pyramids: Biasi 1991, 255; Du Camp 1860, 89.
  – 'ignobly plump': PC 1, 588.
  – 'Instead of forgetting': ibid., 589.
  – It took eleven hours on a donkey: Richardson 1996, 407.
172 Having sat through . . . Napoléon: PC 1, 590.
  – Flaubert turned the conversation: Biasi 1991, 260.
  – 'quite obviously getting it up': PC 1, 602.
  – He was further delighted: Biasi 1991, 260.
  – 'So off we went': ibid., 263.
  – So they haggled her down: ibid., 264.
  – 'Then it was . . . my entire being': ibid., 274.
173 All of Cairo's . . . ever since 1834: Nieuwkerk 1996, 32–5.
  – She had strong shoulders: Du Camp 1860, 116.
  – 'beautiful women dance badly': PC 1, 606.
  – Du Camp thought of the Bacchantes: Du Camp 1860, 118.
  – 'ancient Greek vases': Biasi 1991, 283.
  – 'Second shot with Kuchuk-Hanem: ibid., 285.
174 'How sweet it would be': ibid., 287.
  – Infinitely sad . . . watching the crowds: ibid., 362–3.
  – The moonlight shining on the sand: Biasi 1991, 315.
  – 'He gave a shout': Du Camp 1882, 1, 481.
175 Together they went striding: Biasi 1991, 317.
  – 'sounded like the distant striking': Biasi 1991, 326–7.
176 'We spent the afternoon lying down': HH 10, 505.
  – 'In which case . . . thinking of me': PC 1, 622.
  – 'serpents with several heads': PC 1, 621.
  – Exporting mummies . . . illegal': ibid., 622.
177 'I feel a wild mix of terror': HH 10, 536.
  – When they came down to the Red Sea: ibid., 539.
  – 'It was one of the most voluptuous': PC 1, 636.
178 Here was yet another instance: Du Camp 1882, 490–94.
  – I muse upon my life: PC 1, 627 & 628.
  – 'That night immense nostalgia': HH 10, 549.
  – 'the future of society': PC 1, 645.
  – 'Bizarre psychological phenomenon': ibid., 644.
179 Flaubert had an epileptic attack: Biasi 1991, 446.
  – In preparation for the next stage: PC 1, 697.
  – 'one of the same artist gang': ibid., 661.
  – Characteristically he would challenge: PC 2, 769–70.

CHAPTER FIFTEEN: Countries of the Mind

180 'It was never mentioned between us': Du Camp 1882, 1, 513.
181 'We went in through the Jaffa Gate': HH 10, 562.
  – 'Jerusalem strikes me . . . immensely sad': ibid.
  – 'The Armenians curse the Greeks': PC 1, 665.
  – 'neither religious enthusiasm': HH 10, 562.
  – On their first evening in Jerusalem: PC 1, 1056.

181 'a ruin of a man': HH 10, 565.
  – 'I lingered there': ibid., 569.
182 'they reached Damascus . . . like bandits': PC 1, 674.
  – 'The stones of Baalbek': HH 10, 597–600.
183 'I'm thinking of Homer': HH 11, 30.
  – 'the Oriental who was becoming civilised': Du Camp 1882, 1, 515; Durry 1950, 104–8.
  – ' in a bad mood': HH 11, 36.
  – 'like Siberia': PC 1, 733.
184 'a second style perhaps': ibid., 704.
  – In Constantinople . . . affected him deeply: ibid., 710.
  – 'Women . . . are taught to lie shamelessly': ibid., 711.
  – 'The sound of our horses' hooves': HH 11, 53.
185 'You can portray wine, love': PC 1, 720.
  – 'happy as a child': ibid., 724.
  – 'I am in a positively Olympian state': ibid., 725.
  – 'My journey . . . has bitten deep': ibid.
  – 'I'm not getting any prettier': ibid., 732.
  – 'you must expect to find me three-quarters bald': ibid., 741.
  – 'I'm about to join the ranks': ibid., 750.
186 'What a splendid story': Du Camp 1882, 1, 542–3.
  – It would be very interesting: ibid., 543
  – 'Maxime is sick of it': PC 1, 748.
  – Flaubert was the sweet, delicate: ibid., 738.
187 It was common knowledge . . . political prisoners: ibid., 757.
  – 'No more tent, no more desert': Du Camp 1882, 1, 558.
188 'it had to be so . . . to look at me': PC 1, 756.
  – He was in a peculiar state: ibid., 774.
189 'like a perpetual hallucination': ibid., 770.
  – 'I'm in love with Murillo's Virgin': ibid., 780.
  – The second encounter . . . Murillo's Virgin: Intégrale 2, 697–8.
  – '[. . .] having her portrait painted': HH 11, 157.
190 'My mother . . . holding myself back': PC 1, 782.
191 'We would have cut it in two': ibid., 778.

CHAPTER SIXTEEN: Intimacies

192 'Painful emotions, tears, regret': PC 1, 811.
  – '[. . .] I want to see you . . . course of my life': ibid., 812.
193 an infinitely ambiguous *au revoir*: PC 1, 815; details from Louise Colet's Journal, written a few days after the events described.
  – 'You must have thought me very cold': PC 2, 7.
  – 'Gustave arrives, handsome and charming': ibid., 878.
194 Footnote: Flaubert did lend money: ibid., 1024.
  – It looked as if . . . evening dress: ibid., 6.
  – Once you had seen . . . being a maharajah: Seznec 1951, 9–25.
195 This was to be a literary journal: De Senneville 1996, 209–14.
  – Du Camp . . . Paris single-handed: PC 2, 864.
  – 'used up . . . inside and out': ibid.,13.
  – Tell me what to do: ibid., 8–12.

196 He felt betrayed: ibid., 863–7.
  – 'Nothing at all about me': ibid., 880.
  – 'Only there . . . is the breath of life': ibid., 116.
  – 'good-natured and aggrieved': ibid., 122.
  – 'I find your distress . . . along the same road': ibid.,113 & 120.
  – 'I do not think . . . for some time': ibid., 123.
199 'I'm afraid of lapsing': ibid., 5.
  – 'progressing painfully . . . quantities of paper': ibid., 14–16.
  – 'Her *physique* . . . less venereal': ibid., 16.
  – At some point . . . another woman: ibid., 881.
200 'If you are not resolved to die': ibid., 881–2.
  – 'I was nearly knocked out': ibid., 29.
  – 'that fatal thirtieth year': ibid., 205.
  – 'six weeks of intimacy': ibid., 883.
  – 'Gustave loves me . . . read me his works': ibid., 882.
201 The leper . . . dresses his sores': ibid., 24.

CHAPTER SEVENTEEN: The Pangs of Art

202 Footnote: 'If my book is any good': ibid., 147.
  – 'Only me . . . as if I were still 18': ibid., 35.
203 'I am . . . much more with it': ibid., 42.
  – 'Time to pull it off': ibid., 31.
  – 'What I'd like to do': ibid.
  – 'No lyricism, no digressions': ibid., 40.
  – He was writing tirelessly: ibid., 45.
204 'the terrors that came to me': ibid., 55–6.
  – 'Disperse yourself into everything': ibid., 61.
  – 'somehow manage . . . he never existed': ibid., 62.
  – 'You have to drink up an ocean': ibid., 86.
  – 'Ideally . . . he wanted to be buried': ibid., 66.
  – 'Then they went . . . to watch the dawn': ibid., 885.
205 'The life of a man of letters': Raitt 1994, 12.
  – 'walk on a hair across the double abyss': PC 2, 57.
  – 'imbecile inertia': ibid., 68.
  – 'I think best lying on my back': ibid., 71.
  – 'a permanent state of fury': ibid., 75.
  – 'I had to go and get my handkerchief': ibid., 76.
206 'a large fantastical . . . novel': ibid., 85.
  – In real life . . . triumphant serenity: HH 12, 230–32.
  – 'a novel about madness': PC 3, 59.
  – 'because it is a subject that frightens me': ibid., 290.
207 'jealous selfishness . . . own personality': ibid., 84.
  – 'These things . . . make me feel ill': ibid., 95.
208 'breathless, coughing, spitting': ibid., 886.
  – 'We shall see . . . by the lion's cage': ibid., 887.
209 'It's gripping!': ibid., 118.
  – 'I omitted my momentary lapse': ibid., 889.
  – 'You have truly made me suffer strangely': ibid., 129–30.
  – 'Not a word . . . my heart over to him': ibid., 889.

209 'good relations are henceforth impossible': ibid., 914.
210 It was a feeling of powerlessness: ibid., 131.
- I said to myself . . . make her happier: ibid., 132.
- 'Don't know why my chest . . . layers of brass': ibid., 133.
- 'impossible . . . dramatic narrative': ibid., 136.
- After reading it aloud . . . on edge: ibid., 139.
- 'He begs me not to call for help': ibid., 891-2.
211 'He said . . . follow his advice': ibid., 893.
- 'What's the use?': ibid., 162.
212 Serious art would soon be impossible: ibid., 491.
- In August 1854 . . . to the Emperor: ibid., 566.
- 'Close your door . . . the turkeys are making': ibid., 180.
- in alphabetical order . . . beginning to end: ibid., 208-9.
213 'so perfectly . . . to strangle you: ibid., 245.
- 'done the plan, put it down in writing': ibid., 252.
214 'I stink of my Homais': ibid., 344.
- 'sprawling in every possible position': ibid., 296-7.
- 'My nerves were so on edge': ibid., 210.
- 'People carry a slumbering passion': ibid., 330.
215 'no crude details': ibid., 373.
- 'I've reached the Big Fuck': ibid., 483-4.
216 'It was not the walk or the weight': ibid., 1227.
- 'Just as the pearl . . . a deeper wound': ibid., 431.
- 'Sometimes I curl up so tightly': ibid., 295-6.
- 'a savage obstinacy': ibid., 348.
217 'Yet another year!': ibid., 1216.
- 'If poor old Saint Antony': Bancquart 1967, 69.
- He showed Flaubert . . . complained about him: PC 2, 452.
- which Flaubert found 'upsetting': ibid., 454.
- 'hard, quarrelsome and malicious': ibid., 456.
- 'I'll come and see you more often': ibid., 458.
- She teased him for it: ibid., 461.
218 'though our bodies came together': ibid., 466.
- 'Ever since then . . . you haven't any money': ibid., 500.
- 'when I tried . . . you sent me packing': ibid.
- After a memorably wretched farewell: ibid., 464.
- 'I sense that . . . she drops me': ibid., 475.
- Just had a series . . . attributed to her: ibid., 1234.
- 'acerbic and *abusive*': ibid., 507.
219 'You have made art into a receptacle': ibid., 502.
- 'I shall never reform': ibid., 507.
- 'surly and disagreeable': ibid., 540.
- 'On our last evening . . . *not being intelligent*': ibid., 525.
- She was forever mocking him: ibid., 527.
- The face of suicidal despair . . . tied to his belt: ibid., 498.
220 '[. . .] I always look like a dull bourgeois': ibid., 438.
- A ghostly image . . . 'domineering and brutal': ibid., 1273-5.
221 Footnote: Jean Bruneau has established: ibid., 1253-4.
- 'Exhibitions of human misery': ibid., 377.
- 'behind the scenes in the theatre': ibid., 83.

221 'With any bourgeois subject': ibid., 469.
222 'waving about attached to my body': ibid., 474–5.
  – In the event . . . symptoms had subsided: ibid., 562.
223 Bottles of wine . . . are strewn everywhere: ibid., 621.
  – Flaubert once pictured himself: ibid., 576.
  – 'When I'm in my frock coat': ibid., 355.
  – 'It's a bit of petty malice': ibid., 365.
  – 'is one of the people I don't want to think about': ibid., 485.
  – 'We are their enemies': ibid., 599.
224 Madame Sabatier . . . throughout the 1850s: Pichois & Ziegler 1989, 206–7.
225 'Three great movements': PC 2, 1283.
  – 'No writer allowed to unveil his feelings': Du Camp 1882, 2, 182–4.
  – True to his fantasies: De Senneville 1996, 223.
  – 'To the delightful host': PC 2, 1299.
  – 'three big speeches by Homais': ibid., 613.
226 'Be brave, close your eyes': ibid., 869.
  – 'It has been officially agreed': ibid., 620.
  – Du Camp defended his friend's work: Du Camp 1882, 2, 195.
  – 'dressed like a carpenter . . . sweating': PC 2, 613.
  – 'I shall only feel happy': ibid., 641.
  – 'What a pretty comparison': ibid., 574.
  – They read *Macbeth* together: ibid., 634.
227 It speaks for . . . their friendship: ibid., 871.
  – '[. . .] the subscribers were up in arms': Du Camp 1882, 2, 195.
  – '[. . .] aesthetically I wanted to open it up': PC 2, 635–6.
228 He followed Flaubert around: Du Camp 1882, 2, 186–7.
  – The reviews were good: PC 2, 1326.
  – '[. . .] early in November': Du Camp 1882, 2, 199.
  – 'They had exiled many eloquent men': ibid., 46.
  – 'Your carriage scene is impossible': PC 2, 873.
229 'You are attacking little details': ibid., 650.
  – Footnote: Du Camp tells a different story: Du Camp 1882, 2, 199–200.
  – 'regarding an unpleasant business': PC 2, 650.
  – 'well within conventional rates': Heath 1992, 48.
230 this is exactly how it is: PC 2, 654–5.
  – 'If my book is any good': ibid., 147.
  – 'Excessive sensibility . . . my only consolation': ibid., 695.
231 'Console me, advise me: ibid., 687.
  – 'I love you . . . for your ideas': ibid., 331.
  – 'My trial is *political*': ibid., 657.
  – 'since . . . the punishment of misconduct': ibid.
  – 'hysterical kitchen-maids': ibid., 656.
232 A guilty verdict . . . future elections: ibid., 659.
  – He had female supporters too: ibid., 662.
  – At one point . . . for shame: ibid., 664.
  – Then Senard . . . would proceed: ibid., 666.
  – 'There is *something* . . . invisible and relentless': ibid., 667.
  – Footnote: Jean Bruneau, the most recent editor: ibid., 1334.
  – 'These fellows are naive': ibid., 875.
  – 'I pity the people': ibid., 673.

233 Footnote: . . . and from Flaubert's letters: ibid., 674.
  − 'extremely biased': ibid., 676.
  − A complimentary copy: ibid., 1347; letter from Edmond Pagnèrre to Flaubert.
  − Monsieur Dubarle . . . the imperial prosecutor: Du Camp 1882, 2, 204–6.
234 Rumoured . . . eye for the erotic: HH 15, 586.
  − 'The offence against public morality': Oeuvres 1, 619.
  − 'The beauty of Madame Bovary': ibid., 621.
  − 'What the author is showing you': ibid., 624.
235 'Voluptuous one day . . . to her lover': ibid., 625.
  − '[. . .] the genre . . . realist painting': ibid., 630.
  − Even men of virtue . . . out of danger: ibid., 632.
  − Madame Bovary obviously dies of poison: ibid.
236 'Is there . . . Madame Bovary': ibid., 633.
  − 'spoke for four hours': PC 2, 676–8.
  − Emma escapes into . . . 'endless daydreams': Oeuvres 1, 637.
  − Sénard affirms . . . things that weren't there: ibid., 645.
  − They said . . . with eager curiosity: ibid., 646.
237 'crushed [. . .] writhing in his seat': PC 2, 676–8.
  − 'My cause . . . contemporary literature': ibid., 678.
238 'far from humankind': ibid., 679.
  − 'All the people I've met personally': ibid., 683.
  − Within a week . . . changed his mind: PC 3, 194.
  − 'the elite of contemporary authors': Heath 1992, 48–9.
239 'You Parisians think well': PC 2, 1366.
  − 'absolutely correct': PC 4, 471.
  − 'All this uproar around my first book': PC 2, 678–9.
  − 'selling superbly': PC 2, 711.
240 The brutality . . . was to be deplored: ibid., 1373.
  − 'I have been attacked': ibid., 766.
  − 'The thing seems impossible to me': ibid., 746.
  − 'A masterpiece' . . . Flaubert and his publisher: ibid., 712; PC 3, 222; Oliver 1980, 63 and 66.
  − 'On reflection . . . in the provinces': Sand 1878, 291–2.
  − 'This bizarre androgyne': Baudelaire 1961, 652 & 654.
  − 'You have found your way . . . your own': PC 2, 772.
241 He dresses. . . 'some substance': ibid., 1406.
  − 'Do not put your portrait': ibid., 839.
  − Henri Monnier . . . play Homais: ibid., 1418.
  − They would hire . . . thirty thousand francs: ibid., 797.
  − Footnote: Flaubert wrote to Louis Bouilhet: PC 3, 79.
  − One of them sang comic songs: PC 2, 1415.
242 Flaubert saw them both: ibid., 798.
  − 'Two turpitudes . . . are quite enough': ibid., 794.
  − 'It will be Art, pure Art': ibid.

CHAPTER EIGHTEEN: Barbarians at the Gates

243 'I feel a need for immense epics': ibid., 412.
  − 'novels with a grandiose setting': ibid., 428.
  − Reading Herodotus . . . twelve years old: ibid., 547.

244 'A good subject for a novel': PC 3, 191.
245 'truculent little pleasantry': PC 2, 713.
 – 'ought to be done . . . *lively* style': ibid., 748.
 – 'in a labyrinth': ibid., 751.
 – 'being *truly* moved . . . my heroes': ibid., 749.
 – 'deplorable academic style': ibid., 764.
 – 'without having carried it in my belly': ibid., 779.
 – Demoralised, he withdrew: ibid., 778.
 – 'trying to resuscitate . . . we know nothing': ibid., 781.
 – 'I feel as if . . . the emotion is missing': ibid., 784.
 – 'Living in a house . . . at the stars': ibid., 821.
246 'Chateaubriandesque reflections . . . time': ibid., 808.
 – 'I can smell it once again': HH 11, 181.
 – Le Colonel Caligaris: PC 2, 1446.
 – He remembered dining with a postmaster: HH 11, 182.
247 He remembered evenings in Tunis: PC 2, 811.
 – 'I look at the landscape': ibid., 810.
 – 'I feel as though . . . masked ball': HH 11: 208.
 – 'just like some sea god': PC 2, 818.
 – 'I shall write horrors': ibid.
 – 'All the energies of nature': HH 11: 208.
 – 'Carthage . . . will have to be completely reworked': PC 2, 817.
 – 'a chapter of explanations': HH 12, 276–303.
 – 'wrinkled as a mummy': ibid., 299–300.
248 'I've had it once before': PC 2, 837.
 – 'When I take a look into it': ibid., 830.
 – By December 1858 . . . day of the week: ibid., 843.
 – 'nothing happening, no sound': ibid., 845.
 – The long December nights . . . Hamilcar: ibid., 847.
 – 'For me . . . my slowness': ibid., 846.
 – 'My characters don't talk': PC 3, 11.
 – 'I am convinced' . . . found in all of that: ibid., 16–17.
249 By the autumn of 1859: ibid., 38.
 – 'deep endless sadness': ibid., 894.
 – 'domestic worries and upsets': ibid., 45.
 – On the evening of 18 September: ibid., 40.
 – Resuscitating Carthage . . . inconceivable sadness: ibid., 59.
 – 'For years . . . I have been pondering': ibid., 59.
250 'Is it really the case': ibid., 1078.
 – When Flaubert pictured himself writing: ibid., 120.
 – 'It has to be simultaneously obscene': ibid., 122.
 – 'dreaming about . . . a cloudless sky': ibid.
 – 'human flesh . . . rhinoceros butter': ibid., 152.
251 He had told the de Goncourts: ibid., 875.
 – 'his eyes bulging': ibid., 876; 3, 877; 3, 870.
 – Du Camp recalled: Du Camp 1880, 2, 472.
 – 'You quivered along with him': Commanville 1886, xxxviii.
 – It was the 'moral colouring': PC 3, 877.
252 'Drown the bourgeois': ibid., 157.
 – 'deadly boring': ibid., 164.

252 'I think there are too many soldiers': ibid., 166.
  – 'revolt the sensitive . . . a cannibal': ibid., 170.
  – 'an immense disdain . . . hold it against me': ibid., 172.

CHAPTER NINETEEN: Dining Out

253 'Very tall, very broad': PC 3, 868.
  – He referred to them . . . the little darlings: ibid., 360.
254 'It's the most wonderfully amusing thing': ibid., 867.
  – 'Stories about teachers at the Collège': ibid., 870.
255 'The finest literary description . . . of a thousand women': ibid., 222.
  – Lévy backed down: ibid., 1190.
  – Flaubert accepted: ibid., 239.
  – 'The future is a worry': ibid., 227.
  – 'It's not allowed': ibid., 236.
  – 'I have a great desire': ibid., 254.
256 'He quietly pushes himself forward': Pages, 153.
257 'It scared me': PC 3, 1208.
  – 'should have been printed . . . like a volume of poems': ibid.
  – 'It's an atrocious book': ibid., 1211.
  – 'He's going to do three articles': Pages, 154.
  – 'an attentive and impartial judgement': HH 2, 410.
  – 'For fear . . . cultivates the atrocious': ibid., 431.
258 I must tell you quite frankly: PC 3, 381.
  – In my bloody excesses: ibid., 1244.
  – Berlioz praised it: ibid., 1226.
  – The new director of the Opéra: ibid., 286.
259 The Empress . . . delighted by *Salammbô*: ibid., 1230.
  – 'They have expressed a desire': ibid., 1236.
  – 'We were almost the only three people': Pages, 155.
  – The Empress Eugénie asked Flaubert: PC 3, 881.
  – The bodice of the authentic Salammbô costume: ibid., 1254.
260 An ardent Bonapartist: Bierman 1988, 78.
  – The Princess used to send out: PC 3, 730.
  – 'fitting the ocean into a carafe': ibid., 882.
  – 'working simultaneously on my two plans': ibid., 314.
  – I'm slaving away: ibid., 315.
261 'beginning to take shape': ibid., 318.
  – 'a series of analyses': ibid., 323.
  – 'It's an old idea that I've had': ibid., 320.
  – 'You're like a fish out of water': ibid., 846.
  – 'three very distressing months': ibid., 327.
  – Charles Lambert . . . Flaubert's mood: ibid., 336.
  – 'I am not cheerful enough': ibid., 333.
  – 'I feel as limp as a dog's dick': ibid., 334.
  – 'Mère Schlesinger is mad': ibid., 848.

CHAPTER TWENTY: Tuesday's Child

262 Caroline Hamard's inheritance . . . arranging: ibid., 314.
 – *'C'est ridicule, Gustave!'*: Desportes 1999, 52.
263 Unlike Uncle Achille: ibid., 50.
 – 'a charming fellow': HH 14, 70.
 – The talented . . . worldly tastes: PC 3, 1304.
 – 'a rich man who loves her': ibid., 1306.
 – 'like being thrown off the summit': Desportes 1999, 61.
264 Look and consider: PC 3, 366.
265 'I feel ridiculous': ibid., 367.
 – 'I've broken the ice': ibid., 368.
 – And tell him . . . out of the way: ibid., 1306.
 – 'I shall see you . . . with a young man": ibid., 372.
 – 'tall and well built': ibid., 1302.
 – It may have been a question: ibid., 1310.
266 There were cashmere shawls: Desportes 1999, 62.
 – 'Don't worry . . . everything will be fine': ibid., 63.
 – Caroline Hamard . . . 'sacrificed': ibid.
 – Mother soon fell asleep: PC 3, 389.
267 'you are having a good time': ibid., 387.
 – 'tall, slender and elegant': ibid., 1339.
 – 'The aforesaid Prefect': ibid., 425.
 – 'I committed every indiscretion': Desportes 1999, 76–7.

CHAPTER TWENTY-ONE: Troubadours

270 Everyone pays ten francs: Steegmuller and Bray 1993, 10.
271 'You are the only person': Pages, 75.
 – 'Flaubert impassioned . . . still not sure': Steegmuller & Bray 1993, 9.
 – 'delicately defined . . . gentle and serene': Pages, 72.
 – For a woman . . . gesture of emancipation: Pages, 116.
 – 'Mme Sand . . . intended to rape Flaubert': PC 3, 1383.
 – 'bring me your criticisms of my book': ibid., 501.
 – 'the source of . . . pleasantries': ibid., 514.
272 'I don't know what it is': ibid., 553.
 – Tuesday, 28 August: Steegmuller & Bray 1993, 17–18.
 – 'You are a splendid kind boy': PC 3, 524.
 – 'the final farewell look': ibid., 525.
 – 'We have done nothing but talk': ibid.
 – 'There's lots of it': ibid., 526.
 – 'That is a present': ibid., 527.
273 He was keen to discuss . . . with her: ibid., 532.
 – 'You are' . . . a very mysterious . . . being: ibid., 529.
 – 'If the weather's fine . . . our days and nights': ibid., 534.
 – 'I do so much dreaming': ibid., 535.
 – Unlike you . . . of the Orient too perhaps: ibid., 536.
274 'She worked all day': ibid., 554.
 – 'Superb animals as tame as dogs': Steegmuller & Bray 1993, 32.
 – 'she has insights': PC 3, 554.
 – 'We parted . . . ask you questions': ibid.

274 We're lucky, don't you think: ibid., 555.
275 The only sour note: ibid., 552.
 – 'sings of perfect love': ibid., 564.
276 It was amusing to compare this: ibid.,
 – Great artists are often invalids: ibid., 570–1.
277 'My literary anxieties! . . . exceptions': ibid., 574–5.

CHAPTER TWENTY-TWO: Chevalier Flaubert

278 Dr Cloquet prescribed: PC 3, 287.
 – According to the medical wisdom of the day: Corbin 1995, 75.
 – 'Venus is no doubt partly to blame': PC 3, 850.
 – He was putting on weight: ibid., 358.
 – 'rheumatism, neuralgia . . . melancholy': ibid., 422.
 – 'as big as . . . hen's egg': ibid., 485.
 – 'My only entertainment': ibid., 487.
279 His 'Homeric' rages: ibid., 1476.
 – Flaubert's 'extreme excitability': ibid., 749.
 – Returning to my room: ibid., 749–50.
280 Flaubert was most disconcerted: ibid., 767.
 – 'capable of violent feeling': ibid., 770.
 – 'becoming more and more irritable': ibid., 814–5.
281 'redecorating my study in Croisset': ibid., 430–1.
 – There is a farm near Nogent: ibid., 1341.
282 'so that he may conduct himself': ibid., 1342.
 – 'I don't believe that he owes': ibid.
 – 'Try to persuade her' . . . bad for his nerves: ibid., 431.
 – 'I could have the money immediately': ibid., 563.
283 'She'd think I was on the road': ibid., 636.
 – 'the high point of Flaubert's existence': Du Camp 1882, 2, 369–70.
284 He was always noticed: ibid., 371.
 – 'convinced that he could save everything': Echard 1985, Prince Jérôme Napoléon'.
 – Plon-Plon . . . political speeches: PC 3, 361.
 – In February 1864 . . . in the morning: ibid., 375.
 – 'In the midst of all this': ibid., 374.
285 'a humble request': ibid., 377.
 – The invitation stipulated in uniform: ibid., 392.
 – 'an absolute egotism . . . or an intrigue': Christiansen 1994, 19.
286 'Gustave Flaubert . . . too much wine': PC 3, 1331.
 – 'You have to create a good impression': ibid., 411.
 – In this compliant and straightlaced world: Du Camp 1882, 2, 372.
287 'I expected to be bored': PC 3, 412.
 – 'a classic impersonation of the Emperor': ibid.; Pages, 215.
 – Avoiding a dull quartet of worthies: PC 3, 425.
 – 'Women will never know': ibid., 1400.
 – She was a great admirer of Salammbô: ibid., 1348.
 – 'What do you want': ibid., 1401.
288 'The Princess . . . as her lover': ibid., 884.
 – Footnote: Jean Bruneau . . . have been found: ibid., 1400.
 – 'All this is infinitely flattering': ibid., 490.

288 'done a great deal': ibid., 503.
- He had been made *chevalier*: ibid., 514.
- 'If only . . . at eighteen': ibid., 517.
- It was Sainte-Beuve's doing: ibid., 1396.
- 'As for forgetting about my trial': ibid., 517.
- It was humiliating: ibid., 525.
- But then . . . sharing it with him: Du Camp 1882, 2, 370.

CHAPTER TWENTY-THREE: *L'Education sentimentale*

290 Epigraph:'It's the feeling of *Modernity*': PC 3, 706.
- He worked at it . . . clearer focus: ibid., 393.
- 'I'm beginning to understand it': ibid., 389.
- 'What despots they are': ibid., 400.
- He fumbled his way along: ibid., 408.
- 'I have written fifteen pages': ibid., 410.
291 Since last month: ibid., 409.
- It's like being inside an enormous . . . tomb: ibid., 416.
- 'I go to bed at four': ibid., 421.
- 'Yesterday . . . I spent the whole afternoon': ibid., 478.
- In the summer of 1866: Bierman1988, 279–92; *Encyclopaedia Britannica*, Sadowa, Molkte, Shoulder Weapons, Dreyse Rifle.
292 'It'll be mediocre': PC 3, 518.
293 'When you have nothing else to do': ibid., 559.
- 'obviously the best thing he has done': ibid., 616.
- 'a very naive book': ibid., 579.
- 'I am among the last of that kind': ibid., 580.
- 'Damn me if I have any idea': ibid., 600.
294 'The political horizon is darkening': ibid., 629.
- The bourgeois are frightened of everything: ibid., 629.
- Not even the Magny Dinners: ibid., 631.
- Maxim: hatred of the Bourgeois'
- Forty-three Zingaris: ibid., 1478.
295 This will be the third time: ibid., 653–4.
- 'You must look beyond the People': ibid., 643.
- 'Their majesties being desirous': ibid., 649.
296 'Paris is becoming colossal': ibid., 652–3.
- The outline of a Second Empire novel: Durry 1950, 253–7.
- 'He read Lord Byron and . . . his pipe': PC 3, 693.
297 'I have serious problems': ibid., 734.
- 'moral cohabitation with the bourgeois': ibid., 769.
- 'a great pile of mediocre stuff': ibid., 733.
- 'discovering many things': ibid., 725.
298 George Sand, loyal to the muddlers: ibid., 770.
- 'I rely on you': ibid., 783.
- Rich or poor . . . no objection: ibid., 786.
- 'Here is the one I've adopted': PC 4, 37.
- 'Prime example of beautiful painting': Steegmuller & Bray, 145.
- His head was 'splitting': PC 4, 45.
299 So delighted that she insisted: ibid., 47.

299 In the event . . . the final chapter: ibid., 51.
 – From his rooms on the fourth floor: Baillie & Salmon 1997b, 205.
 – His old quarters . . . rue de Clichy: PC 4, 1069.
300 'He was not the same man': ibid., 71.
 – 'Strange things are happening': Cappello 1996, 699.
 – 'in the antique manner': PC 4, 70.
 – 'died like a *philosophe*': ibid., 74.
 – He called out to Flaubert: ibid., 72–3.
 – 'I say to myself': ibid., 78.
301 'It feels like a major amputation': ibid., 77.
 – 'my literary conscience': ibid., 70.
 – 'You have managed a kind of tour de force': ibid., 1006.
 – Whatever their truth . . . 'annoying': ibid., 78.
 – At this point. . . perilously fragile: ibid., 1090.
 – 'The real progressives . . . will rage': ibid., 126.
 – *L'Education sentimentale* . . . the Suez Canal: ibid., 124.
 – 'about thirty newspapers': ibid., 127.
302 He received some astutely appreciative replies: ibid., 1117–8.
 – 'sad, indecisive and mysterious': ibid., 1124.
 – 'the repetition . . . slightly contrived': ibid., 1128.
 – 'You are the only reader': ibid., 139.
303 'such hatred and such bad faith': ibid., 134.
 – 'Such mysticism in the language': ibid., 1125.
 – Flaubert . . . 'stays on the surface . . . no depths': ibid., 1122.
 – 'a robust piece': ibid., 1126.
 – a crowd that 'goes down on its knees': ibid., 1101.
 – 'sterilised his talent': ibid., 1130.
 – 'For fear of compromising themselves': ibid., 134.
304 'You are too innocent': ibid., 139.
 – 'Come and shake off this persecution': ibid., 144.
 – 'Perhaps you're being rather coy': Steegmuller & Bray 1993, 126.
 – Besides . . . 'all the time': ibid., 171.
 – She would spend the winter days . . . in her life: ibid., 122 & 131.
305 'We met, dined, talked': ibid., 174.
 – On Christmas Day . . . went wild: ibid., 175.
 – Footnote: George Sand's son: PC 3, 713–14.
 – 'They're still attacking your book': PC 4, 1512.
306 His mind, likewise: ibid., 151–2.
 – 'Your friendship blinds you': ibid., 153.
 – 'When I lost my dear Bouilhet': ibid.
 – 'physically broken, shattered' . . . unable to climb stairs: ibid., 160 & 164.
 – 'a dear old confidant': ibid., 164.
 – 'I gobbled up too many books': ibid., 186.
 – 'Everything and everyone . . . I can talk to': ibid., 170.
 – There was always Turgenev: ibid., 185.
 – Flaubert and Turgenev . . . at Croisset: ibid., 827.
307 'I could talk to you for weeks': PC 3, 754.
 – But it was embarrassing: PC 4, 159.
 – 'Though I keep hold of myself': ibid., 173.
 – 'I've been reading enormously': ibid., 178.

307 'When I leave my study': ibid., 193.
- 'an accursed year': ibid., 203.
- Autumnal wisdom . . . the local council: ibid., 194.
- Minimally biographical . . . writers had shared: ibid., 197.
- 'Here in Croisset': ibid.
308 'the terrible Raoul-Duval': ibid., 201.
- Raoul-Duval had 'conceived a passion': HH 14, 152.
- 'with his three horses . . . his two daughters': PC 4, 209.
- 'The moon . . . utterly exquisite': ibid., 210.
- In Paris . . . banned ever since 1850: ibid., 1168.
- 'At last . . . flung into the sewer': Christiansen 1996, 137–8.

CHAPTER TWENTY-FOUR: Into the Dark

309 Epigraph: 'The war with Prussia: PC 4, 308.
- 'I am disgusted': ibid., 211.
- People are going crazy: ibid., 217.
- 'I feel that we are entering into darkness': ibid.,218.
- In her reply . . . marched away: ibid., 220.
310 'My rifle is all ready': ibid., 222–3.
- Meanwhile . . . a thousand a day: ibid., 223, 232.
- 'The house is packed out': ibid., 227.
- 'yet we are supposed . . . to the very end': ibid., 224.
- 'My sadness has turned . . . for a fight': ibid., 225.
- 'Is it . . . the blood of my ancestors . . . breaking out': ibid., 227.
- In Paris . . . the defence of the city: ibid., 1174.
- Princess Mathilde . . . better days returned: ibid., 1173.
- 'quash this idiotic slander': ibid., 233.
- The Third Republic was declared: ibid., 229.
- 'Splendidly energetic': ibid., 1175.
- 'lessons in the art of war': ibid., 233.
- 'Anyone who feels afraid': ibid., 1175.
- The joke was taken seriously: ibid., 236.
- 'What a houseful I have here': ibid., 233.
- 'rivers and oceans of sadness': ibid., 234.
311 The everyday order . . . was crumbling': ibid., 239.
- A neighbour barricaded his garden gate: ibid., 235.
- Within a week they turned nasty: ibid., 238.
- 'Your old windbag . . . almost cheerful': ibid., 240.
- In the village of Mantes . . . with his teeth: ibid., 241.
- 'paying for the great lie . . . act of immorality': ibid., 243.
- By the middle of October . . . thirty miles away: ibid., 246–7.
- Flaubert said . . . overran Italy: ibid., 248.
- 'They shout threats at us': ibid., 252.
- Flaubert . . . sitting in the café: ibid., 256.
- He remembered . . . rue de Courcelles: ibid., 258.
312 He could foresee . . . world to come: ibid., 256.
- Flaubert felt about eighty years old: ibid., 262.
- He waited all through November: ibid., 264.
- 'I spent my nights . . . death-agony': ibid., 281.

312 'Why do they detest us': ibid., 264.
 – 'if only I could escape': ibid., 265.
 – He burnt many of his papers: ibid., 289.
 – 'buried a large box full of letters': ibid., 313.
 – 'I spent . . . first signs of a cancer': ibid., 318.
 – All through December . . . Seine was frozen: ibid., 272.
 – Locked in . . . like a prison: ibid., 281.
 – Anyone found . . . an angry crowd: ibid., 271.
 – Prussian troops were soon billeted: ibid., 408.
 – 'Yesterday I spent three hours searching': ibid., 265–7.
 – 'I can feel my intelligence weakening': ibid., 269.
313 Things got worse . . . Prussian soldiers: ibid., 1188.
 – They were much more threatening: ibid., 273.
 – 'That poor dear house . . . have it demolished': ibid., 275.
 – He spent the days dreaming: ibid., 282.
 – Caroline found him greatly altered: ibid., 1192.
 – 'I was completely off my head': ibid., 302.
 – Ernest Commanville . . . in great distress: ibid., 303.
 – Then Flaubert . . . 'under the Arc de Triomphe': ibid., 284 & 1193.
 – 'What barbarism!': ibid., 288.
314 In Rouen . . . great agitation . . . on both sides: ibid., 290 & 1195.
 – 'behaving abominably': ibid., 291.
 – Commanville had a lucky escape: ibid., 297.
 – A few days later . . . 'shot by the insurgents': ibid., 1201.
 – 'trying to work so as to forget': ibid., 299.
 – 'Contrary to expectation . . . did no damage': ibid., 313.
 – Sunday visitors could be received: ibid., 759.
 – The harbour was full of shipping: ibid., 304.
 – 'the putrescence of the present': ibid., 312.
 – 'just as innocent and as useful': ibid., 310.
 – my whole life's work . . . to do with it: ibid., 532.
315 deaden his sorrows', 'forget about France: ibid., 186, 299.
 – This extravagant book . . . happening in Paris: ibid., 318.
 – Flaubert's exceptional reluctance . . . work of art: Nadeau 1980, 224.
 – It was an 'ignoble experiment': ibid., 311.
 – 'She realises . . . idol was hollow': ibid., 319.
 – 'I find it difficult to stop': ibid., 316.
 – Footnote: Flaubert drew his later social ideas: Steegmuller & Bray 1993, 244.
316 I've just returned from Paris: PC 4, 324.
 – 'It's sinister and marvellous': ibid., 329.
 – The smell of corpses sickened me: ibid., 331–2.
 – 'the infamous Commune': ibid., 336.
 – 'waking from a dream': ibid., 335.
 – 'We parted in such good spirits': ibid.
 – At the end of July . . . for the proletariat: ibid., 351.
 – 'For the first time in her life': ibid., 371.
 – 'Chère maître . . . a golden mist': ibid., 376–7.
 – 'The human race . . . to each other': ibid., 376.
317 'I believe that the poor hate the rich': ibid., 384.
 – 'Our real discussions . . . mysteries too': ibid., 385.

317 Footnote: Flaubert prized this heroic analogy: ibid., 22.
– 'an old elephant stuck in a swamp': ibid., 339.
– 'I have achieved a state of calm': ibid. 368.
– Yet keeping still clashed: ibid., 383.
– *The New Corneille* . . . his monument: ibid., 411.
318 He could deploy everything: ibid., 436.
– Flaubert was soon prodigiously busy: ibid., 420.
– 'I feel as if . . . all day long': ibid., 433.
– He would certainly . . . for Christmas: ibid., 429.
– After a splendid première . . . end of the day: ibid., 470.
– 'A little piece . . . stinking compatriots': ibid., 456.
– In itself this business . . . a stupid bougeoisie: Raitt 1994, 21–2.
319 The local newspaper . . . risk publishing it: PC 4, 464.
– 'It may have been a mistake': ibid., 470.
– '[. . .] now they are afraid': ibid., 471.
– 'At your age . . . your constitution': ibid., 467.
– 'a disdainful serenity': ibid., 469.
320 'to fortify herself': ibid., 501.
– Now she . . . was 'terribly frail': ibid., 313.
– 'So sad . . . their intelligence disappearing': ibid., 383.
– '*At my age* . . . at least once a year': ibid., 362.
– 'I'm afraid . . . not enough': ibid., 194.
– Twice a day . . . city of Babylon: ibid., 350.
– Madame Flaubert died: ibid., 508; detail from Chevalley-Sabatier 1972, 213, n.86.
– 'I think . . . doesn't he?': ibid., 534.
– The memory of his mother . . . 'like a mist': ibid., 519.
– He ate alone at the big table: ibid., 522 & 525.
– 'I'm like an old man': ibid., 525.
– He wondered . . . all on his own: ibid., 516.
– 'I have realised . . . been torn out': ibid., 515.
321 'More than ever . . . my mother's room': ibid., 530.

CHAPTER TWENTY-FIVE: Ghost Love

322 'a modern novel . . . being comic': ibid., 543.
– 'A kind of critical encyclopaedia': ibid., 559.
– 'to vent . . . my indignation': ibid., 583.
– 'so that my beautiful niece . . . seen with me"': ibid., 534.
323 Caroline was 'ill and unhappy': Desportes 1999, 75.
– Flaubert was . . . unsociable: PC 4, 568.
– such was his 'nervous susceptibility': ibid., 548.
– After a few days they moved: ibid., 551.
– He was in "a state of dryness": ibid., 557.
– Then, by a glorious . . . accident . . . *Bouvard et Pécuchet*: HH 6, 598.
– He thought it . . . '*terrifying*': PC 4, 561.
– 'He knew my hurt': Desportes 1999, 75–6.
– 'These revelations . . . to her uncle': Chevalley-Sabatier 1971, 102.
324 'For me the future holds no more dreams': PC 4, 585.
– 'You avoid your friends': ibid., 595.
– He might retaliate . . . political insults: ibid., 597.

324 'The feminine . . . nobody knows about': ibid., 599.
 – 'Sad or cheerful . . . enough for you': ibid., 611.
325 I didn't say that I scorned: ibid.
 – 'You ought to be more in harmony': ibid., 621–2.
 – 'Don't take . . . too seriously': ibid., 624.
 – 'I read difficult books': ibid., 630.
 – In a new twist . . . 'Géant Aplati': ibid., 630.
 – 'Suicide is . . . in comparison': ibid., 607.
 – 'I go from exasperation . . . being annoyed': ibid., 646.
 – 'What has been wrong with me': ibid., 650.
326 I've just dined with Flaubert: Flaubert/Sand, 313–14.
 – *Le Candidat* came to him: PC 4, 691.
 – 'It amuses me *enormously*': ibid., 717 & 719.
 – Thus we find Flaubert . . . one in the morning: ibid., 725.
327 'because it's facile': ibid., 748.
 – He probably thought . . . with a lunatic: ibid., 748.
 – I began reading . . . a great success: ibid., 752–3.
 – 'No indignation . . . even easy-going': ibid., 757 & 766.
 – 'I left the theatre . . . with a stick': ibid., 763.
 – The week before . . . had to be delayed: ibid., 770.
328 'Sitting by my fire' . . . coughing and spitting: ibid., 773.
 – 'All fops . . . the poetic bits': ibid., 779.
 – The author consoled himself: ibid.
 – 'I felt like a criminal': ibid., 781.
 – His friends and the theatre manager . . . out of it: Steegmuller & Bray 1993, 339.
329 'quite philosophical on the surface': PC 4, 1024.
 – They were all failed dramatists: ibid., 815.
 – 'We began with a long discussion': Pages, 207.
 – 'avalanche of stupidity': PC 4, 794.
 – relentlessly boring . . . Faust: Nadeau 1980, 224
 – Beneath it all . . . sign of disdain' PC 4, 795.
 – 'that is how far . . . takes me': ibid., 793.
 – 'to get some air, clear my head': ibid., 799.
 – He felt morose and empty-headed: ibid., 839.
330 'insulting the imbeciles': ibid., 820.
 – 'sweating like a pig . . . every twenty paces': ibid., 819.
 – 'I was tempted . . . express my feelings': ibid., 820.
 – 'You begin to think . . . Most uplifting': ibid., 822.
 – 'I tremble at the thought': ibid., 842.
 – In a gentle mockery . . . authentic relic: ibid., 846.
 – 'the colour of ebony': ibid., 868.
 – Living from hand to mouth: ibid., 871.
 – 'When you have . . . gloomy speculations': ibid., 901.
 – 'trying to put the ocean in a bottle': HH 16, 241.
 – 'I worry about your way of life': PC 4, 883.
 – 'The unhappier . . . childhood is sacred': ibid., 895.
331 'Don't tell me . . . germinate anything': ibid., 899.
 – 'describe your martyrdom': ibid., 904.
 – 'a sign of decrepitude': ibid., 909.
 – 'like a leper': ibid., 917.

331 'The sound was inexpressibly sweet': ibid., 926.
332 'roving twinges of gout': ibid., 924.
  – 'I'm bone-weary': ibid., 800.
  – Upset by the storm . . . the next day: ibid., 931.
  – 'full of sacred memories': ibid., 945.
  – 'I have spent my life depriving my heart': ibid., 931.
  – 'At best we shall have hardly enough': ibid., 940.
  – 'somewhat imprudent . . . very bad luck': ibid., 943.
  – His debts . . . a half-million francs: ibid., 945.
  – 'Dark days are coming': ibid., 942.
  – 'at a most advantageous price': ibid., 952.
  – 'last patch of land': ibid., 955.
333 'save my poor nephew': ibid., 951.
  – Others might . . . get away with it: ibid., 949.
  – He kept choking . . . 'with misery': HH 15, 456.
  – 'I spent Wednesday night . . . that line the road': PC 4, 958.
  – 'a good old-fashioned inn' . . . at every meal: ibid., 966.
  – Flaubert's hands . . . separately: ibid., 959.
  – He kept sobbing: ibid., 958.
  – He went swimming in the sea: ibid., 960.
  – Waking . . . a bitter moment: ibid., 961.
  – Flaubert sat in his room: ibid., 983.
334 'rootless, drifting along': ibid., 961.
  – 'A man weeping over his money': ibid., 970 & 971.
  – 'The idea of accepting . . . repugnant': ibid., 975.
  – 'do something . . . appeal to everyone': ibid., 976.
  – 'I will have finished it . . . February': HH 15, 432.
  – 'There have been such rumours': ibid.
335 'They value everything that I despise': PC 4, 1000.
  – 'One aspect of your life . . . one who doesn't exist': Steegmuller & Bray 1993, 385.
  – I kept telling you: ibid.,
  – 'I've been on the point of throwing it': ibid., 386.
  – You always . . . as its pope: HH 15, 435.
  – 'You will see . . . this little work': Steegmuller & Bray 1993, 398.

CHAPTER TWENTY-SIX: Alchemist with Parrot

337 'I wept like a calf': HH 15, 460.
  – 'In the little country cemetery' . . . of her novels: ibid., 458.
  – 'If I did not stay on longer': ibid., 459.
  – 'being able to settle . . . self-respect': ibid., 504.
  – Returning to Croisset . . . as a child: ibid., 453.
  – 'To tell the truth . . . finish it': ibid., 457.
338 The Story of a Simple Heart . . . being one myself: ibid., 458.
  – 'At the moment . . . his glass eyes': ibid., 471.
  – 'The sight of the thing . . . parrothood': ibid., 476.
  – 'I'm going to bring Julie': ibid., 471.
  – Thin and frail . . . around the garden: ibid., 475.
  – On his table . . . prayer books: ibid., 480.
  – 'Before dinner . . . the Seine': ibid., 473.

338 'like a young man': ibid., 477.
  - 'In the night . . . endless rumbling': ibid., 463.
339 'One day . . . I shall explode': ibid., 481.
  - 'I've been seriously and secretly ill': ibid., 484.
  - As proof of his new powers: ibid., 482.
  - 'Yesterday at one . . . this autumn': ibid., 485.
  - 'an encyclopaedia of human stupidity': HH 16, 150.
340 'Writing was rather like roadmending . . . day after day': HH 15, 583.
  - 'like an old cab-horse, weary but ever willing': HH 16, 61.
  - 'I who detest . . . irony of fate': ibid., 95
  - 'Sometimes . . . so weary': ibid., 358
  - 'Talking about the old days . . . fresh air': HH 15, 529.
  - 'I gaze at her . . . rise up in me': HH 16, 126.
  - A miniature . . . mantelpiece of his study: HH 15, 530.
341 'A gentleman being wanked off . . . the Eastern Question': ibid., 521.
  - Herodias . . . like a Delacroix: Roger des Genettes, Lettres à Gustave Flaubert, 253.
342 Or was it a heart attack . . . the young housemaid: Douchin 1984, 240.
  - Death took him . . . had finished him: Desportes 1999, 166.
  - At Croisset . . . not for a second suspected: Steegmuller 1950, 123–4.
343 This morning Pouchet . . . shelves of the bookcase: Pages, 256–7.
344 'seeing yellow': Lottmann 1989, 336.
  - On Saturday 8th May . . . and died: Du Camp 1882, 2:549–50.
  - Du Camp hinted menacingly . . . epilepsy: ibid., 548.

CHAPTER TWENTY-SEVEN: Endings

346 The document . . . constellation of things: 'Inventaire diplomatique', in Bulletin Flaubert 1: April 2001.

Select Bibliography

Affiches, annonces et avis divers de la ville et arrondissement de Sens, Sens, Société archaéologique de Sens.

Abelanet, R. and Saint-Maur, P. de (1991), 'Le musée Dupuytren, passé et present', *Histoire des Sciences Médicales* 25, 127–31.

Ackerknecht, E. H. (1948), 'Anti-contagionism between 1821 and 1867', *Bulletin of the History of Medicine* XXII, Sept.–Oct. 1948, 562–93.

Ackerknecht, E. H. (1967), *Medicine at the Paris Hospital 1794–1848*, Baltimore.

Agulhon, M. (1981), 'Peut-on lire en historien *L'Education sentimentale?' Histoire et langage dans* L'Education sentimentale, Paris, Soc. d'Ed. d'Enseignement Supérieur, 35–41.

Ahearn, E. (1988), 'The Magic Cigar Case: Emma Bovary and Karl Marx', *Women in French Literature*, Saratoga, CA, Anima Libri, 181–8.

Amelinckx, F. (1978), 'La Réaction de Flaubert au mythe romantique du voyage en Orient', *Travel, Quest, and Pilgrimage as a Literary Theme: Studies in Honor of Reino Virtanen*, Lincoln, Soc. of Sp. & Sp.-Amer. Studies, 191–200.

Andrieu, L. (1969), 'Bouilhet, le fidèle ami', *Les Amis de Flaubert*, (Dec. 1969), 8–13.

Andrieu, L. (1967), 'Les maisons de la famille: Flaubert dans la région rouennaise', *Les Amis de Flaubert* 31, 9–14.

Andrieu, L. D. (1967), 'La nomination du Père de Flaubert comme chirurgien-chef de l'Hôtel-Dieu de Rouen', *Les Amis de Flaubert* 37, 38–42.

Aronson, R. (1988), 'L'Idiot de la famille: The Ultimate Sartre?' *Critical Essays on Jean-Paul Sartre*, Boston, G. K. Hall & Co., 119–36.

Arout, F. (1969), 'Maupassant chez Flaubert', *Europe: Revue Littéraire Mensuelle* 482, 146–62.

Aubé, R. (1885), 'Le cochon de Saint-Antoine', *Journal de Rouen*, 18 November 1885, p. 3.

Auriant, C. (1943), *Koutchouk-Hanem: L'Almée de Flaubert*, Paris, Nizet.

Baehrel, R. (1952), 'La haine de classe en temps d'epidémie', *Annales E.S.C.* 7, 357–60.

Bailbe, J.-M. and J. Pierrot (1981), *Flaubert et Maupassant: Ecrivains normands*, Paris, PU de France.

Bailbe, J.-M. (1982), 'Salammbô de Reyer: du roman à l'opéra', *Romantisme*, no. 38, 4e trimestre, p. 93–106.

Baillie, K. and Salmon, T. (1997a), *France: The Rough Guide*, London, Rough Guides.

Baillie, K. and Salmon, T. (1997b), *Paris: The Rough Guide*, London, Rough Guides.

Baldick, R. (1959), *The Life and Times of Frederick Lemaitre*, London, Hamish Hamilton.

Baldick, R. (1962), *Pages from the Goncourt Journal*, London, OUP.

Bally, Charles (1912), 'Le Style indirect libre en français moderne', *Germanisch-romanisch Monatsschrift*, 4 (1912), 549–56, 597–606.

Bancquart, M.-C. (1969), 'Croisset, haut-lieu de la littérature', *Europe: Revue Littéraire Mensuelle* (485–7) 129–37.

Bancquart, M.-C. (1969), 'Louis Bouilhet le poète, l'auteur dramatique, l'ami', *Les Amis de Flaubert* 34, 5–10.

Bancquart, M.-C. (1983), 'L'Espace urbain de *L'Education sentimentale* interieurs, exterieurs', *Flaubert, la femme, la ville*, Paris, PU de France, 143–57.

Bancquart, M.-C. (1971), 'Un notable rouennais contemporain de Flaubert et de Maupassant. Lettres inédites', *Revue d'Histoire Littéraire de la France* 71, 489–92.

Bardèche, M. (1974), *L'Oeuvre de Flaubert d'après ses carnets, ses études, ses scenarios, sa correspondance inédite*, Paris, Sept Couleurs.

Barnes, H. (1981), *Sartre and Flaubert*, London, University of Chicago Press.

Barnes, J. (1983), 'Flaubert and Rouen', *The Listener*, 18 August 1983, 14–15.

Barnes, J. (1986), 'Dear Mole: Flaubert/Turgenev', *London Review of Books*, VIII, i (23 Jan. 1986), lvi–lviii.

Bargues-Rollins, Y. (1998), *Le pas de Flaubert: une danse macabre*, Paris, Champion.

Barrell, J. (1991), 'Death on the Nile: Fantasy and the Literature of Tourism 1840–1860', *Essays in Criticism*, vol. XLI, no. 2, April 1991, 97–127.

Bart, B. (1953), 'Is Maxime Du Camp a reliable Witness?', *Modern Language Review* XLVII, 17–25.

Bart, B. F. (1963), 'Louis Bouilhet, Flaubert's "accoucheur" ', *Symposium* 17, 183–201.

Bart, B. (1967), *Flaubert*, Syracuse, Syracuse University Press.

Bart, B. (1973), 'Louis Bouilhet and the Redaction of Salammbô', *Symposium* 27, 197–213.

Barthes, R. (1968,1970)), 'Flaubert et la phrase', *Linguistic Studies Presented to André Martinet on the Occasion of His Sixtieth Birthday. Part Two: Indo-European Linguistics*, New York, Ling. Circle of New York, 48–54.

Baruk, H. (1988), 'L'oeuvre d'Esquirol et la régression actuelle', *Histoire des Sciences Médicales* 22, 155–8.

Bascelli, A. (1977), 'Flaubert and the Brothers Goncourt', *Nineteenth Century French Studies* 5, 277–95.

Bassan, F. (1964), 'Chateaubriand, Lamartine, Nerval, and Flaubert in Palestine', *University of Toronto Quarterly* (33), 142–63.

Bassan, F. (1965), 'Chateaubriand, Lamartine, Nerval et Flaubert en Terre-sainte', *Revue des Sciences Humaines* (120), 493–513.

Baudelaire, C. (1961), *Oeuvres complètes*, ed. Y.-G. Le Dantec, Paris, Gallimard.

Beaumont, J.G. (1996), *Blackwell Dictionary of Neuropsychology*, Oxford, Blackwell.

Bellet, R., ed. (1982), *Femmes de lettres au XIXe siècle autour de Louise Colet*, Lyon, Presses Universitaires de Lyon.

Bem, J. (1980), 'Sur des hiatus temporels dans *L'Education sentimentale*', RHLF 80, 626–8.

Benezit, E., ed. (1954), *Dictionnaire des peintres, sculpteurs, dessinateurs et graveurs*, Paris, Librairie Grund.

Benjamin, W. (1989), *Paris capitale du XIXe siècle*, Paris, Editions du Cerf.

Berlioz, H. (1995), *Selected Letters*, London, Faber and Faber.

Bernheimer, C. (1989), *Figures of Ill-Repute: Representing Prostitution in Nineteenth-Century France*, London, Harvard University Press.

Berthier, P. (1981), 'La Seine, le Nil et le voyage du rien', *Histoire et langage dans* L'Education sentimentale, Paris, Soc. d'Ed. d'Enseignement Supérieur, 3–16.

Bevernis, C. (1981), 'Historicité et actualité dans le roman de Flaubert *Salammbô*', *Flaubert et Maupassant: Ecrivains normands*, Paris, PU de France, 255–63.

Biasi, P.-M. D., ed. (1988), *Carnets de travail de Gustave Flaubert*, Paris, Balland.

Biasi, P.-M. D., ed. (1991), *Gustave Flaubert: Voyage en Egypte*, Paris, Grasset.

Bierman, J. (1988), *Napoleon III and his Carnival Empire*, London, John Murray.

Bismut, R. (1979), 'Un Cas privilégié de filiation littéraire: Une Vie de Guy de Maupassant', *Essais sur Flaubert: En l'honneur du professeur Don Demorest*, Paris, Nizet.

Block, H. (1965), 'Flaubert's Travels in Relation to His Art', *North Carolina Folklore Journal* 131–2, 64–72.

Boime, A. (1995), *Art and the French Commune: Imagining Paris after War and Revolution*, Princeton, NJ, Princeton UP.

Bollème, G. (1964, 1972), *La leçon de Flaubert*, Paris, Juillard.

Bollème, G. (1966), *Le Second Volume de* Bouvard et Pécuchet, Paris, Denoel.

Bolster (1977), 'Autour de *L'Education sentimentale*. Flaubert et les évènements de 1848', *Les Amis de Flaubert* 50, 22–6.

Bonaccorso, G. (1963), 'Sulla cronologia del viaggio in Oriente di Flaubert e Du Camp', *Studi Francesi* (7), 495–99.

Bonaccorso, G. (1996), 'Synonymes et l'instrument ronfle', *Voix de l'écrivain*, Toulouse, PU du Mirail. 117–27.

Bonaccorso, G. and R.-M. Di Stefano, ed. (1978), *Lèttres inédites à Gustave Flaubert*, Messina, EDAS.

Bonaparte, M. (1939), 'A Defence of Biography', *International Journal of Psychoanalysis* 20, 231–40.

Bood, M. and S. Grand (1986), *L'Indomptable Louise Colet*, Paris, Pierre Horay.

Bornecque, Jacque-Henry (1964), 'Dans l'intimité des Maupassant. Une femme méconnue: Laure de Maupassant', *RHLF*, Oct.-Dec. 1964, 623–32.

Bosquet, A. (1845), *La Normandie romanesque et merveilleuse traditions, légendes et superstitions de cette province*, Paris, Taschener.

Bosquet, A. (1955), 'Achille-Cléophas Flaubert père Exemption de Service Militaire', *Les Amis de Flaubert* 6.

Bosquet, A. (1965), 'La critique d'Amélie Bosquet sur *L'Education sentimentale*', *Les Amis de Flaubert* 26, 19–23.

Bouilhet, L., *Notes autobiographiques*, Rouen, Bibliothèque municipale de Rouen.

Bouilhet, L. (1967), *Lèttres à Louise Colet*, Rouen, Publications de l'université de Rouen.

Bouquet, F. V. (1895), *Souvenirs du Collège de Rouen par un élève de pension (1829–1835)*, Rouen, Cagniard.

Bouteron, M. (1934), 'Marie Dorval', *Muses romantiques*, Paris, Plon.

Bowie, K. and Polino, M-N. (1993), 'Vies, morts et renaissances de la gare d'Austerlitz', *13e arrondissement, une ville dans Paris*, exhibition catalogue, ed. Langlois, G-A., Paris, 134–47.

Briggs, A. (1961), 'Cholera and Society in the Nineteenth Century', *Past and Present* 19 (April 1961), 76–96.

Brombert, V. (1966), *The Novels of Flaubert: A Study of Themes and Techniques*, Princeton, Princeton UP.

Brombert, V. (1975), *Flaubert*, Paris, Seuil.

Brombert, V. (1979), 'Usure et rupture chez Flaubert: L'Exemple de "Novembre"', *Essais sur Flaubert: En l'honneur du professeur Don Demorest*, Paris, Nizet.

Brombert, V. (1984), *Victor Hugo and the Visionary Novel*, Cambridge, Mass., Harvard UP.

Brown, F. (1996), *Zola*, London, Macmillan.

Bruneau, J. (1962), *Les Débuts littéraires de Gustave Flaubert 1831–1845*, Paris, Armand Collin.

Bruneau, J. (1965), 'Les Deux voyages de Gustave Flaubert en Italie', *North Carolina Folklore Journal* 13(1–2), 164–80.

Bruneau, J. (1968), 'Une lèttre inédite de Henry James à Gustave Flaubert Autour de Monckton Milnes, Lord Houghton', *Revue de Littérature Comparée* 42, 520–33.

Bruneau, J. (1972), *Gustave Flaubert: Les sept fils du derviche conte oriental*, Paris, Editions Denoel.

Bruneau, J. (1972), *Album Flaubert*, Paris, Gallimard.

Bruneau, J., ed. (1973), *Flaubert: Correspondance I (janvier 1830 à avril 1851)*, Paris, Gallimard.

Bruneau, J. (1973), *Le 'Conte oriental' de Gustave Flaubert Documents inédits*, Paris, Denoel, Lettres nouvelles.

Bruneau, J. (1979), 'L'Education sentimentale: Roman autobiographique?' *Essais sur Flaubert: En l'honneur du professeur Don Demorest*, Paris, Nizet.

Bruneau, J. (1980), *Flaubert: Correspondance II (juillet 1851– décembre 1858)*, Paris, Gallimard.

Bruneau, J. (1984), 'Louise Colet, Maxime Du Camp, Gustave Flaubert et Garibaldi', *Mélanges offerts à la mémoire de Franco Simone*, Geneva, Editions Slatkine, 469–83.

Bruneau, J. (1991), *Flaubert: Correspondance III (janvier 1859–décembre 1868)*, Paris, Gallimard.

Bruneau, J. (1998). *Flaubert: Correspondance IV (janvier 1869–décembre 1875)*, Paris, Gallimard.

Burguet, F.-A. (1967), 'Tristesse sanguine', *Cahiers de la Compagnie Madeleine Renaud Jean-Louis Barrault* 59, 106–12.

Butor, M. (1984), *Improvisations sur Flaubert*, Mainz, Editions de la différence.

Butor, M. and F. W. J. Hemmings (1970), 'Special Issue: Gustave Flaubert', *L'Esprit Créateur*, Baton Rouge, LA 101.

Cabanis, G. (1802), *Rapports du physique et du moral de l'homme*, Paris.

Caminiti, L., ed. (1966), Dictionnaire des idées reçues; Ed. diplomatique des trois manuscrits de Rouen. En appendice: Les Idées reçues dans l'oeuvre de Flaubert, Naples; Paris, Liguori; Nizet.

Campbell, S. (1978), *The Second Empire Revisited*, New Brunswick, N.J., Rutgers University Press.

Cappello, M. L., ed. (1996), *Louis Bouilhet: Lèttres à Gustave Flaubert*, Paris, CNRS editions.

Carlut, C. (1979), *Essais sur Flaubert: En l'honneur du professeur Don Demorest*, Paris, Nizet.

Carlut, C., P.-H. Dube, et al. (1979), *A Concordance to Flaubert's* La Tentation de Saint Antoine, New York, Garland.

Carlut, C., P.-H. Dube, et al. (1979). *A Concordance to Flaubert's* Trois Contes, New York, Garland.

Caute, D. (1974), 'The Refusal to Be Good: Sartre on Flaubert', *Collisions: Essays and Reviews*, London, Quartet Books, 73–87.

Cento, A. (1962), 'Flaubert e la Rivoluzione di febbraio', *Rivista di Letterature Moderne e Comparate* (15), 270–85.

Cento, A. (1963), 'Flaubert e la Rivoluzione di febbraio', *Rivista di Letterature Moderne e Comparate* (16), 20–49.

Cervantes, M. (1828), *Le Don Quixote en estampes . . . représentées par 34 jolies gravures, avec un texte abrégé de Florian*, Paris, Eymery, Frugger et Cie.

Chaline, J.-P. (1969), 'A la recherche de la Bourgeoisie Rouennaise du XIXe siècle', *Les Amis de Flaubert* (December 1969), 18–30.

Chaline, J.-P. (1976), 'Rouen au milieu du XIXe siècle la révolution de 1848', *Rouen*, III.

Chaline, J.-P. (1981), 'Le Milieu culturel rouennais au temps de Flaubert', *Flaubert et Maupassant: Ecrivains normands*, Paris, PU de France, 17–25.

Chaline, J.-P. (1982), *Les Bourgeois de Rouen*, Paris, Presses de la Fondation nationale des Sciences Politiques.

Chartier, R. (1984), 'Culture as Appropriation: Popular Cultural Uses in Early Modern France', *Understanding Popular Culture*, Berlin, 229–53.

Chateaubriand, R. (1969), *Oeuvres romanesques et voyages*, 2 vols., ed. M. Regard, Paris, Gallimard.

Chevalier, L., ed. (1958), *Le choléra la première epidémie du xixe siècle*, Bibliothèque de la Révolution de 1848, La Roche-sur-Yon.

Chevalley-Sabatier, L. (1971), *Gustave Flaubert et sa nièce Caroline*, Paris, La Pensée universelle.

Chevreuil, C. (1966), 'Nogent-sur-Seine dans la vie et l'oeuvre de Flaubert', *Les Amis de Flaubert* 28, 5–42.

Chotard, L. (1990), *Nadar, caricatures et photographies*, Paris, Maison de Balzac.

Christiansen, R. (1996), *Tales of the New Babylon: Paris 1869–1875*, London, Minerva.

Clark, T. J. (1973), *The Absolute Bourgeois: Artists and Politics in France 1848–1851*, London, Thames and Hudson.

Clark, T. J. (1985), *The Painting of Modern Life: Paris in the Art of Manet and his followers*, London, Thames and Hudson.

Claudon, F. (1981), 'A propos des voyages de Flaubert Le Voyage en Italie et en Suisse' (1845), *Flaubert et Maupassant: Ecrivains normands*, Paris, PU de France, 91–109.

Clayton, P. A. (1982), *The Rediscovery of Ancient Egypt*, London, Thames and Hudson.

Clébert, J.-P. (1986), *Louise Colet, ou la muse*, Paris, Editions de la Renaissance.

Cogny, P. (1981), 'Flaubert et la qualification de la femme dans *L'Education sentimentale*', *Histoire et langage dans* L'Education sentimentale, Paris, Soc. d'Ed. d'Enseignement Supérieur, 25–33.

Colet, L. (1967), 'Un poème méconnu de Louise Colet', *Les Amis de Flaubert* 37, 19–36.

Collins-Weitz, M. (1979), 'Flaubert et Montaigne Parallèles', *Essais sur Flaubert: En l'honneur du professeur Don Demorest*, Paris, Nizet, 79–96.

Colwell, D. J. (1988), *Bibliographie des études sur G. Flaubert: 1921–1959*, Egham, Runnymede Books.

Colwell, D. J. (1988), *Bibliographie des études sur G. Flaubert: 1960–1982*, Egham, Runnymede Books.

Colwell, D. J. (1989), *Bibliographie des études sur G. Flaubert: 1837–1920*, Egham, Runnymede Books.

Commanville, C. (1895), *Souvenirs sur Gustave Flaubert*, Paris, Ferraud.

Corbin, A. (1978), *Filles de noce: misère sexuelle et prostitution*.

Corbin, A. (1995), *Time, Desire and Horror*, Cambridge, Polity Press.

Cornu, C. (1991), 'Le personnel parlementaire dans l'Eure sous la Troisième République', *Etudes normandes* 3, 17–38.

Crossley, C. (1993), *French Historians and Romanticism*, London, Routledge.

Czyba, L. (1983), *La Femme dans les romans de Flaubert: mythes et idéologie*, Lyon, Presses universitaires de Lyon.

Debray-Genette, R. (1974), 'Flaubert Science et écriture', *Littérature* 15, 41–51.

Debray-Genette, R., C. Duchet, et al. (1980), *Flaubert à l'oeuvre*, Paris, Flammarion.

De Goncourt, E. and J. de Goncourt (1956), *Journal*, Paris, Fasquelle-Flammarion.

De Heureux, A. D. (1995), '*Salammbô*: entre un orientalisme romantique et un orientalisme fin de siècle', *Carthage: l'histoire, sa trace et son echo*, Paris, Paris Musées, 128–37.

De Mandriargues, A.-P. (1967), 'I Une Hallucination merveilleuse', *Cahiers de la Compagnie Madeleine Renaud Jean-Louis Barrault* 59, 3–5.

Demorest, D. (1940), 'Les Suppressions dans le texte de *Madame Bovary*', *Mélanges de philologie et d'histoire littéraire offerts à Edmond Huguet*, Paris, Boivin, 373–86.

Demorest, D.-L. (1967), *L'Expression figurée et symbolique dans l'oeuvre de Gustave Flaubert*, Geneva, Slatkine.

Descharmes, R. (1924), *Alfred Le Poittevin*, Paris, Les Presses Françaises.

De Senneville, G. (1996), *Maxime Du Camp*, Paris, Stock.

Desloges, D. (1981), 'Le Goût du théâtre chez Gustave Flaubert à travers les oeuvres romanesques', *Flaubert et Maupassant: Ecrivains normands*, Paris, PU de France, 127–42.

Desportes, M., ed. (1999), *Gustave Flaubert par sa nièce Caroline Franklin Grout*. Rouen, Publications de l'Université de Rouen.

Dewachter, M. and D. Oster, eds. (1987), *Un Voyageur en Egypte vers 1850 'Le Nil' de Maxime Du Camp*, Paris, Sand/Corti.

Di Stefano, R. (1979), 'Maxime Du Camp d'après sa correspondance avec Flaubert', *Les Amis de Flaubert* 54, 7–18.

Dixon, L. S. (1984), 'Bosch's "St. Anthony Triptych" – An Apothecary's Apotheosis', *Art Journal*, vol. 44, no. 22, 119–31.

Dijkstra, B. (1986), *Idols of Perversity*, New York, Oxford University Press.

Donato, E. (1976), 'Flaubert and the Question of History: Notes for a Critical Anthology', *Modern Language Notes* 91, 850–70.

Donato, E. (1993), 'Flaubert and the Question of History: The Orient', *The Script of Decadence*, New York, OUP.

Donnard, J.-H. (1978), 'George Sand et Gustave Flaubert face à la Révolution de 48', *Europe: Revue Littéraire Mensuelle* 587, 41–7.

Douchin, J.-L. (1981), 'L'Influence des publications populaires sur l'oeuvre de Flaubert', *Flaubert et Maupassant: Ecrivains normands*, Paris, PU de France. 27–38.

Douchin, J. L. (1984), *La vie érotique de Flaubert*, Paris, Carrère.

Dranch, S. (1982), 'Flaubert: Portraits d'un ironiste', *Nineteenth Century French Studies* 111–2, 106–16.

Dubosc, G. (1908), 'La Tentation de Saint Antoine à la foire', *Journal de Rouen*, 1 October 1908, p. 5.

Dubosc, G. (1913), 'La famille de Flaubert', *Journal de Rouen*, 26 May 1913, p. 2.

Dubuc, A. (1962), 'Les quotidiens Rouennais et la mort de Flaubert', *Les Amis de Flaubert* 20, 11–22.

Dubuc, A. (1964), 'La nomination du père Flaubert en 1806 à l'Hôtel-Dieu de Rouen', *Les Amis de Flaubert* 24, 43–6.

Dubuc, A. (1964), 'Une Amitié littéraire: Gustave Flaubert et Emile Zola', *Les Cahiers Naturalistes* (28), 129–36.

Dubuc, A. (1965), 'Flaubert et la Rouennaise Amélie Bosquet', *Les Amis de Flaubert* 27, 19–31.

Dubuc, A. (1969), 'Flaubert, un Rouennais mal-aimé', *Europe: Revue Littéraire Mensuelle* (485–87), 140–50.

Dubuc, A. (1969), 'Une déclaration politique de Bouilhet en 1848', *Les Amis de Flaubert* (December 1969), 14–17.

Dubuc, A. (1970), 'L'enterrement du père de Gustave Flaubert', *Les Amis de Flaubert* 37, 34–6.

Dubuc, A. (1972), 'Trouville-sur-Mer en 1846', *Les Amis de Flaubert* 40, 44–5.

Dubuc, A. (1973), 'Les dessous de la lèttre de Flaubert au Conseil Municipal de Rouen', *Les Amis de Flaubert* 43, 17–25.

Dubuc, A. (1976), 'La critique rouennaise des "Trois contes"', *Les Amis de Flaubert* 48, 29–32.

Dubuc, A. (1978), 'Echos: lèttres de Chéruel à Michelet', *Les Amis de Flaubert* 52, 41–3.

Dubuc, A. (1980), 'La Bibliothèque générale du père de Gustave Flaubert', in *Les Rouennais et la famille Flaubert*, Rouen, Les Amis de Flaubert, 38–49.

Dubuc, A. (1981), 'L'Amitié entre Flaubert, Zola et Maupassant', *Les Cahiers Naturalistes* (55), 24–30.

Du Camp, M. (1860), *Le Nil, Egypte et Nubie*, Paris, Bourdilliat.

Du Camp, M. (1876), *Souvenirs de l'année 1848*, Paris, Hachette.

Du Camp, M. (1882), *Souvenirs littéraires*, Paris, Hachette.

Du Camp, M. (1978), *Lettres inédites à Gustave Flaubert*, Messina, Edas.

Duchet, C. (1980), 'Flaubert premier lecteur de Sade', *La Quinzaine Littéraire* 324, 13, 15.

Duchet, C. (1984), 'L'Ecriture de jeunesse dans le texte flaubertien', *Nineteenth Century French Studies* 123, 297–312.

Duckwood, C. (1968), 'Flaubert and the Legend of St. Julian. A Non-Exclusive View of Sources', *French Studies: A Quarterly Review* 22, 107–13.

Dufour, P. (1988), 'Entendre des voix', *La Revue des Lèttres Modernes* 865–72, 105–122.

Dumesnil, R. (1947), *Gustave Flaubert l'homme et l'oeuvre*, Paris, Desclée Debrouwer & Co.

Dunet, M. (1975), 'Présence normande dans l'oeuvre de Flaubert', *Les Amis de Flaubert* 46, 5–24.

Duquette, J.-P. (1979), 'Flaubert politique', *Essais sur Flaubert: En l'honneur du professeur Don Demorest*, Paris, Nizet.

Durry, M.-J. (1950), *Flaubert et ses projets inédits*, Paris, Nizet.

Echard, W. E., ed. (1985), *Historical Dictionary of the French Second Empire*, New York, Greenwood Press.

Edel, Leon (1961), 'The Biographer and Psychoanalysis', *International Journal of Psychoanalysis* 42, 458–66.

Emelina, J. (1980), 'Théâtre et politique, *Le Candidat* de Flaubert', *Revue d'Histoire du Théâtre* 33, 248–60.

Ender, E. (1995), *Sexing the Mind: Nineteenth Century Fictions of Hysteria*, Ithaca, NY, Cornell UP.

Fairlie, A. (1969), 'Pellérin et le thème de l'art dans *L'Education sentimentale*', *Europe Revue Littéraire Mensuelle* (485–7), 38–51.

Fairlie, A. (1974), 'Flaubert and Some Painters of His Time', *The Artist and the Writer in France: Essays in Honour of Jean Seznec*, London, Oxford UP, 111–25.

Fairlie, A. (1981), 'Flaubert et la conscience du réel', *Imagination and Language: Collected Essays on Constant, Baudelaire, Nerval and Flaubert*, Cambridge, Cambridge UP, 325–37.

Fairlie, A. and A. Green (1973), 'Deciphering Flaubert's Manuscripts: The "Club de l'honnête homme" Edition', *French Studies: A Quarterly Review* 27, 287–315.

Fairlie, A. (1981), *Imagination and Language: Collected Essays on Constant, Baudelaire, Nerval and Flaubert*, Cambridge, Cambridge UP.

Fairlie, A. (1983), 'La Quête de la femme à travers la ville dans quelques oeuvres de Flaubert', *Flaubert, la femme, la ville*, Paris, PU de France, 77–87.

Falconer, G. (1988), 'Le Travail de "débalzacienisation" dans la rédaction de *Madame Bovary*', *La Revue des Lèttres Modernes* 865–72, 123–56.

Falconer, G. (1990), 'Le Statut de l'histoire dans *L'Education sentimentale*', *Littérature et revolutions en France*, Amsterdam, Rodopi. 106–20.

Faure, O. (1984), 'La Médicine gratuite au XIXe siècle: De la charité à l'assistance', *Histoire, économie et société* 3, 593–608.

Favier, J., ed. (1989), *Chronicle of the French Revolution*, Harlow, Essex, Longman.

Felman, S. (1981), 'La Signature de Flaubert: La Légende de Saint Julien l'Hospitalier', *Revue des Sciences Humaines* (181), 39–57.

Felman, S. (1984), 'Flaubert's Signature: The Legend of Saint Julian the Hospitable', *Flaubert and Postmodernism*, Lincoln, Univ. of Nebraska Press, 46–75.

Ferguson, J. A. (1986), 'The Comices and the Fête: A Sadean Allusion in Flaubert's *Madame Bovary*', *French Studies Bulletin* (19), 10–12.

Festa-McCormick, D. (1980), 'Emma Bovary's Masculinization Convention of Clothes and Morality of Conventions', *Women and Literature* 1, 223–35.

Finlay, J. (1983), 'Flaubert in Egypt', *The Hudson Review* 363 (Autumn), 496–509.

Flaubert, A-C. (1810), *De la manière de conduire les malades avant et après les opérations chirurgicales*, Rouen: Musée Flaubert.

Flaubert, G. (1958), *La Queue de la poire de la boule de Monseigneur*, Paris, Nizet.

Flaubert, G. (1967), *Cahiers Intimes [Intimate Notebooks] 1840–1841*, Garden City, NY, Doubleday.

Foucault, M. (1973), *The Birth of the Clinic*, London, Tavistock.

Foucault, M. (1967), 'Un "Fantastique" de bibliothèque', *Cahiers de la Compagnie Madeleine Renaud Jean-Louis Barrault* 59, 7–30.

Fournier, A. (1969), 'De Rouen à Croisset', *Europe Revue Littéraire Mensuelle* (485–7), 252–68.

Fournier, L. (1979), 'Sartre sur Flaubert *Le Dictionnaire des idées reçues*', *Si Que* 4, 169–74.

Fournier, L. (1995), 'Trois lecteurs de *Bouvard et Pécuchet*: Maupassant, Thibaudet, Sabatier', *French Studies* 491 (Jan.), 29–48.

France, P. (1995), *The New Oxford Companion to Literature in French*. Oxford, OUP.

François, A. (1953), 'Gustave Flaubert, Maxime Du Camp et la Révolution de 1848', *RHLF* (Jan.–Mars).

Frank, C. (1995), 'Commemorative Peasants: Sand, Turgenev, and Flaubert's "Un Coeur simple" ', *George Sand Studies*, Hempstead, NY, 141–2 (Fall), 59–73.

Franklin-Grout, C. (1926), 'Souvenirs intimes', *Gustave Flaubert: Correspondance Première Série 1830–1846*, Paris, Conard, v–xlv.

Frère, E. (1908), *Louis Bouilhet*.

Frey, J. (1981), 'Un Inédit de Flaubert "La Lutte du sacerdoce et de l'empire" (1837)', *RHLF* 814–5, 702–719.

Furst, L. (1993), 'Realism and Hypertrophy: A Study of Three Medico-Historical "Cases" ', *Nineteenth Century French Studies* 221–2 (Fall–Winter), 29–47.

Gaignebet, C. (1972), 'Le Cycle annuel des fêtes à Rouen au milieu du XVIe siecle', *Les Fêtes de la Renaissance*, Paris, CNRS, 569–78.

Gaillard, F. and T. Reiss (1980), 'An Unspeakable (Hi)story', *Yale French Studies* 59, 137–54.

Galérant, G. (1969), 'Flaubert vu par les médecins d'aujourd'hui', *Europe Revue Littéraire Mensuelle* (485–7), 107–12.

Galérant, G. (1955), 'Le Docteur Achille-Cléophas Flaubert', *Les Amis de Flaubert* 7, 25–32.

Galérant, G. (1962), 'Quel diagnostic aurions-nous fait si nous avons soigné Gustave Flaubert?', *Les Amis de Flaubert* 20, 6–10.

Galérant, G. (1979), 'Plaidoyer pour Monsieur Homais', *Les Amis de Flaubert* 55, 34–9.

Genette, G. (1963), 'Le Travail de Flaubert', *Tel Quel* 14, 51–57.

Genette, G. (1983), 'Vues de Rouen (Apocryphe)', *Poetique Revue de Théorie et d'Analyse Littéraires* 1455 (Sept.), 378–380.

Genette, G. (1984), 'Demotivation in Hérodias', *Flaubert and Postmodernism, Lincoln, U of Nebraska Press, 193–201*.

Gérard-Gailly, L. (1934), *Les Véhemences de Louise Colet*, Paris, Mercure de France.

Gérard-Gailly, L. (1944), *Le Grand Amour de Flaubert*, Paris, Aubier.

Germain, J. P., ed. (1987), *Gustave Flaubert Cahier intime de jeunesse*, Paris, Nizet.

Gervais, D. (1976), 'James's Reading of *Madame Bovary*', *The Cambridge Quarterly* (7), 36–49.

Gevrey, F. (1996), 'L'Image de Voltaire dans la correspondance de Flaubert', *Voix de l'écrivain*, Toulouse, PU du Mirail, 139–49.

Girard, R. (1966), *Deceit, Desire, and the Novel Self and Other in Literary Structure*, Baltimore, Johns Hopkins UP.

Godfrey, S. (1980), 'The Fabrication of Salammbô: The Surface of the Veil', *MLN* 95, 1005–16.

Goldin, J. (1981), 'La Création flaubertienne dans les comices Déplacements genetiques', *Flaubert et Maupassant: Ecrivains normands*, Paris, PU de France, 237–53.

Goldin, J. (1984), *Les comices agricoles de Gustave Flaubert transcription intégrale et genèse dans le manuscrit g*, Geneva, Droz.

Goldstein, J. (1991), 'The Uses of Male Hysteria: Medical and Literary Discourse in Nineteenth-Century France', *Representations* 34 (Spring), 134–65.

Gothot-Mersch (1986), 'Flaubert, Nerval, Nodier et la Reine de Saba', *La Revue des Lèttres Modernes* 777–81, 125–160.

Gothot-Mersch, C. (1966), *Le Genèse de Madame Bovary*, Paris, Corti.

Gothot-Mersch, C., ed. (1972), *Madame Bovary*, Paris, Garnier.

Gothot-Mersch, C. (1982), 'Aspects de la temporalité dans les romans de Flaubert', *Flaubert: La Dimension du texte*, Manchester, Manchester UP, 6–55.

Gothot-Mersch, C., ed. (1983), *La Tentation de Saint Antoine*, Paris, Gallimard.

Gothot-Mersch, C. (1993), 'La Correspondance de Flaubert: Une Methode au fil du temps', *L'Oeuvre de l'oeuvre: Etudes sur la correspondance de Flaubert*, Paris, PU de Vincennes, 43–57.

Gothot-Mersch, C. (1996), 'Quand un romancier met un peintre à l'oeuvre: Le Portrait de Rosanette dans *L'Education sentimentale*', *Voix de l'écrivain*, Toulouse, PU du Mirail, 103–15.

Goubault, C. (1979), 'Un musicien polonais ami de Flaubert Anton Orlowski', *Les Amis de Flaubert* 54, 19–25.

Gracq, J. (1988), *Proust, Stendhal, Balzac, Flaubert, Zola*, Brussels, Complexes.

Grandpré, C. D. (1991), 'Senecal et Dussardier: La République en effigie', *The French Review: Journal of the American Association of Teachers of French*, Champaign, IL 644 (Mar.), 621–31.

Gray, E. (1980), 'The Clinical View of Life: Gustave Flaubert's *Madame Bovary*', *Medicine and Literature*, New York, Watson.

Gray, F. D. P. (1994), *Rage and Fire: A Life of Louise Colet*, London, Hamish Hamilton.

Green, A. (1980), 'Flaubert, Salgues et le *Dictionnaire des idées reçues*', *Revue d'Histoire Littéraire de la France* 80, 773–7.

Green, A. (1982), 'La Thématique de l'apprentissage chez Flaubert', *Flaubert: La Dimension du texte*, Manchester, Manchester UP, 237–52.

Green, A. (1986), 'Flaubert, Bouilhet and the Illegitimate Daughter: A Source for *L'Education sentimentale*', *French Studies* 403 (July), 304–10.

Green, A. (1993), 'Flaubert Paris, Elsewhere', *Romance Studies* 22 (Autumn), 7–15.

Greene, J. (1981), 'Structure et épistemologie dans *Bouvard et Pécuchet*', *Flaubert et le comble de l'art: Nouvelles recherches sur Bouvard et Pécuchet*, Paris, Société d'Edition d'Enseignement Supérieur, 111–128.

Griffin, R. (1988), 'The Myth of Flaubert's Ritual', *Stanford French Review* 122–3 (Fall–Winter), 287–303.

Griffin, R. (1991), 'Flaubert's Mother Rite Paradigm Lost', *Nineteenth Century French Studies* 192 (Winter), 262–78.

Griffin, R., ed. (1991), *Gustave Flaubert: Early Writings*, Lincoln, U of Nebraska Press.

Gross, D. (1985), 'Sartre's Reading of Flaubert's Politics', *Yale French Studies* 68, 127–51.

Guillemolles, A. (1998), 'Une promenade curieuse au pays d'Emma Bovary', *La Croix*, 13 August 1998.

Haig, S. (1986), *Flaubert and the Gift of Speech Dialogue and Discourse in Four 'Modern' Novels*, Cambridge, Cambridge University Press.

Hamilton, J. (1991), 'The Ideology of Place: Flaubert's Depiction of Yonville–l'Abbaye', *The French Review: Journal of the American Association of Teachers of French, Champaign, IL* 652 (Dec.), 206–15.

Harvey, D. (1985), *Paris, 1850–1870. Consciousness and the Urban Experience*, Baltimore, 63–220.

Heath, S. (1992), *Madame Bovary*, Cambridge, Cambridge University Press.

Helein-Koss, S. (1992), 'Le Trace ironique du "velours vert" dans *Madame Bovary*', *Nineteenth Century French Studies* 211–12 (Fall–Winter, 1992–3), 66–72.

Hemmings, F. (1993), *The Theatre Industry in Nineteenth Century France*, Cambridge, CUP.

Henry, G. (1980), *Promenades en Basse-Normandie avec un guide nommé Flaubert*, Paris, Corlet.

Herschberg-Pierrot, A., 'Le Cliché dans *Bouvard et Pécuchet*', *Flaubert et le comble de l'art: Nouvelles recherches sur* Bouvard et Pécuchet, Paris, Société d'Edition d'Enseignement Supérieur, 31–7.

Herschberg-Pierrot, A. (1988), *Le* Dictionnaire des idées reçues *de Flaubert*, Lille, PU de Lille.

Herschberg-Pierrot, A. (1989), 'Figures de la parodie chez Flaubert', *Dire la parodie: Colloque de Cerisy*, New York, Peter Lang. 213–30.

Herschberg-Pierrot, A. (1995), 'Les Dossiers de Bouvard et Pécuchet', *Romanic Review* 863 (May), 537–49.

Hervouet, Y. (1983), 'Aspects of Flaubertian Influence on Conrad's Fiction', *Revue de Littérature Comparée* 571 (225) (Jan.–Mar.), 5–24.

Hiddleston, J. (1985), 'Flaubert and L'Art Industriel', *French Studies Bulletin* 15 (Summer), 4–5.

Hillenaar, H. (1994), 'George Sand et Gustave Flaubert Comme un roman', *(En)jeux de la communication romanesque*, Amsterdam, Rodopi, 135–49.

L'Illustration (1843), 'Inauguration du Chemin de Fer de Paris à Orléans', samedi 6 mai, 1843, 12–16.

Isherwood, R. M. (1981), 'Entertainment in the Parisian Fairs in the Eighteenth Century', *Journal of Modern History* 53, 24–48.

Isser, N. (1974), *The Second Empire and the Press*, The Hague, Martinus Nijhoff.

Jackson, J. F. (1937), *Louise Colet et ses amis littéraires*, New York, Yale University Press.

Jacobs, A., ed. (1981), *Correspondance Gustave Flaubert–George Sand*, Paris, Flammarion.

Jacquet, C. (1990), 'Joyce et Flaubert', *La Revue des Lèttres Modernes* 8, 5–11, 953–95.

Jacquet, C. and Topia, A. (1990), *Scribble 2: Joyce et Flaubert*, Paris, Minard.

Jacquet, M.-T. (1987), *Les Mots de l'absence ou du 'Dictionnaire des idées reçues' de Flaubert*, Paris, Nizet.

Jameson, F. (1984), 'Flaubert's Libidinal Historicism: *Trois Contes*', *Flaubert and Postmodernism*, Lincoln, U of Nebraska Press, 76–83.

Jameson, M. (1994), 'De Villequier à Pont-L'Evêque: Un Palimpseste flaubertien?', *Revue des Lèttres Modernes* 1165–1172, 169–86.

Jardin, A. and A.-J. Tudesq (1973), *Restoration and Reaction 1815–1848*, Cambridge, Cambridge UP.

Joubert, Jean (1984), *Jules Sénard*, Paris, Les Presses du Palais-Royal.

Kanes, M. (1968), 'Zola, Flaubert et Tourgueniev: Autour d'une correspondance', *Les Cahiers Naturalistes* 36, 173–181.

Kaufmann, V. (1994), *Post-Scripts: The Writer's Workshop*, London, Harvard UP.

Kelly, L. (1976), *The Young Romantics: Paris 1827–27*, London, Bodley Head.

Kempf, R. (1990), *Bouvard, Flaubert et Pécuchet*, Paris, Grasset.

Kennedy, E. (1989), *A Cultural History of the French Revolution*, London, Yale University Press.

Killick, R. (1994), 'Maupassant, Flaubert et *Trois contes*', *Maupassant conteur et romancier*, Durham, Univ. of Durham, 41–56.

Knight, D. (1985), *Flaubert's Characters: The Language of Illusion*, Cambridge, Cambridge UP.

Knight, D. (1985), 'Sartre for Flaubertians: The Case for L'Idiot de la famille', *Neophilologus* 691 (Jan.), 46–58.

Labracherie (1957), 'L'Elève Flaubert au Collège Royal de Rouen', *Les Amis de Flaubert* 10, 2–10.

LaCapra, D. (1982), Madame Bovary *on Trial*, Ithaca, Cornell UP.

Laforge, F. (1985), '*Salammbô*: Les Mythes et la Révolution', *Revue d'Histoire Littéraire de la France* 851, 26–40.

Lagny, J., ed. (1967), *Saint-Amant Oeuvres*, Paris, Didier.

Lanoux, A. (1983), *Flaubert, la femme, la ville*, Paris, PU de France.

Le-Hir, M.-P. (1991), 'Landscapes of Brittany in Chateaubriand, Balzac, and Flaubert', *West Virginia University Philological Papers* 37, 20–31.

Leclerc, Y., ed. (1993), *Flaubert-Maupassant correspondance*, Paris, Flammarion.

Leclerc, Y. (1995), *Plans et scenarios de 'Madame Bovary'*, Paris, Zulma.

Leclerc, Y. (2001), 'Sept années noires', *Revue Flaubert–1*.

Lecuyer, M. (1967), 'I Triple perspectives sur une oeuvre', *Cahiers de la Compagnie Madeleine Renaud Jean-Louis Barrault* 59, 46–65.

Lehouck, E. (1966), 'L'Education sentimentale et la critique en 1869', *Revue Belge de Philologie et d'Histoire* 44, 936–44.

Lemaire, J.-F. (1981), 'Gustave Flaubert, medecin passif', *Nouvelle Revue des Deux Mondes* (Sept.) 580–92.

Leroy, C. (1936), 'Forgerons guerrisseurs', *Revue du folklore français et du folklore colonial* 7, 1–14.

Letellier, L. (1919), *Louis Bouilhet*, Paris, Hachette.

Levin, H. (1963), 'Flaubert', *The Gates of Horn*, New York, Oxford University Press, 214–304.

Levin, H. (1972), 'A Literary Enormity: Sartre on Flaubert', *Journal of the History of Ideas* 33, 643–9.

Loftus, W. (1974), 'The Veracity of Maxime Du Camp's Reminiscences of Gustave Flaubert, 1849–51', *Les Bonnes Feuilles (Penn State)* 31, 61–72.

Lottman, H. (1989), *Flaubert: A Biography*, London, Methuen.

Lowe, M. (1983), ' "Rendre plastique . . . ": Flaubert's Treatment of the Female Principle in "*Hérodias*" ', *Modern Language Review* 783 (July), 551–8.

Lowe, M. (1984), *Towards the Real Flaubert: A Study of* Madame Bovary, Oxford, Clarendon.

Lukacher, M. (1986), 'Flaubert's Pharmacy', *Nineteenth Century French Studies* 141–2 (1985–6, Fall–Winter), 37–50.

McHale, B. (1978), 'Free Indirect Discourse: A Survey of Recent Accounts', *Poetics and Theory of Literature*, 3, 249–87.

Magraw, R. (1993), *A History of the French Working Class. Vol. 1 The Age of Artisan Revolution, 1815–1871*, Oxford, Blackwell.

Mainardi, P. (1993), *Art and Politics of the Second Empire: The Universal Expositions of 1855 and 1867*, New Haven, Yale UP.

Marec, Y. (1981), 'Lendemains de révolution l'agitation ouvrière dans la région rouennaise en 1830', *Etudes normandes* 4, 47–56.

Marotin, F. (1982), '*Les Trois Contes*: Un Carrefour dans l'oeuvre de Flaubert', *Frontières du conte*, Paris, CNRS. 111–118.

Masson, B. (1981), '*Salammbô* ou la barbarie à visage humain', *Revue d'Histoire Littéraire de la France* 814–15, 585–96.

Masson, B. (1983), 'Le Corps d'Emma', *Flaubert, la femme, la ville*, Paris, PU de France, 13–22.

Masson, B. (1981), Paris dans *L'Education sentimentale*: Rive gauche, rive droite, *Histoire et langage dans* L'Education sentimentale, Paris, Soc. d'Ed. d'Enseignement Supérieur, 123–8.

McCarthy, M. (1964), 'On *Madame Bovary*', *Partisan Review* (31), 174–188.

McCauley, E. (1994), *Industrial Madness: Commercial Photography in Paris 1848–1871*, New Haven, Yale UP.

McCrady, J. (1969), 'The Saint Julien Window at Rouen as a Source for Flaubert's Légende de Saint Julien l'Hospitalier', *Romance Notes* 10, 268–76.

McKenna, R. (1987), 'Sartre's Flaubert: A Contribution to Psychoanalytic Theory?', *Sartre: An Investigation of Some Major Themes*, Aldershot, Gower, 86–103.

McWilliam, N. (1993), *Dreams of Happiness: Social Art and the French Left 1830–1850*, Princeton, Princeton UP.

Meyer, E.-N. (1994), 'Facts into Fiction in Flaubert's *Bouvard et Pécuchet*', *Nottingham French Studies* 332 (Fall), 37–46.

Meyer, P. (1995), '*Anna Karenina*: Tolstoy's Polemic with *Madame Bovary*', *The Russian Review: An American Quarterly Devoted to Russia Past and Present* 542 (Apr.), 243–59.

Michel, A. (1983), '*Salammbô* et la cité antique', *Flaubert, la femme, la ville*, Paris, PU de France, 109–121.

Mignot, A. (1888), *Ernest Chevalier et Gustave Flaubert*, Paris, Dentu.

Mill, J. (1821), *A Visit to France in the Year 1820*.

Mitchell, G. (1987), 'Flaubert's Emma Bovary: Narcissism and Suicide', *American Imago: A Psychoanalytic Journal for Culture, Science, and the Arts* 442 (Summer), 107–128.

Mollat, M. (1979), *Histoire de Rouen*, Toulouse, Privat.

Monceaux, H. (1890), *La Révolution dans le département de l'Yonne 1788–1800*, Auxerre, Bonsant.

Mouchard, C. (1993), 'Flaubert critique', *L'Oeuvre de l'oeuvre: Etudes sur la correspondance de Flaubert*, Paris, PU de Vincennes, 87–160.

Moussaron, J.-P. (1981), 'Une Etrange Greffe', *Flaubert et le comble de l'art: Nouvelles recherches sur* Bouvard et Pécuchet, Paris, Société d'Edition d'Enseignement Supérieur, 89–109.

Murphy, T. D. (1979), 'The French Medical Profession's Perception of Its Social Function Between 1776 and 1830', *Medical History* 23, 259–78.

Nadeau, M. (1980), *Gustave Flaubert ecrivain*, Nouvelle edition revue, Paris, Les Lettres Nouvelles.

Naipaul, V. S. (1982), 'A Note on a Borrowing by Conrad', *The New York Review of Books* 2920 (Dec. 16), 37–8.

Nakam, G. (1969), 'Le 18 Brumaire de *L'Education sentimentale*', *Europe Revue Littéraire Mensuelle* (485–7), 239–48.

Neefs, J. (1980), 'Une Lecture nouvelle de La Tentation', *La Quinzaine Littéraire*, 20.

Neefs, J. (1981), 'Descriptions de l'espace et espaces de socialité', *Histoire et langage dans* L'Education sentimentale, Paris, Soc. d'Ed. d'Enseignement Supérieur, 111–22.

Neefs, J. (1982), 'Le Recit et l'edifice des croyances: *Trois Contes*', *Flaubert: La Dimension du texte*, Manchester, Manchester UP, 121–40.

Neefs, J. (1988), 'L'Espace d'Emma', *Women in French Literature*, Saratoga, CA, Anima Libri, 169–180.

Neefs, J. (1990), 'Ecrits de formation: *L'Education sentimentale* de 1845 et le Portrait', *Revue des Lèttres Modernes: Histoire des Idées et des Littératures* (953–958), 85–99.

Neefs, J. (1996), 'L'Illusion du sujet', *Voix de l'écrivain*, Toulouse, PU du Mirail, 129–37.

Neefs, J. and R. Pierrot (1993), 'Editer une correspondance', *L'Oeuvre de l'oeuvre: Etudes sur la correspondance de Flaubert*, Paris, PU de Vincennes, 21–8.

Nieuwkerk, K. (1996), *A Trade Like Any Other: Female Singers and Dancers in Egypt*, Cairo, American University in Cairo Press.

Noiret, C. (1836), *Mémoires d'un ouvrier rouennais*, Rouen.

Oehler, D. (1980), 'L'Echec de 1848', *L'Arc* 79, 58–68.

Ogura, K. (1994), 'Le Discours socialiste dans l'avant-texte de *L'Education sentimentale*', *Revue des Lèttres Modernes* (1165–72), 43–76.

Olby, R. (1990), *Companion to the History of Modern Science*, London, Routledge.

Oliver, H. (1980), *Flaubert and an English Governess*, Oxford, Clarendon Press.

Oliver, H. (1983), 'Flaubert and Juliet Herbert: A Postscript', *Nineteenth Century French Studies* 121–2 (1983–1984, Fall–Winter), 116–23.

Oliver, H. (1988), 'The Calves' Head Club: Notes Sent to Flaubert', *French Studies Bulletin: A Quarterly Supplement* 29 (1988–1989, Winter), 5–7.

Orr, L. (1989), 'Repulsive Recollections After the Revolution, French Romantic Historical Thought', *Stanford Literature Review* 61 (Spring), 29–42.

Orr, M. (1992), 'Reading the Other: Flaubert's *L'Education sentimentale* Revisited', *French Studies: A Quarterly Review* 464 (Oct.), 412–23.

Parent-Duchatelet, A. (1836), *Hygiene publique*, Paris, Baillière.

Parent-Duchatelet, A. (1836), *De la prostitution dans la ville de Paris*, Paris, Baillière.

Pascal, Roy (1977), *The Dual Voice: Free Indirect Speech and Its Functioning in the Nineteenth Century European Novel*, Manchester, Manchester UP.

Pasquet, A. (1949), *Ernest Pinard et le procès de* Madame Bovary, Paris, Editions Savoir Vouloir Pouvoir.

Pelletier-Hornby, Paulette (1995), '*Salammbô*: le Carthage de Flaubert' (1995), *Carthage: l'histoire, sa trace et son echo*, Paris, Paris Musées, 138–44 (ISBN 2–87900–196–X).

Peltre, C. (1996), *L'Atelier du voyage*, Paris, Le promeneur.

Perrone-Moises, L. (1984), 'Quidquid Volueris: The Scriptural Education', *Flaubert and Postmodernism*, Lincoln, U of Nebraska Press, 139–159.

Pichois, C. and J. Ziegler (1989), *Baudelaire*, trans. G. Robb, London, Vintage.

Pickstone, J. V. (1981), 'Bureacracy, Liberalism and the body in post-revolutionary France: Bichat's physiology and the Paris School of Medicine', *History of Science* 19 (1981), 115–42.

Pinkney, D. H. (1986), *Decisive Years in France 1840–1847*, Princeton, Princeton UP.

Platt, M. (1976), 'Nietzsche on Flaubert and the Powerlessness of His Art', *The Centennial Review* 20, 309–13.

Pommier, J. (1967), 'Flaubert et la naissance de l'acteur', *Dialogues avec le passé*, Paris, Nizet, 319–28.

Pommier, J. (1972), 'Les maladies de Flaubert', *Revue d'Histoire Littéraire de la France* 72, 298–9.

Pomponi, F. (1980), 'Vendetta et banditisme', *Le Mémorial des Corses: La Présence française*, 3: 166–88, Ajaccio, Christian Gleizal.

Porter, D. (1984), '*Madame Bovary* and the Question of Pleasure', *Flaubert and Postmodernism*, Lincoln, U of Nebraska Press, 116–38.

Porter, D. (1991), *Haunted Journeys: Desire and Transgression in European Travel Writing*, Princeton, Princeton UP.

Porter, D. (1989), 'The Perverse Traveler: Flaubert's Voyage en Orient', *L'Esprit Créateur* 291 (Spring), 24–36.

Porter, Roy (1997), *The Greatest Benefit to Mankind: A Medical History of Humanity from Antiquity to the Present*, London, HarperCollins.

Prenderghast, C. (1986), *The Order of Mimesis: Balzac, Stendhal, Nerval, Flaubert*, Cambridge, Cambridge UP.

Prenderghast, C. (1992), *Paris and the Nineteenth Century*, Oxford, Blackwell.

Price, R. (1987), *A Social History of Nineteenth-Century France*, London, Hutchinson.

Privat, J.-M. (1988), 'Essai d'ethnologie du texte littéraire: Les Charivaris dans *Madame Bovary*.' *Ethnologie Française Revue Trimestrielle de la Société d'Ethnologie Française* 3 (July–Sept.), 291–5.

Privat, J.-M. (1994), *Bovary Charivari, essai d'ethnocritique*, Paris, CNRS éditions.

Raimond, C. (1983), 'Le Corps feminin dans *L'Education sentimentale*', *Flaubert, la femme, la ville*, Paris, PU de France, 23–37.

Raitt, A. (1965), 'The Composition of Flaubert's Saint Julien l'Hospitalier', *French Studies: A Quarterly Review* (19), 358–72.

Raitt, A., ed. (1979), *L'Education sentimentale*, Paris, Garnier.

Raitt, A. (1981), 'L'Eternel Présent dans les romans de Flaubert', *Flaubert et le comble de l'art: Nouvelles recherches sur Bouvard et Pécuchet*, Paris, Société d'Edition d'Enseignement Supérieur, 139–47.

Raitt, A. (1982), 'La Décomposition des personnages dans *L'Education sentimentale*', *Flaubert: La Dimension du texte*, Manchester, Manchester UP, 157–74.

Raitt, A. (1982), 'Etat présent des études sur Flaubert', *L'Information Littéraire: Revue Paraissant Cinq Fois par An* 345 (Nov.–Dec.), 198–206.

Raitt, A. (1983), 'Etat présent des études sur Flaubert', *L'Information Littéraire: Revue Paraissant Cinq Fois par An* 351, 18–25.

Raitt, A. (1986), ' "Nous étions a l'étude . . . " ', *Revue des Lèttres Modernes: Histoire des Idées et des Littératures* (777–81), 161–92.

Raitt, A. (1988), 'Balzac et Flaubert: Une Rencontre peu connue', *L'Année Balzacienne* 9, 81–5.

Raitt, A. (1991), *Trois contes*, London, Grant & Cutler.

Raitt, A. (1991), 'Le Balzac de Flaubert', *L'Année Balzacienne* 12, 335–61.

Raitt, A., ed. (1994), *Pour Louis Bouilhet*, Exeter, Univ. of Exeter Press.

Raitt, A. (1998), *Flaubert et le théâtre*.

Ramazani, V. (1993), 'Historical Cliché, Irony and the Sublime in *L'Education sentimentale*', *PMLA* 1081 (Jan.), 121–35.

Ramsey, M. (1988), *Professional and popular medicine in France, 1770–1830*, Cambridge, Cambridge UP.

Ratier, H. (1984), 'Le code vestimentiare de la Bourgeoisie au temps de Flaubert et Maupassant', *Les Amis de Flaubert* 65, 31–7.

Reddy, W. (1977), 'The Textile Trade and the Language of the Crowd at Rouen 1752–1871', *Past and Present* 74, 62–89.

Reff, Theodore (1962), 'Cézanne, Flaubert, St Antony and the Queen of Sheba', *Art Bulletin*, vol. XLIV 113–25.

Reichler, C. (1992), 'Les Promesses du paysage: Le Voyage en Suisse', *Etudes de Lèttres, Lausanne–Dorigny, Switzerland* 1 (Jan.–Mar.), 103–14.

Reid, M. (1991), 'Flaubert et Sand en correspondance', *Poetique* 2285 (Feb.), 53–68.

Reid, M. (1995), *Flaubert Correspondant*, Paris, SEDES.

Reynaud-Pactat, P. (1990), 'La Lèttre de rupture de Rodolphe à Emma Bovary: L'Enonciation parle l'économie', *Nineteenth Century French Studie*s 191 (Fall), 83–94.

Richard, J.-P. (1970), *Stendhal–Flaubert: Littérature et sensation*, Paris, Seuil.

Richard, J.-P. (1982), 'Variations d'un paysage', *Poetique* 1251 (Sept.), 345–58.

Richard, J.-P. (1988), 'La Blessure, la splendeur', *Nouvelle Revue Française* 431 (Dec.), 51–67.

Richardson, D. (1996), *Egypt: The Rough Guide*, London, Rough Guides.

Riffaterre, M. (1981), 'Flaubert's Presuppositions', *Diacritics* 114 (Winter), 2–11.

Robert, M. (1982), *En haine du roman: Etude sur Flaubert*, Paris, Balland.

Robert, M. and A. Adamov (1967), 'L'Art et la vie de Gustave Flaubert', *Cahiers de la Compagnie Madeleine Renaud Jean-Louis Barrault* (59), 66–105.

Robertson, I. (1997), *France: Blue Guide*, London, A. & C. Black.

Roe, D. (1989), *Gustave Flaubert*, New York, St. Martin's.

Rouxeville, A. (1987), 'Victorian Attitudes to Flaubert: An Investigation', *Nineteenth Century French Studies* 161–2 (Fall–Winter, 1987–88), 132–140.

Sabiston, E. (1973), 'The Prison of Womanhood', *Comparative Literature* 25, 336–51.

Sagnes, G. (1981), 'Tentations balzaciennes dans le manuscrit de *L'Education sentimentale*', *L'Année Balzacienne* 2, 53–64.

Salgas, J.-P. (1986), 'Julian Barnes n'en a pas fini avec Flaubert', *La Quinzaine-Littéraire*. 463, 16–31, 10–13.

Salgues, J.-B. (1829), *Troisième mémoire pour l'infortuné Lesurques*, Paris, Auguste Mie.

Sand, George (1878), *Questions d'art et de littérature*, Paris, Calmann–Levy.

Sarraute, N. (1966), 'Flaubert', *Partisan Review* (33), 193–208.

Sartre, J.-P. (1966), 'La Conscience de classe chez Flaubert', *Temps Modernes* 21, 1921–1951, 2113–53.

Sartre, J.-P. (1971-2), *L'idiot de la famille: Gustave Flaubert, 1821-1857*, Paris, Gallimard. 3 vols.

Savine, A., ed. (1892), *La censure sous Napoléon III*, Paris, Nouvelle Librairie parisienne.

Schor, N. (1983), 'Salammbô enchaînée, où femme et ville dans *Salammbô*', *Flaubert, la femme, la ville*, Paris, PU de France, 173.

Schor, N. (1988), 'Fetishism and Its Ironies', *Nineteenth Century French Studies* 171–2 (1988–9 Fall–Winter), 89–97.

Schweiger, A. (1984), 'La Lèttre d'Orient', *Revue des Sciences Humaines* 66195 (3) (July–Sept.).

Segal, N. (1991), 'The Sick Son: A Motif in Stendhal and Flaubert', *Romance Studies* 19 (Winter), 7–19.

Seigel, J. (1987), *Bohemian Paris Culture, Politics and the Boundaries of Bourgeois Life 1830–1930*, London, Penguin.

Sewell, W. H. J. (1980), *Work and Revolution in France: The Language of Labor from the Old Regime to 1848*, Cambridge, CUP.

Seylaz, J.-L. (1981), 'Un Aspect de la narration flaubertienne: Quelques reflexions sur l'emploi du "on" dans *Bouvard et Pécuchet*', *Flaubert et le comble de l'art: Nouvelles recherches sur Bouvard et Pécuchet*, Paris, Société d'Edition d'Enseignement Supérieur, 23–30.

Seznec, J. (1947), 'The Temptation of St Antony in Art', *Magazine of Art*, vol. XL, 86–93.

Seznec, J. (1951), *Flaubert à l'exposition de 1851*, Oxford, Clarendon Press.

Sherrington, R. (1971), 'Louise Roque and *L'Education sentimentale*', *French Studies: A Quarterly Review* 25, 427–36.

Sherrington, R. J. (1970), *Three Novels by Flaubert: A Study of Techniques*, Oxford, Clarendon.

Shukis, D. (1980), 'The Dusty World of *Madame Bovary*', *Nineteenth Century French Studies* 7, 213–19.

Siler, D. (1977), 'Autour de Flaubert et Louise Pradier: Lèttres et documents inedits', *Studi Francesi (Torino)* 61–62, 141–50.

Siler, D. (1973), *Flaubert et Louise Pradier*, Paris, Minard.

Siler, D. (1978), 'Du nouveau sur les Mémoires de Madame Ludovica', *Revue d'Histoire Littéraire de la France* 78, 36–46.

Siler, D. (1981), 'La Mort d'Emma Bovary: Sources médicales', *Revue d'Histoire Littéraire de la France* 814–15, 719–46.

Siler, D. (1986), *Statues de chair; sculptures de James Pradier*, Paris, Editions de la Réunion des Musées Nationaux.

Spencer, P. (1953), *Flaubert: A Biography*, London, Faber.

Spitzer, A. (1987), *The French Generation of 1820*, Princeton, NJ, Princeton UP.

Stanley, R. (1986), 'That Obscure Object of (Oriental) Desire, Flaubert's Kuchuk-Hanem', *French Literature Series*, Amsterdam 13, 148–55.

Starkie, E. (1967), *Flaubert: The Making of the Master*, London, Weidenfeld & Nicolson.

Starkie, E. (1971), *Flaubert The Master: A Critical and Biographical Study (1856–1880)*, London, Weidenfeld.

Steegmuller, F. (1950), *Maupassant*, London, Collins.

Steegmuller, F. (1981), *The Letters of Gustave Flaubert*, Cambridge, Harvard UP.

Steegmuller, F. (1983), 'Flaubert to Louise Colet (1851–54)', *Grand Street* 22 (Winter), 136–49.

Steegmuller, F. & B. Bray (1993), *Flaubert–Sand: The Correspondence*, London, Harvill.

Strong, I. (1977), 'Deciphering the Salammbô Dossier, Appendix 4 of the "Club de l'Honnête Homme" Edition', *Modern Language Review* 72, 538–54.

Suffel, J. 'Quelques remarques sur la correspondance de Gustave Flaubert et de Maxime Du Camp', *Essais sur Flaubert: En l'honneur du professeur Don Demorest*, Paris, Nizet.

Suffel, J. (1968), *Flaubert*, Paris, Eds. univs.

Suffel, J. (1969), 'Chronologie de Gustave Flaubert', *Europe Revue Littéraire Mensuelle* (485–87), 268–78.

Sussman, P. (1973), 'Carriers of Cholera and Poison Rumours in France in 1832', *Societas* 3, 17–28.

Tadiar, N.-X. (1995), 'The Dream-Work of Modernity: The Sentimental Education of Imperial France', *Boundary-2: An International Journal of Literature and Culture*, Durham, NC 221 (Spring), 143–83.

Terdiman, R. (1985), *Discourse/Counter-Discourse: The Theory and Practice of Symbolic Resistance in Nineteenth-Century France*, Ithaca, NY, Cornell UP.

Testa, C. (1991), 'Representing the Unrepresentable: The Desexualization of Desire in Flaubert's "Etre la matière!"', *Nineteenth Century French Studies* 201–2 (1991–2 Fall–Winter), 137–44.

Tetu, J.-F. (1974), 'Désir et révolution dans *L'Education sentimentale*', *Littérature* 15, 88–94.

Thibaudet, A. (1935), *Gustave Flaubert*, Paris, Gallimard.

Thomas, J.-J. (1981), 'Poétique de la bêtise: *Le Dictionnaire des idées reçues*', *Flaubert et le comble de l'art: Nouvelles recherches sur Bouvard et Pécuchet*, Paris, Société d'Edition d'Enseignement Supérieur, 129–38.

Thomas, Y. (1994), 'La Tentation du desert chez Flaubert', *La Revue des Lèttres Modernes* (1165–72), 155–67.

Tondeur, C.-L. (1981), 'Flaubert et Sade, ou la fascination de l'excès', *Nineteenth Century French Studies* 101–2 (1981–2, Fall–Winter), 75–84.

Tooke, A. (1985), 'The Manuscripts of "Par les champs et par les grèves"', *French Studies Bulletin* 16 (Autumn), 8–10.

Tooke, A., ed. (1987), *Par les champs et par les grèves*, Geneva, Droz.

Tooke, A. (1994), 'Flaubert on Painting: The Italian Notes (1851)', *French Studies* 482 (Apr.), 155–73.

Tournier, M. (1972), 'La dimension mythologique', *Nouvelle Revue Française* (Oct. 1972), 124–9.

Traughott, M. (1993), *The French Worker: Autobiographies from the Early Industrial Era*, London, University of California Press.

Troyat, H. (1988), *Flaubert*, Paris, Flammarion.

Unwin, T. (1981), 'Flaubert and Pantheism', *French Studies* 354, (Oct.) 394–406.

Unwin, T., ed. (1981), *Trois contes de jeunesse: édition critique*, Exeter, Univ. of Exeter Press.

Unwin, T. (1982), *Flaubert et Baudelaire: Affinités spirituelles et esthétiques*, Paris, Nizet.

Unwin, T. (1982), 'Flaubert's Early Philosophical Development: The Writing of Smarh', *Nottingham French Studies* 212 (Oct.), 13–26.

Unwin, T. (1988), 'Flaubert: Art et infini', *Essays in French Literature*, Nedlands, WA, Australia 25 (Nov.), 53–61.

Unwin, T. (1993), 'Louis Bouilhet, Friend of Flaubert: A Case of Literary Conscience', *Australian Journal of French Studies* 302, 207–13.

VanderWolk, W. (1990), *Flaubert Remembers: Memory and the Creative Experience*, New York, Peter Lang.

Vaucquier Du Traversain, H. (1846), *Physiologie de la foire Saint-Romain par le patriarche Abraham*, Rouen, Haulard, 66p.

Védie, D. (1847), *Notice biographique sur M Flaubert, chirurgien en chef de l'Hôtel-Dieu de Rouen*, Rouen, Brière.

Vercouter, Jean (1998), *A la recherche de l'Egypte oubliée*, Paris, Gallimard.

Vidalenc, J. (1969), 'Gustave Flaubert, historien de la révolution de 1848', *Europe Revue Littéraire Mensuelle* (485–7), 51–71.

Villand, P. (1976), 'Paul Le Poittevin, Grand-Père paternelle de Guy de Maupassant', *Les Amis de Flaubert* 49, 29–41.

Walker, I. (1986), 'Sartre, Flaubert and "L'Imparfait virgilien"', *French Studies Bulletin* 21 (1986–7, Winter), 13–16.

Wetherill, P. (1968), 'Le dernier stade de la composition de *L'Education sentimentale*', *Zeitschrift für Französische Sprache und Literatur* 78, 229–52.

Wetherill, P. (1974), 'Montaigne and Flaubert', *Studi Francesi* 54, 416–28.

Wetherill, P. (1979), 'Les Dimensions du texte Brouillons, manuscrit et version definitive: Le Cas d'*Un Coeur simple*', *Zeitschrift für Französische Sprache und Literatur* 89, 159–71.

Wetherill, P. (1981), 'Flaubert et la cohésion du texte', *Neuphilologische Mitteilungen* 824, 434–42.

Wetherill, P. (1982), 'Flaubert et les incertitudes du texte', *Flaubert: La Dimension du texte*, Manchester, Manchester UP, 253–70.

Wetherill, P. (1983), 'Paris dans *L'Education sentimentale*', *Flaubert, la femme, la ville*, Paris, PU de France, 123–38.

Wetherill, P. (1985), 'The Novel and Historical Discourse: Notes on a Nineteenth-Century Perspective', *Journal of European Studies* 152 (58), 117–30.

Wetherill, P. (1989), 'Flaubert and Revolution', *Literature and Revolution*, Amsterdam, Rodopi, 19–33.

Wetherill, P. (1989), 'Flaubert, l'homme et l'oeuvre!', *Zeitschrift für Französische Sprache und Literatur* 991, 36–46.

Wetherill, P. (1992), 'Roman et histoire – un problème de situation', *Neuphilologische Mitteilungen* 931, 61–73.

Wetherill, P. (1993), ' "C'était le jeudi": L'Emergence de la ville dans *Madame Bovary*', *MRS* (13), 43–66.

Wetherill, P. M. (1967), *Flaubert et la création littéraire*, Paris, Nizet.

Wetherill, P. M. (1985), 'L'Histoire dans le texte', *Zeitschrift für Französische Sprache und Literatur* 952, 163–74.

Wetzel, A. (1988), 'Reconstructing Carthage: Archeology and the Historical Novel', *Mosaic: A Journal for the Interdisciplinary Study of Literature* 211 (Winter), 13–23.

White, H. (1979), 'The Problem of Style in Realistic Representations: Marx and Flaubert', *The Concept of Style*, Ithaca, Cornell UP, 279–98.

Wilcocks, R. (1991), 'The Resurrectionist, or November in Le Havre', *Sartre Alive*, Detroit, Wayne State UP, 240–69.

Wild, N. (1989), *Dictionnaire des théâtres parisiens au XIXe siecle*, Paris, Aux Amateurs de Livres.

Wiley, W. (1979), '*Madame Bovary* et le Théâtre des Arts à Rouen.' *Revue d'Histoire du Théâtre* 32, 280–88.

Williams, A. (1991), 'Une Chanson de Restif et sa reécriture par Flaubert', *Revue d'Histoire Littéraire de la France* 912 (Mar.–Apr.), 239–42.

Williams, D. (1982), 'Le Rôle de Binet dans *Madame Bovary*', *Flaubert: La Dimension du texte*, Manchester, Manchester UP, 90–120.

Williams, J. (1992), 'Emma Bovary and the Bride of Lammermoor', *Nineteenth Century French Studies* 203–4 (Spring–Summer), 352–60.

Williams, R. L. (1957), *Gaslight and Shadow: The World of Napoleon III*, New York, Harper.

Williams, T. (1991), 'Champfleury, Flaubert and the Novel of Adultery', *Nineteenth Century French Studies* 201–2 (1991–2, Fall–Winter), 145–57.

Williams, T. (1992), 'Gender Stereotypes in *Madame Bovary*', *Forum for Modern Language Studies* 282 (Apr.), 130–9.

Williams, T. (1992), L'Education sentimentale: *les scénarios*, Paris, Corti.

Wilson, S. (1988), *Feuding, Conflict and Banditry in Nineteenth Century Corsica*, Cambridge, Cambridge UP.

Wing, N. (1992), 'Reading Simplicity: Flaubert's "Un Coeur simple" ', *Nineteenth Century French Studies* 211–2 (1992 Fall–1993 Winter), 88–101.

Wittig, M. (1967), 'A propos de *Bouvard et Pécuchet*', *Cahiers de la Compagnie Madeleine Renaud Jean-Louis Barrault* 59, 113–22.

Woestelandt, E. (1987), 'Le Corps venal Rosanette dans *L'Education sentimentale*', *Nineteenth Century French Studies* 161–2 (1987–8, Fall–Winter), 120–131.

Wolman, Benjamin B., ed. (1977), *International Encyclopaedia of Psychiatry, Psychology, Psychoanalysis, & Neurology*, New York, Aesculapius (12 vols.).

Wood, P. (1985), 'Sartre's Notes for the Fourth Volume of The Family Idiot', *Yale French Studies* 68, 165–188.

Zviguilsky, A., ed. (1989), *Flaubert–Tourgueniev: Correspondance*, Paris, Flammarion.

Index

409